Sufficiency Economy

Samuel Alexander

SUFFICIENCY ECONOMY: ENOUGH, FOR EVERYONE, FOREVER

Published by the Simplicity Institute, Melbourne, 2015
www.simplicityinstitute.org

Copyright © 2015 Samuel Alexander
Cover design by Andrew Doodson
All rights reserved.
ISBN-13: 978-0-9941606-1-4

WHAT OTHERS ARE SAYING ABOUT *SUFFICIENCY ECONOMY*:

'With the vision of a prophet, the eloquence of a poet, the forensic detail of the scholar, and the engaged passion of an activist, Samuel Alexander offers critique, analysis and strategy for a post-growth society beyond carbon-fuelled, consumer capitalism. It is a truism that 'where there is no vision the people perish'. This book in its comprehensive scope presents a challenging, provocative and absolutely necessary vision, synthesising theoretical and practical considerations related to the current crisis of 'the human condition', and offering informed suggestions as to what comes after the unsustainable growth economy. They say knowledge is power, if so, arm yourself by reading and (re)acting to and on this book, notes from the 'front line' of our crisis-ridden but self-transforming present.'

– John Barry, author of *The Politics of Actually Existing Unsustainability*

'Impressively researched, eloquently argued, and deeply engaging, Samuel Alexander's work sits at the forefront of the degrowth movement. More than just a powerful critique of the capitalist growth economy, this book highlights the promise – and the necessity – of localised, ecological economies as the only means of adequately confronting the crises that are converging upon us. At times his vision of the future may be challenging, but it is never despairing, and ultimately the reader comes away uplifted and inspired. Alexander convinces us that less can indeed be more.'

– Helena Norberg-Hodge, author of *Ancient Futures* and producer of *The Economics of Happiness*

'*Sufficiency Economy* is a fascinating and encompassing work that envisions an affirmative response to the descent of growth-driven societies. It prospects a way forward that is neither overly optimistic, nor bleak. The result is a strategy for transitioning to a steady-state yet vibrant existence that focuses as much on ensuring human dignity as on ending our planetary over-consumption.

– Raymond De Young, co-author of *The Localization Reader: Adapting to the Coming Downshift*

CONTENTS

Acknowledgements

These collected essays are an outgrowth of work initiated in 2006, when I began working on my doctoral thesis, 'Property Beyond Growth: Toward a Politics of Voluntary Simplicity'. Since then the ideas and perspectives they express have developed in the process of establishing and teaching a course called 'Consumerism and the Growth Economy: Interdisciplinary Perspectives', which forms part of the Masters of Environment at the University of Melbourne, Australia. Over this time, most of the essays have been published in peer-reviewed journals, book chapters, or other academic publications, as detailed below, with Chapter 1 being the only journalistic piece:

A version of Ch. 1 was published in *The Conversation* (2 October 2014); a version of Ch. 2 was published in *Real-World Economics Review* (2012) 61: 2-21; a version of Ch. 3, co-authored with Simon Ussher, was published in *Journal for Consumer Culture* (2012) 12(1): 66-86; a version of Ch. 4 was published as a *Simplicity Institute Report* (2012) 12s: 1-31; a version of Ch. 5, co-authored with Paul Yacoumis, was published as a *Simplicity Institute Report* (2015) *15d*: 1-19; a version of Ch. 6 was published in David Humphreys and Spencer Stober, eds, *Transitions to Sustainability: Theoretical Debates for a Changing Planet* (2014) Ch. 19: 296-315; a version of Ch. 7 was published as a *Simplicity Institute Report* (2014) 14h: 1-24; a version of Ch. 8 was published in *Environmental Values* (2013) 22(2): 287-308; a version of Ch. 9 was published in Michelle Maloney and Peter Burdon, eds, *Wild Law – In Practice* (2014) Ch. 3: 31-44; a version of Ch. 10, co-authored with Johnny Rutherford, was published as a *Simplicity Institute Report* (2014) 14a: 1-24; a version of Ch. 11, co-authored with Esther Alloun, was published as a *Simplicity Institute Report* (2014) 14g: 1-24; a version of Ch. 12 was published in *Earth Jurisprudence and Environmental Justice Journal* (2011) 1: 26-59. I am grateful for the opportunity to reprint.

In writing these essays I was encouraged, challenged, and inspired by my colleagues and fellow authors at the Simplicity Institute. I would also like to thank Professor John Wiseman and the Melbourne Sustainable Society Institute for the support offered as I prepared this manuscript for publication. I owe special thanks to Antoinette Wilson and Johnny Rutherford for helping proof and prepare the manuscript. Debts of gratitude and Guinness are also owed to my very good friend, Andrew Doodson, for designing the cover for this book. Your time and creativity are always greatly appreciated.

Finally, to Helen and Laurie – whose love, support, and tolerance make all my efforts possible. Thank you, as always, for everything.

You never change things by fighting the existing reality. To change something, build a new model that makes the existing model obsolete.

– Buckminster Fuller

INTRODUCTION

What is to be done? This is surely one of the central questions for those of us who are animated by what Charles Eisenstein calls 'the more beautiful world our hearts know is possible'; a central question for those of us with the fire of ecological democracy burning in our eyes. Yet, it is a question that demands engagement with three preliminary questions, the answers to which provide the necessary guidance for effective practical action. First, we must adequately understand the nature and extent of the overlapping crises that confront us today. Secondly, we must envision the alternative world, or matrix of alternative worlds, that would adequately dissolve the current crises and provide the foundations for a flourishing human civilisation into the deep future. And thirdly, having provided an accurate critique and having envisioned an appropriate and effective alternative, we must meditate deeply on the question of strategy – the question of how best to direct our energies and resources if we are to maximise our chances of building the new world we have imagined. Then, and only then, are we in a position to ask ourselves the ultimate question: what is to be done? If that question is asked prematurely, or if it is asked having answered any one of the preliminary questions inadequately, then there is a great risk that one's action, motivated by the best of intentions, is directed in ways that fail to effectively produce any positive effect and, indeed, may even be counter-productive to the cause.

The publication of my two volumes of collected essays – PROSPEROUS DESCENT and SUFFICIENCY ECONOMY – represents an attempt to engage these questions as directly and as clearly as possible. The primary motivation for doing so arises from my concern that much of the literature on 'sustainable development' fails to understand the magnitude of our overlapping crises, and for that reason, the envisioned alternatives or solutions widely proposed tend to be fundamentally misconceived. Furthermore, when the critique of the existing world is off target and when the envisioned alternatives are misconceived, it should come as no surprise that the strategies proposed for achieving the stated goals are similarly flawed. If our map is poorly drawn and our compass is broken, we are unlikely to arrive at where we need to go. Is it any wonder humanity seems so lost and directionless?

Over the years of writing these essays my ideas and perspectives have naturally evolved in a dialectical relationship with other people's ideas, and are constantly being refined further as my experience of the ever-changing world is digested and reflected upon. The human condition is such that the sands of thought forever shift beneath our feet. Nevertheless, having now spent the best part of a decade engaging the questions posed above, I notice that the evidential ground upon which I stand is firming up, providing me with confidence that the position I defend – radical though it may seem – is accurate, even if there may be matters of detail that will always be open to revision or refinement.

In this introduction I would like to state some of the fundamental tenets which shape the following essays, in the hope that this will guide the interpretation of those essays, especially at those times when these central ideas lie beneath the surface of a more focused discussion. As I am writing this introduction *after* having written the essays, there is also the luxury of having the full benefit of what I have learned throughout the writing process.

Here are twelve defining theses that shape my work:

1. **Pursuing limitless growth on a finite planet is a recipe for ecological and humanitarian catastrophe.** Despite the controversy that still surrounds the 'limits to growth' perspective, there is something strikingly obvious about the idea that if human population keeps growing, if our resource and energy demands on the natural environment continue expanding, and if our streams of waste and pollution keep growing, then eventually we will undermine the ecological foundations of our civilisation so violently that nature will fight back and bring things into balance. Let us face the fact, too, that 'bringing things into balance' is a euphemism for mass population die-off, signifying a prospective tragedy of unspeakable proportions. So the question is not so much *whether* there are limits to growth – of course there are limits to growth! – but rather *when* those limits will begin to impose themselves on our current ways of living and force us to live differently. It would be far better for people and planet that we anticipate these limits and begin working toward a post-growth economy now. Needless to say, this will not be easy. We have developed two centuries of industrial, growth-orientated momentum that will make it incredibly difficult to consciously redirect the economic trajectory so fundamentally. But transitioning 'beyond growth' is a transformation that is coming, one way or another. Better it be by design than disaster.

2. **'Green growth' is a dangerous myth that entrenches the status quo.** When the limits to growth are raised in objection to the growth model of progress, many people seem comforted by the fantasy that science and technology will save the day. Current forms of growth may have ecological limits, these people acknowledge, but they then insist that the global economy can and should keep growing forever, if only we learn how to produce and consume more efficiently. This is nice in theory, perhaps, but it is biophysically naïve. It is of the utmost importance, of course, that we use the best of our technological knowledge to help us achieve a sustainable way of life through efficiency improvements. It would be foolish to argue other-wise. But efficiency alone cannot 'decouple' economic growth from ecological impact sufficiently to produce a sustainable way of life. The extent of decoupling required is simply too great. To be effective, the drive for efficiency must be shaped and limited by an ethics of sufficiency. That is to say, our aim should not be to do 'more with less' (which is the flawed paradigm of green growth), but to do 'enough with less' (which is the paradigm of sufficiency).

3. **'Degrowth' (i.e., planned contraction of resource and energy demands) is necessary in the developed nations in order to move toward a just and sustainable economy that operates within the sustainable carrying capacity of the planet.** When the extent of ecological overshoot is understood, and bearing in mind the fact that ecological room must be left for poorest nations to attain a dignified existence, there is no escaping the fact that degrowth is required in the developed – or rather *over*developed – regions of the world. This is not a popular thesis, but it does reflect a biophysical reality.

4. **Addressing poverty within a degrowth framework implies a redistribution of wealth and power on a much more egalitarian basis.** Within the growth model it is assumed that poverty will be eliminated through continued growth of the global economy via some 'trickle down' effect. This is an ecologically unsupportable pathway to poverty elimination, because it relies on continued growth on an already overburdened planet. Once it is recognised that growth cannot solve the problem of poverty and in fact threatens to exacerbate it through climate change, continued ecological degradation, or economic collapse, it becomes clear that the only coherent pathway beyond poverty lies in a more

egalitarian distribution of wealth and power within a degrowth model of progress. This is not the place to argue *how* that could be achieved – there are many options. The present point is simply to acknowledge that it is a *necessary* feature of any transition to a just and sustainable world.

5. **Degrowth implies radically reduced energy and resource requirements compared to overdeveloped nations.** Among other things, degrowth means giving up affluent, consumer lifestyles and embracing 'simpler ways' of living that provide for mostly local needs using mostly local resources. This is an implication of the environmental predicament that few dare to acknowledge, since most people seem resistant to giving up the comforts and conveniences of consumer affluence. But given the extent of ecological overshoot, there is no way that the consumer way of life could be universalised. Consumerism was an experiment that failed. It led civilisation down a dead end. We are now being called to reimagine the good life beyond consumer culture and explore new conceptions of progress and prosperity. This does not necessarily mean hardship. It means focusing on what is *sufficient* to live well – and pursuing that goal with all the wisdom, creativity, and compassion we can muster.

6. **It is not enough merely to live more simply within existing structures and systems.** While challenging ourselves to live more simply is necessary, the even greater challenge is to begin building new systems and structures that support and encourage 'simpler ways' of life. We cannot wait for governments to do this for us. First and foremost, we must organise and network at the grassroots level and begin building the new world within the shell of the world.

7. **At some point, when the social movement becomes powerful enough, there will need to be some democratic social planning of the economy to ensure that the necessary degrowth transition does not collapse the economy.** Accordingly, to advocate for degrowth is ultimately to embrace a reconceived form of eco-socialism. This means that the most fundamental questions about what is produced and how it is distributed cannot be left primarily to market forces. While there will inevitably be a place for forms of private property and market exchange, any successful transition to a degrowth economy is going to require democratic planning of the economy, preferably in highly

decentralised and localised ways. Many wasteful or damaging sectors of the existing economy – such as advertising, fossil fuel production, private motor vehicle production, and the finance industries – will need to be greatly reduced or repurposed. Other sectors – such as organic farming, renewable energy production, and public transport – will need to be ramped up.

8. **Degrowth is thus incompatible with capitalism.** Admittedly, this is a realisation that I resisted for some time, hoping that the social, economic, and environmental crises that human beings face would not require such terrifyingly fundamental change. Couldn't we just reform capitalism? Eventually, however, I realised that there was no honour in deceiving myself and potentially others just because the challenge of replacing capitalism seemed, and still seems, like an impossible pipe dream. The first question to grapple with is whether capitalism *needs* to be replaced, not whether we will ever *succeed* in doing so, and the nature of capitalism is such that it is unable to deal with the crises we face. Capitalism has a 'grow or die' imperative built into its very structure. At every turn participants in the market economy are more or less compelled to pursue profit or else risk being destroyed by competitors running them out of business. The technologies and products that are developed under capitalism are the one's that promise the best return, not the one's that are most needed. Similarly, the distribution of resources is determined by who has the most money, not who needs the resources the most. The structures and incentives of capitalism also create constant pressure for individuals and businesses to externalise environmental and social costs, making it impossible to price commodities in a way that ensures 'optimal' consumption and production. The consequence is that the justifications of capitalism based on wealth-maximisation and efficiency are rarely if ever reflected in reality. Furthermore, the vast amounts of private and public debt that have been taken on in recent decades depend on continued growth for those debts to be repaid. For all these reasons, the idea of reforming capitalism in a way that deals with the crises of civilisation entails irresolvable contractions. Perhaps the most compelling reason for why capitalism cannot produce a just and sustainable world, however, is because capitalist economies would collapse if existing structures tried to deal with the necessary degrowth of resource and energy consumption. This is especially so in a globalised economy where it is becoming increasingly difficult for one capitalist economy to defy the neoliberal world order.

Localisation and contraction of national economies in such a context will require democratic planning of the economy.[1]

9. **A swift transition to renewable energy is necessary to respond to climate change and peak oil.** Be that as it may, renewable energy will be unable to sustain a growth-orientated, consumerist society. A society based on renewable energy is a moderate energy society, which means energy-intensive societies must prepare for energy descent. Given the close connection between energy and economic activity, the required energy descent necessarily means economic contraction.

10. **Climate change and peak oil are not the fundamental problems.** Rather, they are the symptoms of the cultures and systems of consumer capitalism. While it is absolutely necessary to work toward responding to climate change and peak oil as effectively as possible, we should not lose sight of the more fundamental challenge of replacing the cultures and systems that produce those problems. Otherwise we will find ourselves hacking at the branches of the problems, when we should be aiming for the roots. After all, a post-carbon capitalism would still be a growth economy that degraded the natural environment, alienated workers, and distributed wealth so unjustly.

11. **Material sufficiency in a free society provides the conditions for an infinite variety of meaningful, happy, and fulfilling lives.** Perhaps this thesis is the most fundamental, because any political or economic system is inevitably shaped by some conception of the good life.

---

[1] But as John Holloway warns: 'Revolution is not about destroying capitalism, but about refusing to create it. To pose revolution as the destruction of capitalism is to reproduce the abstraction of time that is so central to the reproduction of capitalism: it is self-defeating. To think of destroying capitalism is to erect a great monster in front of us, so terrifying that we either give up in despair or else conclude that the only way in which we can slay the monster is by constructing a great party with heroic leaders who sacrifice themselves (and everyone around them) for the sake of the revolution... To pose revolution as the destruction of capitalism is to distance it from ourselves, to put it off into the future. The question of revolution is not in the future. It is here and now: how do we stop producing the system by which we are destroying humanity?' See John Holloway, *Crack Capitalism* (2010, London: Pluto Press), p. 254.

Currently, global capitalism conceives of human beings as consumers who can achieve happiness by purchasing goods and services in the market economy. On that basis, global growth is seen as the most direct pathway to human flourishing. By contrast, degrowth arises out of an alternative conception of what it means to be human. It poses the question, 'What is it that makes life worth living?' and answers that question by saying, 'Something *other* than the limitless consumption of material things.' Consumerism just does not satisfy the universal human craving for meaning, and the sooner the world realises this the better it will be for everyone and the planet. In short, I argue that the simple life can be a good life.

12. **Chances of success do not look good.** Despite the increasingly robust case for the necessity of a post-capitalist politics and economics – for the necessity of degrowth – we should not pretend that this revolutionary project shows many signs of achieving its ambitious goals. Although there are nascent movements based on notions of degrowth – permaculture, Transition Towns, intentional community, and voluntary simplicity – in the greater scheme of things these subcultures, promising though they are, remain small. Furthermore, despite the increasing prominence environmental issues are given in the mainstream media, there is a pervasive techno-optimism that shapes the discussion of these issues, meaning that the reality of the crises are understated and the proposed solutions (typically market-based) are misconceived. Under these conditions, a mass movement for degrowth seems highly unlikely. But does this mean that we should throw our hands up in the air and distract ourselves with television and consumer trinkets while the curtain closes on our civilisation? Surely not. As Wendell Berry says, we should not focus on the question of whether we will succeed; we should focus on the question of what is the right thing to do. And that means doing everything in our power to resist the forces that are degrading people and planet by prefiguring ways of living that respect people and planet. We should do this irrespective of our chances of realising the ideal of a degrowth society. We should do this because it is the right thing to do. Fortunately, there are two silver linings to this approach. First, even if we fail to stop the growth economy from growing itself to death, we should still be trying to prefigure a 'simpler way' to live here and now, because if we are to face economic collapse, then the more systems and practices of sufficiency we can get in place today, the better prepared and more resilient we will be should the

status quo be disrupted for one reason or another. Secondly, and most promising of all, working on building the new world promises, if not a life free from strife and hard work, at least a life full of meaning, passion, and love. And that is something we can cling to even if it transpires that the story of civilisation does not have a happy ending.[2]

◆ ◆ ◆

Before outlining the content of the chapters to come, a few more words are required on the vocabularies of degrowth, steady state economy, and sufficiency economy, which I use throughout these chapters, sometimes interchangeably. To avoid confusion, let me offer some clarification here, although context should also generally assist with interpretation. Degrowth, as I use the term, refers primarily to a macroeconomic model that is defined by planned contraction of the resource and energy requirements of over-developed economies. Obviously, degrowth is a transitional phase, not an end-sate, because an economy could not and should not 'degrow' indefinitely. Accordingly, the basic vision of sustainability that I subscribe to and defend is one in which overgrown economies initiate a degrowth process of planned economic contraction, a process that would eventually stabilise in a steady state economy operating within the sustainable carrying capacity of the planet. I do not argue that this is likely, only that it is necessary. The poorest nations may need to increase their energy and resource demands to

---

[2] To again draw on the words of John Holloway (2010: 253):

> How I wish I could write a book with a happy ending. That I could offer all the answers. That the good would triumph over evil. That we could close the dialectic, end with a synthesis, arrive Home. That we could say with certainty that history is on our side. That, sure as eggs is eggs, communism will take the place of capitalism. That the darkest hour is just before dawn. That our cracks, for sure and certain, are the harbingers of a new society.
>
> But no, it is not like that. There is no certainty. The dialectic is open, negative, full of danger. The hour is dark, but it may be followed by a darker one, and dawn may never come. And we, the fools who live in the cracks, may be just that: fools.
>
> And yet, fools that we are, we think we can see something new emerging. We are standing in the dark shade of a threshold and trying to see and understand that which is opening in front of us. We do not understand it very well, but we can hear, especially in the previous theses, fragments of new melodies of struggle emerging, see glimpses of a new direction in the flow of revolt.

attain a dignified standard of living, but eventually they too would need to stop growing and also transition to a steady state economy. Within this broad framework, a 'sufficiency economy', as I use the term, is essentially a form of steady state economy, but I choose to employ the vocabulary of sufficiency to emphasise some issues that I find misleading or problematic in the work of most ecological economists, whom I otherwise admire greatly.

First of all, ecological economists rarely discuss the radical lifestyle implications of 'one planet' living. By employing the notion of a 'sufficiency economy', therefore, I hope to emphasise the fact that one planet living involves abandoning affluence in favour of a radically simpler way to live based on material sufficiency. Secondly, ecological economists have not always discussed the limits of renewable energy or the economic implications of energy descent in much detail, and in this regard I consider the 'biophysical economists' to have made an important contribution to the debate. A sufficiency economy is an economy based primarily or entirely on renewable energy, but due to the inability of renewable energy systems to replace fossil fuels entirely, this means significantly reducing energy consumption compared to the richest nations today. As noted above, given the close connection between energy and economy, significant energy descent has huge economic implications that have been insufficiently discussed by most ecological economists. Thirdly, most ecological economists, to my mind, tend to have too much faith in market mechanisms. As discussed above, if degrowth is truly what is required, then significant social control over the economy will be needed if economic contraction is to avoid an unstable descent into economic and social chaos. Primarily for these three reasons I use the term 'sufficiency economy' to refer to a degrowth economy that culminates in a steady state economy – but a steady state economy that is shaped by the three points of difference just outlined.

◆ ◆ ◆

As with the first volume of collected essays, I will provide a brief outline of the chapters to come. These chapters have been ordered roughly to reflect steps in an argument, however they all stand alone well enough, so there is no need, necessarily, to read them in order. To provide context, certain lines of argument, in places, are repeated or summarised, as are certain turns of phrase, but I hope this serves primarily to emphasise key points and weave the essays together into a coherent whole. Readers are encouraged to skim over summary paragraphs if the point being made is sufficiently well understood.

Chapter 1 provides a short, accessible summary of the central themes of this book. A slightly abridged version of this chapter was originally published in the *The Conversation*, under the title 'Life in a "degrowth" economy, and why you might actually enjoy it'. The article received a significant amount of attention – it was viewed more than 50,000 times – making it one of the most widely read pieces on degrowth. I include this journalistic piece as a means of introducing questions that are explored in more depth throughout the book. Readers familiar with growth skepticism, degrowth, and voluntary simplicity, may wish to begin at Chapter 2.

Chapter 2 begins by reviewing the empirical studies that have examined the correlation between income and self-reported happiness. While the scholarly debate is not conclusively settled, the weight of evidence suggests that once people have their basic material needs adequately met, the correlation between income and happiness begins to fade. Put otherwise, there comes a point where rises in income become less important as means of increasing wellbeing, and other features of life, such as more meaningful employment, more leisure time, and more social engagement, become increasingly important. This has been called the 'income-happiness paradox', because it contradicts the widely held assumption that more income and more economic growth will always contribute positively to human wellbeing. After reviewing the empirical literature, the analysis proceeds to consider the various explanations for this apparent 'paradox', and I also consider what implications this paradox might have for people and nations that are overconsuming. The chapter concludes by outlining what I call an 'economics of sufficiency', drawing on the perspectives of degrowth and steady state economics.

Chapter 3 analyses the results of the most extensive multi-national survey of the Voluntary Simplicity Movement, conducted by the Simplicity Institute. The Voluntary Simplicity Movement can be understood broadly as a diverse social movement made up of people who are resisting high consumption lifestyles and who are seeking, in various ways, a lower consumption but higher quality of life alternative. If it is true that post-consumerist lifestyles of reduced and restrained consumption are a necessary part of any transition to a just, sustainable, and flourishing human civilisation, then gaining extensive empirical insight into this movement is a matter of some importance. The results of the survey are preceded by a summary of the 'limits to growth' perspective, which serves to contextualise the analysis.

Chapter 4 is probably the key chapter of the book, for it attempts to envision in some detail the contours of a 'sufficiency economy'. The fundamental aim of a sufficiency economy, as I define it, is to create an economy that provides 'enough, for everyone, forever'. In other words, economies should seek to universalise a material standard of living that is sufficient for a good life but which is ecologically sustainable into the deep future. Once that is achieved, further growth in material wealth would not be an economic priority and, indeed, would need to be deliberately restrained. For individuals and economies that are already overconsuming, the attainment of sufficiency implies not merely resisting further growth, but first entering a phase of planned economic contraction. Once sustainable sufficiency has been attained, prosperity should be sought in various low-impact, non-materialistic forms of wellbeing, such as enjoying social relationships, experiencing connection with nature, engaging in meaningful work or spiritual practice, or exploring various forms of peaceful, creative activity. There are no limits to the scale or diversity of qualitative improvement of life in a sufficiency economy, but to achieve sustainability in a world of seven billion people (and counting), material standards of living must not aim for consumer affluence but only for what is minimally sufficient for a good life. How would we feed ourselves? What clothes would we wear? What forms of transport and technology would we use? How much and what types of energy would we require? And what material standard of living would we have if we were to successfully decarbonise the economy? Most importantly, perhaps, what would the quality of daily life be like? These are some of the concrete questions to which this chapter offers some tentative answers.

Chapter 5 presents an energy analysis and review of various alternative technologies. Energy is often called the 'lifeblood' of civilisation, and yet the overconsumption of fossil energy lies at the heart of two of the greatest challenges facing humanity today: climate change and peak oil. While transitioning to renewable energy systems is an essential 'supply side' strategy in response to climate change and peak oil, the extent of the problems and the speed at which decarbonisation must occur means that there must also be a 'demand side' response. This means consuming much less energy not just 'greening' supply, at least in the most developed regions of the world. In that context, this chapter provides an energy analysis of various 'low tech' options – such as solar shower bags, solar ovens, washing lines, and cycling – and considers the extent to which these types of 'simple living' practices could reduce energy consumption if widely embraced. It is demonstrated that low-tech options provide a very promising means of significantly reducing energy (and water) consumption. While the focus of this chapter is on the direct energy and water savings of low-tech living, the subtext of the analysis is that prefiguring a simpler way to live has deeper significance too, in that it helps create the cultural conditions needed for a post-capitalist politics and economics to emerge, which I maintain is a necessary part of the decarbonisation project. Lifestyle change is far from enough.

Chapter 6 reviews some of the most promising social movements that have the potential to change the current trajectory of industrial civilisation acutely in the direction of a low-carbon world. If there is any hope for rapid decarbonisation today, it surely lies, at this late stage, in movements, innovations, or technologies that do not seek to produce change through a smooth series of increments, but through an ability to somehow 'disrupt' the status quo and fundamentally redirect the world's trajectory toward a low-carbon, post-growth future. This chapter considers movements based on such things as fossil fuel divestment, Transition Towns, collaborative consumption, the sharing economy, voluntary simplicity, and direct democracy.

Chapter 7 considers the economic implications of carbon budget analysis. Building on the work of climate scientists Kevin Anderson and Alice Bows, it is argued that the logic of the carbon budget numbers leads to conclusions that most people, including most climate policy makers, refuse to accept, acknowledge, or understand. Most significantly, the carbon budget arithmetic indicates that rapid decarbonisation may well be incompatible with continuation of current global economic growth trends and paradigms. Even more challengingly, carbon budget analysis seems to imply that in the most highly developed regions of the world, keeping within the carbon budget will require 'degrowth' strategies of significantly reduced energy and resource consumption. In the final sections of this chapter an attempt is made to outline the main elements of an integrated socio-economic and political strategy consistent with keeping emissions within the confines of the carbon budget. The aim is not to present something that is politically or culturally palatable, but to explore *what needs to be done* to adequately respond to the challenge of climate change.

Chapter 8 explores what role social or cultural evolution may need to play in providing the necessary *preconditions* for fundamental structural change of society. The central argument of this chapter is that the Voluntary Simplicity Movement (or something like it) will almost certainly need to expand, organise, radicalise, and politicise, if anything resembling a degrowth or steady state economy is to emerge through democratic processes. In a sentence, that is the 'grassroots' or 'bottom-up' theory of structural transformation that will be expounded and defended in this chapter. The essential reasoning here is that legal, political, and economic structures will never reflect a post-growth ethics of macroeconomic sufficiency until a post-consumerist ethics of sufficiency is embraced and mainstreamed at the cultural level. Conversely, a micro-economics of 'more' will always generate, or try to generate, a macroeconomics of 'growth'. Only by changing consumerist cultures of consumption, I conclude, is there any hope of transcending and socially reconstructing the structures of growth.

Chapter 9 examines what I call the 'anarchist challenge' to the promising new legal movement, Earth Jurisprudence. This new movement seeks to reconceive law in a way that treats ecological sustainability as a fundamental legal principle of governance, focusing attention on what the legislature and judiciary could do to achieve that noble end. The central issue this chapter seeks to raise for Earth jurists, and for oppositional thinkers and activists more generally, is the question of 'strategy'. That is, the chapter raises the question of how best to direct our limited energies and resources, for if transformative change is truly what we desire, our energies and resources must be used to their fullest practical effect. To do justice to the 'ends' for which we struggle, surely we must take care that the 'means' we employ are the best we have available. It is not enough to have good intentions. We must also be as effective as possible. This chapter considers whether 'top-down' change is where we should be directing our energies or whether we should be directing most of our energies toward building the new society at a grassroots level; building it beneath the legal structures of the existing society with the aim that one day new societal structures will emerge 'from below' to replace the outdated forms we know today.

Chapter 10 analyses the most prominent strategies that have been put forth to bring the sufficiency economy into existence. In other words, the vision of a deep green alternative society is taken for granted, focusing instead on how such an alternative may be realised. The chapter begins by outlining the alternative society – a sufficiency economy – with a very broad brush, in order to give the more critical and substantive sections some context. It seems that there is some interesting and heartening overlap with respect to the envisioned 'end state' of the deep green school, and yet there is fierce debate over how to get there. The primary purpose of this chapter, therefore, is to examine these various theories of transition or transformation – ranging from parliamentarianism to socialism to anarchism – in order to highlight the most important factors at play, and hopefully shed some further light on the question of 'strategy'.

Chapter 11 presents a sympathetic critique of the Transition Towns Movement. The fundamental aims of this movement are to respond to the twin challenges of peak oil and climate change by decarbonising and relocalising the economy through a community-led model of change based on permaculture principles. As promising as the movement may be, there are crucial questions it needs to confront and reflect on if it wants to fully realise its potential for deep societal transformation. The Transition Towns Movement is ostensibly 'inclusive'; this chapter examines this self-image in order to assess whether it is as inclusive and as diverse as it claims to be, and what this might mean for the movement's prospects. The chapter also considers the issue of whether a grassroots, community-led movement can change the macro-economic and political structures of global capitalism 'from below' through (re)localisation, or whether the movement may need to engage more directly in political activity if it is to have any chance of achieving its ambitious goals. Finally, we raise the question of whether the movement is sufficiently radical in its vision. Does it need to engage more critically with the broader paradigm of consumer capitalism, its growth imperative, and social norms and values? Is building local resilience within this paradigm an adequate strategy? And does the movement recognise that decarbonisation almost certainly means giving up many aspects of affluent, consumer lifestyles? The chapter does not expect to be able to offer complete answers to these probing questions, but by engaging critically with these issues one hopes to advance the debate around a movement that may indeed hold some of the keys to transitioning to a just and sustainable world.

Chapter 12, the final chapter, tells a story of the future, a possible future that was conceived of in between the poles of pessimism and optimism but which is ultimately based upon a faith in the human spirit to meet the challenges of creating an Ecozoic era. The chapter looks back on the 21st century from the vantage point of the year 2099. It takes the form of an essay, entitled 'The Path to Entropia', written for the journal *Possibility* by Lennox Kingston, a 90-year-old retired Professor of Legal and Political History. The essay reviews how attitudes toward consumption and economic growth underwent a radical shift over the course of the 21st century and how this affected, through legal transformation, the social, political, and economic order of late capitalism. Particular attention is given to the evolution of property rights and the cultural movements that made this evolution possible.

I close this introduction, as I closed the introduction to PROSPEROUS DESCENT, by acknowledging that the essays in this book do not answer all questions and, in fact, may raise as many questions as they answer. The first volume of essays, I hope, fills some of the gaps (as summarised in the Appendix to this volume).

1

FRUGAL ABUNDANCE IN AN AGE OF LIMITS
A simpler way for an energy descent future

Our understandings and expectations of the world have been shaped by our experience of economic growth. The dynamic stability of that growth has habituated us to what is 'normal'. That normal must soon shatter.
— David Korowicz

1. Introduction

What would genuine economic progress look like, today? The orthodox answer is to say that growth in the production of goods and services is the most direct path to advancing the interests of individuals and society – that higher incomes, and a bigger economy, are always better. It would seem to follow that growth means progress, and progress means growth, on the assumption that more money means more power to satisfy human needs and desires. But this dominant perspective is increasingly strained by the knowledge that, on a finite planet, the economy cannot grow forever (Turner, 2012). What is more, the benefits of growth, far from being directed to those in most need, are primarily being channelled into the hands of a privileged few, creating socially corrosive inequalities (Wilkinson and Pickett, 2010). Even those who have attained the consumerist ideal tend to discover that the pursuit of affluence fails to fulfil its promise of a happy and meaningful life (Kasser, 2002).

In recent decades critical thinkers have been exploring how to move beyond growth economics towards some form of steady state economy (Daly, 1973; Jackson, 2009). But what is a steady state economy? Why is it desirable or necessary? What would it be like to live in? And how might we get there? This short, introductory chapter sketches an outline of this alternative economic paradigm, raising questions which the remaining chapters will develop and explore in more detail (see also, Alexander, 2015).

1

2. The Global Predicament

We used to live on a planet that was relatively empty of humans; today it is full to overflowing, with more people consuming more resources. We would need one and a half Earths to sustain the existing economy into the future (Vale and Vale, 2013). Every year this ecological overshoot continues, the foundations of our existence, and that of other species, are undermined.

At the same time, there are great multitudes around the world who are, by any humane standard, under-consuming, and the humanitarian challenge of eliminating global poverty is likely to increase the burden on ecosystems still further.

Meanwhile, the population is forecast to hit 11 billion this century. Despite this, the richest nations still seek to grow their economies without apparent limit.

As if governed by the ideology of a cancer cell, our growth-orientated civilisation suffers from the delusion that there are no environmental 'limits to growth'. But rethinking growth in an age of limits cannot be avoided. The only question is whether it will be by design or disaster.

3. Degrowth to a Steady State Economy

The idea of the steady state economy – the idea of an economy that deliberately stops growing in resource and energy use – presents us with an alternative. This idea is somewhat misleading, however, because it suggests that we simply need to maintain the size of the existing economy and stop seeking further growth.

But given the extent of ecological overshoot – and bearing in mind that the poorest nations still need some room to develop their economies *in some form* and allow the poorest billions to attain a dignified existence – the transition will require the richest nations to downscale radically their resource and energy demands.

In recent years this realisation has given rise to calls for economic 'degrowth' (Latouche, 2009). To be distinguished from recession, degrowth means a phase of planned and equitable economic contraction in the richest nations, eventually reaching a steady state that operates within Earth's biophysical limits.

At this point, mainstream economists will accuse degrowth advocates of misunderstanding the potential of technology, markets, and efficiency gains to 'decouple' economic growth from environmental impact. But there is no misunderstanding here. Everyone knows that we could produce and consume more efficiently than we do today. The problem is that efficiency without sufficiency is lost.

Despite decades of extraordinary technological advancement and huge efficiency improvements, the energy and resource demands of the global economy are still increasing. This is because within a growth-orientated, capitalist economy, efficiency gains tend to be reinvested in more consumption and more growth, rather than in reducing impact (see Polimeni *et al*, 2009).

This is the defining, critical flaw in growth economics: the false assumption that all economies across the globe can continue growing while radically reducing environmental impact to a sustainable level. The extent of decoupling required is simply too great. As we try unsuccessfully to 'green' capitalism, we see the face of Gaia vanishing.

The very lifestyles that were once considered the definition of success are now proving to be our greatest failure. Attempting to universalise affluence would be catastrophic. There is absolutely no way that today's 7.2 billion people could live the Western way of life, let alone the 11 billion expected in the future. Genuine progress now lies beyond growth (Kubiszewski *et al*, 2013). Tinkering around the edges of capitalism will not cut it (Smith, 2010).

We need an alternative.

4. Enough, for Everyone, Forever

When one first hears calls for degrowth, it is easy to think that this new economic vision must be about hardship and deprivation; that it means going back to the stone age, resigning ourselves to a stagnant culture, or being anti-progress. Not so.

Degrowth would liberate us from the burden of pursuing material excess. We simply do not need so much stuff – certainly not if it comes at the cost of planetary health, social justice, and personal wellbeing. Consumerism is a gross failure of imagination, a debilitating addiction that degrades nature and does not even satisfy the universal human craving for meaning.

Degrowth, by contrast, would involve embracing what has been termed the 'simpler way' – producing and consuming less (Trainer, 2010). This would be a way of life based on very modest material and energy needs but nevertheless rich in other dimensions – a life of frugal abundance. It is about creating an economy based on sufficiency, knowing how much is enough to live well, and discovering that enough is plenty (Princen, 2005).

The lifestyle implications of degrowth and sufficiency are far more radical than the 'light green' forms of sustainable consumption that are widely discussed today. Turning off the lights, taking shorter showers, composting, and recycling are all necessary parts of what sustainability will require of us, but these measures are far from enough.

This does not mean, however, that we must live a life of painful sacrifice. Most of our basic needs can be met in quite simple and low-impact ways, while maintaining a high quality of life.

5. What Would Life Be Like in a Degrowth Society?

In a degrowth society we would aspire to localise our economies as far and as appropriately as possible. This would assist with reducing carbon-intensive global trade, while also building resilience in the face of an uncertain and turbulent future.

Through forms of direct or participatory democracy we would organise our economies to ensure that everyone's basic needs are met, and then redirect our energies away from economic expansion. This would be a relatively low-energy mode of living that ran primarily or entirely on renewable energy systems.

Renewable energy cannot sustain an energy-intensive global society of high-end consumers. A degrowth society embraces the necessity of 'energy descent' in the rich nations, turning our energy crises into an opportunity for civilisational renewal.

We would tend to reduce our working hours in the formal economy in exchange for more home-production and leisure. We would have less income, but more freedom. Thus, in our simplicity, we would be rich.

Wherever possible, we would grow our own organic food, water our gardens with water tanks, and turn our neighbourhoods into edible landscapes as the Cubans have done in Havana. As my friend Adam Grubb so delightfully declares, we should 'eat the suburbs', while supplementing urban agriculture with food from local farmers' markets on the urban periphery.

We do not need to purchase so many new clothes. Let us mend or exchange the clothes we have, buy second-hand, or make our own. In a degrowth society, the fashion and marketing industries would quickly wither away. A new aesthetic of sufficiency would develop, where we creatively re-use and refashion the vast existing stock of clothing and materials, and explore less impactful ways of producing new clothes.

We would become radical recyclers and do-it-yourself experts. This would partly be driven by the fact that we would simply be living in an era of relative scarcity, with reduced discretionary income.

4

But human beings find creative projects fulfilling, and the challenge of building the new world within the shell of the old promises to be immensely meaningful, even if it will also entail times of trial. The apparent scarcity of goods can also be greatly reduced by scaling up the sharing economy, which would also enrich our communities.

One day, we might even live in cob houses that we build ourselves, but over the next few critical decades the fact is that most of us will be living within the poorly designed urban infrastructure that already exists. We are hardly going to knock it all down and start again. Instead, we must 'retrofit the suburbs', as leading permaculturalist David Holmgren (2013) argues. This would involve doing everything we can to make our homes more energy-efficient, more productive, and probably more densely inhabited.

This is not the eco-future that we are shown in glossy design magazines featuring million-dollar 'green homes' that are prohibitively expensive. Degrowth offers a more humble – and I would say more realistic – vision of a sustainable future.

6. Making the Change

A degrowth transition to a steady state economy could happen in a variety of ways. But the nature of this alternative vision suggests that the changes will need to be driven from the 'bottom up', rather than imposed from the 'top down' (Trainer, 2010).

What I have written above highlights a few of the personal and household aspects of a degrowth society based on sufficiency. Meanwhile, the Transition Towns Movement is exploring how whole communities can engage with the idea (Hopkins, 2008).

But it is critical to acknowledge the social and structural constraints that currently make it much more difficult than it needs to be to adopt a lifestyle of sustainable consumption. For example, it is hard to drive less in the absence of safe bike lanes and good public transport; it is hard to find a work-life balance if access to basic housing burdens us with excessive debt; and it is hard to re-imagine the good life if we are constantly bombarded with advertisements insisting that 'nice stuff' is the key to happiness.

Actions at the personal and household levels will never be enough, on their own, to achieve a steady state or degrowth economy. We need to create new, post-capitalist structures and systems that promote, rather than inhibit, a simpler way of life (Alexander, 2015). These wider changes will never emerge, however, until we have a culture that demands them. So first and foremost, the revolution that is needed is a revolution in consciousness.

I do not present these ideas under the illusion that they will be readily accepted. The ideology of growth clearly has a firm grip on our society and beyond. Rather, I hold up degrowth up as the most coherent framework for understanding the global predicament and signifying the only desirable way out of it.

The alternative is to consume ourselves to death under the false banner of 'green growth', which would not be smart economics.

References

Alexander, S. 2015. *Prosperous descent: Crisis as opportunity in an age of limits*. Melbourne: Simplicity Institute.

Daly, H. 1973. *Toward a steady-state economy*. San Francisco: W.H. Freeman.

Holmgren, D. 2013. 'Crash on demand: Welcome to the brown tech future'. *Simplicity Institute Report* 13c: 1-23.

Hopkins, R. 2008. *The transition handbook: From oil dependency to local resilience*. Totnes, Devon: Green Books.

Jackson, T. 2009. *Prosperity without growth: Economics for a finite planet*. London: Earthscan.

Kasser, T. 2002. *The high price of materialism*. Cambridge, MA: MIT Press.

Kubiszewski, I., Costanza, R., Franco, C., Lawn, P., Talberth, J., Jackson, T., and Aylmer, C. 2013. 'Beyond GDP: Measuring and achieving global genuine progress'. *Ecological Economics* 93: 57-68.

Latouche, S. 2009. *Farewell to growth*. Cambridge, UK: Polity Press.

Polimeni, J. et al. 2009. *The myth of resource efficiency: The Jevons paradox*. London: Earthscan.

Princen, T. 2005. *The logic of sufficiency*. Cambridge (MA): MIT Press.

Smith, R. 2010. 'Beyond growth or beyond capitalism'. *Real-World Economics Review* 53: 28-42.

Turner, G. 2012. 'Are we on the cusp of collapse? Updated comparison of *The limits to growth* with historical data'. *Gaia* 21(2): 116-124.

Trainer. T. 2010. *The transition to a sustainable and just world*. Sydney: Envirobook.

Vale, R. and Vale, B. 2013. *Living within a fair share ecological footprint*. London: Earthscan.

Wilkinson, R. and Pickett, K. 2010. *The spirit level: Why greater equality makes socieities stronger*. London: Penguin.

2

THE OPTIMAL MATERIAL THESHOLD
Toward an economics of sufficiency

He who knows he has enough is rich.
– Lao Tzu

1. Introduction

Increasing material wealth has been, and remains, one of the dominant goals of humankind – perhaps *the* dominant goal, even if for most people historically it was a goal that would never be realised. Given the extremely low material standards of living endured by most people throughout history, and indeed, by great multitudes around the world even today, the desire for more wealth is hardly surprising. When people are hungry, they understandably desire more food; when people are cold, warmer clothing and adequate housing are critically important; when people are ill, they naturally want access to basic medical supplies, etc. In conditions of material destitution, the pursuit of more material wealth seems wholly justifiable.

But what about those of us in the highly developed regions of the world who generally have our basic material needs for food, shelter, clothing, etc., adequately met, and who even have some discretionary income to purchase things like alcohol, microwave ovens, non-essential clothing, take-out food, movie tickets, books, and even the occasional holiday? In these relatively comfortable material circumstances, is more material wealth a goal for which we should still be striving? Or should we now be dedicating more of our time and energy to other, less materialistic pursuits? In other words, when it comes to material wealth – money, possessions, assets, etc.

– how much is actually needed to live a meaningful, free, and happy life?

These questions are of the highest importance, today more than ever before. At a time when Earth's ecosystems are already trembling under the weight of overconsumption (Turner, 2012), increasing the consumption levels of those who are already materially well off seems to be a highly questionable objective, despite it being an objective whose legitimacy is widely taken for granted. Furthermore, the extent of global poverty strongly suggests that the wealthier sectors of the global population (say, the richest one billion people) should restrain their consumption in order to leave more resources for those in much greater need. This is especially so given that the global population is expected to exceed nine billion by mid-century. We could call these the 'ecological' and 'social justice' arguments for consuming less.

In recent decades, however, a large body of sociological and psychological research has emerged which indicates that people living high consumption lifestyles might actually find that *it is in their own, immediate self-interest to consume less*, irrespective of the moral arguments for reduced consumption. Given the urgency with which overconsuming societies need to reduce their consumption, an argument from 'self-interest' should be taken very seriously indeed, for the reason that such an argument may prove to be more persuasive than more 'moralistic' arguments. On that basis, this chapter explores whether, or to what extent, it is in the self-interest of people in the global consumer class to voluntarily embrace lifestyles of reduced and restrained consumption. This will strike some people as a counter-intuitive hypothesis, at best, but it will be seen that the evidence indicates that such an intuition may well be based on false assumptions.

The analysis begins by reviewing the empirical studies that have examined the correlation between income and self-reported happiness. While the scholarly debate is not conclusively settled, the weight of evidence suggests that once people have their basic material needs adequately met, the correlation between income and happiness begins to fade. Put otherwise, there comes a point where rises in income become less important as means of increasing wellbeing, and other features of life, such as more meaningful employment, more leisure time, and more social engagement, become increasingly important (Helliwell, Layard, and Sachs, 2012). This has been called the 'income-happiness paradox', because it contradicts the widely held assumption that more income and more economic growth will always contribute positively to human wellbeing. After reviewing the empirical literature, the analysis proceeds to consider the various explanations for this apparent 'paradox', and it also considers what implications this paradox might have for people and nations that are overconsuming. The chapter concludes by outlining what will be called an 'economics of sufficiency', drawing on the perspectives of degrowth and steady state economics.

2. The Income-Happiness Paradox: Is More always Better?

It is often assumed that income growth will always contribute positively and directly to human wellbeing. The following inquiry considers what empirical evidence exists for this assumed correlation, in the following three situations: (1) across nations; (2) between individuals within a nation; and (3) over time. This scientific literature will be used to assess whether, or to what extent, individuals who are leading high consumption lifestyles could reduce their consumption while maintaining or even increasing their quality of life. The macroeconomic implications of this literature will also be explored.

For many decades now social scientists have been using surveys to assess empirically the wellbeing of human beings in different places, situations, and times (Easterlin, 1974; Diener, 1999). These surveys have been crafted in a variety of ways, asking such questions as, 'Taken all together, how happy would you say you are: very happy, quite happy, not very happy, or not happy at all'. Another prominent approach involves asking people to consider such statements as 'The conditions of my life are excellent' and then asking them to provide a response from 1-7 ranging from 'strongly agree' to 'strongly disagree'. Scientists have also sought to measure human wellbeing using a number of different methods – for example, using physiological and neurobiological indicators, observing social behaviour, and non-verbal behaviour – but prominent researchers Bruno Frey and Alois Stutzer (2002: 26) conclude: 'Self-reported happiness has turned out to be the best indicator of happiness. Extensive research has shown that people are capable of consistently evaluating their own state of wellbeing'. The following analysis proceeds on that basis.

A variety of terms have been used to denote overall wellbeing, including 'happiness', 'utility', 'subjective wellbeing', 'reported wellbeing', and 'life satisfaction'. The following analysis will follow Frey and Stutzer (2002) in using these terms interchangeably. It should be noted, however, that some recent work has drawn a distinction between two aspects of subjective wellbeing, as Daniel Kahneman and Angus Deaton (2010: 16489) explain:

> Emotional wellbeing refers to the emotional quality of an individual's everyday experience – the frequency and intensity of experiences of joy, stress, sadness, anger, and affection that make one's life pleasant or unpleasant. Life evaluation refers to the thoughts that people have about their life when they think about it.

While this distinction is valid, most studies into wellbeing are based on 'life evaluation' surveys, rather than 'emotional wellbeing' assessments, and so the former approach should be assumed for the purposes of the following literature review, unless stated otherwise.

Although surveys on happiness and life evaluation cannot provide an exact accounting of a notion as complex as 'human wellbeing', if their results are received critically and cautiously then they can still provide a good deal of insight into the state of human wellbeing and provide valuable information with which individual, social, economic, and political decisions can be made (Kruger and Schkade, 2008; Diener *et al.*, 2009; Bok, 2010). It would be quite unjustified to ignore the vast empirical research into the state of human wellbeing simply because the subject of wellbeing defies exact accounting. It would be especially unjustified given that in recent years a vast amount of research has been dedicated to this subject,[1] suggesting that these studies ought to be taken seriously, despite the fact that there is 'still more work to be done' (Diener and Biswas-Diener, 2009).

2.1 *The correlation between income and wellbeing across nations*

There is now a substantial body of research that has assessed the correlation between income and wellbeing across nations (Diener, Helliwell, and Kahneman, 2010; Helliwell, Layard, and Sachs, 2012). If ever there were people who seriously subscribed to the romantic notion of poor nations being happier than rich nations, rigorous studies over recent decades have convincingly dispelled such a myth. On average, persons living in rich countries are demonstrably happier than those living in the poorest countries. This unsurprising result has been established by Ed Diener and colleagues (2009) in an extensive study covering 55 nations. Their study was based on data from the *World Values Survey*, which is one of the best sources for international comparisons of life

---

[1] Kruger and Schkade (2008) note that between 2000 and 2006, 157 scholarly articles and numerous books were published in the economics literature alone, using data on life satisfaction or subjective wellbeing. See also, Diener and Seligman (2004) (reviewing hundreds of studies on wellbeing).

satisfaction over such a large number of countries. Many other studies, comparing various sets of nations, have found the same positive association between per capita income and life satisfaction (Deaton, 2008).

When the results of these studies are illustrated graphically, however, with average per capita income in a nation (across the horizontal axis) and average life satisfaction (on the vertical axis), a curious relationship is observable. While life satisfaction indeed rises with income up to a point, many researchers have observed a distinct *curvilinear* relationship between the two variables, suggesting that increases in income have a more or less direct and positive impact on life satisfaction at low levels of income, but beyond a surprisingly modest threshold point the correlation between income and life satisfaction weakens significantly (Inglehart and Klingemann, 2000). In one of the most comprehensive reviews of this body of literature, Frey and Stutzer (2002: 75) point out that 'there is no sizeable correlation between wealth and satisfaction with life above an average income level of US$10,000'. This is not to suggest, necessarily, that there is no correlation at all above that surprisingly low level, only that income above that level has a diminishing marginal utility (Layard *et al.*, 2008; Inglehart, 1996; Helliwell, Layard, and Sachs, 2012).

When comparing only the richest nations, however – which is the focus of this chapter – the correlation between income and life satisfaction is evidently negligible. Clive Hamilton, for example, has studied data on the richest 17 nations, and found that 'there is no relationship at all between higher incomes and higher reported appreciation of life' (Hamilton, 2003: 26). Similarly, Richard Layard (2005: 32) concludes: 'If we compare the Western industrial countries, the richer ones are no happier than the poorer ones.' In a recent study, Layard and his colleagues (2010) provide further evidence for this position and rigorously respond to their critics (Deaton, 2008; Stevenson and Wolfers, 2008). This new study essentially corroborates Ronald Inglehart's (1996: 509) thesis that 'although economic gains apparently make a major contribution to subjective wellbeing as one moves from societies at the subsistence level to those with moderate levels of economic development, further economic growth seems to have little or no impact on subjective wellbeing'. And as another commentator notes, even people who argue that economic growth still brings happiness in prosperous countries 'often find that the rate of increase is very slight' (Bok, 2010: 14).

To those people or governments who assume that income per capita is a proxy for social progress, these research findings present a challenging anomaly. Indeed, it is suggested that they provide credible grounds for doubting whether growth in Gross Domestic Product (GDP) should still be a dominant policy objective for rich nations, since it would seem getting richer is no longer contributing much, if anything, to wellbeing (Jackson, 2009). After reviewing more than 100 scholarly studies, Ed Diener and Martin Seligman (2004: 1) conclude:

> economic indicators were extremely important in the early stages of economic development, when the fulfilment of basic material needs was the main issue. As societies grow wealthy, however, differences in wellbeing are less frequently due to income, and are more frequently due to factors such as social relationships and enjoyment at work.

When considering this body of social research one must, of course, allow for the possibility that any perceived correlation between income and happiness may be produced by factors other than income, as such. To some extent this will almost certainly be the case. Frey and Stutzer (2002: 75) note, in particular, that 'countries with higher per capita incomes tend to have more stable democracies than poor countries' and so 'it may well be that the seemingly observed positive association between income and happiness is in reality due to the more developed democratic conditions'. Or perhaps the perceived association is actually due to more secure human rights or better average health. Controlling as far as possible for these and several other possibly misleading factors, Frey and Stutzer (2002: 75-6) still hold that 'there is substantial evidence that it is indeed income that produces subjective wellbeing, at least for countries below a certain threshold of wealth'.

Once that threshold has been crossed, however – and the rich Western nations already seem to have crossed it – evidence suggests that further growth in GDP has a fast-diminishing marginal utility. What this means, in other words, is that beyond the threshold, income per capita is an increasingly poor indicator of human wellbeing. This is a cause for concern because, despite this evidence, rich nations persist in using the growth model in their decision-making, consciously or unconsciously (Purdey, 2010), and this means that they continue to endorse and seek growth, and structure institutions accordingly, even though growth has seemingly stopped contributing significantly to their wellbeing (see Kubiszewski *et al.*, 2013; Diener, Helliwell, and Kahneman, 2010). This is all the more troubling given that growth is the primary cause of ecological degradation.

2.2 *The correlation between income and wellbeing within a nation*

Within any nation, are rich people happier? One might have thought the answer would be simple. When people have lots of money, they seem to have more opportunities to achieve whatever they desire: they can purchase more luxurious consumer goods and services; they can afford better healthcare, receive a better education, and are more likely to enjoy higher status, etc. And if for some reason rich people think that living in poverty will make them happier, they are free to dispose of their money at no cost (Frey and Stutzer, 2002). These are no doubt the kinds of reasons that led the great utilitarian economist Jeremy Bentham (2005: 468) to assert: 'Money is the most accurate measure of the quantity of pain or pleasure that a person can be made to receive... It is from his money that a man derives the main part of his pleasures.' But are things that simple?

It seems not. When we actually consider the extensive empirical evidence on this subject, rather than just uncritically accept the perhaps 'commonsense' assumptions of conventional economics, we find a much more nuanced relationship between income and wellbeing. The evidence generally confirms that, on average, rich people report higher levels of life satisfaction than poor people (Frey, 2008). But upon closer inspection, the research shows that, although more money increases wellbeing at low levels of income, with further increases in income there soon comes a point when the correlation between income and wellbeing tends to fade, at times even to vanishing point (Lane, 2000). In their US study, for example, Kahneman and Deaton (2010) argue that there comes a point when getting richer *is not correlated at all* with emotional wellbeing. While they conclude that life satisfaction does rise with the log of income (see also, Stevenson and Wolfers, 2008), this should not be interpreted to mean that pursuing money is the most direct path to life satisfaction, because evidence has consistently shown that as people get richer, things *other than income* become more influential causes of happiness and life satisfaction (see, e.g., Helliwell, Layard, and Sachs, 2012; Helliwell, Layard, and Sachs, 2013). In other words, while income growth might sometimes lead to happiness, it seems that the richer and more secure one gets in material terms, the more likely it is that further increases in happiness are going to come from things such as more meaningful work, social engagement, and leisure. This point seems to be lost on those who simplistically argue that 'money buys happiness'.

The positive effects of increasing income seem to be stronger within the poorest nations, for the reason that more people subsist in conditions of material destitution. But, as David Myers (2000a: 131) puts it, 'within affluent countries, where nearly everyone can afford life's necessities, increasing affluence matters surprisingly little'. Similarly, Frey and Stutzer (2002: 83) conclude that '[a]t low levels of income, a rise in income strongly raises wellbeing. But once an annual income of about US$15,000 has been reached, a rise in income level has a smaller effect on happiness'.

The diminishing correlation between income and wellbeing within nations has also been observed by Inglehart in his 16-nation study of the US, Canada, and Western Europe, where he concludes that the correlation between income and happiness is 'surprisingly weak (indeed, virtually negligible)' (Inglehart, 1990: 242). Commenting on this weak or even non-existent relationship between income and happiness, Michael Argyle (1999: 353) pays tribute to the theory of declining marginal utility of money: 'The reason for the rather weak effect of income [on happiness] in the USA may be that many Americans are above the level at which income affects happiness.' It seems this reasoning now applies to most if not all the advanced capitalist societies (Lane, 2000; Layard, 2005).

The central insight here is that the rich are not much more satisfied with their lives than the merely comfortable, who in turn are only slightly, if at all, more satisfied with their lives than the lower middle classes. And there is now considerable research on these issues (see also, Kahneman and Deaton, 2010; Helliwell, Layard and Sachs, 2012; Helliwell, Layard, and Sachs, 2013). It seems that once a moderate threshold has been reached – which some theorists argue is essentially when 'basic needs' have been satisfied (Di Tella and MacCulloch, 2010) – a higher income will tend to have less impact on human wellbeing. The point is summarised well by John Talberth (2008: 10):

> An increasingly large and robust body of hedonics research confirms what people know intuitively: beyond a certain threshold, more material wealth is a poor substitute for community cohesion, healthy relationships, a sense of purpose, connection with nature, and other dimensions of human happiness.

It is suggested that this research casts further doubt on the received wisdom that increases in income per capita will benefit people in affluent societies. It even suggests that some people could increase their wellbeing by directing less of their time and energy toward materialistic pursuits, and more time toward non-materialistic pursuits – a point to which we will return.

2.3 *The correlation between income and wellbeing over time*

A final way to assess the correlation between income and wellbeing is to compare the wellbeing of an individual or a society over different points in time, in different financial circumstances. If we assume that increasing per capita incomes will have a direct and positive bearing on life satisfaction, we would expect to see this relationship reflected over time as an individual or a society gets richer. Again, there is a large and growing empirical literature providing insight into this issue (e.g., Hinte and Zimmerman, 2010).

As documented above, rich nations tend to report higher levels of subjective wellbeing than the poorest nations, where poverty is widespread. From this it can be fairly inferred that as a poor nation's economy grows over time and secures more basic material needs for its inhabitants, the wellbeing of those inhabitants also tends to rise.[2] This initially strong correlation between income and wellbeing is arguably the main reason the growth paradigm is so deeply entrenched today. It is no wonder, given the many benefits derived from economic growth since the Industrial Revolution, that the growth imperative structures our politics, our outlook, even our identities. And since increasing income tends to increase wellbeing significantly when nations or individuals are very poor, it is easy to infer that, beyond poverty, further income will keep on increasing wellbeing in the same direct and positive fashion. That inference, however, turns out to be false. Richard Easterlin (2013) argues that long term trends in growth and happiness are not related, while others argue it is related, but only up to a point (see generally, Diener, Helliwell, and Kahneman, 2010).

In the US and UK, to begin with two of the most notorious examples, research shows that the 'income-happiness paradox' has developed (Blanchflower and Oswald, 2004). The 'paradox', so-called, is this: over the last half century, average per capita incomes have grown several times over, but despite this tremendous rise in the material standard of living, inhabitants are slightly less happy or no more happy today than they were 50 years ago. Similarly, if we look to Japan, evidence indicates that between 1958 and 1991 real GDP per capita increased six-fold, yet reported satisfaction

---

[2] While this suggests that there are powerful arguments for more economic growth *of some form* in countries where a large proportion of the population lives in poverty, Clive Hamilton (2003: 27) is correct to warn that 'this should not be construed as an unalloyed endorsement of growth at all costs. The nature of the growth process matters'.

with life did not change at all (Frey, 2008: 39; Layard *et al.*, 2010; Easterlin, 2013).

Let us dwell on these points for a moment. Three of the richest economies in the world have grown considerably over the last 50 years and yet the wellbeing of their inhabitants, which surveys have quite consistently recorded, has tended to stagnate (or, in the case of the US, decline). In other words, the affluence delivered by growth in GDP within these nations has evidently stopped serving human wellbeing. *Getting richer is no longer making people happier.* As mentioned above, this phenomenon can be labelled the 'income-happiness paradox', a paradox because it fundamentally contradicts what conventional 'more is better' economics would have predicted. And it calls for reflection: 'If the economy is up,' ask Clifford Cobb *et al.* (1995: 1), 'why is America down?' In his review of the scholarly literature, Hamilton (2003: 30) is surely right to insist: 'The implications of the figures cannot be brushed aside: if a sharp rise in personal incomes does not result in any increase in personal life satisfaction, why do we as societies give such enormous emphasis to economic growth?'

Evidently, it is not just the US, UK, and Japan that must confront this deeply challenging state of affairs. Many other developed societies are showing distinct signs of confronting a very similar paradox, as evidenced by the recent studies based on the 'extended accounts' of the Index for Sustainable Economic Welfare (ISEW) or the Genuine Progress Indicator (GPI) (Lawn, 2006; Kubiszewski *et al.*, 2013). These analytical tools, among others (e.g., the Human Development Index, the Happy Planet Index, the Measure of Domestic Progress, etc.), have been developed in response to growing discontent with the inadequacies and narrowness of GDP as a measure of welfare (see Stiglitz, Sen, and Fitoussi, 2010). As much more nuanced measures of welfare, the ISEW and the GPI take into consideration extremely important social and environmental factors that GDP, as a measure of welfare, does not and cannot reflect. For example, the ISEW and the GPI begin with total private consumption expenditure and then make deductions for such things as resource depletion, pollution, income inequality, loss of leisure, 'defensive expenditures' etc, and make additions for such things as public infrastructure, volunteering, and domestic work (Daly and Cobb, 1989). The aim of these indexes is to measure genuine progress as accurately as possible, not just total market activity.

What, then, do these 'extended accounts' of welfare show? Avner Offer (2006) helpfully reviews the key findings of the ISEW in relation to many nations. Offer shows that the US and UK ISEW declined significantly between 1975 and 1990, even though GDP grew significantly. Furthermore, ISEW measures are now available for Australia, Austria, Chile, Germany, Italy, the Netherlands, Sweden, as well as the US and UK. Offer (2006: 19) reports that, 'All except Italy record ISEW growth until the 1970s, with stagnation or decline afterwards.' Other studies suggest that Italy is also in decline (D'Andrea, 1998).

Although there is still room to improve the ISEW and the GPI, it is suggested that they are undoubtedly better measures of national progress than GDP (Lawn, 2003; Lawn 2005). It is heartening to observe that these types of extended accounts are approaching official recognition, albeit slowly (Stiglitz, Sen, and Fitoussi, 2010). The message they convey, however, is a rather disconcerting one, especially for the developed nations. After all, they show that economic growth since about the mid-1970s has done little or no good in terms of aggregate welfare. On that basis, Offer (2006: 20) seems justified in concluding that 'the pursuit of further growth has been irrational. It is only myopia and habit which allow it to continue in the face of negative welfare returns'.

Interestingly, this message is even being acknowledged by some conservative political parties, which typically have been the bastion of 'more is better' growth economics. In 2007, for example, the UK Conservative Party issued a landmark report, *Blueprint for a Green Economy* (Gummer and Goldsmith, 2007), which is one of the first attempts by a major political party in the industrialised world to refocus attention away from economic growth and toward a much broader and more inclusive conception of wellbeing. In a startling admission, the authors (Gummer and Goldsmith, 2007: 8) state:

> ...beyond a certain threshold – a point which the UK reached some time ago – ever increasing material gain can become not a gift but a burden. As people, it makes us less happy, and the environment upon which all of us, and our economy, depend is increasingly degraded by it.

More recently, UK Prime Minister, David Cameron – hardly known for his progressive economics – has stated, 'It's time we admitted that there's more to life than money and it's time we focused not just on GDP but on GWB – general well-being' (see Stratton, 2010). Of course, this has remained at the level of rhetoric merely, but it does indicate that cultural attitudes toward income growth may be shifting toward less materialistic perspectives.

In light of all this evidence, the question about the effects of rising incomes on wellbeing over time can be answered as follows: getting richer over time makes people and societies better off *up to a point*, but once a moderate level of wealth has been attained – a level which the developed nations, as detailed above, already seem to have surpassed – getting richer makes little, if any, positive difference to wellbeing (Kubiszewski *et al.*, 2013; Helliwell, Layard, and Sachs, 2012; Helliwell, Layard and Sachs, 2013). When that point has been reached – which cannot be precisely defined and is likely to be context-dependent – individuals and societies, if they wish to increase their wellbeing, should dedicate their energies toward non-materialistic sources of meaning and fulfilment. In a consumerist age that celebrates the limitless pursuit of material wealth, this is admittedly a counter-intuitive point. But that just makes it all the more important that the complex relationship between income and happiness is given due attention.

3. Explaining the Income-Happiness Paradox

Before exploring the implications of these findings, it is important to consider the question of why it might be that, beyond a moderate threshold, more income 'paradoxically' stops contributing much to wellbeing. Understanding this paradox, so-called, might provide some insight into how best to respond to it. Seven of the more prominent explanations for the 'income-happiness paradox' are outlined below, none of which are mutually exclusive.

3.1 *Relative income vs. absolute income*

Some theorists, going at least as far back as Thorstein Veblen (1965 [1899]), have highlighted the fact that once a person's basic material needs are satisfied, *relative* income often has much more effect on subjective wellbeing than *absolute* levels of income. This issue has been the subject of many sociological studies (e.g., Ball and Chenova, 2008; Layard *et al.*, 2010), and the studies have tended to show that, not so far beyond the poverty line, people generally assess their individual wellbeing in relation to how others in a similar social group are doing, such that if our incomes rise relative to those around us we are likely to become happier; but if everyone else's incomes rise at the same time as our own, we are less likely to become happier. Moreover, if your increase in income causes envy in those around you, your increased happiness (through status) might be offset by dissatisfaction in others, so that aggregate happiness across the nation may not change at all (Jackson, 2006: 10). For these reasons, there may come a time when economic growth is wasteful or self-defeating, much like when everyone stands on tip toes in a crowd and nobody's position improves. Status competition, after all, is a zero-sum game, in the sense that if someone's status increases, someone else's must have relatively decreased. Many theorists argue that this struggle over social positioning is why economic growth has stopped contributing much to wellbeing in affluent societies (Hirsch, 1976; Layard *et al.*, 2010).

3.2. *Hedonic adaptation*

Other theorists point to the impact of 'hedonic adaptation' as the cause, or a contributing cause, of the income-happiness paradox (Di Tella and MacCulloch, 2010). The central idea here is that as people get richer they generally become more accustomed to the pleasure of the goods and services their new income affords them. Accordingly, if people want to maintain the same level of happiness, they must achieve ever-higher levels of income in the future just to stay in the same place, hence the metaphor of the 'consumerist treadmill' (Jackson, 2006:10). As Myers (2000b: 60) notes, 'Thanks to our capacity to adapt to ever greater fame and fortune, yesterday's luxuries can soon become today's necessities and tomorrow's relics.' This phenomenon of hedonic adaptation, just like the struggle over social positioning, is nullifying the projected or anticipated benefits of income growth in rich nations.

3.3 *Rising expectations*

In a similar fashion, the benefits of income growth can be nullified if people continually raise their material expectations about what is needed to attain contentment. One example of this is known as the 'Diderot Effect' (named after the philosopher Denniss Diderot, who first wrote about it). This phenomenon refers to how consumer purchases can induce the desire for other purchases, which can induce further desires, and so on. The purchase of some new shoes looks out of place without a new outfit to match; a new car looks out of place parked in front of a shabby old house; painting the lounge can make the kitchen look even older; and replacing the sofas tempts one to replace the chairs too. This striving for uniformity in cultural standards of consumption can function to lock people onto a consumerist treadmill that has no end and attains no lasting satisfaction.

Richard Easterlin (2001: 465) argues that 'people project current aspirations to be the same throughout the life cycle, while income grows. But since aspirations actually grow along with income, experienced happiness is systematically different from projected happiness. Consequently, choices turn out to be based on false expectations'. This type of reasoning prompted Easterlin (1995) to ask, 'Will raising the incomes of all increase the happiness of all?', and he answered this question in the negative, on the grounds that the material norms on which judgements of wellbeing are made tend to increase in the same proportion as the actual income of the society. Derek Bok (2010: 13) makes essentially the same point when he suggests that 'people's aspirations are forever beyond their reach, leaving them perpetually unsatisfied'. Once again, the anticipated benefits of increased income will never be realised if material expectations keep rising.

3.4 *Overwork*

Another reason why income growth has generally stopped contributing to wellbeing in affluent societies can be attributed to the fact that many of those societies have developed cultures of overwork, despite the fact that technological advances have made the workforce considerably more productive per hour than in earlier eras. In terms of wellbeing, Charles Siegel (2008: 8) poses the critical question: 'Should we take advantage of our increasing productivity to consume more or to have more free time?' If people keep raising their material standards of living every time they come into more money – through a pay rise, for example, or through some new technology which increases productivity per hour – working hours will never decrease and may even rise. Indeed, many Westerners, especially North Americans, Britons, and Australians, are working longer hours today than they were in the 1970s, despite being considerably more productive (de Graaf, 2003; Hamilton and Denniss, 2005). Generally speaking, they have directed all their wealth and productivity gains into consuming more and have not taken any of those gains in terms of increased free time. Arguably, quality of life could have been increased if more of those productivity gains were converted into more time and less consumption (see also, Helliwell, Layard, and Sachs, 2012; Helliwell, Layard, and Sachs, 2013).

To make matters worse, there are structural biases in many affluent societies that function to promote overwork (i.e., working hours that are not 'optimal' or 'utility maximising'), such as laws that treat the 40-hour work week as 'standard' or which exclude part-time workers from many of the non-pecuniary benefits enjoyed by those who work full-time (Robinson, 2007). The effect of these structural biases is essentially to force or coerce many people to work longer hours than they want or need to, which gives rise to cultures that tend to overconsume resources and under-consume leisure. This might lead to higher GDP per capita, but at the cost of quality of life and planetary health (Hayden, 1999).

3.5. The high price of materialism

Many ancient wisdom traditions, both 'philosophical' and 'spiritual', tell us that materialistic values can be dangerous; that focusing on attaining material possessions and social renown can detract from what is meaningful about life (Vanenbroeck, 1991). Tim Kasser (2002, 2009) has explored the science beneath such ancient wisdom, and he shows that research on the effects of materialism yields clear and consistent findings: 'People who are highly focused on materialistic values [i.e., people who orientate their lives around the acquisition of money, fame, and image] have lower personal wellbeing and psychological health than those who believe that materialistic pursuits are relatively unimportant' (Kasser, 2002: 22). What is more, Kasser shows that these relationships have been documented in samples of people ranging from the wealthy to the poor, from teenagers to the elderly, and from Americans to Russians, from Australians to South Koreans. If this is true then today's growth-obsessed, consumer cultures are inculcating people with values that are not conducive to their own wellbeing. After reviewing the evidence, Kasser concludes that when people in affluent societies subscribe to materialistic values and organise their lives around the pursuit of wealth and possessions, 'they are essentially wasting their time as far as wellbeing is concerned. By concentrating on such a profitless style of life, they leave themselves little opportunity to pursue goals that could fulfil their needs and improve the quality of their lives' (Kasser, 2002: 47-8).

3.6. The limits to purchasing happiness

A related reason for why income does not contribute much to wellbeing in affluent societies concerns the limits of market consumption. Whatever it is that makes life meaningful or fulfilling, evidently it is not the limitless consumption of goods and services (Scitovsky, 1976; Csikszentmihalyi, 1999). Robert Lane expresses the idea as follows: 'the richer the society and its individuals become, *the less purchasable are the goals that bring them happiness* – although they may still pursue wealth with their accustomed vigor' (Lane, 2000: 63, emphasis added). And, indeed, continuing the pursuit seems to be the way of many individuals in affluent societies today, as Kasser (2002: 59) explains: 'The sad truth is that when people feel the emptiness of either material success or failure, they often persist in thinking that more will be better, and thus continue to strive for what will never make them happy'. This 'sad truth' manifests itself politically in affluent societies as an insatiable desire for economic growth.

3.7. *Inequality is socially corrosive*

One final explanation for why per capita income growth is failing to contribute much to wellbeing in rich countries is that in recent decades, especially, the rewards of growth have gone mainly to the richest few per cent of the population. Kate Picket and Richard Wilkinson (2010) have discussed this issue in depth, presenting an impressive body of evidence showing the social benefits of a broad-based distribution of wealth. These studies show that great economic inequality in a society is socially corrosive – a point that supports a more egalitarian distribution of wealth in societies where wealth is highly polarised. In short, beyond a certain threshold, it seems that distributive equity matters more, in terms of overall human wellbeing, than continuous growth.

4. The Radical Implications of the Income-Happiness Paradox

At first instance the widespread assumption that real income growth will always contribute positively to human happiness seems intuitively plausible. As noted earlier, money provides people with power to purchase some of the things that they desire, whether those things are goods (big houses, nice clothes, expensive food, etc.) or services (hired help, luxurious holidays, massages, etc.). The advertising industry plays on this materialistic assumption in highly sophisticated and manipulative ways, implicitly or explicitly reinforcing the idea that people need this or that product if they want to be satisfied with life (PIRC, 2011). If it were the case that subjective wellbeing always increased in proportion with real income growth, this would provide some grounds for arguing that human beings have an ongoing interest in being materialistic, and that governments are correct to treat growth in GDP as a proxy for social progress. But the evidence reviewed above shows that such arguments are either false or in need of significant qualification.

We have seen that income growth tends to contribute positively and directly to human wellbeing when people and societies have very low levels of material wealth. But once basic material needs have been met – as they generally have been in the most developed regions of the world – further increases in income have diminishing marginal returns. The evidence even suggests that there comes a point – a threshold which the most developed nations have already crossed – where the anticipated benefits of growth are nullified by social and psychological phenomena such as status competition, hedonic adaptation, rising expectations, etc. While it is true that within a nation, the richest people are generally happier than those less well off, it seems that once a moderate level of wealth has been attained, further increases in wealth play only a minimal role raising wellbeing. What this means is that if people whose basic material needs have been met continue to dedicate their lives to the pursuit of more and more wealth, they may find that they are essentially wasting their time so far as wellbeing is concerned. As Tim Jackson (2006: 10) puts it:

> Far from making us happier... the pursuit of material things damages us psychologically and socially. Beyond the satisfaction of our basic material needs for housing, clothing and nutrition, the pursuit of material consumption merely serves to entrench us in unproductive status competition, disrupts our work/life balance and distracts us from those things that offer meaning and purpose to our lives.

When considering the body of evidence reviewed above, it is commonplace to acknowledge that relatively affluent individuals and societies are unlikely to increase their wellbeing significantly by getting richer. The lesson typically drawn from this is that those individuals and societies should not seek *further* income growth (e.g., Jackson, 2009). Given that the world economy today is governed by the profit-maximising logic of growth economics, this lesson is a challenging one.

It is my contention, however, that the implications of the literature are more radical still. After all, the evidence does not merely show that the richest nations are consuming at the material threshold in an 'optimal' way. That is to say, the richest nations are not consuming 'just enough' to maximise their wellbeing. Instead, the sociological evidence (to say nothing of the ecological evidence) implies that the richest nations, and many people within those nations, have actually gone *beyond* the optimal material threshold; they are now dedicating 'too much' of their time and energy toward materialistic pursuits (Max-Neef, 1995; Lawn and Clarke, 2010; Kubiszewski *et al.*, 2013). This implies that those nations and individuals who have gone beyond the optimal material threshold could actually *increase their wellbeing by reducing their consumption*. That is the central thesis this chapter is advancing.

For example, if people in affluent societies were to rethink their relationships with money and reduce their outgoings, they might be able to free up more time for things that truly make them happy, such as more time with friends and family, or more time to engage in their private passions. This type of reasoning has even led one theorist, Kate Soper (2008), to coin the term 'alternative hedonism', in order to highlight the many joys and pleasures that come with living a simpler, post-consumerist existence.

Could it be that many people in affluent societies can actually live better, happier, and more pleasurable and engaged lives by reducing and restraining their income and consumption?

5. Toward an Economics of Sufficiency

Fortunately, we no longer need to rely on theories or abstract arguments to show that people can live well on less. A growing number of people in the Voluntary Simplicity Movement are choosing to reduce and restrain their consumption – not out of sacrifice or deprivation, but in order to be free, happy, and fulfilled in a way that consumer culture rarely permits (see generally, Alexander, 2009). By limiting their working hours, spending their money frugally and conscientiously, growing their own vegetables, sharing skills and assets, riding bikes, rejecting high-fashion, and generally celebrating life *outside* the shopping mall, these people are new pioneers transitioning to a form of life beyond consumer culture.

This post-consumerist social movement, it could be said, is exemplifying an 'economics of sufficiency', one that seeks to attain 'enough' to live well, while resisting the counter-productive urge to increase consumption without limit. Given that overconsumption is the driving force behind many of today's social and ecological crises (Lane, 2000; Trainer, 2010), the emergence of a social movement that is increasing social wellbeing by embracing sufficiency in consumption is an omen whose positive potential can hardly be overstated.

Significantly, the largest multi-national survey analysis of the Voluntary Simplicity Movement (Alexander and Ussher, 2012) reports that almost all participants in the movement are happier for embracing lifestyles of reduced or restrained income. Quite remarkably, only an insignificant number (0.3%) said that they were 'less happy'. These results, which support the analysis above, are important because they indicate that a 'double dividend' can flow from reducing consumption, or even a 'triple' or 'quadruple' dividend, etc. (Jackson, 2005; Brown and Kasser, 2005; Kasser 2009). That is to say, the results suggest that the arguments for reduced consumption based on environmental, humanitarian, and population concerns, etc., are supported also by an argument based on increased happiness. People have a reason to live simply for their own sakes, the evidence suggests, but by doing so, it may be inferred, they are also likely to benefit others and the planet. If this is indeed so, it is extremely good news, because an argument based on 'self-interest' is likely to be more persuasive than arguments based on more 'moralistic' concerns arising from environmental or humanitarian concerns.

Of course, these results do not 'prove' that living simply will make people happier. But they do suggest that the overwhelming majority of participants in the Voluntary Simplicity Movement are notably happier for living more simply. And this means that simpler living is providing many people with a viable and desirable alternative to higher consumption lifestyles – an alternative that other people may also find it in their interest to explore.

The most promising thing about this emerging social movement is that it may provide a solution to one of the greatest problems of our age – the problem of growth. Despite the global economy far exceeding the planet's sustainable limits (Vale and Vale, 2013), even the richest nations on the planet still seek to grow their economies further (Purdey, 2010). This growth imperative arises because our economies are dependent on growth to function, for when growth-based economies do not grow, people suffer – as evidenced by the ongoing Global Financial Crisis, especially in Europe. One is struck here by a painful contradiction arising from the need to consume *less* for ecological and hedonic reasons, but consume *more* for the sake of a strong economy. Can this contradiction be resolved?

Perhaps, but only perhaps. If more people came to place self-imposed limits on their own consumption, rather than always seeking an ever-higher material standard of living, then this could well open up space to rethink the growth imperative that defines our economies. In other words, if an economics of sufficiency were ever embraced at the personal and social levels, there is no reason to think that an economics of sufficiency could not also arise at the macroeconomic level (Alexander, 2011a; Alexander, 2013). This may sound like science fiction to those who cannot think beyond the growth model. But times they are a-changing.

The following sections outline, in a preliminary way, the basic structure of what could be called a 'macroeconomics of sufficiency'. It will be argued that there are social, ecological, and even economic reasons to support the proposition that continuing growth in the developed nations is: (1) increasingly wasteful, and arguably counter-productive, in terms of social wellbeing; (2) ecologically unsustainable; and (3) uneconomic. So far as this analysis is correct, it arguably follows that an equitable downscaling of production and consumption – or degrowth (Latouche, 2009; Kallis, 2011; Alexander, 2012a) – is the most appropriate and desirable response to the failings of growth economics. This is especially so given that growth in the richest parts of the world has proven to be an extremely inefficient and environmentally unsupportable means of eliminating global poverty (Woodward and Simms, 2006).

5.1. Degrowth for social wellbeing

As we have seen, the social critique of growth holds that growth in GDP is often strongly correlated with wellbeing at low levels of per capita income, but that once a society attains a moderate level of wealth, further growth has little, if any, positive impact on overall wellbeing. This has significant implications for high income societies like those in the developed world today. Most notably, it suggests that those societies could dedicate considerably less time to producing and consuming goods and services without negatively affecting overall wellbeing. Indeed, it is likely that wellbeing would be positively affected if they did so, since a considerable amount of time and energy otherwise spent on wasteful production and consumption would be freed up for more meaningful and fulfilling activities (Trainer, 2013). For this reason, some degrowth scholars argue that degrowth should not be considered a 'forced option' in the face of the ecological crisis; instead, degrowth should be seen as a choice to be made even without the crisis, 'simply to be human' (Fournier, 2008: 536).

Although trading money for time implies a lower material 'standard of living' (in terms of income/consumption), the above reasoning indicates that this would nevertheless lead to increased 'quality of life' (measured by subjective wellbeing). On that basis, it is argued that developed societies could increase overall wellbeing by initiating a degrowth process of planned economic contraction, in the sense of developing and implementing policies to reduce wasteful production and consumption and facilitate the exchange of money for time. To the extent that governments cannot be relied on to initiate this process, it follows that it must be driven from the grassroots (Trainer, 2010; Alexander, 2012a; Alexander, 2012b). Ideally, the degrowth process should continue until overgrown societies produce and consume to an optimal degree – not too much, not too little. Whether a society has attained this optimal social state, of course, may be forever contestable and unclear, but it is suggested that the notion of macroeconomic 'sufficiency' itself guards against the mistake of thinking that more production and consumption are always going to improve wellbeing (which is the defining flaw in the ideology of growth). The notion of macroeconomic 'optimality' also provides the theoretical space needed to argue that a downscaling of production and consumption could increase wellbeing, which is indeed an aspect of the case for degrowth (Latouche, 2003).

5.2. Degrowth for ecological sustainability

The ecological critique of growth holds that the global economy already significantly exceeds the regenerative and absorptive capacities of Earth's ecosystems, a crisis driven by the developed nations which are demonstrably overconsuming their fair share of Earth's resources (Meadows *et al.*, 2004). This situation is especially troubling since the poorest nations still need to develop their economic capacities in some form simply to provide for themselves a dignified standard of living. In response to the argument that techno-efficiency improvements will 'decouple' growth from ecological impact – and thus allow for 'sustainable development' or 'green growth' – evidence shows absolute ecological impacts are still increasing, despite the relative decoupling achieved by techno-efficiency improvements (Jackson, 2009; Alexander, 2014). For these reasons, it is argued that to achieve ecological sustainability, the developed nations need to initiate a degrowth process of planned economic contraction, in the sense of reducing the absolute level (not merely per unit level) of ecological impact caused by economic activity. Ideally, this process should continue until ecological sustainability has been achieved, at which point the developed nations should adopt a 'zero growth' or 'steady state' economic model (Trainer, 2010; Daly, 2008). In the poorest nations, a phase of clean, efficient, and equitable economic development is still required to achieve a dignified standard of living – facilitated, ideally, by some global redistribution of wealth – but eventually those developing nations too will need to transition to a steady state economy (Lawn and Clarke, 2010). The steady state model is of a physically non-growing but qualitatively developing economy which is maintained by a sustainable rate of resource throughput. Within a steady state economy, renewable resources would be harvested at rates that do not exceed regeneration rates; the rate of depletion of non-renewable resources would not exceed the rate of creation of renewable substitutes; and waste emission rates would not exceed the natural assimilative capacities of ecosystems into which they are emitted (Daly, 1990). These guiding principles would help ensure that an economy remains within the sustainable carrying capacity of the environment.

5.3. Degrowth for optimal macroeconomic scale

The economic critique of growth begins by pointing out that growth of an economy, measured by a rise in GDP, is not 'economic growth' unless the benefits of growth exceed the costs, all things considered. The critique then shows that most of the developed nations have entered or are entering a phase of 'uneconomic' growth (Daly, 1999); that is, a phase in which the costs of growth exceed the benefits, all things considered. This argument is based primarily on the extended accounts of the ISEW and GPI, discussed earlier, which are tools that seek to internalise many of the significant social and environmental externalities that GDP, as a measure of progress, fails to take into account. Since the ISEW and GPI indicate that the developed economies seem to have already exceeded their optimal macroeconomic scale (Kubiszewski et al., 2013), to achieve optimality those economies should initiate a degrowth process of planned economic contraction, a process which could be described as 'economic' degrowth. This would not involve deliberately reducing GDP per capita for its own sake, however, since degrowth for its own sake is no more sensible than growth for its own sake (Latouche, 2009: 7). Rather, degrowth for optimal macroeconomic scale would involve explicitly giving up the pursuit of growth and directly pursuing more specific welfare-enhancing objectives – such as eliminating poverty, lessening inequality, and protecting the environment – even if this led to lower GDP per capita. Planned economic contraction should continue until the costs are equal to the benefits, a situation which would represent an optimal macroeconomic scale and ideally would be maintained in the form of a steady state economy.

This is the vision of a macroeconomics of sufficiency, and the purpose of this chapter has been to provide some of its sociological foundations.[3] The present socio-economic argument has been that it

---

[3] The details on what precise structural form a macroeconomics of sufficiency would take is an important issue, but one beyond the scope of the present chapter.

is possible for affluent nations, and many people within those nations, to increase quality of life by reducing and restraining consumption. At the personal and community levels, this involves rejecting consumerism and transitioning to lifestyles of voluntary simplicity. At the macroeconomic level, it involves moving away from the dangerously flawed growth model of progress and implementing some degrowth process of planned economic contraction. If, on the other hand, the world continues to pursue growth without limits, on the flawed assumption that money buys happiness, then soon enough our civilisation will resemble a snake eating its own tail – and, in fact, one could say this is already the defining metaphor of our industrial age.

6. Conclusion

Over the last century, the majority of individuals in affluent societies have essentially been freed for the first time in history from the threat of material destitution and, indeed, now live lives of relative comfort (Offer, 2006). These individuals could now be confronting what the great economist John Maynard Keynes (1963: 362) called our 'permanent problem' – the problem of what to *do* with the radical freedom that material comfort provides. This chapter has made no attempt to answer that question; a question which, in any case, we must each answer for ourselves. The analysis above does suggest, however, that the meaning of human existence does not and cannot consist in the consumption and accumulation of ever more material things. Perhaps that is obvious, but what then of growth capitalism? In the apt verse of William Wordsworth (1994): 'Getting and spending, we lay waste our powers.'

The motivating aim of this chapter was to prompt self-reflection in the following terms: Could it be that it is now in our self-interest to voluntarily embrace 'simpler' lifestyles of reduced and restrained consumption? And could it be that it is also in the self-interest of developed nations to give up growth economics and transition by way of degrowth to a steady state economy? In an age that glorifies consumption and fetishises growth as never before, these might seem like counter-intuitive proposals. But the growing voluntary simplicity and degrowth movements – which represent two complementary dimensions of an economics of sufficiency – are indicating that such intuitions may well be false.

Consume less, live more. Just perhaps this is a way of life whose time has come.

References

Alexander, S. (ed.) 2009. *Voluntary simplicity: The poetic alternative to consumer culture*. Auckland: Stead & Daughters.

Alexander, S. 2011. *Property beyond growth: Toward a politics of voluntary simplicity*. Doctoral thesis, Melbourne Law School. Available at: http://papers.ssrn.com/sol3/papers.cfm?abstract_id=1941069 (accessed 10 September 2013).

Alexander, S. 2012a. 'Planned economic contraction: The emerging case for degrowth'. *Environmental Politics* 21 (3): 349-368.

Alexander, S. 2012b. 'Ted Trainer and the simpler way'. *Simplicity Institute Report* 12d, 1-19.

Alexander, S. 2013. 'Voluntary simplicity and the social reconstruction of law: Degrowth from the grassroots up'. *Environmental Values* 22: 287-308.

Alexander, S. 2014. 'A critique of techno-optimism: Efficiency without sufficiency is lost'. Melbourne Sustainable Society Institute Working Paper (WP 1/14, January 2014).

Alexander, S. and Ussher, S. 2012. 'The voluntary simplicity movement: A multi-national survey analysis in theoretical context'. *Journal of Consumer Culture* 12(1): 66-88.

Argyle, M. 1999. 'Causes and correlates of happiness'. In Kahneman, D., Diener, E., and Schwartz, N. (eds). *Well-being: The foundations of hedonic psychology*. New York: Russell Sage Foundation.

Bentham, J. 2005. 'The principles of penal law'. In *The works of Jeremy Bentham: Vol. I*. London: Elibron.

Blanchflower, D. and Oswald, A. 2004. 'Well-being over time in Britain and the USA'. *The Journal of Public Economics* 88: 1359.

Bok, D. 2010. *The politics of happiness: What government can learn from the new research on well-being*. Princeton: Princeton University Press.

Brown, K. and Kasser, T. 2005. 'Are psychological and ecological well-being compatible? The role of values, mindfulness, and lifestyle'. *Social Indicators Research* 74: 349-368.

Cobb, C., Halstead, T., and Rowe, J. 1995. 'If GDP is up, why is America down?' *The Atlantic Monthly*: 1 October.

Csikszentmihalyi, M. 1999. 'If we are so rich, why aren't we happy?' *American Psychologist* 54(10): 821.

D'Andrea, S. 1998. 'Italian quality of life'. *Social Indicators Research* 44(1): 5.

Daly, H. 1990. 'Toward some operational principles of sustainable development'. *Ecological Economics* 2(1): 1.

Daly, H. 1996. *Beyond growth: The economics of sustainable development*. Boston: Beacon Press.

Daly, H. 1999. 'Uneconomic growth in theory and fact'. *The First Annual Feasta Lecture*, 26 April 1999. Available at: http://www.feasta.org/documents/feastareview/daly.htm (accessed 1 February 2014).

Daly, H. and Cobb, J. 1989. *For the common good: Redirecting the economy toward community, environment, and a sustainable future*. Boston: Beacon Press.

Deaton, 2008. 'Income, health, and well-being around the world: Evidence from the Gallup World Poll'. *Journal of Economic Perspectives* 22(2): 53

De Graaf, J. (ed.) 2003. *Take back your time: Fighting overwork and time poverty in America*. San Francisco: Berret-Koehler.

Di Tella, R. and MacCulloch, R. 2010. 'Happiness adaptation to income beyond "basic needs"'. In Diener, E., Helliwell, J., and Kahneman, D. (eds). *International Differences in Well-Being*. Oxford, New York: Oxford University Press.

Diener, E., Diener, M., and Diener, C. 2009. 'Factors predicting the subjective well-being of nations'. In *Culture and well-being: The collected works of Ed Diener*. London: Springer.

Diener, E., Helliwell, J., and Kahneman, D. 2010. *International differences in well being*, Oxford University Press, Oxford: New York.

Diener, E. and Seligman, M. 2004. 'Beyond money: Toward an economy of well-being'. *Psychological Science in the Public Interest* 5: 1-31.

Easterlin, R. 1974. 'Does economic growth improve the human lot?' In David, P. and Reder, M. (eds). *Nations and households in economic growth: Essays in honor of Moses Abramovitz*. New York: Academic Press.

Easterlin, R. 1995. 'Will raising the incomes of all increase the happiness of all?' *Journal of Economic Behavior & Organization,* 27: 35.

Easterlin, R. 2001. 'Income and happiness: Towards a unified theory'. *Economic Journal* 111(473): 465.

Easterlin, R. 2013. *Happiness and economic growth: The evidence.* Discussion Paper No. 7187, January 2013: 1-30.

Easterlin, R. and Angelescu, L. 2010. 'Happiness and growth the world over: Time series evidence on the happiness – Income paradox'. In Hinte, H. and Zimmerman, K. (eds). *Happiness, growth and the life cycle*. Oxford: Oxford University Press.

Fournier, V. 2008. 'Escaping the economy: The politics of degrowth'. *International Journal of Sociology and International Research* 28: 528-545.

Frey, B. and Stutzer, A. 2002. *Happiness and economics: How the economy and institutions affect human well-being.* Princeton, NJ: Princeton University Press.

Frey, B. 2008. *Happiness: A revolution in economics.* London: MIT Press.

Gummer, J. and Goldsmith, Z. 2007. *Blueprint for a green economy: Submission to the shadow cabinet.* Available at: http://conservativehome.blogs.com/torydiary/files/blueprint for a green economy110907b.pdf (accessed 14 December 2013).

Hayden, A. 1999, *Sharing the work, sparing the planet: Work time, consumption, and ecology.* Annandale, Toronto, Ont: Pluto Press.

Hamilton, C. 2003. *Growth fetish.* Crows Nest, NSW: Allen & Unwin.

Hamilton, C. and Denniss, R. 2005. *Affluenza: When too much is never enough.* Crows Nest, NSW: Allen & Unwin.

Helliwell, J., Layard, R., and Sachs, J. (eds). 2012. *World happiness report 2012.* New York: Sustainable Development Solutions Network.

Helliwell, J., Layard, R., and Sachs, J. (eds). 2013. *World happiness report 2013.* New York: Sustainable Development Solutions Network.

Hinte, H. and Zimmerman, K. (eds). 2010. *Happiness, growth and the life cycle.* Oxford: Oxford University Press.

Hirsch, F. 1976. *Social limits to growth.* Cambridge, Mass: Harvard University Press.

Inglehart, R. 1990. *Culture shift in advanced industrial society.* Princeton, NJ: Princeton University Press.

Inglehart, R. 1996. 'The diminishing marginal utility of economic growth'. *Critical Review* 10: 509.

Inglehart, R. 1997. *Modernization and postmodernization: Cultural, economic, and political change in 43 societies.* Princeton, NJ: Princeton University Press.

Inglehart, R. and Klingemann, H-D. 2000. *Genes, culture, and happiness.* Boston: MIT Press.

Jackson, T. 2005. 'Live better by consuming less? Is there a double dividend in sustainable consumption?' *Journal of Industrial Ecology* 9: 19-36.

Jackson, T. (ed.) 2006. *Sustainable consumption.* London, Sterling, VA: Earthscan.

Jackson, T. 2009. *Prosperity without growth: Economics for a finite planet.* London: Earthscan.

Kahneman, D. and Deaton, A. 2010. *High income improves evaluation of life but not emotional well-being.* PNSA 107(38): 16489-16493.

Kallis, G. 2011. 'In defence of degrowth'. *Ecological Economics* 70: 873.

Kasser, T. 2002. *The high price of materialism*. Cambridge, MA: MIT Press.

Kasser, T. 2009. 'Psychological need satisfaction, personal well-being, and ecological sustainability'. *Ecopsychology* 1(4): 175.

Keynes, J.M. 1963. *Essays in Persuasion*. New York: Norton.

Kruger, A. and Schkade, D. 2008. 'The reliability of subjective well-being measures'. *Journal of Pub. Economics* 92: 1833.

Kubiszewski, I., Costanza, R., Franco, C., Lawn, P., Talberth, J., Jackson, T., and Aylmer, C. 2013. 'Beyond GDP: Measuring and achieving global genuine progress'. *Ecological Economics* 93: 57-68.

Lane, R. 2000. *The loss of happiness in market democracies*. New Haven: Yale University Press.

Latouche, S. 2003. 'Would the west actually be happier with less? The world downscaled'. *Le Monde Diplomatique (English Version)*. Available at: http://www.hartford-hwp.com/archives/27/081.html (accessed 10 November 2011).

Latouche, S. 2009. *Farewell to growth*. Cambridge, UK: Polity Press.

Layard, R. 2005. *Happiness: Lessons from a new science*. New York: Penguin Press.

Layard, R., Mayraz, G., and Nickell, S. 2008. 'The marginal utility of income'. *Journal of Public Economics* 92: 1846-1857.

Layard, R. *et al.* 2010. 'Does relative income matter? Are the critics right?' In Diener, E., Helliwell, J., and Kahneman, D. (eds). *International differences in well-being*. Oxford, New York: Oxford University Press.

Lawn, P. 2003. 'A theoretical foundation to support the index of sustainable economic welfare (ISEW). Genuine Progress Indicator (GPI), and other related indexes'. *Ecological Economics* 44(1): 105.

Lawn, P. 2005. 'An assessment of the valuation methods used to calculate the Index of Sustainable Economic Welfare (ISEW), Genuine Progress Indicator (GPI), and Sustainable Net Benefit Index (SNBI)'. *Environment, Development, and Sustainability* 2: 185-208.

Lawn, P. 2006. *Sustainable development indicators in ecological economics*. Cheltenham: Edward Elgar Publishing.

Lawn, P. and Clarke, M. 2010. 'The end of economic growth? A contracting threshold hypothesis'. *Ecological Economics* 69: 2213.

Max-Neef, M. 1995. 'Economic growth and quality of life: A threshold hypothesis'. *Ecological Economics* 15(2): 115.

Meadows, D., Randers, J., and Meadows, D. 2004. *Limits to growth: The 30-year update.* White River Junction, Vt., Chelsea Green Publishing.

Myers, D. 2000a. *The American paradox: Spiritual hunger in an age of plenty.* New Haven: Yale University Press.

Myers, D. 2000b. 'The funds, friends, and faith of happy people'. *American Psychologist* 55(1): 56.

Offer, A. 2006. *The challenge of affluence: Self-control and well-being in the United States and Britain since 1950.* Oxford; New York: Oxford University Press.

Pickett, K. and Wilkinson, R. 2010. *The spirit level: Why greater equality makes societies stronger.* London: Penguin.

PIRC (Public Interest Research Centre), 2011. 'Think of me as evil? Opening the ethical debates in advertising'. Surrey, Public Interest Research Centre and WWF-UK.

Purdey, S. 2010. *Economic growth, the environment, and international relations: The growth paradigm.* Routledge, New York.

Robinson, T. 2009. *Work, leisure, and the environment: The vicious circle of overwork and overconsumption.* Cheltenham: Edward Elgar Publishing.

Scitovsky, T. 1976. *The joyless economy: The psychology of human satisfaction and consumer dissatisfaction.* Oxford: Oxford University Press.

Siegel, C. 2008. *The politics of simple living.* Berkeley: Preservation Institute.

Soper, K. 2008. 'Alternative hedonism, cultural theory and the role of aesthetic revisioning'. *Cultural Studies* 22(5): 567.

Stevenson, B. and Wolfers, J. 2008. 'Economic growth and subjective well-being: reassessing the Easterlin paradox'. *Brookings Papers on Economic Activity*, 1.

Stiglitz, J., Sen, A., and Fitoussi, J.P. 2010. *Mis-measuring our lives: Why GDP doesn't add up.* New York: The New Press.

Stratton, A. 2010. 'Cameron aims to make happiness the new GDP'. *The Guardian* (15 November 2010). Available at: http://www.theguardian.com/politics/2010/nov/14/david-cameron-wellbeing-inquiry?intcmp=239 (accessed 15 December 2013).

Talberth, J. 2008. 'A new bottom line for progress'. In *State of the world.* Available at: http://www.worldwatch.org/files/pdf/SOW08_chapter_2.pdf (accessed 10 September 2010).

Trainer, T. 2010a. *The transition to a sustainable and just world.* Sydney: Envirobook.

Trainer, T. 2013. 'Your delightful day: The benefits of life in the simpler way'. *Simplicity Institute Report* 13b: 1-8.

Turner, G. 2012. 'On the cusp of global collapse? Updated

comparison of the *Limits to growth* with historical data'. *Gaia*, 21(2): 116-124.

Vale, R. and Vale, B. 2013. *Living within a fair share ecological footprint*. London: Earthscan.

Vanenbroeck, G. (ed.) 1991. *Less is more: An anthology of ancient and modern voices raised in praise of simplicity*. Vermont: Inner Traditions.

Veblen, T. 1965 [1899]. *The theory of the leisure class*. New York: A. M. Kelley.

Woodward, D. and Simms, A. 2006. 'Growth isn't working: The uneven distribution of benefits and costs from economic growth. *New Economics Foundation*. Available at: http://www.neweconomics.org/publications/entry/growth-isnt-working (accessed 10 September 2013).

Wordsworth, W. 1994. 'The world is too much with us; Late and soon'. In Hayden, J. *William Wordsworth: Selected Poems*.

3

THE VOLUNTARY SIMPLICITY MOVEMENT
A multi-national survey analysis in theoretical context

Superfluous wealth can buy superfluities only.
– Henry Thoreau

1. Introduction

The Voluntary Simplicity Movement can be understood broadly as a diverse social movement made up of people who are resisting high consumption lifestyles and who are seeking, in various ways, a lower consumption but higher quality of life alternative (Grigsby, 2004; Alexander, 2009, 2011a). In 2011 a multi-national online survey was launched for the purpose of gaining empirical insight into this 'post-consumerist' social movement. Presently 2268 participants in the movement have completed our 50-question survey and that makes it by far the most extensive sociological examination of the movement available (Elgin and Mitchell, 1977; Schor, 1998; Pierce, 2000; Kasser, 2002; Craig-Lees and Hill, 2002; Grigsby, 2004; Brown and Kasser, 2005; Hamilton and Denniss, 2005). This chapter presents a foundational analysis of these survey results.[1]

---

[1] This chapter is a lightly revised version of the paper that appeared in the *Journal of Consumer Culture* (2012), co-authored by Samuel Alexander and Simon Ussher. Although the original paper was based on 2268 participants, at the time of writing this revised version (March 2015) that number had grown to 3708 participants. The results have not changed in any significant way by these extra participants, however to remain consistent with the peer-reviewed paper the results below remain based on 2268 participants. The survey is still open, collecting more data. See here:

2. Why Examine the Voluntary Simplicity Movement?

Before turning to the survey and its results, we wish to provide some theoretical context to this research by outlining briefly why we chose to examine the Voluntary Simplicity Movement (hereafter, the 'Simplicity Movement'). As Directors of the Simplicity Institute – which is a research institute focusing on issues related to sustainable consumption – we feel it is important to be explicit about the presuppositions that we bring to this research project. All researchers have potential biases that may result from studying a subject from a particular viewpoint, but we feel that one means of being reflexive and transparent in this regard is for us to state our presuppositions from the outset.

2.1. *Ecological overshoot*

Many credible scientific studies have shown that the human economy is degrading the planet's ecosystems in ways that are unsustainable (Wackernagel, 2002; Millennium Ecosystem Assessment, 2005; Hansen, 2011; Turner, 2012). While this is hardly news, the full implications of the ecological crisis are rarely acknowledged or understood, at least with respect to what it means for the 'Western-style' consumption practices of the global consumer class.[2] It is clear enough that human beings need to consume *differently* and produce commodities more *efficiently*. But few people (and no governments – in the developed world, at least) are prepared to accept that attaining an ecologically sustainable global economy requires the global consumer class to consume *less*. On the contrary, the mainstream position on sustainability seems to be that economies around the world simply need to adopt 'sustainable development', which in theory means continuing to pursue economic growth (i.e., increases in GDP per capita) while employing science and technology to produce and consume more cleanly and efficiently (e.g., UNDP, 2007/8: 15).

---

http://simplicityinstitute.org/phpQ/fillsurvey.php?sid=2

[2] We use the phrase 'Western-style' rather than 'Western' to acknowledge that the high consumption, energy intensive lifestyles that originated in the West are practised today in many regions of the globe, such as the growing consumer classes in nations like China, India, Brazil, etc. We will refer to those living such high consumption lifestyles throughout the world as the 'global consumer class'. While this phrase obviously homogenises a diversity of lifestyles, it is sufficiently suggestive of a referent for immediate purposes.

This mainstream vision of how to achieve a sustainable world is coherent in theory, at best, but demonstrably it does not reflect empirical reality (Alexander, 2014a). Although many economies around the world are indeed getting better at producing commodities more cleanly and efficiently (a process known as 'relative decoupling'), overall ecological impact is nevertheless *still increasing*, because every year increasing numbers of commodities are being produced, exchanged, and consumed as a result of growing economies (Jackson, 2009, Ch. 5). We might have more fuel-efficient cars, for example, but the rebound effect is that we are also driving more and buying more cars. This is but one example of the 'Jevons Paradox' that permeates market societies and beyond (Polimeni *et al.*, 2008) – a paradox, so-called, because a per unit reduction in the throughput of commodities does not actually lead to reduced ecological impact, since those efficiency improvements are outweighed by the increasing amounts of commodities that are consumed (Holm and Englund, 2009). The obvious implication of this is that technology and efficiency improvements are not going to solve the ecological crisis, as their most optimistic advocates suggest they can – at least, not unless the global consumer class also downshifts to some significant extent from its currently unsustainably high levels of consumption and moves beyond the 'growth economy' (Trainer, 2010). Since voluntary simplicity as a way of life generally implies 'choosing to live with less', we see the mainstreaming of its ethos into the global consumer class as an absolutely necessary part of any effective response to the ecological crisis.

2.2. *Poverty amidst plenty*

The fact that the global economy is already in significant ecological 'overshoot' is even more challenging when we bear in mind that in the poorest parts of the world today great multitudes are living lives oppressed by extreme poverty (World Bank, 2008). The global challenge, therefore, in terms of humanitarian justice and ecological sustainability, can be stated as follows: The human community must find a way to *raise* the material standards of living of the world's poorest people – who surely have a right to develop their economic capacities in some form – while at the same time *reducing* humanity's overall ecological footprint (Meadows *et al.*, 2004: xv). We feel this provides a further and equally compelling justification for the adoption of lifestyles of reduced consumption among the global consumer class. A moral philosopher might be interested in writing a sophisticated argument along these lines, but perhaps

Mahatma Gandhi put it best when he called for human beings to live simply so that others may simply live (see Gandhi, 1997: 306-7).

2.3. *Overpopulation*

What exacerbates the ecological and humanitarian crises outlined above is the fact that, according to the United Nations, global human population is expected to exceed nine billion by mid-century (UNDSEA, 2012). Obviously, this will intensify greatly the already intense competition over access to Earth's limited natural resources and it will put even more pressure on Earth's fragile ecosystems (Ehrlich and Ehrlich, 1990). The problem of an expanding human population, therefore, provides further support for the proposition that any transition to a just and sustainable world will need to involve the global consumer class transitioning away from high consumption lifestyles.

Needless to say, getting the global population under control in some equitable way will also be a *necessary* part of the equation. We have concerns, however, that focusing on overpopulation as the primary cause of the ecological crisis can lead to population being used as a 'scapegoat'; that is, as a means of deflecting attention away from what we see as the more substantial cause of environmental harm – namely, overconsumption by the global consumer class, particularly in the developed nations. Non-coercive measures to stabilise and reduce population worldwide should certainly be taken (education, provision of contraception, incentives not to procreate, etc.). But the developed nations cannot lecture the developing nations about how expanding populations are putting immense strain on Earth's ecosystems *while at the same time indulging in ever-higher levels of consumption*. If the developed nations are serious about reducing global impact on the environment, then before looking overseas it can be argued they must first show the world that they are prepared to step more lightly themselves.

2.4. *The limitless pursuit of economic growth*

There is also a complex macroeconomic problem that may also depend for its resolution upon more people in the global consumer class embracing lifestyles of reduced or restrained consumption. Essentially every nation on the planet currently aims to grow its economy, and for the poorest nations, growth of some form is justifiable (Purdey, 2010). If it is accepted, however, that the global economy already exceeds the sustainable carrying capacity of the planet; and if it is also accepted that techno-efficiency improve-ments are leading to 'relative' but not 'absolute' decoupling of the economy, then this casts considerable doubt on whether economic growth is still an appropriate goal for the richest nations on the planet. Indeed, there is a vast body of literature on ecological and post-growth economics which argues forcefully that the richest nations should immediately give up the pursuit of growth and move toward a 'steady state' economy – that is, an economy that develops qualitatively but does not grow quantitatively (Daly, 1996; Victor 2008; Jackson, 2009). There is also an emerging body of literature on 'degrowth' which argues more radically that, due to the fact of ecological overshoot (among other reasons, such as global population growth), the richest nations will need to move through a period of *planned economic contraction* before seeking to achieve a steady state economy (Latouche, 2009; Kallis, 2011; Alexander, 2011b, 2012a).

While we cannot enter into the intricacies of this macroeconomic debate here, our position is that eventually, if not today then tomorrow, the economies of our world, starting with the richest ones, are indeed going to have to learn how to stop growing, and to stop growing in a way that is stable and deliberate, not the result of unplanned recession or ecosystemic collapse (Woodward and Simms, 2006; Victor, 2008; Turner, 2012). The great obstacle that lies in the way of a macroeconomics 'beyond growth', however, is the dominant paradigm of growth economics that quite explicitly treats growth in GDP as the best measure of national progress and politico-economic competency (Purdey, 2010). In fact, the growth paradigm is so deeply entrenched in mainstream political discourse in the developed nations (and increasingly elsewhere) that it is hard to imagine any of the major political parties, whether on the Left or the Right, daring to pursue or even seriously consider a post-growth alternative (Hamilton, 2003a). In the developed world, at least, this arguably gives rise to an acute and disturbing contradiction: we must give up the pursuit of growth, but cannot.

Given the hegemony of growth economics in the political sphere, we maintain that any realisation of a macroeconomics beyond growth will need to be built from the grassroots up. More specifically, the Simplicity Movement – or something like it – will almost certainly need to expand, organise, radicalise, and politicise, if a steady state or degrowth economy is ever to emerge through democratic processes (Alexander, 2013a).

2.5. *Peak oil*

Even if the developed nations never *choose* to question the growth imperative – which admittedly seems to be a real likelihood – the issue of 'peak oil' suggests that the era of growth may be coming to an end nevertheless (Murphy and Hall, 2011a; Murphy and Hall, 2011b; Murphy, 2014; Heinberg, 2011). The International Energy Agency reported in November 2010 that the production of conventional oil peaked in or around 2006 (IEA, 2010), and prominent energy analysts have also acknowledged the same (Miller and Sorrell, 2014). While there is still some debate about when the peak of total 'liquid fuels' will arrive, it is now widely accepted that if they have not already peaked, they will peak sometime in the foreseeable future, and then, after an undulating plateau, enter terminal decline. Since oil *demand* is expected to keep on rising, however, the reduction of oil *supply* will inevitably lead to sharply increasing oil prices (Hirsch *et al.*, 2010). The issue is not that human beings will ever run out of oil, therefore; the issue is that we will soon run out of cheap oil, and indeed it seems we already have (Alexander, 2014b; Alexander, 2015).

This is hugely significant because oil is not just another commodity – it is the lifeblood of modern industrial civilisation. If the price of oil continues to rise, no one is quite sure what will happen to the global economy that is so dependent on it. Many of the most prominent experts in the field argue that if immediate steps are not taken to mitigate the effects of peak oil, the consequences are likely to be extremely grim (Heinberg and Lerch, 2010; Tverberg, 2012). The world seems to be recovering (at least superficially) from the 'credit crunch', but the 'oil crunch' may well come to tell a different story.

Again, the intricacies of this highly complex issue cannot be explored here. Our purpose in raising the issue of peak oil is simply to highlight the fact that breaking free from industrial civilisation's addiction to oil will entail breaking free from high consumption lifestyles that in so many ways depend upon oil. The Transition Movement, co-founded by Rob Hopkins (2008), provides the most prominent example of people responding to peak oil at the grassroots level, and in their attempts to re-localise economies and become less oil-dependent those involved are in many ways exemplifying 'simpler lives' of reduced consumption. This is a strong indication that, if there is to be a voluntary transition to a world beyond cheap oil, it is very likely to be informed by the post-consumerist ethos of voluntary simplicity.

Moreover, as Ted Trainer (2013a; 2013b) has argued, renewable energy, even if it is embraced whole-heartedly and on a global scale, will never be able to sustain the expansion of high consumption, energy-intensive consumer lifestyles, especially with the global population growing. If Trainer is correct, and he presents a powerful case that ought to be taken seriously, this provides further grounds for thinking that the global consumer class will need to adopt simpler lifestyles of reduced consumption in the foreseeable future. Whether this transition occurs voluntarily or is imposed by force of biophysical limits remains to be seen. It scarcely needs remarking that a voluntary transition would be the desired path.

2.6. *Consumer malaise*

Finally, what makes the problems outlined above all the more troubling is the fact that high consumption lifestyles, so often held up as the peak of human development, are in many cases engendering an unexpected discontent or malaise among those who live them (see, e.g., Lane, 2000; Myers, 2000; Putnam, 2000; McCormack, 2001; Pickett and Wilkinson, 2010). There is in fact a mounting body of sociological and psychological evidence (Kasser, 2002; Alexander, 2012b) indicating that lives orientated around achieving high levels of consumption often result in such things as time poverty, stress, physical and mental illness, wasteful status competition, loss of community, disconnection from nature, a sense of meaninglessness or alienation in life, and general unhappiness (not to mention ecological degradation).

This evidence, however, troubling though it is, arguably provides something of a silver lining to the admittedly gloomy problems outlined above (Jackson, 2005; Brown and Kasser, 2005). If high consumption lifestyles are not even a trustworthy path to personal wellbeing, this raises the tantalising possibility that members of the global consumer class could live more fulfilling and meaningful lives by *reducing* their consumption (while at the same time reducing their ecological footprint, reducing their dependence on oil, and leaving more resources for those in greater need). Determining whether this possibility is a romantic myth or an emerging empirical reality is another factor that motivated our examination of the Simplicity Movement.

2.7 *The coherency of voluntary simplicity as a response*

If we are correct that post-consumerist lifestyles of reduced and restrained consumption will indeed be a necessary part of any transition to a just, sustainable, and flourishing human civilisation, then gaining some extensive empirical insight into the contemporary Simplicity Movement is a matter of some importance. Among other things, studying the Simplicity Movement is of value because it contributes to our understanding of counter-cultural consumption choices in contemporary consumer societies. In particular, it is important that we understand who the participants in this movement are, how they are living, and what motivates them, as well as what prospects the movement has for expanding into the mainstream and engendering significant social, economic, and political change. Furthermore, by acquiring a better understanding of what *challenges* participants in the contemporary Simplicity Movement face, governments, NGOs, and think-tanks, etc. will be better able to develop appropriate and effective policy proposals for the purpose of transcending high consumption lifestyles and facilitating the transition to lower consumption, but higher quality of life, alternatives. Primarily for these reasons, we created the online 'simple living' survey with the aim of acquiring some of the information needed to answer these important questions.

3. The 'Simple Living' Survey

3.1. *Outline of content and method*

In the broadest terms, the survey was designed to gain some empirical insight into the lives of people who are choosing to move away from high consumption lifestyles and who are embracing lifestyles of reduced or restrained income and consumption. In its preamble the survey states that it seeks participants who are living a 'simpler life', which is defined as a lifestyle of 'reduced or restrained income, consumption, and/or working hours' (Simplicity Institute Study, 2011). Parents who had reduced or stopped paid employment to care for children, and students were asked to fill out the survey only if they considered their simpler lifestyle (as defined above) was a *long-term* way of life. It was also made clear that the survey was not intended for people who were *involuntarily* living simply. We note that Brown and Kasser (2005: 356) provide evidence that when people self-categorise themselves as 'voluntary simplifiers' they do so accurately.

The survey was launched with 50 questions. The survey begins with demographic questions and moves onto questions of lifestyle, behaviour, values, and motivations. There are also questions relating to happiness, income, community, and politics. The survey includes some open text questions where participants are asked to comment on what they find best about living simply, what challenges they face in doing so, and what steps they think government could take to better support simple living. The final question provides a space for further comments.

Once the survey was created, the next task was to seek as many participants as possible. We began by promoting the survey through every willing organisation, website, or 'blog' we could find related to simple living, voluntary simplicity, downshifting, etc., on the assumption that many people living simply (according to our definition stated above) would be interested in and likely to browse those online resources. We then contacted academics, educators, and activists who are involved in the Simplicity Movement (or involved in closely related subjects such as sustainable consumption) and asked them to promote the survey to relevant networks. The response was positive and soon we had a steady flow of participants.

Although a 'control' sample would maximise the usefulness of some of the survey results, the results in themselves remain useful as a description of the Simplicity Movement, especially due to the unprecedented sample size. We note also that statistics on populations at large (regarding income, education, demographics, energy consumption, etc.) are available already in many cases, thus making a control sample unnecessary in such circumstances. Furthermore, we note Brown and Kasser's (2005) controlled study of voluntary simplifiers which, although based on far fewer participants, supports some of the findings below (most notably, the findings on happiness and ecological value orientations).

4. Overview of Results

Below we will outline and provide a preliminary analysis of the most significant findings of the survey results as they currently stand. Before doing so, however, we will provide an overview of the results pertaining to, first, demographics, and second, the practice of simplicity.

4.1. Demographics

The participants in the survey came from all around the world, but primarily from the developed regions of the world. Of the 2268 participants, 970 were from North America, 871 were from Australia, 147 were from the UK; 108 were from Western Europe (excluding the UK); 77 were from New Zealand; 4 were from Japan;

and 91 were from 'other' parts of the globe. Since we are primarily interested (at least presently) in how people are living simply in the most developed regions of the world, the analysis below excludes all those participants who answered 'other'. In the future, however, we hope to broaden or refocus the analysis to include those participants. We also excluded participants who stated that voluntary simplicity was not a long-term lifestyle decision. We did this because we are interested primarily in voluntary simplicity as a 'way of life', rather than a temporary engagement. This means that the analysis below is based on the answers provided by 2131 participants.

In terms of more specific geographic locality, 28% of participants lived in large cities (over 500,001 people); 18% lived in medium sized cities (between 100,000 and 500,000 people); 16% lived in small cities (between 15,001 and 99,999 people); 17% lived in small towns (under 15,000 people); and 21% lived rurally (i.e., non-urban or farm). This dispels the myth that simple living is the reserve of those who live rurally. In an increasingly urbanised world, it is promising to see the Simplicity Movement existing pre-dominantly in cities, for if it only manifested as a predominantly rural lifestyle, it would probably lose any prospect of impacting significantly on mainstream, urbanised culture (Shaw and Moraes, 2009; Ambrose, 2010).

With respect to other demographics, the participants fell into all age brackets, with nothing particularly noteworthy about the distribution. 68% were married or in a de facto relationship; and 69% owned their own home. 42% had no children, 40% had one or two children; and 18% had three or more. In terms of annual household income (converted into US dollars), there was also a significant range. 19% of households lived on less than $20,000 per annum; 17% of households had an annual income that fell between $20,001-$35,000; 27% fell between $35,001-$60,000; 23% fell between $60,000-$100,000; and 14% were over $100,000.

Obviously, much more detailed analyses of income could be provided if we isolated the participants into regions of the world and compared their incomes with national medians. For now, however, we just wish to note that 67% of participants acknowledged that they had *reduced* their incomes from what they had been in the past. This confirms that the Simplicity Movement generally represents a movement of people who are moving toward lifestyles of reduced and restrained income and consumption (Brown and Kasser, 2005).

4.2. *Some characteristics of the practice of simplicity*

The issue of how participants are actually practising simplicity is obviously complex and could never be captured completely in a 50-question survey. But the survey results do provide some interesting insights. In terms of participants taking action for the purpose of living more simply, the results show that 38% changed jobs or careers; 48% reduced working hours; 16% moved city or suburb; 23% moved house; 21% moved rurally; and 22% sold or changed their car. Furthermore, when asked whether they took steps to reduce household energy consumption, 46% said they did so 'at every opportunity;' 41% did so 'often', and 12% did so 'sometimes'; with less than 1% saying they did 'not often' do so.

The values of frugality (defined as minimising expenditure) and minimalism (defined as valuing fewer possessions) also proved to be a part of most people's practice of simple living. For example, 50% said that minimising expenditure plays a 'large part' in their practice of simple living, while 35% said that it plays a 'moderate part'. 15% said that it plays only a 'small part' or that it was 'not particularly' important. In the comments box, however, many people also acknowledged in various ways that 'it is more about where and what the money is spent on' than just being frugal, or that they were prepared to spend extra for 'long-lasting quality items'. Others noted that purchasing things like 'land', 'solar panels', 'water tanks', 'tools', and 'carbon offsets', while part of living simply for them, were expensive. As one participant put it, 'buying locally and ecologically [is] more important than minimising expenditure', a point to which we will return.

In terms of possessions, many also acknowledged that while decluttering life can secure 'the energy to focus on what is important', it's 'the type of possessions' that matters most and the 'attitude' one has toward them, 'not the number'. Several also commented on the pleasure they derived from things they had made, purchased second-hand, or salvaged. It would seem, then, that the 'simple' values of frugality and minimalism resist simplistic interpretation. For example, it is clearly not enough to say that voluntary simplicity 'means spending less', even though spending less and decluttering is often considered an important part of it (Cherrier, 2009; Ballantine and Creery, 2010).

Home food production also plays an important role in living simply. 83% of participants grow some of their own fruit and/or vegetables, with 17% saying they grow more than half of what they eat. This provides some evidence for the conception of the Simplicity Movement as a 'local food' movement, one that values self-sufficiency and self-reliance. It also provides some evidence for the view that the Simplicity Movement operates in many ways 'outside' the formal marketplace. This is ratified by the finding that 36% of participants are involved in barter or 'informal' exchange systems (e.g., food swaps, sharing networks, etc.). In terms of diet, 11% said they eat a typical diet (e.g., most foods) while 63% said that they emphasised fresh and unprocessed foods. 9% eat fish but are otherwise vegetarian; 13% are vegetarian and 4% are vegan.

50% of participants noted that they would bike or walk, and 8% would take public transport, when travelling locally (i.e., defined as within 5km). 37% would usually drive. This question prompted 5% of participants to answer 'other' and leave a comment, with many people noting that they were often required to drive due to such things as 'harsh winters', 'rural living', 'health conditions', or 'lack of public transport'. Others noted that they drove a 'hybrid car' or that when they drove locally they would plan to do 'everything in one trip', 'carpool', or even 'hitch hike'. These comments and others suggest that many participants desire to escape the car culture, but for various reasons find it difficult or impossible to do so.

With respect to clothing, 51% said that living simply 'significantly' affected their clothing choices (e.g., wearing second-hand, homemade, or repaired clothing); 44% said that it affected their choices moderately or mildly; and only 5% say that it didn't affect their clothing choices at all. As for recycling, 82% said that they do so 'at every opportunity', with 12% saying that they recycle 'usually'. 5% said that they recycle occasionally and 1% said they 'almost never' recycle. 77% of participants compost.

We can also report on a few miscellaneous points that may be of some interest. 67% of participants were involved in a community organisation. On the subject of spirituality, 52% said that spiritual practice of some sort is a regular part of life. The survey results also dispel any conception of the Simplicity Movement as a movement of luddites, with 80% stating that advanced technology has a role to play in living simply.

5. A Statement and Preliminary Analysis of the Central Findings

We will now state and offer a preliminary analysis of what we consider to be the central findings of the survey.

5.1. *Diversity of motivations*

The Simplicity Movement is sometimes described, occasionally even by its advocates, as a 'leisure expansion movement' (Segal, 1999:

13). The criticism sometimes implicit in this description is that voluntary simplicity is a self-centred, narrowly hedonistic philosophy of life. While it may well be that a life of voluntary simplicity is merely a means to greater leisure *for some*, the results of our survey demonstrate that the Simplicity Movement is comprised of people who are motivated by a diversity of issues – not simply leisure expansion or personal happiness.

Figure 1 (below) illustrates the results regarding what motivates people to live simply. Participants were provided with an array of options (see *x* axis) – including an 'other' option with a text box available for comments – and were asked to select all that applied to them (with the percentage of participants who selected each motivation noted on the *y* axis).

Figure 1. Percentage of participants listing specific motivations for living simply

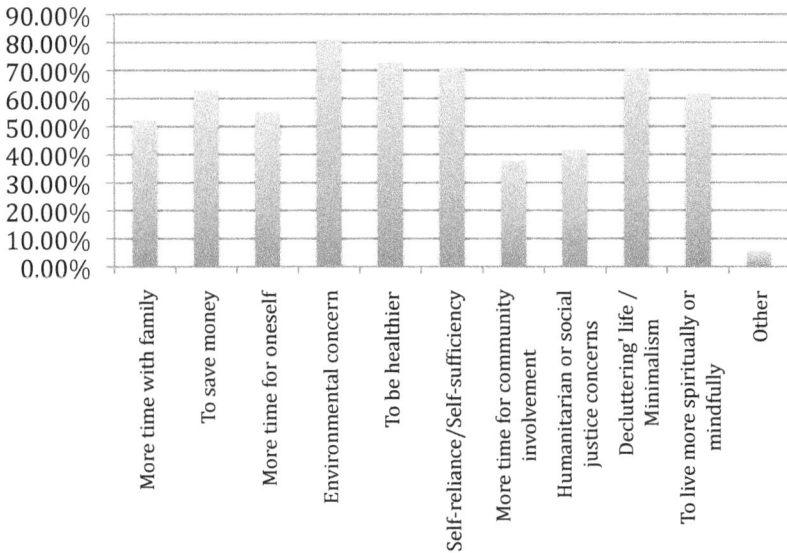

While this particular inquiry did not seek to evaluate the *relative importance* given to each of these motivations – and space does not presently permit an analysis of each of these motivations – the broad range of issues motivating participants nevertheless illustrates that the Simplicity Movement cannot be fairly pigeon-holed as a movement driven by a single issue or small range of issues. While many are motivated by the desire for more time (e.g., with family and/or for oneself), it is clear that many are also motivated by more ethically based factors (e.g., environmental concern, humanitarian or social justice, and/or community involvement). Others are motivated by the desire to declutter their lives; to live healthier lives; or to live more spiritually or mindfully, etc. A separate question (answered by 1306 participants) also asked whether participants were motivated by the notion of 'peak oil': 65% said that they were; 20% said that they were not; and 15% said that they were not aware of the issue.

Once it is acknowledged that the Simplicity Movement is motivated by diverse array of issues (including ethically based ones), the fact that simpler lifestyles can also be described as a means to 'leisure expansion' or as a form of 'alternative hedonism' (i.e., low consumption pleasure seeking), seems to provide not grounds for criticism but further support for the Simplicity Movement (Soper, 2008; Kasser, 2009).

5.2. *Happiness*

The survey also inquired into whether participants in the Simplicity Movement were happier now that they were living more simply. This question was aimed at participants who had once lived less simply and had made a transition toward a simpler life, so an option was needed for participants to answer 'not applicable' if they had always lived a simple life. 10% indicated that this was so.

Of those who *were* living more simply than they once had – the remaining 90% of participants – the results overwhelmingly showed that the transition toward a simpler life increased happiness. Overall, 87% reported that they were happier living more simply. More specifically, 46% said they were 'much happier' and 41% said they were 'somewhat happier'. 13% said that they were 'about as happy' as they were previously. Quite remarkably, only an insignificant amount (0.3%) said that they were 'less happy'.

These results are potentially important because they indicate that a 'double dividend' can flow from living simply, or even a 'triple' or 'quadruple' dividend, etc. (Jackson, 2005; Brown and Kasser, 2005; Kasser 2009). That is to say, the results suggest that the arguments for simpler living based on environmental, human-itarian, population, limits to economic growth, and peak oil concerns, etc., are supported also by an argument based on increased happiness. People have a reason to live simply for their own sakes, the evidence suggests, but by doing so, it may be inferred, they are also likely to benefit others and the planet. If this is indeed so, it is extremely good news.

Of course, these results do not 'prove' that living simply will make a person happier. But they do show that the overwhelming majority of participants in this extensive study are notably happier for living more simply. And this suggests that simpler living is providing some people with a viable and desirable alternative to higher consumption lifestyles – an alternative that those in the global consumer class may find it in their interest to explore also. Furthermore, if increasing amounts of people come to see simpler living as being a path to increased personal happiness, and those people actually begin exploring lifestyles of voluntary simplicity *en masse*, this may well put pressure on governments to do more to support the transition. Should such a cultural shift ever occur, we would surely find ourselves living in a very different world (Alexander, 2011c; 2013b).

5.3. Voting with money

The idea that how a person spends their money is how they vote on what exists in the world is often held up as one of the central tenets of the practice of simplicity, in market societies, at least (Dominguez and Robin, 1999). Our results seem to confirm this, although they also confirm that there remains room for participants in the Simplicity Movement to take greater efforts to spend their money in socially or ecologically conscientious ways. When asked how often participants directed their expenditure toward organic, local, fair-trade, or 'green' products, 31% said 'almost always' and 43% said 'often'. 21% said they 'sometimes' would do so and only 5% said they would 'not often' do so. With respect to the specific question of energy consumption, 60% obtain all or some of their energy from renewable sources, with 19% of participants producing some of their own energy at their homes (e.g., solar). A control sample would enhance the meaning of these figures, but we can say, with respect to the question of energy consumption, at least, that participants in the Simplicity Movement seem to use their powers of expenditure to 'vote for renewable energy' to a much higher degree than the social norm.[3] This is in line with the earlier findings that environmental concern is a leading motivation among participants in the Simplicity Movement.

---

[3] For data on renewable energy use in Australia, see Australian Bureau of Statistics, at: http://www.abs.gov.au/AUSSTATS/abs@.nsf/Lookup/4102. 0Main+Features80March%202009 at 10 April 2011 (reporting that 8% of energy used by households in Australia was renewable). Our results show that 17% of Australian participants purchase 100% renewable energy; 35% purchase partially renewable energy; and 34% produce some or all of their own renewable energy. Overall, 73% of simple living Australians in our survey obtain at least some of their energy from renewable sources.

Arguably the most interesting thing about these results is what they imply about the potential impact the Simplicity Movement could have on the world if it expanded into the mainstream and radicalised. Imagine, for example, if the greater part of an entire nation 'almost always' or 'often' directed their money toward organic, local, fair-trade, and 'green' products. Purchasing something sends a message, consciously or unconsciously, to the marketplace, affirming the product, its social or ecological impact, its process of manufacture, etc. And when the demand for goods increases or decreases, basic economic principles dictate that the supply tends to increase or decrease proportionately. This implies that the global consumer class, with its vast powers of expenditure, has the potential to become a non-violent revolutionary class and change the world, partly by changing its spending habits (Micheletti, 2010).

Our research provides some grounds for thinking that, as well as 'voting with their money', participants in the Simplicity Movement are 'voting with their time' in ways that differ from the general population. Research has shown that in North America and Britain, at least, the activity to which people dedicate most of their time (aside from working and sleeping) is watching television, averaging around 25 hours per week (Layard, 2005: 86). Contrast this with participants in the present study: 19% said that they watch no television at all, with 12% saying that they watch less than one hour per week and a further 28% saying that they watch between 1 and 4 hours per week. While this finding does not indicate how those in the Simplicity Movement *do* spend the time, we think these results are interesting in themselves for showing that there is significant *difference* in leisure activities.

5.4. *Greatest obstacles*

One of our leading motivations for conducting the 'simple living' survey under analysis was to gain some empirical insight into what are the greatest obstacles people face when trying to live simply. We feel such information will be critically important should policy makers ever decide they will try to reduce overall national consumption practices by promoting and facilitating the emergence of 'simpler' lifestyles.

Participants were asked what was the *greatest* obstacle they faced in trying to live simply, and Figure 2 (below) illustrates the results.

Figure 2. Greatest obstacle to living simply vs. percentage of participants

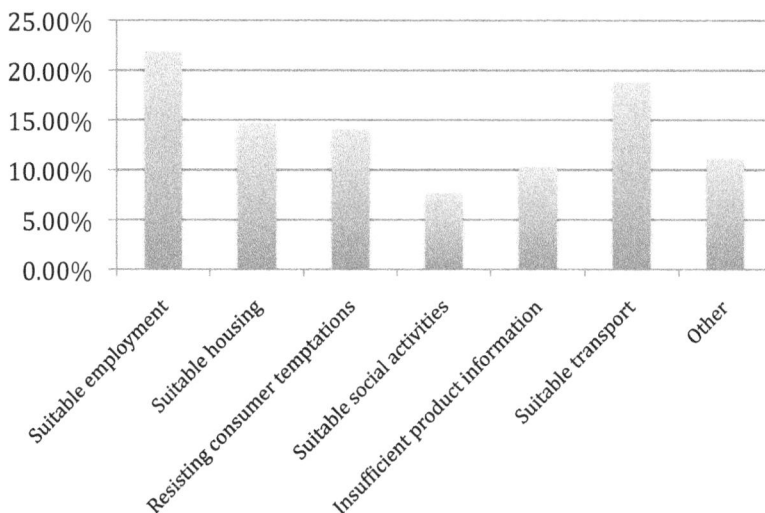

Those who selected 'other' left comments highlighting a wide variety of other obstacles. We will not list them comprehensively here, but some of the recurring points included having family members (e.g., spouse) with a different 'worldview'; health or disability issues; paying for education; and the expense of 'green' consumer products (e.g., solar panels, organic food, etc.). Since only 11% answered 'other', however, it can be inferred that the six obstacles suggested by the survey quite accurately expose some of the greatest challenges people face living simply. This finding in itself should provide some guidance to policy makers who wish to lessen the obstacles people face when trying to live more simply.

For example, many people reported that they find 'the lack of information needed to buy responsibly' as their greatest challenge to living simply, and this suggests that a politics of simple living would involve increasing the mandatory information on product labels (Oates *et al.,* 2008). To provide a second example, the fact that many people find 'resisting consumer temptations' a great obstacle suggests that a politics of simple living might involve taking steps to reduce people's exposure to advertising. We will not, however, try to expound a politics of simple living here; nor do we suggest that devising policies to help people overcome the obstacles to simple living will be 'simple'. Indeed, it may well be that background structural issues (tax policies, state subsidies, government investment, banking systems, property law, contract law, international law, etc.) need to be reformed before the structure of society could facilitate the expansion of the Simplicity Movement (Alexander, 2011b). But the information provided by participants about their greatest obstacles to simply living certainly provides a good place to start thinking about the question of what a politics of simple living would look like.

One point that deserves further comment is the issue of finding employment that suits one's values and lifestyle requirements. As seen from Figure 2, more participants highlighted this as their greatest obstacle to simple living than any other. One aspect to the problem that is particularly important is how to address the structural biases in modern capitalist societies that function systematically to promote overwork (de Graaf, 2003).

Economic theory posits that actors in an economy should be free to maximise their happiness (or 'utility') by selling as much or as little of their time (or 'labour power') as they want (Kimmel and Hoffman, 2002). Currently, however, there are structural biases in advanced capitalist societies that function to promote overwork (i.e., working hours that are not 'optimal' or 'utility maximising'), such as laws that treat the 40-hour work week as 'standard' or which exclude part-time workers from many of the non-pecuniary benefits enjoyed by those who work full-time (Grant, 2010). The effect of these structural biases is essentially to force or coerce many people to work longer hours than they want or need to, which gives rise to cultures that tend to overconsume resources and under-consume leisure. This might lead to higher GDP per capita, but at the cost of quality of life and planetary health (Robinson, 2007).

The problem of structural biases promoting overwork is one that our survey suggests participants in the Simplicity Movement are confronting in significant numbers. 55% report that if they could, they would reduce their current paid working hours and accept a proportionate reduction in income. This is not, however, a problem faced only by participants in the Simplicity Movement. It is a problem endemic to many modern market societies and may be a significant structural barrier inhibiting the expansion of the Simplicity Movement. For example, 28.7% of full-time Australian workers in Australia work 50 hours per week or more; and of these workers, 46% claim they would prefer to work fewer hours, accepting a drop in pay (Australian Conservation Foundation, 2010: 11).

One way to respond to this issue would be to introduce a shorter 'standard' work week, such as the 35-hour work week that exists (to a decreasing degree) in France (New Economics Foundation, 2010); another option would be to ensure that part-time workers enjoy the same non-pecuniary benefits that full-time workers receive (on a pro-rata basis). We feel these are policy reforms that deserve serious attention. Perhaps more importantly still, however, is the policy response that has taken hold in Holland in the form of the Working Hours Adjustment Act 2000. This path-breaking act allows employees to reduce their hours to part-time simply by asking their employers. As explained by leading work reductionist John de Graaf (2009, p. 274):

> Unless there is a clear hardship for the firm – something shown in less than 5% of cases – the employer must grant the reduction in hours. Workers keep the same hourly salary, full health care, and pro-rata additional benefits like vacation time and pensions. This law, in the most concrete terms, allows workers to trade money for time, without losing their jobs or health care. As a result, more than a third of Dutch employees work part-time, the highest ration in the world.

Some may object that industrial relations policies such as this will not maximise GDP per capita. But that is to miss the point. The point of an economy, arguably, is to efficiently promote quality of life for all, and if a smaller economy promotes quality of life by providing increased leisure but less income and consumption for its participants, then a smaller economy is the most economically rational option to choose. In a word, this is the rationality of degrowth (Latouche, 2009), and in many ways it would also seem to be implicit to a politics of simple living (Alexander, 2011b).

Participants noted that 'suitable transport' was the second greatest obstacle to living simply, and this also raises an important point about structural barriers. For example, people may *desire* to escape car culture, but in the absence of safe and accessible bike lanes, or good public transport, many people can find themselves 'locked in' to high consumption, environmentally damaging practices (Sanne, 2002). This highlights the extremely important point that our personal lifestyle decisions always take place within structures of constraint, a point that provides further support for why a politics of simple living is necessary. If current structures are locking people into consumerist lifestyles, as they seem to be, those structures will need to be changed if there is to be any hope of an extensive behaviour-shift in the direction of voluntary simplicity.

5.5. *An emerging group consciousness and political sensibility*

For present purposes, the final empirical insight to report on that we feel is of some significance – that we feel might be of the most significance – concerns what seems to be an emerging 'group consciousness' and political sensibility among participants in the Simplicity Movement. Often in the literature on voluntary simplicity the movement is criticised for being 'escapist' or 'apolitical', a criticism that arguably has some weight, so far as it is true. Mary Grigsby, for example, one of the more prominent sociologists on voluntary simplicity, reports (2004: 12) that in her experience participants in the Simplicity Movement 'don't generally talk about policy initiatives, instead focusing on the individual as the primary mechanism for change'. In line with the conventional view, this characterises the Simplicity Movement as a movement of people who are seeking to 'escape' the system at a personal level, rather than 'transform' it at a collective level.

Our results put this conventional view into question. To begin with, 68% of participants state that they conceive of themselves as part of a 'simple living' movement (based on 1564 responses). This is significant because before a social movement can ever act collectively for a social or political purpose – that is, before it can organise and mobilise to advance some collective aims – the participants arguably have to conceive of themselves as being part of a collective enterprise with collective power, and not simply as isolated and unrelated individuals. There is still a significant body of participants who seem to conceive of voluntary simplicity primarily as an 'individualised' way of life and less as a social movement (see Maniates, 2002). But from the fact that more than two thirds now see themselves as part of a social movement, it would seem that the Simplicity Movement has acquired the 'group consciousness' that it is often thought to lack (or historically did lack). Much social movement theory suggests that the emergence of group con-sciousness is an important and necessary phase in the maturation of a social movement into a more potent social and political force (McCann, 2006). Whether that proves to be true of the Simplicity Movement remains to be seen.

Perhaps more significant still, however, are the results showing, first, that 90% of participants state that they would vote for a political party that was dedicated to promoting simple living, and second, that 94% feel that local and/or national governments currently do not do enough to support simple living. These figures suggest that the Simplicity Movement is an unmobilised con-stituency whose political preferences potentially could be influential if an avenue opened up for their expression on the political scene. Influence would also depend on the overall size of the movement, of course, but at least three studies show that the numbers may be far higher than one might first have thought. With respect to the US, for example, The Merck Family Fund (1995) estimates on the basis of their study that approximately 28% of US citizens are downshifting to some extent. Furthermore, a study conducted by Clive Hamilton and Richard Denniss (2005: 154) concludes that 23% of Australian citizens are downshifting to some extent. In another study, but with respect to Britain, Clive Hamilton (2003b: 12) reports that 25% of people aged between 30-59 are downshifting. If we extrapolate (crudely) and say that all the developed nations are downshifting to a similar degree – even if we make the conservative estimate that merely 20% are downshifting overall – then in the developed world of roughly one billion people, *there are approximately 200 million participants in the global Simplicity Movement.*

Obviously there will be a wide diversity of lifestyles within this group, with some taking relatively minor steps to downshift and others taking more radical steps (McDonald *et al.,* 2006). And the diversity of participants and their personal motivations make any attempt to manage or understand notions of 'group identity' within the movement a complex challenge (Sandlin and Walther, 2009). But if these participants are connected by their attempt to reduce or restrain their consumption – and if they also *feel* connected – then together they are a social movement of considerable collective power and political import, potentially, at least. If the movement were to organise, radicalise and expand in coming years, its collective power and political import would obviously increase.

Our study also indicates that the Simplicity Movement is not merely a movement of social and political aspirations without any action. 67% of participants report that they are involved in a community organisation and, more specifically, 41% report that they are engaged in a community or political organisation related to simple living. Before all else, perhaps, this can be interpreted as the emerging 'politicisation' of the Simplicity Movement, albeit one driven from the grassroots up rather than the top down. When one looks at the world today, however, it is clear that more action is needed if a politics of voluntary simplicity is ever to reorientate the world's trajectory into the future.

6. Conclusion

When one recognises the multi-faceted problem of over-consumption for what it is – the root or contributing cause of environmental degradation; global poverty; uneconomic growth; peak oil; and consumer malaise – voluntary simplicity presents itself as an approach to life that has the potential to respond to all of those great problems. With the prospect of nine billion people on the planet by mid-century, it may be that voluntary simplicity is a living strategy whose time has come. We hope that this study has provided some deeper empirical insight into this important subject.

At the same time, there is little that is 'simple' about living simply in a consumer society, a point that should not be understated. Certainly, having the desire to live more simply is not enough. For this reason, theorists like Daniel Miller (2005) offer insightful warnings about the dangers of demonising consumption. Those who present critiques of 'consumerism' or 'materialism' – simplicity theorists, in particular – must be wary of treating consumption one-dimensionally, as nothing but a means to status distinction, for example, or just the manifestation of hedonism and greed. Things are much more complex, as every participant in the Simplicity Movement probably knows very well (Sandlin and Walther, 2009). Miller is one of very few consumption theorists brave enough to acknowledge, or perceptive enough to see, that much of the literature on consumption is 'saturated by a pervasive anxiety most acutely felt by fairly well-off academics... about the possibility that they may be too materialistic' (Miller, 2005: 223). It would be hypocritical, of course, as Miller notes self-reflectively, to see 'the aspiration of any other person to at least the same level of consumption that I enjoy with my family as anything other than reasonable' (Miller, 2005: 223). But, at the same time, if the universalisation of such standards of living would be, for example, ecologically catastrophic, then the problem that comes to the fore is the quite confronting one of knowing that lifestyles of reduced consumption may be necessary, but finding the realisation of such lifestyles extremely challenging.

Consequently, the task at hand is the patently *practical* one of learning how to live more simply in a world that, in many ways, makes doing so very difficult. Part of this involves figuring out how best to restructure societies to facilitate patterns of sustainable consumption and build an economy not based on perpetual growth (Trainer, 2010). But the 'social' nature of consumption makes any such transition very challenging. As Mary Douglas (2005: 243) puts it, 'An individual's main objective in consumption is to help create the social universe and to find in it a creditable place'. Any injunction to consume less, therefore, ought to acknowledge that commodities play a symbolic role in the social world that go well beyond their material functionality. For this reason, among others, the problem of how to *practise* lifestyles of reduced or restrained consumption will surely not have any 'simple', silver-bullet solution; instead, it will require the rethinking of almost every aspect of life, at the personal, social, and political levels, as well as every level in between and beyond. This is, it could be said, the defining challenge of our age, and we hope that our survey results and analyses provide some of the groundwork needed to advance this important debate.

We do not, however, hold up the Simplicity Movement as it exists as the answer to all problems. It hardly needs stating that the movement will need to radicalise to some significant extent and expand into the social, economic, and political mainstream if it is ever to respond effectively to the problems outlined at the beginning of this chapter. But we maintain that there is a coherency to the ethos of voluntary simplicity that hacks at the root of those problems, while other responses (such as technology and economic growth) seem merely to be hacking at the branches.

References

Alexander, S. (ed.) 2009. *Voluntary simplicity: The poetic alternative to consumer culture.* Whanganui: Stead & Daughters.

Alexander, S. 2011a. 'The voluntary simplicity movement: Reimagining the good life beyond consumer culture'. *International Journal of Environmental, Cultural, Economic, and Social Sustainability* 7(3): 133.

Alexander, S. 2011b. 'Property beyond growth: Toward a politics of voluntary simplicity'. Doctoral thesis, Melbourne Law School. Available at: http://papers.ssrn.com/sol3/papers.cfm?abstract_id=1941069 (accessed 10 September 2013).

Alexander, S. 2011c. 'Looking backward from the year 2099: Ecozoic reflections on the future'. *Earth Jurisprudence and Environmental Justice Journal* 1(1): 25.

Alexander, S. 2012b. 'Planned economic contraction: The emerging case for degrowth'. *Environmental Politics* 21 (3): 349-368.

Alexander, S. 2012. 'The optimal material threshold: Toward an economics of sufficiency'. *Real-World Economics Review* 2-21.

Alexander, S. 2013a. *Entropia: Life beyond industrial civilisation.* Melbourne: Simplicity Institute Publishing.

Alexander, S. 2013b. 'Voluntary simplicity and the social reconstruction of law: Degrowth from the grassroots up'. *Environmental Values* 22(2): 287-308.

Alexander, S. 2014a. 'A critique of techno-optimism: Efficiency without sufficiency is lost'. *MSSI Working Paper* (WP 1/14): 1-21.

Alexander, S. 2014b. 'The new economics of oil'. *MSSI Issues Paper* No. 2: 1-16.

Alexander, S. 2015. 'The paradox of oil: The cheaper it is, the more it costs'. *Simplicity Institute Report 15a* 1-17.

Ambrose, M. 2010. *Voluntary simplicity as an urban lifestyle: Resisting consumer economy.* Doctoral thesis, University of Calgary, NR64103.

Australian Bureau of Statistics, Nov. 2009. *Average weekly earnings.* ABS, Canberra. Available at: http://www.abs.gov.au /AUSSTATS/abs@.nsf/mf/6302.0 (accessed 10 April 2010).

Australian Conservation Foundation (ACF). 2010. *Better than growth.* ACF, Melbourne. Available at: http://www.acfonline. org.au/uploads/res/ACF_BetterThanGrowth.pdf (accessed 5 May 2011).

Ballantine, P. and Creery, S. 2010. 'The consumption and disposition of voluntary simplifiers'. *Journal of Consumer Behaviour* 9(1): 45.

Brown, K. and Kasser, T. 2005. 'Are psychological and ecological well-being compatible? The role of values, mindfulness, and lifestyle'. *Social Indicators Research* 74: 349-368.

Cherrier, H. 2009. 'Disposal and simple living: Exploring the circulation of goods and the development of sacred consumption'. *Journal of Consumer Behaviour* 8(6): 327.

Chhetri, P., Stimson, R., and Western, J. 2009. 'Understanding the downshifting phenomenon: A case of southeast Queensland, Australia'. *Australian Journal of Social Issues,* 44(4): 345-362.

Craig-Lees, M. and Hill, C. 2002. 'Understanding voluntary simplifiers'. *Psychology and Marketing* 19(2): 187-210.

Daly, H. 1996. *Beyond growth: The economics of sustainable development.* Boston: Beacon Press.

De Graaf, J. (ed.). 2003. *Take back your time: Fighting overwork and time poverty in America.* Berret-Koehler: San Francisco.

De Graaf, J. 2009. 'Political Prescriptions'. In Alexander, S. (ed.) *Voluntary simplicity: The poetic alternative to consumer culture.* Whanganui: Stead & Daughters.

Dominguez, J. and Robin, V. 1999, Revised edn. *Your money or your life.* New York: Penguin.

Douglas, M, 2005. 'Relative poverty – relative communication'. In T. Jackson (ed.). *Sustainable Consumption.* London: Earthscan.

Ehrlich, P. and Ehrlich, A. 1990. *The population explosion.* Australia, Brookvale, NSW: Simon & Schuster.

Elgin, D. and Mitchell, A. 1977. 'Voluntary simplicity'. *Co-evolution quarterly* (Summer) 2: 5-18.

Gandhi, M. 1997. 'My quest for simplicity'. In Rahnema, M. & Bawtree, V. (eds). 1997. *The Post-Development Reader.* London: Zed Books.

Grant, L. 2010. 'Sustainability: From excess to aesthetics'. *Behaviour and Social Issues* 19: 5-45.

Grigsby, M. 2004. *Buying time and getting by: The voluntary simplicity movement*. Albany: State University of New York Press.

Hamilton, C. 2003a. *Growth fetish*. Crows Nest, NSW: Allen & Unwin.

Hamilton, C., 2003b. 'Downshifting in Britain: A sea change in the pursuit of happiness'. Australia Institute Discussion Paper No. 58.

Hamilton, C. and Denniss, R. 2005. *Affluenza: When too much is never enough*. Crows Nest, NSW: Allen & Unwin.

Hansen, James, 2011. *Storms of my grandchildren*. London: Bloomsbury.

Heinberg, R. 2011. *The end of growth: Adapting to our new economic reality*. Gabriola Island: New Society Publishers.

Heinberg, R. and Lerch, D. 2010. *The post-carbon reader*. Healdsburg, CA: Watershed Media.

Hirsch, R. *et al.* 2010. *The impending world energy mess*. Burlington: Apoge Prime.

Holm, S.-O. and Englund, G. 2009. 'Increased eco-efficiency and gross rebound effect: Evidence from USA and six European countries 1960-2002'. *Ecological Economics* 68: 879-887.

Hopkins, R., 2008. *The transition handbook: From oil dependency to local resilience*. Totnes, Devon: Green Books.

International Energy Agency. 2010. *World energy outlook*. Available at: http://www.iea.org/weo/ [accessed 20 December 2011].

Jackson, T. 'Live better by consuming less? Is there a double dividend in sustainable consumption?' *Journal of Industrial Ecology* 9: 19-36.

Jackson, T. 2009. *Prosperity without growth: Economics for a finite planet*. London: Earthscan.

Kallis, G. 2011. 'In defence of degrowth'. *Ecological Economics* 70: 873-80.

Kasser, T. 2002. *The high price of materialism*. Cambridge, MA: MIT Press.

Kasser, T. 2009. 'Psychological need satisfaction, personal well-being, and ecological sustainability'. *Ecopsychology* 1(4): 175.

Kimmel, J. and Hoffman, E. 2002. *The economics of work and family*. Kalamazoo, MI: John Institute Press.

Lane, R. 2000. *The loss of happiness in market democracies*. New Haven: Yale University Press.

Latouche, S. 2009. *Farewell to growth*. Cambridge, UK: Polity Press.

Layard, R. 2005. *Happiness: Lessons from a new science.* New York: Penguin Press.

Maniates, M. 2002. 'Individualization: Plant a tree, buy a bike, save the world?' In Princen, T., Maniates, M., and Conca, K. (eds). 2002. *Confronting consumption.* MIT Press: London: Ch. 3.

McCann, M. 2006. 'Law and social movements: Contemporary perspectives'. *Annu. Rev. Law. Soc. Sci.* 2: 17-38.

McCormack, G. 2001, Revised edn. *The emptiness of Japanese affluence.* New York: Armonk, M.E. Sharpe.

McDonald, S., Oates, C., Young, W., and Hwang, K. 2006. 'Toward sustainable consumption: Researching voluntary simplifiers'. *Psychology and Marketing* 23(6): 515.

Meadows, D., Randers, J., and Meadows, D. 2004. *Limits to growth: The 30-year update.* White River Junction, Vt: Chelsea Green Pub.

Merck Family Fund. 1995. *Yearning for balance: Views of Americans on consumption, materialism, and the environment.* Milton, MA: Author.

Micheletti, M. 2010. *Political virtue and shopping: Individuals, consumerism, and collective action.* Basingstoke: Palgrave Macmillan.

Millennium Ecosystem Assessment. 2005. Available at: http://www.millenniumassessment.org/en/index.aspx. [accessed 10 April 2010].

Miller, D. 2005. 'The poverty of morality'. In Jackson, T. (ed.) *Sustainable Consumption.* London: Earthscan.

Murphy, D. 2014. 'The implications of the declining energy return on investment of oil production'. *Philosophical Transactions of the Royal Society* 372, 20130126: 1-19.

Murphy, D. and Hall, C. 2011a. 'Adjusting to the new energy realities of the second half of the age of oil'. *Ecological Modelling* 223: 67-71.

Murphy, D. and Hall, C. 2011b. 'Energy return on investment, peak oil, and the end of economic growth'. *Annals of the New York Academy of Sciences* 1219: 52-72.

Myers, D. 2000a. *The American paradox: Spiritual hunger in an age of plenty,* New Haven: Yale University Press.

New Economics Foundation. 2010. *21 hours: Why a 21-hour work week can help us all flourish in the 21st century.* Available at: www.neweconomics.org [accessed 10 May 2011].

Pickett, K. and Wilkinson, R. 2010. *The spirit level: Why greater equality makes societies stronger.* London: Penguin.

Pierce, L.B. 2000. *Choosing simplicity: Real people finding peace and fulfilment in a complex world.* Carmel, CA: Gallagher Press.

Princen, T., Maniates, M., and Conca, K. (eds). 2002. *Confronting consumption*. London: MIT Press.

Polimeni, J. *et al.* 2009. *The myth of resource efficiency: The Jevons paradox*. London: Earthscan.

Purdey, S. 2010. *Economic growth, the environment, and international relations: The growth paradigm*. New York: Routledge.

Putnam, R. 2000. *The collapse and revival of American community*. New York: Simon and Schuster.

Robinson, T. 2007. *Work, leisure, and the environment: The vicious circle of overwork and overconsumption*. Cheltenham: Edward Elgar Publishing.

Sanne, C. 2002. 'Willing consumers – Or locked in? Policies for a sustainable consumption'. *Ecological Economics* 42: 273.

Sandlin, J. and Walther, C. 2009. 'Complicated simplicity: Moral identity formation and social movement learning in the voluntary simplicity movement'. *Adult Education Quarterly* 59(4): 298.

Schor, J. 1998. *The overspent American: Upscaling, downshifting, and the new consumer*. New York: Basic Books.

Segal, J. 1999. *Graceful simplicity: Toward a philosophy and politics of the alternative American dream*. New York: H. Holt & Co.

Shaw, D. and Moraes, C. 2009. 'Voluntary simplicity: An exploration of market interactions'. *International Journal of Consumer Studies* 33(2): 215.

Simmons, M. 2005. *Twilight in the desert: The coming Saudi oil shock and the world economy*. NJ: John Wiley and Sons, Hoboken.

Simplicity Institute. 2011. *Simplicity Institute study*. Available at: http://simplicityinstitute.org/phpQ/fillsurvey.php?sid=2 [accessed 5 May 2011]

Soper, K. 2008. 'Alternative hedonism, cultural theory and the role of aesthetic revisioning'. *Cultural Studies* 22(5): 567.

Trainer, T. 2010. *The transition to a sustainable and just world*. Sydney: Envirobook.

Trainer, T. 2013a. 'Can Europe run on renewable energy? A negative case'. *Energy Policy* 63: 845-850.

Trainer, T. 2013b. 'Can the world run on renewable energy'. *Humanomics* 29(2): 88-104.

Turner, G. 2012. 'Are we on the Cusp of Collapse? Updated Comparison of *The limits to growth* with historical data'. *Gaia* 21(2): 116-124.

Tverberg, G. 2012. 'Oil supply limits and the continuing financial crisis'. *Energy* 37(1): 27-34.

United Nations Development Program, 2007/8. *Human Development Report*. Available at: http://hdr.undp.org/en/reports/global/hdr2007-2008/ [accessed 10 April 2010].

United Nations Department of Social and Economic Affairs (UNDSEA). 2012. *World population prospects: The 2012 revision*. Available at: http://esa.un.org/wpp/Documentation/pdf/WPP2012 Press Release.pdf [accessed 10 September 2013].

United Nations Education Scientific, and Cultural Organization, Institute for Statistics, 2010. *Global education digest*. Available at: http://www.uis.unesco.org/template/pdf/ged/2010/GED 2010 EN.pdf 231 [accessed 10 April 2011].

Victor, P. 2008. *Managing without growth: Slower by design, not disaster*. Cheltenham: Edward Elgar Publishing.

Wackernagel, M. 2002. 'Tracking the ecological overshoot of the human economy'. *Proceedings of the National Academy of Sciences of the United States of America,* 99, 9266-9271.

Woodward, D. and Simms, A. 2006. *Growth isn't working: The uneven distribution of benefits and costs from economic growth*. Available at: http://www.neweconomics.org/publications/growth-isn%E2%80%99t-working [accessed 10 April 2010].

World Bank, 2008. *World development indicators: Poverty data*. Available at: <http://siteresources.worldbank.org/DATASTATISTICS/Resources/WDI08supplement1216.pdf> [accessed 5 September 2010].

4

SUFFICIENCY ECONOMY

Envisioning a prosperous descent

When [we have] obtained those things necessary to life, there is another alternative than to obtain superfluities; and that is, to adventure on life now, [our] vacation from humbler toil having commenced.
– Henry Thoreau

1. Introduction

If a society does not have some vision of where it wants to be or what it wants to become, it cannot know whether it is heading in the right direction – it cannot even know whether it is lost. This is the confused position of consumer capitalism today, which has a fetish for economic growth but no answer to the question of what that growth is supposed to be *for*. It is simply assumed that growth is good for its own sake, but of course economic activity is merely a means, not an end. It can only ever be justified by some goal beyond itself, but that is precisely what consumer capitalism lacks – a purpose, a reason for existence. It is a means without an end, like a tool without a task. What makes this state of affairs all the more challenging is that the era of growth economics appears to be coming to a close, due to various financial, ecological, and energy constraints, and this is leaving growth-based economies without the very capacity for growth which defined them historically. Before long this will render consumer capitalism an obsolete system with neither a means nor an end, a situation that is in fact materialising before our very eyes. It seems that today we are living in the twilight of growth globally, which implies that the dawn of a new age is almost upon us – is perhaps already upon us. But as we turn this momentous page in history we find that humanity is without a narrative in which to lay down new roots. We are the generation in between stories, desperately clinging to yesterday's story but uncertain of tomorrow's. Then again, perhaps the new words we need are already with us; perhaps we just need to live them into existence.

It is not the purpose of this essay to offer another critique of growth economics, the details of which have been laid down comprehensively many times before (Schumacher, 1973; Meadows *et al.*, 2004; Jackson, 2009; Latouche, 2009; Trainer, 2010). Instead, this essay will attempt to describe in some detail an alternative economic system, which I will call 'the sufficiency economy'. This term is typically applied to so-called 'developing economies', which either have not yet industrialised or are still in the early phases of industrialisation (see e.g., Suwankitti and Pongquan, 2011). These economies are sometimes called sufficiency economies because they do not or cannot produce material abundance, or do not seek material abundance. Instead, sufficiency economies are focused on meeting mostly local needs with mostly local resources, without the society being relentlessly driven to expand by growth-focused ethics and structures of profit-maximisation. My point of differentiation in this essay will be to consider the notion of a sufficiency economy within the context of the most highly developed regions of the world – where an economics of sufficiency is most desperately needed – and to explore what such an economy would look like, how it might function, and how the transition to such an economy might transpire. I address this subject having been convinced that the growth paradigm has no future and that some alternative vision is therefore needed as humanity begins its inevitable transition to a world beyond growth. I put forward the sufficiency economy as the most promising alternative model, although it is one that I believe may ultimately be imposed upon us whether we want it or not. We can go the easier way or the harder way, so to speak, depending on our attitudes and actions. The harder way – the way of collapse – will not be desirable.

Defined and defended in more detail below, a sufficiency economy can be understood in direct contrast to the dominant macroeconomic paradigm based on limitless growth. Whereas existing economies in our increasingly globalised world are predicated on the assumption that 'more production and consumption is always better', the sufficiency economy described below is shaped by an acceptance that 'just enough is plenty'. As will be seen, the implications of this alternative economic perspective are nothing short of revolutionary. Rather than progress being seen as a movement toward ever-increasing material affluence, the sufficiency economy aims for a world in which everyone's basic needs are modestly but sufficiently met, in an ecologically sustainable, highly localised, and socially equitable manner. When material sufficiency is achieved in these ways, further growth would not continue to be a priority. Instead, human beings would realise that they were free from the demands of continuous economic activity and could therefore dedicate more of their energies to non-materialistic pursuits, such as enjoying social relationships, connecting with nature, exploring the mysteries of the universe, or engaging in peaceful, creative activity of various sorts. How to spend this 'freedom from want' is the exhilarating and perhaps terrifying question all human beings would face in a well-established sufficiency economy, so defined.

Such an economy recognises that there are fundamental limits to growth (Meadows *et al.*, 2004), and in this it obviously shares some conceptual ground with the notion of a 'steady state' economy developed by ecological economists in recent decades (e.g., Daly, 1996). But to date the steady state economy has remained largely at the level of theoretical abstraction, and this has made it difficult to envision the alternative society it vaguely implies. Even the most insightful policy prescriptions for a steady state economy have not given due attention to what *life* would be like in such an economy. Unfortunately, this neglect has hurt the movement for change, because if people cannot picture the alternative society, it is very difficult to desire it; and if we do not desire it, no social or political movement will arise to bring it into existence. Many have been persuaded, as I have been, by the insight that economies are a subset of the natural environment, not the other way round, as neoclassical economists assume. Very little attention, however, has been given to describing in detail what life would be like if an ecologically sustainable economy actually emerged. How would we feed ourselves? What clothes would we wear? What forms of transport and technology would we use? How much and what types of energy would we require? And what material standard of living would we have if we were to successfully decarbonise the economy? Most importantly, perhaps, what would the quality of daily life be like? These are some of the concrete questions to which this essay will offer some tentative answers, acknowledging all the while that the nature of the sufficiency economy described, like any economy, must ultimately be shaped and understood in context-specific ways.

The analysis begins in the next section by briefly outlining the multi-faceted problems the world finds itself facing, not for the purpose of providing a thorough review of the global situation but simply to contextualise the discussion that follows. Unless one understands the magnitude of the overlapping problems we face, the relevance, importance, or even the necessity of the sufficiency economy may not be immediately apparent. Once the global predicament is outlined, the analysis proceeds to define in more detail the principles that underpin the sufficiency economy, although again this will be more a matter of exposition than comprehensive defence. The main part of the analysis then explores in some detail what economic life might be like if citizens in the developed nations gave up the pursuit of growth and transitioned to some form of highly localised 'sufficiency economy' based on far lower resource and energy consumption. It is hoped that this analysis might provide some guidance on what it will actually take to transition to a just and sustainable society, as well as provide some deeper insight into what life might be like if we were ever to succeed.

2. Embracing Life after Growth (Before it Embraces Us)

The growth paradigm has reached, more or less, the 'limits to growth', and this means that we must move away from growth-based economies if we are to avoid exacerbating existing ecological crises to the point of catastrophe (Turner, 2012). Billions of lives are potentially at stake, as are the biodiversity and climatic balance of our planet. But even if we do not choose to give up on growth, energy and resource constraints seem to be in the process of bringing growth to an end all the same, and no amount of 'quantitative easing' or technological advances are going to provide an escape from this biophysical reality. When, in the foreseeable future, the world reaches the 'end of growth', we will have a form of 'sufficiency economy' imposed upon us, in the sense at least that we will have to make do, as best we can, without further growth, and probably with swift, unplanned and uncontrollable economic contraction. This may well imply radically reduced consumption, compared to levels prevalent in consumer societies today, because when growth-based economies do not grow, debts cannot be repaid, and economic contraction, not merely stagnation, tends to ensue (Tverberg, 2012). If this situation is not well managed – for example, if we persist blindly with expectations of limitless growth and continue to structure our economies accordingly – then this phase in history is probably going to be a catalyst for civilisational collapse, although it is impossible to be sure whether this would be a rapid breakdown of the existing order (Korowics, 2012) or a slow deterioration over many decades or even a century (Greer, 2008).

Nevertheless, the fact that there are biophysical limits to growth from which we cannot escape sometimes obscures the fact that living within those limits is something that we should *want to do*, simply to be good and wise stewards of Earth. It is obviously in our self-interest to preserve the life-support systems upon which all life depends, a point that is too often overlooked. Furthermore, much social and psychological evidence (see Alexander, 2012a; Jackson, 2005; Brown and Kasser, 2005; Kasser, 2002) implies that 'the good life' does not actually consist in the limitless consumption of material things, contrary to the promises of advertisements, and this means that denying ourselves consumer lifestyles need not be considered a hardship, as the Voluntary Simplicity Movement, for example, already understands (Alexander and Ussher, 2012). Certainly, consumer culture must not be accepted as the peak of civilisation. We must explore alternative ways to flourish without relying on material abundance, and I will argue that embracing a sufficiency economy is one means of doing so, and probably a necessary means. I will now briefly elaborate on some of the values underlying the sufficiency economy, then proceed to unpack their practical implications in some detail.

2.1. The principle of sufficiency – 'enough, for everyone, forever'

The fundamental aim of a sufficiency economy, as I define it, is to create an economy that provides 'enough, for everyone, forever'. In other words, economies should seek to universalise a material standard of living that is sufficient for a good life but which is ecologically sustainable into the deep future. Once that is achieved, further growth in material wealth would not be an economic priority and, indeed, would need to be deliberately restrained. As noted above, for individuals and economies that are already overconsuming, the attainment of sufficiency implies not merely resisting further growth, but first entering a phase of planned economic contraction. Once sustainable sufficiency has been attained, prosperity should be sought in various low-impact, non-materialistic forms of wellbeing, such as enjoying social relationships, experiencing connection with nature, engaging in meaningful work or spiritual practice, or exploring various forms of peaceful, creative activity. There are no limits to the scale or diversity of qualitative improvement of life in a sufficiency economy, but to achieve sustainability in a world of seven billion people (and counting), material standards of living must not aim for consumer affluence but only for what is minimally sufficient for a good life. The basic economic reasoning here is that once basic material needs are met, human beings are not so strictly bound by materialistic concerns and are thus free to dedicate more of their energy and attention to things other than increasing material living standards. 'As wealth increases', John Hicks (1959: xiii) once wrote, 'wealth itself becomes (or should become) less important', a dynamic that Hicks mischievously called 'the diminishing marginal significance of economics'.

These broad comments obviously require (and will receive below) more concrete expression, but they nevertheless provide a normative starting point that contrasts sharply with the materialistic 'more is better' ethos underpinning existing growth economies. The sufficiency economy is based on an alternative economic perspective that accepts that 'just enough is plenty', and this alternative perspective implies that producing more than is sufficient is not required for an individual or society to flourish. In the words of Henry Thoreau (1982: 568): 'Superfluous wealth can buy superfluities only.' Furthermore, the growth paradigm has produced high-impact economic systems that are grossly unsustainable and certainly not universalisable, so the sufficiency economy treats consumer lifestyles, and the growth economies that are required to support them, as neither desirable nor sustainable.

Determining exactly what level of material provision is 'sufficient' cannot be defined with any analytical precision, and will always be context and culturally specific (Sen, 1998). But material sufficiency can be broadly understood to include meeting basic biophysical needs for food and water, shelter, and clothing, as well as having access to basic medical services and some minimal level of social education. Access to extra energy supplies for heating will also be required in certain climates, and since energy is required to sustain any level of social complexity, some indeterminate level of energy supply, beyond food, fire, and labour, should also be considered a basic requirement for a full, human life. (Only those anarcho-primitivists, I presume, who think hunter-gathering is the only acceptable form of social organisation, would object to there being a basic need for energy beyond food, fire, and labour.) Sustainability may not necessarily mean living like the Amish – I am sure people will creatively salvage the 'wastes' and existing material stocks of industrial civilisation to live in ways that lie beyond the Amish lifestyles for some time. But using the Amish as a rough touchstone or benchmark may be worthwhile. At least this evokes a serious image of what low-consumption 'simple living' could look like in an energy descent context, a scenario that is entirely absent from mainstream sustainability discourse (perhaps because such simplicity of life is politically unpalatable). The most important point to understand is that nothing much resembling consumer lifestyles today is sustainable or universalisable.

Although these comments on sufficiency remain highly indeterminate – especially with respect to the amount of energy required – my position is that the concept of sufficiency is so important to sustainability discourse that its indeterminacy must not be a reason to reject it. I contend that universal sufficiency, like justice, is a fuzzy goal toward which humanity should be moving, and the most important thing is that there is a debate over the meaning of sufficiency and an attempt to practise our theory as best we can (Princen, 2005). Currently, in the developed nations, at least, sufficiency does not enter our economic or political vocabulary, which is why so few are asking the question, 'How much is enough?', and why fewer still are trying to answer it.

In an age that has done so much to link 'the good life' with material abundance, some will think the pursuit of sufficiency means giving up happy and fulfilling lives, but such an objection is based on a particular conception of human beings that the sufficiency perspective I am outlining rejects. If it were true that happiness and fulfilment consisted in the consumption and accumulation of ever more material things, then, admittedly, a sufficiency economy would seem to be inconsistent with 'the good life'. But that is far too narrow a conception of the good life (Alexander, 2012a) and it is based on a misunderstanding of human beings. It may be that affluence *can* produce wellbeing, but that does not prove that wellbeing *depends* on affluence. Indeed, the conception of human beings upon which the sufficiency economy is based is one in which there are an infinite variety of fulfilling lives that can be lived while consuming no more than an equitable share of nature. Put more directly, the sufficiency economy is based on the premise that 'a simple life' can be 'a good life', a truth that is obscured only to those who have not sufficiently explored their imaginations. Since consumerist conceptions of 'the good life' are causing devastating social and ecological problems, it follows that our economies should promote conceptions of the good life based on far lower resource and energy consumption, and that is the defining characteristic of the sufficiency economy.

2.2 *The macroeconomic and lifestyle implications of energy descent*

The necessity of highly reduced energy consumption is perhaps the critical issue (Odum and Odum, 2001; Murphy and Hall, 2011; Alexander, 2012c). Such a reduction will arise whether it is enforced by declining oil supplies (and the consequent high prices) or voluntarily embraced as a response to climate change. However, even the most progressive ecological economists who argue for decarbonising the economy do not seem to realise quite how revolutionary this proposal is – which is not to say decarbonisation is misconceived (Hansen *et al.*, 2008), only that its economic implications are widely misunderstood. If the global economy managed to wean itself off fossil fuels over the next few decades in response to climate change, then a 'steady state' economy would be impossible, if a steady state is meant to imply maintaining anything like existing levels of affluence. It would be impossible because fossil fuels currently make up around 80% of global energy supply (IEA, 2010b: 6), and given the close relationship between energy and economics, nothing like existing production or distribution could be maintained when we are talking about that level of energy reduction. Renewable energy sources do not seem capable of fully or affordably replacing the dense energy sources of coal, gas, and oil – with oil for transport being the hardest fossil fuel to replace (Trainer, 2013a; 2013b). As for nuclear energy, the world would need approximately 14,500 nuclear power plants to meet current energy demand (Pearce, 2008) – currently there are only 435 plants – and in a post-Fukushima world, especially, this upscaling presents an impossible challenge, whatever one otherwise thinks of nuclear. Furthermore, it would be foolish to produce so many nuclear facilities in an era of resource scarcity, when the prospects of geopolitical conflict is destined to increase (Klare, 2012). Without fossil fuels, therefore, and with limited nuclear, the world just would not have the energy supply to maintain a steady state of economic output; the economy would have to contract significantly. This is not a consequence many people seem to understand or dare to acknowledge, but it is a reality that we must not shy away from if a post-carbon world is indeed what we seek.

The implication of drastically reduced energy consumption primarily means two things for economies. First, it means significantly reduced production and consumption, commensurate with the available energy supply. In order to meet basic needs for all, this will require much more efficient use of energy and a radical reassessment of how best to use what limited energy is available. In the context of Joseph Tainter's (1988) theoretical framework, this implies 'voluntary simplification' (Alexander 2012b). Secondly, energy descent will mean an inevitable transition to highly localised forms of economic activity, for the reason that trade over large distances would be simply too energy-intensive and costly to afford, especially in an era of stagnating or declining oil supplies and rising prices (Rubin, 2009).

In short, a sufficiency economy is an economy that has low energy and resource requirements (relative to developed economies) but which sufficiently provides for mostly local needs using mostly local resources. These defining features of a sufficiency economy may receive some vague support in certain areas of the 'deep green' literature on sustainability, but to date almost no attention has been given to describing in any detail what economic life would be like if such an economy were ever to arise (but see Morris, 2004; Trainer, 2010; Burch, 2012a; Alexander, 2013). Accordingly, the remainder of this essay is dedicated to providing some of those details, in the hope of advancing the debate about what 'one planet living' actually means for daily life. Until we have some clearer vision of the alternative society, it is very difficult to work effectively and prosperously toward its realisation.

3. Envisioning a Prosperous Descent

Focused broadly on urban contexts in the developed world, the following analysis is structured by considering various aspects of the sufficiency economy, for the purpose of presenting a vision of the alternative way of life it implies. It is not intended to be a blueprint; it is simply an envisioning exercise intended to explore what living sustainably actually means in an age of limits.

3.1. *Water*

I will begin with the issue of water security, this being one of the most essential biophysical needs. The first point to note is that in most urban (including suburban) contexts, the amount of roof space available to collect water would be insufficient to secure the necessary water supplies for such dense populations.[1] What this means is that urban contexts *require* the water mains to exist – at least for the foreseeable future – for if they failed for more than a day or so, most people would quickly perish. Given that most people now live in urban contexts, it is fair to say that the first thing a sufficiency economy must do is ensure that the water mains

---

[1] It may be that tar-sealed roads and existing water infrastructure can be reimagined into decentralised water management systems, but for present purposes I will treat that as a distant possibility on the grounds that the systems for distributing and treating water collected in this manner are still undeveloped. Furthermore, I do not have the knowledge to understand how difficult it would be to secure water for consumption in this manner.

continues to function. This may sound like a trite observation, and it is, but since our present exploration is considering the economic foundations of a very different way of life, the foundations are where we must start. Accordingly, a sufficiency economy must at least have the energy supply and stability to maintain the water mains at a sufficiently high level of regularity and safety, something resembling the existing model.[2] The alternative is mass population die-off and probably significant re-ruralisation (where there would be more room for large water tanks).

Despite the mains system in a sufficiency economy remaining something close to what we have today, attitudes to water consumption and collection would undergo a revolution. To provide some hard numbers, average household water consumption in the US is around 370 litres; in Australia it is around 230 litres per day; and in the UK it is about 150 litres. At the other end of the spectrum, institutions like the United Nations and the World Health Organisation hold that 20 litres per person, per day, is close to the minimum needed for bare subsistence, and that figure is sometimes used as a baseline in refugee camps. In a sufficiency economy, I propose that domestic water consumption per person would need to fall to somewhere between 50-70 litres per person, per day, which is enough to live a dignified existence without leaving much room for waste.

Reduced water consumption should occur partly out of the desire for ecological preservation – for example, a desire to preserve river systems – but I should expect economic incentives to play a large part too. Assuming fresh water becomes increasingly scarce as populations increase and the climate warms (Brown, 2011), the price of water must inevitably rise, and rise significantly.[3] Currently, water is grossly underpriced.[4] In itself, expensive water will provide a strong incentive for people to reduce their wasteful consumption, and much of this can occur with very little hardship at all.

---

[2] I will not argue against privatisation models here, other than to note that in the sufficiency economy I envision, private companies that serve narrow shareholder interests cannot be left in charge of the provision of basic needs. Instead, the universal provision basic needs, such as water, must be considered a social responsibility that ultimately remains under social control. No one, for example, should be denied water on the grounds that they are too poor.

[3] I will assume, here, the continuation of some form of monetary economy, an issue given further attention below.

[4] Between 2008-9, water in Australia (where I am writing) was on average $1.93 per 1000 litres, and for industry water averaged $0.12 per 1000 litres. See Australian Bureau of Statistics: http://www.abs.gov.au/ausstats/abs@.nsf/Lookup/by%20Subject/1301.0~2012~Main%20Features~Water~279

Government rationing or community regulation of some sort may have to provide further incentives, in certain contexts, at least, as well as some baseline supply guarantees, irrespective of ability to pay. Eventually – and as soon as possible – key resources such as water should not be allocated on the basis of markets but come under social control.

In order to reduce water consumption (for either ecological or economic reasons, or both), various steps would be taken. First of all, every household would maximise its roof water collection via water tanks. Those households that prepare first will easily be able to purchase water tanks and pipes from hardware stores, but as times get tougher (e.g., plastics and concrete become harder to produce, source, or afford), more people will have to creatively use whatever containers and pipes they can salvage or make themselves.⁵ We will all become proficient in creating and connecting systems of water collection and reuse. Greywater systems, for example, will become the household norm, including the use of tank water to flush the toilet or simply collecting water – for example, when showering – to flush the toilet. Eventually, composting toilets that use almost no water will be widely used (at least in suburbia), with huge implications on water consumption.

In order to reduce charges from the increasingly expensive mains supply, tank water will be used whenever possible, especially for watering productive gardens (more on food below). In those times when people are required to draw from the mains, there is much room for conservation. Being conscientious of water consumption when preparing food and cleaning dishes is one space for conservation, and never watering (or even having) lawns is another. But perhaps the largest savings in the domestic sphere can come from how we wash ourselves and our clothes. Showers could easily be reduced to a minute or two without interfering with their primary goal of keeping us clean and hygienic. In fact, if required we could remain sufficiently hygienic by cleaning ourselves with a bucket of water and some soap. It may be a requirement of a dignified life to be able to wash oneself regularly – achievable with a bucket of water and some soap – but we could live with dignity without showering or bathing in the accustomed fashion. Clothes would probably be washed less regularly, which might bring some balance to a culture that is arguably excessively concerned with cleanliness.

---

⁵ In the longer term, of course, a good economy would ensure that essential infrastructure like water tanks would be produced and distributed on a 'needs' basis.

Innumerable other water-saving strategies could easily demonstrate that high water consumption is really a product of wastefulness, such that great reductions would not take away from us anything that is actually necessary for a good life. The critical point to note, which applies to all aspects of life discussed below, is that the same reductions in consumption (whether voluntary or enforced) would be experienced in totally different ways, depending on the mindset that was brought to experience. Fortunately, that mindset is within our control, even if the circumstances may not always be.

3.2 *Food*

A foundational issue for any economy is how it sources and produces its food, and this issue sits next to water on the list of essential needs. The globalised, industrial food production system currently in existence is highly unsustainable for various reasons. Not only are industrial farming techniques causing the severe and widespread erosion of nutrient-rich topsoil (which takes many hundreds of years to rejuvenate), but also the industrialised system is extremely fossil fuel dependent. Natural gas is needed to produce commercial fertilisers, and oil is needed to produce commercial pesticides, to fuel farm machinery, and to create the plastics used in packaging. Most importantly, however, are the extremely long supply chains that reach all around the world and which are dependent therefore on oil for transport. In Australia, for example, a basket of food from the supermarket typically travels 70,000 kilometres from producer to consumer, if the distance each item travels is aggregated (Salleh, 2007). With respect to the UK, one study has the figure at 241,000 kilometres (Sustain, 2001). This fossil fuel dependency is highly problematic not only due to its link to climate change, but also because it will not be economically sustainable as oil continues to get more expensive (Rubin, 2009).

In a sufficiency economy, food production would be highly localised and organic, and based on permaculture or 'biointensive' principles (Holmgren, 2002; Jeavons, 2012). Ideally this transition would be voluntarily embraced at once, but more likely is that it will be ushered in by the pressures of declining oil supplies and increasing prices. Cuba, during its 'special period', provides a real world example of some such transition (Percy *et al.*, 2010; Friedrichs, 2010). When the Soviet Union collapsed, Cuba almost over night found itself with drastically reduced oil supplies, and this necessitated an immediate shift away from energy-intensive, industrialised food production, toward a system of local and organic production. Notably, the government played a large role in facilitating this transition, but the driving force for change came from the grassroots level, as people realised they had to produce their own food or starve. The Cuban experience has some parallels with the 'relief gardens' that arose during the Great Depression and the 'victory gardens' during World War II. Necessity has always been a great motivator to grow food.

One of the most significant implications of the transition away from industrial food production is the increased labour needed for organic production. Environmentalists too often overlook this issue. While it is widely accepted that organic production can be more productive *per acre* than industrial food production (Jeavons, 2012), organic production is also vastly more *labour intensive*. The increased labour requirements arise primarily from the less frequent use of mechanised farm machinery, but organic fertiliser production and pest control are also typically more time intensive than industrialised techniques (although permaculture practices can reduce this disparity through things like companion planting, chop and drop fertilising, greywater systems, etc.). What this means is that organic food production is entirely capable of feeding the world, but to do so it will require a huge increase in the provision of agricultural labour. This must be accepted as an implication of the transition to a sufficiency economy, however it is one that has a large silver lining. Not only will it reconnect communities with the local land base upon which they depend for subsistence, but many health benefits will flow from moving away from sedentary office or factory work toward the more active and outdoor work of farming. To help get this transition underway, governments must do everything they can to support localised, organic agriculture, starting by putting an accurate price on carbon.

As well as a proliferation of organic farms on the urban periphery, a sufficiency economy would aim to maximise organic food production *within* the urban boundary. This would involve digging up lawns and turning them into productive vegetable gardens, and planting fruit trees in all available spaces. Nature strips would be cultivated; parks would be turned into small farms or community gardens; suitable roofs would become productive, herbs would grow on balconies and windowsills, and generally all food-producing potential would be realised. Most suburban backyards would keep chickens for eggs, and perhaps even small livestock, such as goats for milk and cheese. Animals are also a great source of manure for compost, and many permaculturalists build animals into their organic systems. While it will probably be far too energy intensive to dig up tar-sealed roads, there is still great potential for building raised beds on driveways, some footpaths or roads, and car parks. Mushrooms could be cultivated on the shady side of the house, and household or neighbourhood aquaculture systems could provide urban centres with some of their fish supply.

Even in a sufficiency economy, however, we can expect our households to 'import' various foods in various forms, if not from around the world, then certainly from rural contexts. This, in fact, would be an absolute necessity in urban contexts, because growing space simply does not permit anywhere near strict self-sufficiency. A recent study of Toronto, Canada, for example, concluded that the city could *possibly* produce 10% of its own fruit and vegetables, if available public growing space within the city's boundaries were converted to agriculture (MacRae *et al.,* 2010). This implies that even if urban agriculture were enthusiastically embraced, the city would still need to import 90% of its fruit and vegetables, to say nothing of its meat, minerals, and other goods. While some cities may be able to do somewhat better (e.g., Havana), the Toronto study clearly shows that urbanites around the world are extremely dependent on functioning food production and distribution systems.

Food consumption, not just production, would change drastically in a sufficiency economy. As already implied, the consumption of food would be organic and highly localised, and this also means that people would eat 'in season' in order to avoid having to import non-seasonal foods from other parts of the world. Preserving foods in season would be the most appropriate way to access those foods out of season. Generally, food would be unprocessed and require no disposable packaging, and people would eat much less meat (especially red meat) or become vegetarian, due to the intolerable environmental impacts of excessive meat and fish consumption. This reduction in meat consumption could also open up huge tracts of land for human food production that are currently used to produce grain for animals. Much land could also be 'rewilded'. People would also eat less meat and fish because the sufficiency economy would internalise all externalities, therefore greatly increasing their relative price and thus their relative demand.

Finally, as well as composting human waste for 'humanure' via composting toilets (Jenkins, 2005), a sufficiency economy would vigilantly compost all its organic food wastes in order to supply the growing need for organic fertilisers, and this would also vastly reduce the amount of so-called 'waste' that is currently 'wasted' by being sent to landfill. One might even say that in a sufficiency economy a good bag of compost will typically be more valuable than a bag of gold, and if readers cannot understand that, perhaps they will not understand much about the sufficiency economy.

3.3 *Clothing*

With a 'sufficient' supply of water and food secured, the next item on the list of basic material needs is clothing. The primary function of clothing is to keep us warm, and its secondary function, at least in our state of society, is to cover nakedness. However, those functions are all but forgotten in consumer societies today, where clothing's purpose has evolved to become primarily about expressing one's identity or social status. In a sufficiency economy, the fashion industry would be considered a superfluous luxury, one costing more than it was worth, and accordingly it would be amongst the first industries to disappear. At the same time, it must be acknowledged that human beings always have, and probably always will, want to express themselves through what they wear, so 'style' would not disappear so much as evolve in a sufficiency economy. A new aesthetic of sufficiency would develop, and soon enough the social expectation to look fashionably 'brand new' would become a quirk of history that would seem incomprehensible to the new generation.

In the short-to-medium term – say, over the next couple of decades – a sufficiency economy of clothing could arise in the developed world simply by people refusing to buy any new clothing. There are mountain ranges of discarded or unused, second-hand clothing already in existence, and these resources can easily provide for basic clothing needs for many years to come. Indeed, most adults could probably survive a decade or even a lifetime without adding to their existing wardrobes, for it is arguably the case that most people in the developed world have superfluous clothing. In a sufficiency economy, we would salvage, swap, and reuse clothing diligently, as well as get very good at sewing and mending. In terms of keeping us warm and covering nakedness, our clothing requirements would be easily and sufficiently met. The attitude to clothing I envisage in a sufficiency economy is nicely summed up in a passage from Thoreau (1982: 278): 'A [person] who has at length found something to do will not need a new suit to do it in,' adding that 'if my jacket and trousers, my hat and shoes, are fit to worship God in, they will do; will they not?' Thoreau's point here (which is not a religious one) is that a full, dignified, and passionate life does not depend on having 'nice' clothes.

Over the longer term, of course, it would not be enough simply to reuse and mend existing clothing. New clothing would need to be produced, and in a sufficiency economy the primary aims of production would be functionality and sustainability, not profit-maximisation or the pernicious desire for ever-changing styles. Fabrics like nylon and polyester would be minimised as they are made from petrochemicals and are non-biodegradable; and cotton requires extensive use of pesticides. Functional, low-impact fabrics would be used instead, such as agricultural hemp, nettles, and wool. Although this form of sustainable clothing production would certainly end up looking quite different from today's styles, it must be remembered that the consumption of clothing, like all consumption, is a culturally relative social practice, so as more people came to wear second-hand or sustainably designed clothing, new social standards would be quickly established. A time will come, no doubt, when those who continue wearing 'high fashion' will be the ones perceived as lacking style and taste, at which time we will realise that a new era has dawned.

3.4 *Housing*

The issue of housing is particularly difficult and complex. Sometimes well-meaning 'green' people like to imagine that the eco-cities of the future are going to look either like some techno-utopia, where everyone is living in million-dollar eco-houses such as those glorified in glossy environmental architecture magazines, or else like some agrarian village, where everyone is living in cob houses or 'earthships' they built themselves. The fact is, however, that over the next few critical decades, most people are going to find themselves living in an urban environment that already exists – suburbia. In other words, the houses and apartment blocks that already exist are, in most cases, going to be the very dwellings that will still exist in 20, 30, or 40 years, or more. So while it is important to explore what role technologies and environmental architecture could play in building new houses in more resource and energy efficient ways, and while there is certainly a place for cob houses and earthships for those who have such alternatives as an option, the existing urban and suburban housing stock is still going to be here for the foreseeable future. We are hardly going to knock down the suburbs and start again, just to try to be greener the second time around. It is important to recognise this reality, and not get too carried away with dreaming of a fundamentally new urban infrastructure. The foreseeable future is going to look much less romantic, and the sufficiency perspective outlined here accepts and embraces this.

Rather than dreaming eco-fairytales, a more important and urgent task is to figure out how to make the best of existing infrastructure – a task David Holmgren (2012) refers to as 'retrofitting the suburbs for the energy descent future'. This might involve things like taking in boarders or putting a caravan in the driveway to help resist further urban sprawl, or putting up curtains and sealing gaps in windows and doors to increase energy efficiency. It might involve changing all the light bulbs or going to the expense of getting an energy efficient fridge or another water tank. It would certainly involve refusing to spend large amounts of money renovating for purely aesthetic reasons or extending the house to create a games room. There is much that can be done (or not done) to improve the existing situation and trajectory.

It is also worth acknowledging that there are limits to what can be done. The existing housing stock is, more or less, what it is. That is, a poorly designed house will never evolve into an earthship, no matter how well it is 'retrofitted'. Perhaps the deeper problem, however, one that cannot be solved here, is the fact that the price of housing in many urban and suburban centres is so high that in order to own a house, or even rent in desirable areas (e.g., close to work), people are often locked into working long hours in jobs they do not like, simply to have a roof over their heads. This is capitalism at its most insidious – ensuring that people who want to escape the system and live differently cannot afford to do so. This structural 'lock in' is a very real problem (Alexander, 2012c), and the price of housing has much to do with it. The best way to escape it, in the absence of significant changes to the laws of property, is to avoid living in cities or towns with expensive real estate. I recognise that this will be very difficult for some people, whose jobs or families are already established in expensive or relatively expensive areas. For these people, the best option, arguably, is to live more densely, in order to share the price amongst more people. On the way to a sufficiency economy, however, more and more people will avoid places with expensive housing, and this is likely to result in a revitalisation of small towns and some significant re-ruralisation. Both of those phenomena will be a welcome relief to the overly dense metropolitan areas whose concrete boundaries continually expand further into the wild.

Over time the existing housing stock will need to be replaced, and a sufficiency economy would have certain expectations about how to do this. Materials should be sourced as locally as possible, and designed for long-term durability and to the highest standards of energy efficiency. Straw-bale or mud-brick houses may become common – but remember that the replacement of existing stock will take many, many decades. More people and communities would take part in the construction of their own homes to reduce costs. To limit the resources required, as well as limit the spaces needed to heat and cool, houses would be much smaller than are typically the case in developed nations today, and they would be more densely inhabited. They would be very modest – not much like the 'eco-houses' in glossy magazines – but they would be sufficient.

A sufficiency economy would also encourage creative, less conventional approaches to housing. 'Retired' shipping containers can be easily converted into humble abodes, and students could easily spend their student years or beyond living simply in a shed or a tent in someone's backyard (Alexander, 2010). To again draw on the words of Thoreau (1982: 283): 'Consider first how slight a shelter is absolutely necessary'. Thoreau reminds us that while 'civilised' people often spend decades toiling to pay for their homes, the American Indians of his day lived contently in tepees or wigwams that in the first instance were constructed in a day or two at most, and taken down and put up in a few hours; and every family owned one, or had a place in one. Thoreau (1982: 284) even quotes from a man called Gookin, being the superintendent of the Indians subject to the Massachusetts colony, who wrote in 1674 that 'I have often lodged in their wigwams, and found them to be as warm as the best English houses'. Would the Indians have been wise to give up those wigwams in exchange for the 40 years' labour required to pay for a more 'civilised' dwelling? In a sufficiency economy, where the full costs and benefits of housing would be taken into account, people would tend to choose something far closer to the wigwam or the yurt than the McMansion, and the only problem this would present for those dwelling in simpler housing is figuring out how to spend their extra decades of freedom. The possibilities for creative renewal of the existing housing stock are limited only by our imaginations.

3.5 *Energy*

It is an inescapable law of nature that economic activity requires energy, from which it can be inferred correctly that the amount of energy required to sustain an economy depends on the nature and extent of its economic processes. Energy therefore lies at the heart of all economies, and a sufficiency economy would be no different. But in terms of energy, the contrast between a growth economy and a sufficiency economy could hardly be starker. Whereas growth economies seek as much energy as possible at the lowest market price, a sufficiency economy requires only enough energy to provide a modest but sufficient material standard of living for all. This means much lower energy requirements, primarily through renewable sources, although the exact levels cannot be known with any precision. As a very rough guideline, energy consumption per capita in a sufficiency economy may be in the vicinity of half that of Western European economies today, and possibly even less (Trainer, 2012a).

Growth-based economies, especially the most highly developed ones, are perilously dependent on a cheap and abundant supply of oil – a finite, non-renewable fuel source, the production of which must inevitably peak and decline. Furthermore, the overwhelming consensus amongst the scientific community is that the carbon emissions from all fossil fuels (oil, gas, and coal) are a major contributor to climate change. These issues mean that economies should urgently work towards: (1) becoming resilient in the face of declining oil supplies and much higher oil prices; and (2), decarbonising their economies as far as possible in response to climate change. That is obviously what is required, and it is very easy to pontificate about the general solution! But since fossil fuels, especially oil, are such potent sources of energy and thus such potent fuels for economic activity, giving them up essentially means giving up the growth economy. That, of course, is precisely what no nation on the planet seems prepared to do – at least, not yet. Mother Nature may soon prove to be a powerful persuader, however, and her case is in the process of being made (Gilding, 2011; Turner, 2012).

The sufficiency economy, on the other hand, if it were ever embraced, would seek to be a post-carbon or very low-carbon economy, and in transitioning thereto we would have to accept that this would imply significantly reduced production and consumption. This would not necessarily be a problem, however, because as has already been made clear, consumption levels in a sufficiency economy would be considerably lower than in consumer societies today, thus requiring much less energy to support them. As well as economic contraction, efficiency improvements and conservation efforts would also lessen the energy requirements of a sufficiency economy.

The major obstacle in the way of completely decarbonising the economy is the fact that, currently, fossil fuels are required to make renewable energy systems, such as solar panels and wind turbines. I do not know of any such systems that have been produced purely from renewable energy. This is because solar panels and wind turbines, etc., depend on materials that are not all accessible, at least not yet, through machines powered by electricity/batteries. Until that time arrives, if it ever arrives, producing renewable energy systems will require the use of fossil fuels, and in the sufficiency economy I envision, this will have to be a necessary evil, so to speak. This, however, is among one of the only justifiable uses of fossil fuels. Aside from producing renewable energy systems, the broad goal must be to electrify the rest of the economy as far as possible, and in many cases return to manual labour. In time, perhaps, even renewable energy systems could themselves be produced from renewable energy, although presently that is far from certain.

I do not wish to understate the challenges that would be faced in attempting the transition toward a low-energy economy. I certainly do not have all the answers about how such a transition would or could successfully transpire. For example, the evidence is uncertain about what role nuclear should or could play in this transition (although I am very sceptical about it being the silver bullet). All I know is that if we are to avoid the dire economic and ecological consequences that are expected to flow from runaway climate change and/or unmitigated peak oil, reducing energy consumption, especially oil, and decarbonising the economy more generally, must be our primary energy aims. Meeting these aims, I contend, depends on the emergence of a sufficiency economy.

3.6 Transport

One of the largest demands for energy today comes from transporting people and materials from place to place. The energy demands are especially high in our globalised economy, where commodities are often consumed thousands of kilometres away from where they were produced. The fact that there are now over one billion cars and light vehicles on the roads makes the energy demand for transport much greater still. It is important to note, however, that the globalised economy and car-dependent cultures only emerged over the last century because oil was so cheap and abundant. It seemed to make economic sense, for instance, to grow apples in Australia and ship them to Alaska for consumption, or to drive to the corner store to pick up some milk, because the transport costs were so cheap. But as the price of oil continues to rise, people will be forced to rethink their driving habits, and much global trade will become uneconomic, priced out of the market through the embedded costs of expensive oil or the pricing of carbon. These processes are already underway, and in a sufficiency economy they would be embraced, even actively encouraged.

The first issue here is the relocalisation of economies (Rubin, 2009). As many parts of the global economy get suffocated from expensive oil, local producers will regain the competitive advantage. Many things once imported from all around the world will now be able to be produced more economically at the local level. This especially applies to food production, for as we have already noted, industrial food systems are highly dependent on oil not only for transport, but also for things like pesticides and plastic packaging. When the costs of oil increase, these methods will no longer be affordable. The consequence will be more localised, organic food production, and therefore vastly reduced energy requirements for transport and production.

These same economic forces will eventually apply to all oil-dependent commodities in the globalised economy. As soon as the extra costs of shipping the commodity outweigh the savings that flow from cheap labour overseas, the commodity will once again be produced locally.[6] Relocalisation, therefore, may well come about, not because of any top-down initiative, nor from a critical mass of people convincing the mainstream of the environmental or social benefits of local production. Rather, relocalisation will arise because the costs of globalised trade simply become unaffordable. If the costs of climate change were internalised to the price of oil, as they would be in a sufficiency economy, this process of relocalisation would occur even faster. The critical point, however – irrespective of the economics – is simply that the sufficiency economy seeks to minimise its energy requirements, and reducing the energy demands of the transport sector will require relocalising the vast majority of production. To the minimal extent that global trade continues, it will probably be conducted in the main by sail, as it was prior to the petroleum age. Food for cities would be imported from rural contexts mainly by electric trains.

The second issue anticipated above relates to driving cars. In order to decarbonise the economy, it is required that people drive much less, or not at all. Electric cars will not be able to escape this imperative, because producing them depends on fossil fuels, and also for most people electric cars remain unaffordable. Just as importantly, it would take many decades or even a century to replace the one billion petroleum-powered vehicles on the roads today with electric vehicles, and we do not have that much time (or money) to mitigate the effects of peak oil and climate change. The only solution is driving less. In many cases, driving less would cause no hardship at all, for various studies have estimated that around half of all car trips are less than 5 kilometres,[7] and around one third

---

[6] To provide a real-world example, when oil rose to $147 in 2008, it became cheaper to make steel in the US, since the high price of oil added $90 per ton to steel production, making Chinese imports less economic than local production. See Jeff Rubin (2009: 150). See also, Peter North, 2010, 'Eco-localisation as a Progressive Response to Peak Oil and Climate Change – A Sympathetic Critique'. *Geoforum* 42: 585.

[7] http://www.transport.wa.gov.au/mediaFiles/AT_TS_P_Thetruthabouttravelin Perth.pdf

are less than 3km.[8] In many cases those could be replaced with walking, cycling, or public transport.

There are, however, deep structural complications underlying the requirement to stop driving as much, which should not be ignored. For many people today driving is the only way of getting to work, so the injunction to 'get out of your car' may frustrate those people who would love to drive less but cannot, due to a lack of viable alternatives. Suburbia was built on the basis of cheap oil, which meant that 'sprawl' was not seen as much of a problem. But now that oil is getting more expensive, the long commutes are becoming increasingly problematic, not only from a cost perspective, but also from an environmental perspective. There is no silver bullet solution to this problem, but the first thing that must happen is to invest as heavily as possible in a good system of electricity-powered public transport, such as light trains or trams, as well as a good system of bike lanes. Putting a price on carbon will also provide economic incentives to drive only when absolutely necessary. To the extent driving persists, car-pooling must increase dramatically (which will be especially necessary in places with poor public transport options).

But there is a more fundamental change that must occur, which is linked to the issue of relocalisation discussed above. The focus above was on how the sufficiency economy would move away from global trade and toward local production on the grounds that the energy required for transport and production is both increasingly expensive and environmentally destructive. With respect to driving, however, the issue is not so much about moving production within regional boundaries but about moving more production within the household or the immediate local community. This is in fact a necessary feature of the sufficiency economy (discussed further below). If this transformation were to occur, driving would be unnecessary for many people, as their place of work would be either at home or a short walk down the road. Longer distances would be covered on bicycle or public transport, and perhaps the occasional horse and cart might even return to our streets. As a general rule, however, people and materials in a sufficiency economy would have to travel far less than is common in developed nations today (Moriarty and Honnery, 2008). In short, a sufficiency economy is by and large a local economy.

---

[8] E.g., http://www.planning.org.au/documents/item/363

3.7 *Work and Production*

A sufficiency economy can also be understood with respect to the fundamental changes that would take place in terms of work and production. The most significant of these changes, noted immediately above, is that the household would once again become a place of production, not merely consumption. This transition would be driven partly by choice, but in tough economic times (e.g., with high unemployment) many households might find that home production would become more of an economic necessity. Rather than hiring other people to grow our food, cook our meals, make our clothes, build our furniture, look after our children, maintain our houses, etc., in a sufficiency economy we would generally take care of such things ourselves, so far as it were possible. Furthermore, households would sometimes produce goods for trade or barter, such as furniture, crockery, clothes, or food, and thereby contribute to the broader local economy. Artisans might also produce speciality goods at the household level, such as musical instruments, paintings, or various tools.

It was not so long ago, we should not forget, when these forms of home production were the norm, and the necessary skills must be passed down to the younger generations, or else the transition back to home production will prove much more difficult as we find ourselves having to reinvent the wheel. Unfortunately, home production has rarely received the respect it deserves, and that is why it is not as highly valued as it should be. It was an unfortunate consequence of the Feminist Movement that home production was often denigrated. Certainly, when women were forced through cultural expectations to be the home-maker while men went out and ran the formal economy and governed the nation, it is perfectly understandable why liberating women seemed to imply leaving the home, joining the formal workforce, and outsourcing home production. But the importance of being given equal freedoms should not have implied, as it too often did, that staying at home was somehow a sign of oppression or failure. There is honour in home production, provided it is not imposed upon one gender. In a sufficiency economy, home-based production (whether undertaken by women or men, or both) would be recognised for what it is – the heart of any economy (Astyk, 2012).

Nevertheless, the sufficiency economy should not be understood to mean strict self-sufficiency at the household level. In most cases, that would be neither desirable nor possible. Much production would still take place beyond the household, but the nature of what would be produced and the values motivating production would be very different. The provision of basic needs –

such as food, clothing, shelter, tools, and medicine – would be the primary focus of production, and the motivation would be to produce what was necessary and sufficient for a good life, rather than to produce luxuries or superfluous abundance. While some large factories would probably remain in order to provide certain materials or hi-tech equipment, small private businesses and worker cooperatives would in most cases replace the mega-corporation, with the local grocer and hardware store returning to Mainstreet, and community-owned-and-operated farms providing much of the community's sustenance.

Since the levels of consumption in a sufficiency economy would be so much lower than is common in consumer societies today, it is worth emphasising that the levels of production would be considerably lower too. This would imply reduced working hours for most people, in the formal economy, at least, creating far more time for leisure and the necessary home production. One consequence of this would be a blurring of the distinction between work and leisure, as people would spend far more time working on their own livelihoods at home, at their own pace and in their own way. It is also worth acknowledging, however, that in some respects – such as food production – much more labour would be required, due to the minor role fossil fuel energy would play in production. In a sufficiency economy, it would be certain that many more people would work as farmers, but far from being a regressive step, there are many reasons to think that this would be a positive advance away from office or factory work. People would be working outdoors with their hands in the soil, once again connected with the natural systems upon which their most basic needs depend.

3.8 *Money, Markets, and Exchange*

The question of what role money, markets, and exchange would play in a sufficiency economy is complex, and cannot be fully addressed here. It is also likely that such issues would play out differently in different contexts, as is the case with all aspects of the sufficiency economy. Nevertheless, some broad comments can be made on these subjects.

First of all, it is worth noting that throughout history, human beings have exchanged goods and services with each other, either by way of barter, gift, or through the use of money. These practices are going to continue in a sufficiency economy, although the nature of money, markets, and exchange will have to evolve greatly, as will our attitudes toward them. As noted above, a sufficiency economy does not mean that everyone would be strictly self-sufficient.

Households will be as self-sufficient as possible, but there will remain 'markets' for various goods that cannot be produced within the household. Money is likely to remain the most convenient tool for 'keeping accounts', so to speak, but in a sufficiency economy non-monetary forms of exchange, such as gift and barter, are likely to become much more prominent modes of economic activity. Since profit-maximisation would not be the aim of market activity in a sufficiency economy, less attention would be given to producing things that fetch the highest price, and more attention would be given to producing what the community most needs.

The fact that markets of some variety would probably still remain in a sufficiency economy implies that some forms of private property are likely to endure, although it is just as likely, and desirable, that more of the economy comes under social control. That is to say, ultimately a sufficiency economy would be defined by a reconceived eco-socialism. The balance between private and social control of the economy, however, could unfold in an infinite variety of ways (so the tripartite distinction between private property/ socialism/ the 'third way' is not unhelpful). This unfolding will depend partly on the extent to which communities come together to decide for themselves how their local economies should run – which I would like to insist is every community's right – but it is also likely to depend, at least at first, on how we deal with the emergence of systemic shocks, such as financial crises, or the impacts from climate change and peak oil. In the event of long-term crises or even a collapse scenario, central governments may lose much of their ability to enforce national law effectively, and some more localised property frameworks would likely arise in very disruptive and unpredictable ways. Even in a less disruptive future, local governments or new forms of community authority could well come to prominence in a sufficiency economy (Trainer, 2010). Whatever the case, a sufficiency economy must be designed, through collective planning and organising, so that everyone has enough, and this means that communities would have to take responsibility for ensuring that basic needs were universally met. This will require a significant degree of social control of the economy, in the sense at least that the provision of basic needs for all would be considered a social responsibility and could not be left to market forces. Some form of rationing may be required, especially in times of crisis and adjustment. The most important issue would be that everyone had access to land, and communities might have to experiment with how best to ensure this occurred (see, e.g., Alexander, 2011a: chs 2 and 5).

With respect to existing monetary systems in developed nations, one of the greatest problems is that money is loaned into existence as debt that accrues interest, and for such systems to function they require economic growth in order for the debts *plus* the interest to be paid back (Sorrell, 2010). Interest payments imply an expansion of the money supply. A sufficiency economy, being a degrowth-cum-zero-growth economy, could not by definition have a monetary system that required growth, so it follows that interest-bearing loans could not be the primary means of money creation in a sufficiency economy (Trainer, 2011). But what should replace this debt-based system – and how the transition beyond such a system would play out – are open questions that have not received the attention they deserve. It may be that as economies are suffocated by expensive oil in coming years, and find themselves at the 'end of growth', debt-based systems which require growth will collapse under the weight of their own debts and the alternative system will arise in a very unplanned, ad hoc, and possibility decentralised way. It is important that more attention is given to this eventuality, for the public debate over what should replace debt-based, fractional reserve systems should be occurring now, prior to the existing crises deepening. I will leave the details to be worked out by those more competent, but the alternative may have to look something like Ted Trainer's proposal for community owned banks to be the source of money, banks which provide zero-interest credit for ventures that have been selected on the basis that they serve community interests (Trainer, 2010).

3.9 *Miscellaneous*

I will close this sketch of the sufficiency economy with some even briefer comments on a range of miscellaneous issues that, like all the issues outlined above, deserve far more attention than space presently allows. The purpose of this essay, however, has not been to provide comprehensive details on every aspect of the sufficiency economy – I am the first to admit that most issues discussed above deserve a book-length treatment. Rather, my purpose has been to link to the dots that have already been formed in order to provide some glimpse of the 'big picture'. I ask that this be taken into consideration should the reader be frustrated (justifiably) that I have raised more questions than I have answered.

To begin with, we should remember that the sufficiency economy, should it ever emerge, would arrive in the wake of industrial civilisation's deterioration. This will mean that vast quantities of industrially produced goods, tools, and materials will already be in existence, and for many decades, perhaps centuries, this would mean we would be living in what some have called the 'salvage economy' (Greer, 2009). In other words, the wastes of industrial civilisation will very quickly become the new materials for life at the end of Empire, and human beings will doubtless prove to be exceedingly creative in the use and reuse of existing materials. Furthermore, recycling in the sufficiency economy will not involve, for example, melting down existing glass bottles and making new glass bottles, but simply reusing glass bottles in the form in which they already exist (Holmgren, 2002). The old ethics of the depression era will return, as people learn to 'use it up, wear it out, make it do, or do without'.

With respect to technology, the first point to note is that we do not need new technological advances to create a better world. We have everything we need already, so the fundamental problem is not a lack of technological know-how; the fundamental problem is the value-system that consumer capitalism currently has adopted to direct the technology we already have. When those values change and are put to the task of providing 'enough, for everyone, forever', then we will realise all at once that we already have the tools that we need to achieve this ambitious task. Technology is only a means, not an end.

The second point to note on technology is that in a sufficiency economy, life will be such that a great many technological conveniences we know today will largely disappear. Microwave ovens, vacuum cleaners, electronic kitchen gadgets, mobile phones, etc., may all become relics of history, but without causing much hardship at all. The clothesline will generally replace the clothes dryer; the bike will largely replace the car; and the television will essentially disappear. I suspect that washing machines and fridges will be the last things we give up, but life would go on even if they became unavailable or unaffordable. Hopefully computers will remain to do some important tasks (primarily information sharing and community organising), although private computers might become much less common. It is also worth remembering that people survived well enough in the 1950s and 60s without computers, and we would survive well enough if we were without them again. At the same time, in the short term computers may be a necessary tool for advancing the sufficiency economy through critical education and the organisation of mass social movements. Education itself would need to undergo a radical transformation, moving away from the goal of training people to maintain the existing growth economy, toward an education that prepares people practically for life in a sufficiency economy (see, e.g., Trainer, 2012b; Burch, 2012b; Burch, 2012c).

There are countless other avenues that this analysis could explore: what would become of existing health systems, or pension schemes, in the sufficiency economy? How would people spend their leisure and what art forms might flourish? How would the sufficiency economy differ in urban centres as opposed to rural settings? And how would sufficiency in the global North affect the global South? These are all issues that deserve further attention, but I must defer those discussions for another occasion. I will, however, finish the current discussion with a comment on politics and power (at risk of opening up a can of worms I cannot close). Some readers might have found themselves sympathising with at least some aspects of the preceding discussion but at the same time asking how the transition could ever transpire, *given existing power structures.* This is a daunting issue to consider, because certainly there are many powerful people and institutions around the world that have an interest in maintaining the status quo, and who will use all their power and resources to inhibit the emergence of a sufficiency economy.

Part of the problem here is that our personal lifestyle choices take place within political and economic structures of constraint, and those structures inevitably make some lifestyle decisions easy or necessary and other lifestyle decisions difficult or impossible (Alexander, 2012c). The existing structures of consumer capitalism are functioning to 'lock' people into high consumption, consumer lifestyles, even if they desire a different way of life. What this means is that personal action alone is never going to be enough to bring about a sufficiency economy; structural change will be necessary. But this draws us into the vexed question: how do we change the fundamental structures of global capitalism?

From the mainstream liberal-democratic perspective, the solution to this problem depends on a culture shift. That is to say, a sufficiency economy will not arise in liberal democracies until there is a culture that wants it, at which time those cultural values will be embraced by representative politicians and used to shape public policy in order to keep or win office. This understanding of representative democracy might be nice in theory, but it assumes that democracies are functioning well, and a strong case can be made that many so-called democracies are under the undue influence of corporate interests (e.g., Tham, 2010). If that is so, even a culture shift in favour of sufficiency would not necessarily bring about structural change, because we can be sure that corporate interests influencing public policies are not interested in a sufficiency economy. They want infinite growth.

The Marxist perspective essentially accepts this critical view of liberal democracy, arguing that the capitalist state is merely a tool for maintaining the status quo and for furthering the narrow interests of the economic elites. From this perspective, the revolution that is needed depends not so much on a cultural shift but on the working classes taking control of the state in order to socialise the means of production. Since the economic elites will never voluntarily give up their hold on power, it follows that the Marxist revolution must be a violent revolution. The problem with this understanding of social change, however, is that Marxism, and socialism more generally, have almost without exception remained embedded within the growth model of progress that the sufficiency economy rejects (but see, e.g., Sarkar, 1999; Smith, 2010). In other words, socialists have tended to seek state power, not to use that power to move away from the growth economy, but to facilitate continued growth only in more socially just ways and with a broader distribution. While it is possible to imagine a 'state socialism of sufficiency' – certainly it is easier than imagining a 'state capitalism of sufficiency'! – there arguably remains the concern that states of *any type* – whether capitalist, socialist, or some other variety – are in and of themselves structurally inclined to be pro-growth. The basic critique here is that all states are dependent for their existence on a taxable economy, and the larger the tax-base, the more funds the state can draw from to carry out its policies.

This leads to a third, broad vision of social change, arising out of the anarchist tradition – the environmental anarchists, in particular, such as Peter Kropotkin, Murray Bookchin, and Ted Trainer. Although these theorists have their important differences, they essentially agree with the Marxists that state capitalism is unjustifiable on the grounds that it is being used unjustly as a tool to maintain the existing order. But unlike the Marxists, they do not think the solution is taking control of the state. They think the solution is building the new society at the local, grassroots level, where communities create self-governing, localised, participatory democracies. Part of the disagreement with the Marxists here is because these 'deep green' anarchists think that the state is inextricably intertwined with economic violence against nature, and so from this perspective, no state, not even state socialism, is going to lead to sustainability. But even if there were hope of a green state, these theorists would not advocate that people direct their energies toward top-down change, because they think that state governance is an unjustifiable form of hierarchy and rule, no matter how green it might be. Accordingly, they believe that if a just and sustainable society is to emerge, it has to be built without much or any help from the state (and probably with a lot of resistance).

While this brief review does a disservice to the richness of the ideas and thinkers discussed, it does serve the purpose of raising questions about how any transition to a sufficiency economy could unfold. Would it (or could it) be somehow voted in through the mechanisms of parliamentary democracy? Would it require a political revolution and the introduction of some form of eco-socialism? Or would it require grassroots movements to essentially do it mostly themselves, building the new economy underneath the existing economy, without state assistance? While I have much sympathy with the latter approach, I think it would be unwise to commit ourselves unconditionally to any one strategy. While this open-mindedness is not theoretically tidy or distinct, it may be the best strategy. The future is highly uncertain, and the conditions for change are always shifting beneath our feet. Who knows what might be possible tomorrow? Who knows what events or crises or leaders might one day shift the balance of power between strategies? My view is that the Transition Towns Movement, while not homogenous in its approach, currently has something of the right strategic balance here. Adopting what I would call 'participatory democracy', the movement basically accepts that change must be driven at the grassroots, community level, while at the same time being prepared to press on governments (mainly local governments) to assist in the transition whenever that seems to be a good use of limited energies. Furthermore, if the Transition Towns Movement were ever to succeed in achieving its ambitious and diverse goals, I believe something resembling the sufficiency economy may well be the result. My primary aim in writing this chapter was to provide some more detail on what that alternative economy might look like.

4. The Ambiguous Charge of Utopianism

This time, like all times, is a very good one, if we but know what to do with it.
— R.W. Emerson

With the notion of a sufficiency economy now broadly sketched out, and some issues about the transition raised for consideration, it may be worthwhile stepping back from the analysis to consider the vision as a whole. This should provide a new perspective and perhaps raise new issues that deserve attention. One objection that can be easily anticipated is that the notion of a sufficiency economy, as I have described it, is fundamentally utopian in its outlook, and in this section I will respond to this objection briefly.

4.1. *Four responses*

The charge of utopianism can be dealt with in at least the following four ways. First, if the charge is meant to imply that the goal of economic sufficiency, as opposed to economic growth, is unrealistic, then there is a sense in which that charge must be turned on its head. It is limitless growth on a finite planet that is unrealistic. After all, what could be more utopian, in the pejorative sense, than the neoclassical growth model which takes as 'given' certain non-physical parameters (e.g., market pricing, preferences, technology, wealth distribution, etc.), but on that basis purports to be independent of the biophysical laws of nature? Recognising the biophysical (and other) limits to growth may indeed require a radical new approach to how economies are structured, as I have argued it does; but this would be in *recognition* of certain realities, not in any attempt to *transcend* them.

In a second sense, however, the charge of utopianism should be embraced, not as an indictment, but as a defence. 'Without the hypothesis that a different world is possible', Genevieve Decrop has stated, 'there can be no politics, but only the administrative management of men [sic] and things' (as quoted in Latouche, 2009: 32). In this sense, the sufficiency economy is indeed a utopian vision, arising out of a defiant faith that a different world is possible, and indeed, that forthcoming crises must be embraced as opportunities. But as Serge Latouche (2009: 32) has aptly explained with respect to the degrowth movement, 'Far from representing a flight of fancy, it is an attempt to explore the objective possibility of its implementation.' With a nod to Latouche, the sufficiency economy described above should be understood in similar terms. Imagining the alternative is the first step toward its realisation.

But there is a third sense in which the sufficiency economy is not utopian at all – not if 'utopia' refers to that which does not and could never exist. Granted, there is no economy that resembles closely the one described above, which is of a growth economy that has gone through the transition to sufficiency. Nevertheless, almost all the features of the sufficiency economy do find reflection in existing economies in the developed world (and elsewhere). Indeed, real-world examples of sufficiency in practice are everywhere bubbling beneath the surface, threatening to expand into the mainstream; some are in the process of doing so, albeit slowly. For example, there are nascent movements based on notions such as voluntary simplicity, eco-villages, permaculture, Transition Towns, collaborative consumption, slow food, degrowth, steady state economics, etc., all of which can be understood to be exemplifying the practice of sufficiency in disparate but overlapping ways. What this indicates is that a sufficiency economy is not at all a utopian fantasy, but rather an embryonic, fragmented reality struggling away beneath the existing economy, trying to replace that economy with something fundamentally different. It is easy to forget that social movements constantly surprise us, often moving from tiny subcultures to the cultural mainstream with startling speed. Rather than despair, we should proceed on the assumption that more surprises could still lie in store for us.

Finally, some might claim that the sufficiency economy is utopian – again, in the pejorative sense – for the reason that it posits a transformation of economy that relies on a cultural embrace of low consumption lifestyles of sufficiency, or rather lifestyles of voluntary simplicity. Human beings are essentially consumers with insatiable material desires, the objection might run, and the sufficiency economy will never voluntarily emerge because voluntary simplicity asks people to act against their personal interests. Any response to this point should begin with the social critique of consumer culture, which would be based on the large and robust body of hedonics research ratifying what many people, perhaps, know intuitively, namely, that 'beyond a certain threshold, more material wealth is a poor substitute for community cohesion, healthy relationships, a sense of purpose, connection with nature, and other dimensions of human happiness' (Talberth, 2008: 21). Since the evidence suggests that many people in affluent societies are above such a 'threshold', there are strong grounds for thinking that reducing consumption in such cases would actually increase personal happiness. Relying on the expansion of the Voluntary Simplicity Movement would be more problematic, of course, if voluntary simplicity were a living strategy founded solely upon altruism, or if it implied sacrificing personal wellbeing for the sake of ecological health or social justice. But plainly its foundations are less demanding. Although many in the Voluntary Simplicity Movement are indeed motivated by humanitarian and ecological concerns, the most promising sign for the expansion of the movement lies in the fact that almost all those who practise simplicity report being happier in their lifestyle choice, *despite a voluntary reduction or restraint in income and consumption* (Alexander and Ussher, 2012). A utopian theory of economic transformation seems much less utopian, I would suggest – as would any theory of social reorganisation – when it is based upon a living strategy that is demonstrably in people's best interests, including their own happiness.

For all these reasons, I contend that the sufficiency economy is not utopian in any problematic sense. The prospects of its imminent realisation, I admit, seem slim; and certainly it will depend on human beings working relatively well together as the challenges ahead intensify. But human beings share a universal desire to work toward a better life, and if that energy can be harnessed and the transition wisely negotiated, then the sufficiency economy will be quite achievable. Seemingly impossible things have happened before.

5. Conclusion

The challenges that will be faced on the path to a sufficiency economy can hardly be overstated. One of them not considered above is our genetic composition, which is not well suited to dealing effectively or thoughtfully with long-term issues. Historically we had to worry about immediate dangers such as tigers, other tribes, staying warm, and getting enough food; now we also have to get our heads around and respond effectively to the seemingly distant and abstract issues of climate change and peak oil. Evidently, this does not come easy to us. Secondly, the very task of decarbonising our economies as far as possible will be much harder and more unsettling than most people think. As you read these words, look around your room and consider what material artefacts are not, in some way, the product of fossil fuels. Is there anything? My point is that the sufficiency economy described above is not about turning off the lights and taking shorter showers. It is about embracing a fundamentally different way of life and a fundamentally different economy. If we do not voluntarily embrace these differences, however, and instead persist with the goal of universal affluence, then soon enough ecological and/or economic systems will collapse and we will be faced with fundamental change all the same, only with much more suffering. As I noted earlier, we can go the easier way (which will not be easy), or the harder way (which will be unspeakably tragic), depending on our attitudes and actions. We are free to choose our fate, and presently we are in the process of doing so.

I have hardly presented the full picture of the sufficiency economy and I acknowledge that various issues, probably most issues, are controversial and will be contested. That is the way it will be, and that is the way it should be. What is important is that the debate gets drawn away from the question of how to *maintain* the existing system, toward the urgent and necessary question of what new system should *replace* the existing system. In this sense the humble notion of a sufficiency economy can be seen as the revolutionary proposal that it is. It will not, of course, be easy to build a new, simpler way of life from within industrial civilisation. Everything will conspire against us. But various social movements already in existence provide a glimmer of hope in these dark times, and that glimmer is everyday growing brighter.

In all movements for change, including the broad movements for justice and sustainability, it is important occasionally to hold up for examination what one understands to be the clearest expression of one's highest hopes and ideals. That is what I have tried to do in this essay, albeit in an incomplete way. No doubt some will find the threads of underlying positivity utterly indigestible. But let them fester in their own negativity, while the rest of us (including the constructive critics) set about building the new economy out of the emerging ashes of Empire. All we can do is our best, and we should die trying, not because we think we will succeed, but because if we do not try, something noble in our hearts and spirits will be lost.

References

Alexander, S., ed. 2009. *Voluntary simplicity: The poetic alternative to consumer culture*. Whanganui: Stead & Daughters.

Alexander, S., 2010. 'Deconstructing the shed: Where I live and what I live for'. *Concord Saunterer: The Journal of Thoreau Studies* 18: 125.

Alexander, S. 2011a. 'Property beyond growth: Toward a politics of voluntary simplicity'. Doctoral thesis, Melbourne Law School, University of Melbourne. Available at http://papers.ssrn.com /sol3/papers.cfm?abstract_id=1941069 (accessed 5 May 2011).

Alexander, S.. 2012a. 'The Optimal Material Threshold: Toward an Economics of Sufficiency'. *Real-World Economics Review* 2-21.

Alexander, S. 2012b. 'Resilience through simplification: Revisiting Tainter's theory of collapse'. *Simplicity Institute Report* 12h.

Alexander, S. 2012c. 'Degrowth, expensive oil, and the new economics of energy' *Real-World Economics Review* 40.

Alexander, S. 2012d. 'Degrowth implies voluntary simplicity: Overcoming barriers to sustainable consumption'. *Simplicity Institute Report* 12b.

Alexander, S. 2013. *Entropia: Life beyond industrial civilisation*. Melbourne: Simplicity Institute Publishing.

Alexander, S. and Ussher, S. 2012. 'The voluntary simplicity movement: A multi-national survey analysis in theoretical context'. *Journal of Consumer Culture* 12(1): 66-88.

Astyk, S. 2012. *Making home: Adapting our homes and our lives to settle in place*. Gabriola Island: New Society Publishers.

Brown, L. 2011. *World on the edge: How to prevent environmental and economic collapse*. New York: W.W. Norton and Co.

Brown, K. and Kasser, T. 2005. 'Are psychological and ecological well-being compatible? The role of values, mindfulness, and lifestyle. *Social Indicators Research* 74: 349-368.

Burch, M. 2012a. 'Simplicity and economy'. *Simplicity Institute Report* 12q: 1-23.

Burch, M. 2012b. 'Educating for simple living'. *Simplicity Institute Report* 12j: 1-32.

Burch, M. 2012c. 'The simplicity exercises: A sourcebook for simplicity educators'. *Simplicity Institute Report* 12k: 1-207.

Daly, H. 1996. *Beyond growth: The economics of sustainable development*. Boston: Beacon Press.

Friedrichs, J., 2010. 'Global Energy Crunch: How Different Parts of the World Would React to a Peak Oil Scenario' 38 *Energy Policy* 4562.

Gilding, P. 2011. *The Great Disruption: How the climate crisis will transform the global economy*. London: Bloomsbury.

Global Footprint Network, 2012. Reports available at: http://www.footprintnetwork.org/en/index.php/GFN/ [accessed 31 March 2012].

Greer, J.M. 2008. *The Long Descent*. Gabriola Island: New Society Publishers.

Greer, J.M. 2009. *The ecotechnic future*. Gabriola Island: New Society Publishers.

Hansen, J. *et al.* 2008, 'Target Atmospheric CO2: Where Should Humanity Aim? Available at http://www.columbia.edu/~jeh1/2008/TargetCO2_20080407.pdf [accessed 31 March 2012].

Hicks, J., 1959. *Essays in world economics*. Oxford: Clarendon Press.

Heinberg, R. 2011. *The end of growth: Adapting to our new economic reality*. Gabriola Island: New Society Publishers.

Holmgren, D. 2002. *Permaculture: Principles and pathways beyond sustainability*. Hepburn: Holmgren Design Services.

Holmgren, D. 2012. 'Retrofitting the suburbs for the energy descent future'. *Simplicity Institute Report* 12i.

Hopkins, R. 2008. *The transition handbook: From oil dependency to local resilience*. Totnes, Devon: Green Books.

International Energy Agency (IEA). 2010a. *World Energy Outlook 2010: Executive Summary*, IEA Report. Available at http://www.iea.org/Textbase/npsum/weo2010sum.pdf (accessed 22 December 2011).

International Energy Agency (IEA), 2010b. *Key World Energy Statistics*. Available at: http://www.iea.org/textbase/nppdf/free/2010/key_stats_2010.pdf [accessed 20 June 2012].

Jackson, T. 2005. 'Live better by consuming less? Is there a double dividend in sustainable consumption?' *Journal of Industrial Ecology* 9: 19-36.

Jackson, T. 2009. *Prosperity without growth: Economics for a finite planet*. London: Earthscan.

Jeavons, J. 2012. 8th edn. *How to grow more vegetables*. Berkeley: Ten Speed Press.

Jenkins, J. 2005. 3rd edn. *The humanure handbook: A guide to composting human manure*. White River Junction, VT: Chelsea Green Publishing.

Kasser, T. 2002. *The high price of materialism*. Cambridge, Mass: MIT Press.

Klare, M., 2012. *The race for what's left: The global scramble for the world's last resources*. New York: Picador.

Korowics, D. 2012. 'Trade-off: Financial system supply-chain cross-contagion: A study in global systemic collapse'. Metis Risk Consulting, 30th June, revised, 2012.

Latouche, S. 2009. *Farewell to growth*. Cambridge, UK: Polity Press.

MacRae, R. *et al.* 2010. 'Could Toronto provide 105 of its fresh vegetable requirements from within its own boundaries? Matching consumption requirements with growing space'. *Journal of Agriculture, Food Systems, and Community Development* 1(2).

Meadows, D., Randers, J., and Meadows, D. 2004. *Limits to growth: The 30-year update*. White River Junction, Vt: Chelsea Green Publishing.

Moriarty, P. and D. Honnery. 2008. 'Low-mobility: The future of transport'. *Futures* 40: 865.

Morris, W. 2004. *New from nowhere and other writings*. London: Penguin.

Murphy, D. and Hall, C. 2011. 'Energy return on investment, peak oil, and the end of economic growth'. *Annals of the New York Academy of Sciences* 1219: 52.

North, P. 2010. 'Eco-localisation as a progressive response to peak oil and climate change – A sympathetic critique'. *Geoforum* (2010) 42: 585.

Odum, E. and Odum, H. 2001. *A prosperous way down: Principles and policies*. Colorado: University Press of Colorado.

Pearce, J. 2008. 'Thermodynamic limitations to nuclear energy deployment as a greenhouse gas mitigation technology'. *International Journal of Nuclear Governance, Economy and Ecology* 2(1): 113-130.

Percy, E. *et al.* 2010. 'Planning for peak oil: Learning from Cuba's "Special Period"'. *Urban Design and Planning* 163(4): 169.

Princen, T. 2005. *The logic of sufficiency*. Cambridge, Mass: MIT Press.

Purdey, S. 2010. *Economic growth, the environment, and international relations: The growth paradigm*. New York: Routledge.

Rubin, J. 2009. *Why your world is about to get a whole lot smaller*. London: Virgin.

Salleh, A. 2007. 'Food miles can mislead'. ABC Science, available at: http://www.abc.net.au/science/articles/2007/11/28/2103395. htm [accessed 10 January 2012].

Sarkar, S. 1999. *Eco-socialism or eco-capitalism: A critical analysis of humanity's fundamental choices*. London: Zed books.

Schumacher, E. 1973. *Small is beautiful: Economics as if people mattered*. London: Blond and Briggs.

Sen, A. 1998. 'The living standard'. In Crocker, D. and Linden, T. (eds). *Ethics of consumption*. Rowman and Littlefield, New York.

Seneca. 2004. *Letters from a Stoic*. London: Penguin.

Smith, R., 2010. 'Beyond growth or beyond capitalism'. *Institute for Policy Research & Development*. Available at http://iprd.org.uk/wp-content/uploads/2011/02/Beyond-Growth-or-Beyond-Capitalism-by-Richard-Smith-2011.pdf (accessed 16 October 2013).

Sorrell, S. 2010. 2 'Energy, economic growth, and environmental sustainability: Five propositions'. 1784.

Sustain. 2001. 'Eating oil – Food in a changing climate'. *A Sustain/Elm Farm Research Centre Report*. Available at: http://www.sustainweb.org/pdf/eatoil_sumary.PDF (accessed 10 March 2014).

Suwankitti, W. and Pongquan, S. *Enhancement of rural livelihoods in Thailand: An application of sufficiency economy approach in community economic development*. Saarbrucken: Lambert Academic Publishing.

Tainter, J. 1988. *The Collapse of Complex Societies*. Cambridge: Cambridge University Press.

Talberth, J. 2008. 'A new bottom line for progress'. In *State of the World*. Available at: <http://www.worldwatch.org/files/pdf/SOW08_chapter_2.pdf> (accessed 10 September 2010).

Tham, J-C. 2010. *Money and politics: The democracy we can't afford*. Sydney: University of New South Wales Press.

Thoreau, H. 1982. *The portable Thoreau*. Bode, C. (ed.). New York: Penguin.

Trainer, T. 2010. *The transition to a sustainable and just world*. Sydney: Envirobook.

Trainer, T. 2011. 'The radical implications of zero growth economy'. *Real World Economics Review* 57: 71.

Trainer, T. 2012a. 'How cheaply could we live and still flourish?' In Alexander, S., Trainer, T., and Ussher, S., 'The simpler way: A practical action plan for living more on less'. *Simplicity Institute Report* 12a.

Trainer, T. 2012b. '"Education" under consumer-capitalism, and the simpler way alternative'. *Simplicity Institute Report* 12m.

Trainer, T. 2013a. 'Can Europe run on renewable energy? A Negative Case'. *Energy Policy* 63: 845-850.

Trainer, T. 2013b. 'Can the world run on renewable energy'. *Humanomics* 29(2): 88-104.

Turner, G. 2012. 'Are we on the cusp of collapse? Updated Comparison of *The limits to growth* with historical data'. *Gaia* 21(2): 116-124.

Tverberg, G. 2012a. 'Oil supply limits and the continuing financial crisis'. *Energy* 37(1): 27-34.

5

LOW-TECH LIVING AS A DEMAND-SIDE STRATEGY

Simplicity is the ultimate sophistication

1. Introduction*

Energy is often called the 'lifeblood' of civilisation, and yet the overconsumption of fossil energy lies at the heart of two of the greatest challenges facing humanity today: climate change and peak oil. While transitioning to renewable energy systems is an essential 'supply side' strategy in response to climate change and peak oil, the extent of the problems and the speed at which decarbonisation must occur means that there must also be a 'demand side' response. This means consuming much less energy not just 'greening' supply, at least in the most developed regions of the world. In that context, this chapter provides an energy analysis of various 'low tech' options – such as solar shower bags, solar ovens, washing lines, and cycling – and considers the extent to which these types of 'simple living' practices could reduce energy consumption if widely embraced. We demonstrate that low-tech options provide a very promising means of significantly reducing energy (and water) consumption.[1]

---

* This chapter is a lightly revised version of *Simplicity Institute Report 15d* (2015), co-authored by Samuel Alexander and Paul Yacoumis.
[1] While our focus herein is on the direct energy and water savings of low-tech living, it is our view that prefiguring a simpler way to live has deeper significance too, in that it helps create the cultural conditions needed for a post-capitalist politics and economics to emerge, which we maintain is a necessary part of the decarbonisation project. In this paper, however, space does not permit any sustained engagement with those underlying political or macroeconomic issues.

2. Technology Fetishism

All problems have hi-tech solutions. This is one of the defining assumptions of our technocratic, industrial civilisation, and yet it is an assumption that seems to be failing on its own terms. As the world continues to celebrate the most 'advanced' and 'profitable' technologies, we find our ecosystems being degraded and our communities fragmented more so now than ever before. Unfortunately, it seems that technology often just helps us get better at doing the wrong things, or the right things in unnecessarily harmful, energy-intensive ways.

Without denying the obvious *benefits* of many advanced technologies – such as the Internet, medical procedures, labour-saving machinery, etc. – humanity must nevertheless develop a more critical understanding of the *costs* of our technologies, costs that are often hidden or indirect, escaping our notice as we marvel at the latest invention. It is naïve to think that advanced technologies can solve all societal problems, and yet this naivety permeates contemporary understandings of what 'progress' and 'sustainable development' mean (Huesemann and Huesemann, 2011). The most pernicious consequence of this blind faith in technology is that it deflects attention away from the need to rethink our lifestyles, our economic structures, or our systems of governance, because it is assumed that technology will solve our problems without the perceived inconvenience of having to change the way we live. In this light, technology becomes an ethical void, one in which our societies are expected to become just and sustainable, without us having to live justly or sustainably ourselves. Even ethical problems are assumed to have hi-tech rather than behavioural solutions. This is techno-fetishism.

But what is technology? Technology can be defined simply as any tool, invention, technique, or design that assists in achieving certain goals. It follows that even the most primitive human societies were, in a sense, technological. The prehistoric tribes that used fragments of stone to create axes were developing technology, just as the engineers that design spacecraft today are. Technology is a broad term, therefore, and so it makes no sense to be either for or against technology without stating what types of technology are being considered. Moreover, technology can only be judged according to some goal or end that the technology is supposed to help us achieve. A technology may be very good at achieving a certain goal, but if the goal is dubious or comes at too great a cost, then the technology's appropriateness is questionable, no matter how effectively or efficiently it achieves that goal. In fact, when the goal is misconceived, the effectiveness or efficiency of a technology is more of a flaw than a feature.

Technology, in short, is a means to an end. This calls on us to assess the ends that our technologies are serving, and not merely get lost admiring the often dazzling means. As Henry Thoreau said: 'Our inventions are wont to be pretty toys, which distract our attention from serious things. They are but improved means to an unimproved end' (Thoreau, 1982: 306). Granted, we have become very good at cutting down rainforests and emptying the oceans in the pursuit of economic growth and more affluent lifestyles, using machinery and techniques that would have amazed earlier generations. It is not clear, however, whether all such inventions have been a positive advance. Just because we *can* do something does not mean that we *should*.

Have our communities, for example, been enriched by Facebook? Or is there more alienation today than ever before? Should the development and refinement of 'fracking' techniques be considered progress? Or are they merely feeding an addiction to fossil fuels and hastening climate disruption? Instead of saying that all problems have hi-tech solutions, perhaps it would be closer to the truth to say that many of our greatest problems have hi-tech *causes*. At least, advanced technology has allowed our misguided ethics to devastate the biosphere in unprecedented ways. As we continue to degrade our planet ever more efficiently, and live in the shadow of nuclear weapons that still threaten to turn on us, homo sapiens may come to be described as the species that was more clever than wise; the species that chose to destroy the foundations of its own existence, spellbound by its own technological power but lacking the maturity to wield it responsibly.

Despite the ominous dark side of many of our inventions, many people still think that the problems we face are not because of too much advanced technology, but too little (see, e.g., Nordaus and Schellenberger, 2011). Entranced by the many wonderful inventions that have genuinely advanced the human situation, techno-optimists think that all our problems therefore must have hi-tech solutions (for a critique, see Alexander, 2014a). Geo-engineering is perhaps the most perverse example of this techno-fetish – a so-called 'solution' to climate change that risks causing greater problems without necessarily stabilising the climate (see generally, Hamilton, 2013). But geo-engineering is merely an extreme example of a more insidious and generalised *zeitgeist*. The underlying assumption, once more, is that we do not need to change our ways of living or capitalist structures to solve our environmental and social ills. Instead, it is assumed that we must simply get better at forcing nature to do what she is told through the application of technology within a market-based society.

In an age so enamoured with hi-tech thinking, any consideration of low-tech solutions – which are the focus of this essay – will immediately be dismissed by some as being 'Luddite'. Regrettably, it is often considered an affront to human ingenuity to think that we cannot solve all problems with technological innovation and application. Low-tech is reproached as being primitive or 'just for hippies'. But could it be that various low-tech options are actually more civilised, all things considered, than some of their hi-tech replacements? Could 'advancement' or 'progress' today actually involve a move toward, rather than away from, some low-tech alternative technologies? These are some of the questions we explore in this essay by attempting to assess the potential energy savings of various low-tech options. By doing so we hope to understand the extent to which a society could reduce its energy consumption if various low-tech options were broadly embraced.

It is important to point out at once that the following review of low-tech options must not be interpreted to be a blanket rejection of appropriate hi-tech options. The key word there, of course, is 'appropriate' (see Schumacher, 1973). There is surely a place for hi-tech innovations like solar PV and wind turbines, and arguably computers should or could be a part of the good, sustainable, interconnected society. Without doubt, many medical treatments are genuine 'goods' also, and the list could go on. We must not throw out the baby with the bathwater. But this essay attempts to examine with some analytical rigour the question of whether, or to what extent, various low-tech options provide an effective and available means of reducing energy demand. In an age when the overconsumption of energy underlies some of our most pressing problems – climate change and peak oil, in particular (as outlined below) – it should be clear that this analysis is about looking forwards, not backwards.

3. Living in an Age of Limits

Before beginning the substantive analysis we wish to outline the broad context in which this analysis takes place. First and foremost, this means acknowledging that we are living at the 'limits to growth' (Meadow *et al.*, 2004; Turner, 2012). If once we lived on a relatively 'empty' planet, that planet is now 'full'. There are now more than seven billion people trying to live on a planet that has declining biocapacity (Global Footprint Network, 2013). Indeed, we are living in an age frequently described by scientists as the Anthropocene, signifying the first geological epoch that has been induced by human impacts on the planet. Geological timeframes are normally measured in millions or tens of millions of years, but the Anthropocene refers merely to the last 300 years of indust-rialisation. During this geological blink-of-an-eye, humanity has degraded Earth's ecosystems in unprecedented ways and at unprecedented speed. Among a host of other ecological aberrations, this has induced what has been called 'the sixth great extinction' (Kolbert, 2014). Over the last 40 years we have destroyed over 50% of Earth's vertebrae wildlife (mammals, birds, reptilians, amphibians, and fish) (WWF, 2014). As George Monbiot (2014) asks: 'Who believes that a social and economic system which has this effect is a healthy one? Who, contemplating this loss, could call it progress?' Strangely, the last few decades are in fact widely considered a time of great progress, despite this continuing holocaust of biodiversity. It seems the dominant conception of progress is deeply flawed.

Humanity's impact has been so devastating because fossil fuels have given us extraordinary powers, at a time when our ethical vision has been narrow and short-sighted. With this one-off inheritance of dense, stored, non-renewable energy, we have been able to use machines and other technologies and techniques to do things we simply could never have done without a cheap and abundant supply of energy. But this power has come at a devastating ecological cost. Not only is global capitalism destroying the ecological foundations of the planet's declining biodiversity, but the vast amount of carbon being emitted into the atmosphere is destabilising the climate in ways that is threatening the viability of the planet for human civilisation. Current trends suggest we are facing a future 4°C hotter or more by 2100 (Potsdam, 2012; Christoff, 2013), which climate scientist Joachim Shellnhuber argues could reduce the carrying capacity of the planet to below one billion people (Kanter, 2009). This presents us with a foreseeable moral tragedy almost unfathomable in its enormity. We may try to understand this scenario intellectually, but it is doubtful whether there are any among us with the emotional capacity to truly absorb the meaning of it (Gardiner, 2011).

In international climate negotiations, it has been agreed that humanity must avoid a temperature rise of more than 2°C above pre-industrial levels (UNFCCC, 2011). For this goal to be achieved, however, it has been shown that the wealthy 'Annex 1' nations need to decarbonise their economies by 8-10% p.a. over coming decades, starting immediately (see Anderson, 2013). The problem is that historically, long-term emissions reductions of more than 1% p.a. have been associated with recession (Stern, 2006), and while surely greater reductions could be achieved if we seriously *planned* for decarbonisation, it nevertheless seems clear enough that reductions of 8-10% year on year are incompatible with continued economic growth (for the details of this argument, see Alexander, 2014b). The basic reasoning here is that decarbonising by 8-10% p.a. will mean a significant reduction in overall energy consumption, and given the close connection between energy and the economy (Ayres and Warr, 2009), an economy cannot continue growing in terms of GDP while also reducing energy consumption so significantly.

Therefore, effectively responding to climate change means transcending the growth paradigm that has defined industrial civilisation and embracing 'degrowth' strategies of planned economic contraction. Not only does this mean transitioning to renewable energy systems and producing goods and services more efficiently, which can be understood as 'supply side' responses. It also requires that the most developed regions of the world simply consume less energy and resources, which is a 'demand side' response that must supplement 'supply side' strategies.

As well as climate change, there is also the looming problem of peak oil (and other peak resources). Peak oil refers to the point at which the rate of oil production cannot be increased (whether for geological, economic, or political reasons, or some mixture of such reasons). When this happens, and while oil demand continues to grow, the price of oil will inevitably increase. In fact, this is the dynamic we have seen unfolding since the mid-2000s, when the growth of conventional crude oil began to plateau (Alexander, 2015), forcing producers to extract unconventional oils that are far more expensive due to their lower energy returns on investment (Murphy, 2014).

Oil, however, is often called the 'lifeblood' of industrial economies, and when it gets expensive, everything dependent on oil (which is pretty much everything) gets more expensive too. This begins to suffocate oil-addicted economies, as there is less and less discretionary income to spend paying back our debts, or to consume in ways that help grow our economies. And when debts do not get paid back, and when growth-based economies do not grow, life begins to fray in undesirable ways (see, e.g., Tverberg, 2012).

Many analysts think that this process of civilisational deterioration is already underway (see Heinberg, 2011; Gilding, 2011; Greer, 2008), a process that is likely to intensify in coming years as oil becomes scarcer; as climate change worsens; and as the broader limits to growth tighten their grips on the global economy (Turner, 2012). In this broad context, the notion of 'deindustrial' civilisation can be better understood. It refers to an industrial civilisation in the process of deteriorating or collapsing as the supply of cheap and abundant fossil energy comes to an end, fundamentally changing the conditions of development. Deindustrialisation can also refer to the voluntary process of building a new, low-carbon civilisation as a means of dealing with energy descent and turning crisis into opportunity. That latter definition can sit within the former, and this chapter is based on the view that low-tech living will become increasingly necessary as industrial civilisation continues its inevitable decline.

There is one point deserving of further emphasis. In response to the problems of climate change and peak oil, many people naturally hold up renewable energy as the salvation of civilisation, arguing that all we need to do is transition to renewable energy and the problems of peak oil and climate change will be resolved. The problem is that it is highly doubtful that renewable energy will ever be able to sustain a growth-orientated, industrial civilisation. Although it may be technically feasible from an engineering perspective, the problems of intermittency and storage make renewable energy supply much more expensive and problematic than most analysts think (see Moriarty and Honnery, 2012; Trainer, 2013a; Trainer, 2013b). Even if electricity could be affordably supplied by renewables, electricity only constitutes about 18% of final energy consumption (IEA, 2012), meaning that there is still around 82% of energy to replace, including oil used for transport, pesticides, and plastics, etc. If we try to produce that remaining segment of energy with biofuels, the production of biofuels would compete with land for food production, a conflict that also seems to be already underway, despite the relatively low levels of biofuels production today (Timilsina, 2014). Biofuels also have a very low energy return on investment – between 1 and 3 (Murphy, 2014: 12), suggesting that they will never be able to sustain an industrial civilisation, as we know it today.

What all this means is that responding to today's energy, economic, and ecological crises is not simply a matter of transitioning to renewable energy systems, necessary though that is. It also requires that we (in the developed world) simply consume *far less energy*. Given the close relationship between energy and economics, a radical reduction in energy consumption implies embracing a post-growth macroeconomic framework and materially sufficient but non-affluent ways of living (see Alexander, 2013a; Trainer, 2010). Again, this radically new way of life should be understood in a context of deindustrialisation, which involves trying to retain the best parts of the existing civilisation, and creatively using its existing products and waste streams, while eliminating (or letting wither away) those parts that simply cannot be sustained in an energy and resource constrained world (see Holmgren, 2012;

Greer, 2009). While this will involve using the most appropriate forms of advanced technologies to help us decarbonise our economies, the equally important but neglected part of the equation involves a deep behavioural shift away from high-consumption, energy-intensive ways of living.

We do not, however, assume that mere 'lifestyle' responses to climate change and peak oil are enough to address those problems. The subtext of our analysis is that the revolution that is needed must begin with individuals and communities prefiguring a 'simpler way' to live and beginning to build the structures that support that way of life (Trainer, 2010). The relevance of low-tech living therefore goes beyond its immediate energy and water savings, significant though they are. Low-tech living can also play a part in creating the cultural conditions needed for the fundamental structural transformation of our economies to take place (Alexander, 2013b).

For present purposes, the essential point can be summarised as follows. Addressing the world's problems cannot simply be solved from the 'supply side'. That is, we cannot just transition to renewable energy and more efficient productive processes and expect the growth model of global capitalism to persist more or less as usual. Rather, we also need to consume far less energy and resources – that is, we must confront our problems from the 'demand side' too. This is the essential framework within which the following analysis takes place. Low-tech options are being considered in this chapter as a means of reducing energy con-sumption from the 'demand side'. It will also be seen that low-tech options can lead to significant water savings, which, along with energy savings, is a necessary part of a sustainable way of life (for a justification for water conversation, see Brown, 2011). We show that low-tech options are full of potential and should be receiving far more attention than they do. They also provide paths to increased resilience – the ability to withstand shocks – in ways that will be explained.

4. A Review of Low-Tech Living

Having outlined why energy consumption must be reduced, the analysis will now explore various low-tech options that have the potential to assist in that critically important societal goal. This is particularly relevant to the energy-intensive lifestyles prevalent in the most highly developed regions of the world, but they are also relevant to the poorer parts of the world. With respect to the latter, the argument is not so much that they need to reduce energy consumption so much as they should embrace low-tech as one means of escaping the conventional development path that is in the process of 'locking' them into high-carbon, industrial modes of existence.

The following review will consider such low-tech options as solar shower bags, hand-washing clothes, washing lines, simple warming and cooling techniques, cycling, solar ovens, non-electric fridges, composting toilets etc., in the attempt to understand the extent to which these options could help achieve the goal of minimising energy consumption, if they were broadly embraced across a culture. Low-tech can also refer simply to behaviour change, as opposed to relying on technological solutions of any variety. While much has been written on low-tech or alt-tech options, the following analysis represents the first attempt to quantify with some analytical rigour the potential energy savings of a range of such options. We hope that over time these tentative figures and analyses can be refined, updated, and expanded upon.

A few words on methodological issues are required. As will be seen, some of the low-tech options below are more or less effective depending on weather conditions. For example, a solar shower bag will be more effective (and much more pleasant!) in warmer months or regions, and non-electric fridges may be more effective over a longer period in cooler months or regions. What this means is that an analysis of low-tech options is ultimately context-dependent, and this means universal statements cannot always be made with much confidence. Nevertheless, by clearly stating the assumptions of the analysis, we provide the methodological framework for this type of analysis to be applied in various contexts.

Furthermore, although this type of analysis is ultimately context-dependent, there will obviously be much overlap between contexts, insofar as most regions of the world, to varying degrees, have something resembling the four seasons. Indeed, we have chosen Melbourne, Australia as the case study for the following analysis precisely because it is a good example of a region that has four seasons (and also because it is our home region, which means we have been able to personally test and apply the following low-tech options).

Finally, the fact that different regions of the world have different weather patterns does not mean that the final energy conclusions from the analysis are only relevant to Melbourne. This is because there is something of a balancing effect that flows from different weather patterns. For example, a region that has more hot days each year than Melbourne might allow solar shower bags to be used more often, while this warmer region might not be able to use a non-electric fridge so effectively; similarly, a region much cooler than Melbourne may be able to use a non-electric fridge for more

SAMUEL ALEXANDER

months of the year (or all year), but find it more difficult to use solar shower bags. Not only that, several of the low-tech options (e.g., composting toilets) are not usually linked to weather patterns at all, meaning that the analysis is more or less universally applicable. For these reasons, we would argue that the analysis below, while often shaped by a particular context, is of more general significance. As will be seen below, each of the low-tech options considered also requires more specific methodological assumptions, which will be stated as the analysis proceeds.[2]

We begin our investigation by calculating a baseline 'reference' scenario for each of the technologies discussed; that is, what might be considered the 'typical' use of the conventional technology in the Melbourne area today. Our reference household is a unit or semi-detached dwelling situated in the inner-northern suburbs and has two occupants, the most common occupancy rate in greater Melbourne.[3] We conduct our calculations using publicly available data on appropriate usage metrics related to each technology under consideration (discussed on a per-technology basis below). We then develop multiple scenarios representing varying levels of adoption of the low-impact technologies discussed, and calculate the energy and water consumption under each scenario. These 'alternative' scenarios range from moderate to radical levels of low-tech adoption, which are also described on a per-technology basis. Finally, we compare the reference and alternative scenarios to calculate the potential water and energy savings afforded by adoption of the various low-tech options.

The following analysis is intended to be illustrative of potential solutions in a general sense. We will, however, present our assumptions and the sources used to inform them.

4.1 Showering

The conventional method of showering is to heat water with electricity or gas. But using electricity or gas is unnecessary on

---

[2] One final general point is that we've chosen to ignore the embedded energy in the alternative technologies we discuss, on the assumption that the embedded energy is likely to be negligible in comparison to the potential energy savings they provide. Most of the low-tech options we discuss can be made from recycled or salvaged materials, and others, such as a solar shower bag, have low embedded energy. In any case, low-tech options have vastly lower embedded energy than their hi-tech alternatives (e.g., a washing machine compared to a washing line). This means that ignoring the embedded energy does not distort the following analysis in any significant way.
[3] http://profile.id.com.au/australia/household-size?WebID=260.

112

warm days when water can be heated directly from the sun. Most readers will be familiar with 'solar shower bags', often used when camping, which are black plastic or canvas bags that are filled with water and heated in the sun (see Figure 1). After a few hours in the sun the water is warm enough to use for a comfortable shower, without requiring energy inputs other than free, zero-carbon sunlight. But why should solar shower bags only be used when camping?

Figure 1: A solar shower bag heating water using sunlight

In the reference scenario, based on conventional methods of showering, we assume an average shower duration of 5.6 minutes[4] and an average flow rate of 6.5 litres per minute[5] (L/min), giving us an average of 36 litres of water use per shower. In line with actual observations, we assume that our occupants shower 5.6 per week on average.[6]

A reasonable estimate is that half (18L) of the water used for showering is heated.[7] Assuming the household hot water system must heat water by 45°C to reach the set thermostat temperature of 60°,[8] and that the water is heated with a 'task efficiency' of 73%

---

[4] Average between winter and summer median duration: M. Redhead. 2013. Melbourne Residential Water End Uses Winter 2010/Summer 2012. Final Report June 2013. 24.

[5] Average between winter and summer median flow rates. Ibid.: 25.

[6] Average between winter and summer average frequency. Ibid.: 26.

[7] S.J. Kenway *et al.* 'Energy use in the provision and consumption of urban water in Australia and New Zealand'. 10 December 2008: 19.

[8] Ibid. p19

(using an electric storage system),[9] we estimate that the end-use energy consumption for a single shower is 1.3 kilowatt-hours (kWh).

In terms of the alternative scenarios, we also make several assumptions. We suppose, firstly, that 20L is a sufficient volume of water when using the solar shower – a reasonable estimate based on personal experience.[10] We recognise that weather conditions can render a solar shower either uncomfortable or impossible on some days, so we consider only days between October and April (the warmer months in Australia), with a maximum temperature over 22°C, and with more than four hours of sunlight, as suitable for the purposes of solar showering. According to the Australian Bureau of Meteorology, these criteria yielded 108 suitable days for solar showering in Melbourne over the 2013-2014 period.[11] For simplicity, we assume that whenever a solar shower is possible (108 days), it will be taken.

The reference scenario yielded a result of 21,199 litres of water and 851kWh of energy consumed by our two-person household annually. Five alternative scenarios are described as follows:

- Moderate 1: Reducing shower time to three minutes with no use of a solar shower.
- Moderate 2: Using a solar shower when possible, but showering regularly otherwise.
- Strong 1: Using a solar shower when possible, and reducing shower time to three minutes otherwise.
- Strong 2: Using a solar shower when possible, otherwise reducing shower time to three minutes, and reducing shower frequency by one third (equivalent of showering around four times per week).
- Radical: Using a solar shower when possible, otherwise reducing shower time to three minutes, and reducing shower frequency by two-thirds (equivalent of showering around two times per week).

The results, based on a two-person household, are summarised in Table 1:

---

[9] George Wilkenfeld & Associates Pty Ltd. 2008. Victoria's Greenhouse Gas Emissions 1990, 1995, 2000 and 2005: END-USE ALLOCATION OF EMISSIONS, report to the Department of Sustainability and Environment, February 2008: 84.

[10] See also, M. Redhead. 2013. Melbourne Residential Water End Uses Winter 2010/Summer 2012, Final Report June 2013.

[11] http://www.bom.gov.au

	Annual water saving (L)	**Annual water saving (%)**	Annual energy saving (kWh)	**Annual energy saving (%)**
Moderate 1	9842.6	46%	352.8	46%
Moderate 2	3542.4	17%	281.8	37%
Strong 1	9734.6	46%	503.8	66%
Strong 2	13556.2	64%	589.2	78%
Radical	17377.8	82%	674.5	89%

Table 1: Potential water and energy savings from low-tech showering practices

It is clear that changing our showering behaviour, in terms of shower duration and frequency, has an enormous impact on our water and energy consumption. Under the 'radical' scenario our two-person household is saving over 17,000 litres of water per year, and reducing shower-related energy consumption by nearly 90%. An interesting point to note is that reducing shower time to three minutes, without using a solar shower, actually saves more water and energy than simply replacing conventional showers with a solar shower when possible. Nevertheless, the low-tech solar shower bag clearly provides a way to save significantly more energy and water when combined with taking shorter and less frequent showers.

4.2 Heating

Conventional heating methods involve using gas or electricity to heat living areas. Low-tech alternatives can reduce the need for such energy-intensive heating methods by wearing woollen clothing, insulating one's home well, and, when heating is deemed necessary, heating fewer spaces.

Our reference household is equipped with a wall-mounted gas space heater. A commonly accepted value for average household heating demand is 0.1kW per square metre,[12] which we adopt in this chapter. We assume heating is required in an area of the house with a floor area totalling 60 square metres. According to the Australian Bureau of Statistics most Victorian households use heating for more

---

[12] SA government, 'Energy efficient heating, https://www.sa.gov.au /topics/water-energy-and-environment/energy/saving-energy-at-home/household-appliances-and-other-energy-users/heating-and-cooling/energy-efficient-heating

than three months, but less than six months, of the year.[13] We take a baseline of 150 days (approximately five months) as our reference scenario and assume that the heater is in operation for an average of eight hours on each of these days. In addition, based on SA government figures, we assume a heater efficiency of 75%. We acknowledge that insulation varies greatly in housing across Melbourne, as does the health status of individuals, so we leave scope for the necessity of artificial heating in times of temperature extremes.

This reference scenario sees our household consuming 9,600kWh of energy annually for heating, a figure that aligns closely with CSIRO estimates.[14] Three alternative scenarios are described as follows, all of which assume appropriate clothing:

- Moderate: Insulating house well, and halving the amount of time each day heating is used (i.e., three hours instead of six).
- Strong: Insulating house well, heating only on days between May and September (Australian winter) with a maximum temperature below 15°C (41 days in total for 2014, according to the Bureau of Meteorology), and halving the amount of time heating is used on these days.
- Radical: Insulating house well, heating only on the 10 coldest days, and halving the amount of time heating is used on these days.

The results are summarised in Table 2:

	Annual energy saving (kWh)	**Annual energy saving (%)**
Moderate	4800	*50%*
Strong	8288	*86%*
Radical	9280	*97%*

Table 2: Potential energy savings from low-tech heating practices

From this analysis we see that we can save upwards of 90% of our energy consumption for heating space by simply adopting the

---

[13] ABS, 'Heating and cooling', http://www.abs.gov.au/ausstats/abs@.nsf/0/85424ADCCF6E5AE9CA257A670013AF89?opendocument
[14] CSIRO, 'Zero Emission House', available at:
http://joshshouse.com.au/wp-content/uploads/2014/10/Zero_emission_house_ETF_factsheet-Standard-1.pdf

humble sweater as our *modus operandi* in order to keep warm, rather than relying on energy-intensive heating appliances. This would obviously require a 'reframing' of our attitude to keeping warm, but if that inner work was done (see generally, Burch, 2013) then staying warm in a low-carbon world would be achievable in many climates without hardship. Well-designed, passive solar houses with good insulation would also assist greatly. Other low-tech heating options include highly efficient rocket stove thermal mass heaters, which could be especially useful in colder regions of the world. But the best place to start is with appropriate clothing (Havenith, 1999).

4.3 *Cooling*

The conventional means of cooling houses on hot days is to use air-conditioners, which are energy-intensive to operate. Low-tech and low-energy alternatives exist, such as closing curtains or blinds to keep the sun out, or using simple fans rather than air-conditioners.

Data made available by the South Australian government suggests that ducted evaporative air conditioners consume approximately 1.5kW of energy and 24 L of water every hour on average,[15] which we take as representative of the Victorian context also. According to the Australian Bureau of Statistics almost half of all Victorian households use their air conditioners between one and three months of the year.[16] We take a point of 60 days as our reference scenario and, in addition, assume that the air conditioner is in operation for an average of six hours on each of these days.

For the low-tech scenarios, we assume a mid-range value of energy consumption for ceiling and portable fans based on SA governments data (0.0667kW per hour). In calculating the use of fans, we assume our occupants require three rooms to be artificially cooled. We acknowledge that insulation varies greatly in housing across Melbourne, as does the health status of individuals, so we leave scope for the necessity of artificial cooling in times of temperature extremes.

---

[15] SA government, 'Energy efficient cooling', https://www.sa.gov.au/topics/ water-energy-and-environment/energy/saving-energy-at-home/household-appliances-and-other-energy-users/heating-and-cooling/energy-efficient-cooling

[16] ABS, 'Heating and cooling', available at: http://www.abs.gov.au/ausstats/abs@.nsf/0/85424ADCCF6E5AE9CA257A67 0013AF89?opendocument

The reference scenario sees our household consuming 540kWh of energy and 8,640 litres of water annually to cool the house in hot temperatures. Three alternative scenarios are described as follows:

- <u>Moderate</u>: Using blinds as insulation from sunlight/external heat, and halving the amount of time each day air conditioning is used (i.e., three hours instead of six).
- <u>Strong</u>: Using blinds as insulation and air conditioning only on days with a maximum temperature above 35 degrees Celsius (10 days in total for 2014, according to the Bureau of Meteorology).
- <u>Radical</u>: Using blinds as insulation, and fans instead of air conditioning on days above 35 degrees Celsius.

The results are summarised in Table 3:

	Annual water saving (L)	**Annual water saving (%)**	Annual energy saving (kWh)	**Annual energy saving (%)**
Moderate	4320	50%	270	50%
Strong	7200	83%	450	83%
Radical	8640	100%	528	98%

Table 3: Potential water and energy savings from low-tech cooling practices

We can see that, by significantly increasing our reliance on blinds to keep out heat and restricting our reliance on air conditioning to days when temperatures soar, we can reduce our cooling-related energy and water usage by well over three-quarters. Moreover, if we choose fan cooling instead of air conditioning on such days, we eradicate nearly all cooling-related energy and water consumption.

4.4 *Drying clothes*

The conventional way to dry clothes is to use an electric clothes dryer, which is very energy-intensive. A low-tech alternative is to use a simple washing line to dry clothes outside.

According to Sustainability Victoria, the average dryer use by Victorian households is 78 cycles per year, or 1.5 cycles per week.[17]

---

[17] Sustainability Victoria, 'Washers and Dryers', http://www.sustainability. vic.gov.au/~/media/resources/documents/services%20and%20advice/househol

Taking a mid-range approach to their energy data, we calculate an average per-cycle energy consumption of 4.6kWh, and an annual energy consumption of 359kWh, which represents our reference scenario.

Three alternative scenarios are described as follows:

- Moderate: Reducing electric drying to the four coldest and wettest months of the year, and using a clothesline otherwise.
- Strong: Running the dryer for only five cycles per year (say, on the wettest and coldest days), and using a clothesline otherwise.
- Radical: Using only a clothesline throughout the year (some days may necessitate indoor clothes drying racks).

The results are summarised in Table 4:

	Annual energy saving (kWh)	**Annual energy saving (%)**
Moderate	239.2	67%
Strong	335.8	94%
Radical	358.8	100%

Table 4: Potential energy savings from low-tech clothes drying practices

The decision to dry clothes by clothesline rather than electric dryer can save a significant amount of energy, up to 100% if adopted as a complete replacement. From experience we know this can be achieved without hardship in Melbourne. At most it requires some planning in winter to ensure that washing is done on sunny days.

4.5 Television

The conventional way to spend leisure time is to watch many hours of television each day, often on large, energy-intensive plasma screens. The low-tech alternative is to turn off the TV and spend leisure in ways that do not depend on energy-intensive technologies (e.g., reading a book, playing the guitar, talking with friends, doing craft, etc.).

ds/smarter%20choice/fact%20sheets%20june%202014/rse017_sc_fact%20she et_a5_washers%20and%20dryers_lr.pdf

Our reference scenario assumes two televisions in the household, reflecting the national average,[18] both of which are 32-inch LCD screens (the most popular TV in terms of sales in 2009).[19] The average number of hours of TV each occupant watches in the house also reflects the national average: approximately 3 hours per day.[17] Energy consumption for a TV in use is estimated at 0.15kW,[17] and standby energy consumption is 0.001kW.[16]

We have assumed the occupants watch two hours of TV together, plus one hour separately each day. This equals a daily total of four hours of TV operation. The reference scenario energy consumption therefore totals 235kWh per year.

Three alternative scenarios are as follows:

- <u>Moderate</u>: Halving TV watching time, but keeping TVs in standby mode when not in use.
- <u>Strong</u>: Watching only five hours per week, and switching TVs off at wall when not in use.
- <u>Radical</u>: Removing TVs altogether (or watching negligible amounts).

The results are summarised in the following table:

	Annual energy saving (kWh)	**Annual energy saving (%)**
Moderate	108.77	*46%*
Strong	196.06	*83%*
Radical	235.06	*100%*

Table 5: Potential energy savings from low-tech (non-television) leisure activities

It's clear that reducing TV watching time is a much more effective energy-saving behaviour than simply ensuring the TV is switched off at the wall when not in use. Not only would this transition reduce energy consumption directly, it would also mean less exposure to consumerist messages from advertising that promotes energy-

[18] Energy Use in the Australian Residential Sector 1986-2020, http://industry.gov.au/Energy/EnergyEfficiency/Documents/04_2013/energy-use-australian-residential-sector-1986-2020-part1.pdf
[19] Baseline TV Power Consumption 2009, http://www.energyrating.gov.au/wp-content/uploads/Energy_Rating_Documents/Library/Home_Entertainment/Televisions/200919-tv-power-consump.pdf

intensive lifestyles. This means there would likely be indirect energy savings too.

4.6 *Driving*

The conventional means of transporting ourselves to and from work and leisure activities is to drive in a private motor vehicle. In many parts of the world, however, there are public transport options available, as well as the option of cycling. Shorter trips could be walked.

Perhaps the most involved analysis, the following calculations largely draw on 'average usage' statistics for private vehicles and public transport (PT) published by the Victorian Government Department of Transport and the Public Transport Users Association. Many of these details, while crucial to our calculations, are not vital for describing the various scenarios, and so will be included (for more details, see Alexander and Yacoumis, 2015: 19)

There are several assumptions that we should note at this stage, however, to set the context for our reference scenario. We are first assuming that both our occupants are of working age, own a car each, and drive to work separately. We assume that each work trip is a 16km round trip, half of all trips made are shorter than 5km (corresponding closely with data for Melbourne published by Deakin University),[20] and of those shorter trips the average is 3km. The total distance each occupant travels per day is 33km, 83% of which is by car and a further 12.5% by a mix of PT modes – bus, train, and tram. Some trips are shared. We also assume that a greater shift to cycling and PT is feasible for the occupants of our household, which is not unreasonable for most inner-suburban residents in fair health.

The reference scenario for our household yields an annual energy consumption of 18,773kWh for transport, which is one of the largest contributors to household energy consumption.

Three alternative scenarios are described as follows:

- Moderate: Switching to public transport for all work trips.

---

[20] Deakin University, Environmental benefits of cycling:
https://www.deakin.edu.au/travelsmart/docs/theenvironmentabenefitsofcycling
_fact%20sheet.pdf

- Strong: All trips under 5km are walked or cycled, a car is used for one trip per week (an average of 5km per week) by each occupant, public transport is used for all other trips.
- Radical: Shared car usage totalling 100km over the course of a year, all other trips are walked or cycled.

The results are summarised as follows:

	Annual energy saving (kWh)	**Annual energy saving (%)**
Moderate	8361.6	45%
Strong	15504.0	83%
Radical	18659.2	99%

Table 6: Potential energy savings from low-tech transport practices

We can see that even with a modest change to our travel decisions – for example, shifting from private vehicle to public transport for work trips only – we can potentially save a significant amount of fossil fuel energy. By choosing the bicycle as our preferred mode of transport we are able to realise an even greater energy benefit.

4.7 Five Other Low-Tech Options (In Brief)

The above analysis has demonstrated that low-tech options can lead to huge energy and water savings, depending on the degree to which they are adopted. We conclude this part of the analysis with a more conceptual discussion of several more low-tech options, which in the future could also receive the same type of analysis we have undertaken above. For present purposes, we simply highlight some of the more interesting and promising options:

- Solar ovens/parabolic solar dishes: The conventional means of cooking food is with gas or electric ovens and stoves. Solar ovens and parabolic solar dishes provide a hugely promising means of replacing those methods, on suitable days, using free energy from the sun and without hi-tech PV solar panels.

- Fridge/Freezer: The conventional means of keeping food sufficiently cold or frozen is to use a fridge and freezer, both of which are energy intensive. However, in many parts of the world, including Melbourne, the winter months are sufficiently cold to keep food from spoiling too quickly without a fridge, and there are other low-tech options that can help keep food for longer even in warmer months and warmer regions of the world (e.g., evaporative coolers). Behavioural and dietary changes (e.g., eat less meat and dairy or purchase meat on the day it is to be consumed) can also make it easier to turn off your fridge/freezer. While this low-tech option may indeed find fewer supporters than the others, we nevertheless feel this deserves to be included because the fridge-freezer is a significant category of energy consumption in the household. This also challenges us to think through whether we could cope well enough even if something as seemingly indispensable as a fridge-freezer were not available. It can be helpful to remember that the fridge/freezer is a relatively new innovation, and our ancestors survived without one.

•   Hand-washing clothes and dishes: The conventional means of washing clothes and dishes is to use an electric washing machine. Dishes can be washed by hand, and clothes can be washed in a tub with a manual agitator, especially in the warmer months when a spin-dryer is not necessary.

•   Organic food: Industrial methods of food production and global distribution are incredibly complex and energy-intensive. Local, organic food production – a low-tech option which was used throughout history – is far less-energy intensive, but does require more human labour. Any transition to a low-carbon world is going to require industrial and globalised methods to be replaced by local and organic methods (Jeavons, 2012).

•   Composting toilets: Following on from the last point, in order to replace the fossil fuel-dependent fertilisers used widely in industrial food production today, we are going to need a huge increase in organic fertilisers. One promising low-tech option is to compost human waste for 'humanure' via composting toilets (see Jenkins, 2005). Currently most people conceive of human waste as a problem, but it could be part of the solution if we compost it responsibly. This would significantly reduce or eliminate the need for fossil fuel-dependent fertilisers as well as hugely reduce or eliminate the amount of water required in flushing toilets. As these systems become universally adopted, we would also lessen the need for complex and centralised sewage infrastructure that currently depend on fossil fuels.

5. Conclusion

Although the analysis above has much room for refinement and development in context and household specific ways, it has been demonstrated that what we have called low-tech options have the potential to significantly reduce the energy intensity (and water intensity) of our ways of living. Our personal experience practising all of these low-tech options at times, many of them often, and some of them always, also gives us confidence that the results above are broadly correct. Indeed, when low-tech 'demand side' strategies are applied in conjunction with hi-tech 'supply side' strategies (e.g., solar PV), our personal experience confirms that people can be net-producers of renewable electricity, provided ordinary consumption of energy is significantly reduced. Moreover, we know that this can be done without diminishing quality of life, although low-tech practices do often demand a greater time investment than their conventional alternatives, which can call for broader lifestyle and structural changes to accommodate this increased time commitment (see Ch. 4).

Adopting low-tech options certainly requires a rethinking of conventional practices and attitudes, but if we are serious about a 'demand side' response to climate change and peak oil – which is a *necessary* part of any effective response – then these low-tech options are likely to be a critical part of any future adaptation to an energy descent context. Many people will resist this conclusion, no doubt, and insist that we can universalise the conventional 'affluent' ways of living as well as create a post-carbon world. But this is an unjustifiable assumption, one that may arise in part from a blind faith in technological solutions, or perhaps from a natural human aversion to change. A post-carbon world means a world far less energy-intensive than developed regions of the world, and transitioning to such a world probably implies, whether we like it or not, the embrace of some low-tech options.

Importantly, these low-tech options deserve consideration not just as a means of *voluntarily* responding to climate change and peak oil. They can also be seen as ways of becoming more resilient in circumstances of economic shock, recession, disruption or collapse, where it may be that the conventional ways of living simply aren't available or affordable (see De Young and Princen, 2012). In other words, the low-tech options demonstrate ways to adapt to challenging circumstances, even if they are not freely chosen in advance. Of course, it would be far better to begin working toward these low-tech options now, because prevention of energy crises would be more desirable than dealing with them when they arrive. Accordingly, we ought to be giving these low-tech options more consideration now, because energy and economic crises are already unfolding, and deeper crises seem to be on the horizon (Friedrichs, 2013; Turner, 2012; Gilding, 2011).

This analysis sits in the broader context of a world facing social and environmental crises that cannot be solved within consumer capitalism. Low-tech options are part of an alternative vision of progress that involves rejecting affluent lifestyles for environmental and social justice reasons, and moving toward a 'simpler way' of life based on material sufficiency, highly-localised economies, and self-governing communities (see Trainer, 2010; Alexander, 2012; Alexander, 2013a). Our argument must not, however, be interpreted as a blanket rejection of advanced technology, which certainly has its place. Nor have we argued that the energy crises we face have mere 'lifestyle' solutions. There are a great many structural issues that must be addressed too. But we hope this analysis helps provoke a broader conversation about which technologies are 'appropriate' for our times. When the humble washing line is compared with the electric clothes' dryer, one can certainly sympathise with Leonardo Da Vinci's famous decree: 'Simplicity is the ultimate sophistication'.

References

Alexander, S. 2012. 'The sufficiency economy: Envisioning a prosperous way down'. *Simplicity Institute Report* 12s: 1-31.

Alexander, S. 2013a. *Entropia: Life beyond industrial civilisation.* Melbourne: Simplicity Institute.

Alexander, S. 2013b. 'Voluntary simplicity and the social reconstruction of law: Degrowth from the grassroots up'. *Environmental Values* 22(2): 287-308.

Alexander, S. 2014a. 'A critique of techno-optimism: Efficiency without sufficiency is lost'. *Post-Carbon Pathways* (Working Paper Series, 1/14): 1-21.

Alexander, S. 2014b, 'Degrowth and the carbon budget: Powerdown strategies for climate stability'. *Simplicity Institute Report* 14h: 1-24.

Alexander, S. 2015. 'The paradox of oil: The cheaper it is, the more it costs'. *Simplicity Institute Report* 15a: 1-17.

Alexander, S. and Yacoums, P. 2015. 'Low-tech living as a "demand-side" response to climate change and peak oil'. *Simplicity Institute Report* 15d: 1-19.

Anderson, K. 2013. 'Avoiding dangerous climate change demands de-growth strategies from wealthier nations'. Available at www.kevinanderson.info (accessed 15 July 2014).

Ayres, R. and Warr, B. 2009. *The economic growth engine: How energy and work drive material prosperity.* Cheltenham: Edward Elgar Publishing.

Brown, L. 2011. *World on the edge: How to prevent environmental and economic collapse.* New York: W. W. Norton and Company.

Burch, M. 2013. *The hidden door: Mindful sufficiency as an alternative to extinction.* Melbourne: Simplicity Institute Publishing.

Christoff, P. (ed.). 2013. *Four degrees of global warming.* London: Taylor and Francis.

De Young, R. and Princen, T. (eds). 2012. *The localization reader: Adapting to the coming downshift.* Cambridge, MA: MIT Press.

Friedrichs, J. 2013. *The future is not what it used to be: Climate change and energy scarcity.* Cambridge, MA: MIT Press.

Gardiner, S. 2011. *The perfect moral storm: The ethical tragedy of climate change.* Oxford: Oxford University Press.

Greer, J.M. 2008. *The long descent.* Gabriola Island: New Society Publishers.

Greer, J.M. 2009. *The ecotechnic future: Envisioning a post-peak world.* Gabriola Island: New Society Publishers.

Hamilton, C. 2013. *Earthmasters: Playing God with the climate.* Crows Nest, NSW: Allen & Unwin.

Havenith, G. 1999. 'Heat balance when wearing protective clothing'. *Annals of Occupational Hygiene* 43(5): 289-296.

Heinberg, R. 2011. *The end of growth: Adapting to our new economic reality.* Gabriola Island: New Society Publishers.

Holmgren, D. 2012. 'Retrofitting the suburbs for the energy descent future'. *Simplicity Institute Report* 12i: 1-8.

International Energy Agency (IEA). 2012b. *Key World Energy Statistics 2012.* Available at: http://www.iea.org/publications/freepublications/publication/kwes.pdf (accessed 1 July 2014).

Gilding, P. 2011. *The great disruption: How the climate crisis will transform the global economy.* London: Bloomsbury.

Global Footprint Network. 2013. Reports available at: http://www.footprintnetwork.org/en/index.php/GFN/ (accessed 3 September 2013).

Huesemann, M. and Huesemann, J. 2011. *Techno-fix: Why technology won't save us or the environment.* Gabriola Island: New Society Publishers.

Jeavons, J. 2012 (8th edn). *How to grow more vegetables.* Berkeley: Ten Speed Press.

Jenkins, J. 2005 (3rd edn). *The humanure handbook: A guide to composting human manure*. White River Junction, VT: Chelsea Green Publishing.

Kanter, J. 'Scientist: Warming could cut population to 1 billion'. *New York Times*. 13 March 2009.

Kolbert, E. 2014. *The sixth great extinction: An unnatural history*. New York: Henry Holt.

Meadows, D., Randers, J. and Meadows, D. 2004. *Limits to growth: The 30-year update*. White River Junction, Vt: Chelsea Green Publishing.

Monbiot, G. 2014. 'It's time to shout stop on this war on the living world'. *The Guardian*. 2 October, 2014.

Moriarty, P. and Honnery, D. 2012. 'What is the global potential for renewable energy?' *Renewable and Sustainable Energy Reviews* 16 (1): 244-252.

Murphy, D. 2014. 'The implications of the declining energy return on investment of oil production'. *Philosophical Transactions of the Royal Society A*, 372, 20130126: 1-19.

Nordaus, T. and Schellenberger, M. 2011. 'Evolve: A case for modernization as the road to salvation'. *Orion Magazine* (September/October 2011). Available at: http://www.orion magazine.org/index.php/articles/article/6402/ (accessed 10 September 2013).

Potsdam Institute. 2012. *Turn down the heat: Why a 4° warmer world must be avoided*. Published by the World Bank. Available at: http://documents.worldbank.org/curated/en/2012/11/17097815/turn-down-heat-4%C2%B0c-warmer-world-must-avoided (accessed 15 July 2014).

Schumacher, E. 1973. *Small is beautiful: A study of economics as if people mattered*. Sydney: Vintage.

Stern, N. 2006. *Stern review on the economics of climate change*. Her Majesty's Treasury. Cambridge: Cambridge University Press.

Thoreau, H. 1982. *The portable Thoreau*. Bode, C. (ed.). Penguin, New York.

Timilsina, G. 2014. 'Biofuels in the long-run global energy supply mix for transportation'. *Philosophical Transactions of the Royal Society A*, 372, 20120323: 1-19.

Trainer, T. 2010. *The transition to a sustainable and just world*. Sydney: Envirobook.

Trainer, T. 2013a. 'Can Europe run on renewable energy? A negative case'. *Energy Policy* 63: 845-850.

Trainer, T. 2013b. 'Can the world run on renewable energy'. *Humanomics* 29 (2): 88-104.

Turner, G. 2012. 'Are we on the cusp of collapse? Updated comparison of *The limits to growth* with historical data'. *Gaia* 21(2): 116-124.

Tverberg, G. 2012. 'Oil supply limits and the continuing financial crisis', *Energy* 37(1): 27-34.

UNFCCC. 2011. *The Cancun Agreements*. Available at: http:// unfccc.int/resource/docs/2010/cop16/eng/07a01.pdf#page=2 (accessed 1 July 2014).

6

DISRUPTIVE SOCIAL INNOVATION FOR A LOW-CARBON WORLD
Evaluating prospects for a Great Transition

We think we can see something new emerging. We are standing in the dark shade of a threshold and trying to see and understand that which is opening in front of us. We do not understand it very well, but we can hear fragments of new melodies of struggle emerging, see glimpses of a new direction in the flow of revolt.
> – John Holloway

1. Introduction

It is becoming increasingly clear that small, incremental changes to the way humans use and produce energy are unlikely to catalyse a transformation to a low-carbon civilisation, at least, not within the ever-tightening time frame urged by the world's climate scientists. In September 2013, the IPCC published its fifth report, in which it was estimated that the world's 'carbon budget' – that is, the maximum carbon emissions available if the world is to have a good chance of keeping global warming below 2° – is likely to be entirely used up within two or three decades, based on current trends (IPCC, 2013). If 'business as usual' continues, the trends indicate that we may be facing a future that is 4° hotter, or more (see World Bank, 2012; Christoff, 2013). It is not clear to what extent civilisation is compatible with such a climate.

This calls for an urgent and committed re-evaluation of dominant strategies for transitioning beyond fossil fuels. If there is any hope for rapid decarbonisation today, it surely lies, at this late stage, in movements, innovations, or technologies that do not seek to produce change through a smooth series of increments, but through an ability to somehow 'disrupt' the status quo and fundamentally redirect the world's trajectory toward a low-carbon, post-growth future.

The phrase 'disruptive innovation' will be used in this chapter to refer to rapid and far-reaching societal change that is provoked by the abrupt emergence of a social movement, technology, business model, or confluence of such phenomena. This usage draws loosely on the work of Clayton Christensen (1995), who coined the term 'disruptive innovation' to describe times when commercial enterprises develop new business models or technologies that rapidly change the market in ways that are both unexpected and game-changing. In Christensen's work, a disruptive innovation is contrasted with a 'sustaining innovation', which is less about changing the game and more about competing more effectively in the same game.

While there may be a certain irony to using terminology from commercial discourse to refer to socio-technical innovations that could potentially shake the very energy basis of the global economy, the language of 'disruptive innovation' aptly describes the extent and speed at which any transition to a low-carbon world must proceed. With the carbon budget shrinking as business as usual persists – to say nothing of the myriad other ecological crises worsening by the day – a progression of 'sustaining innovations' seems unlikely to affect the changes necessary. The task is too urgent; the extent of change needed, too great.

As implied above, disruptive innovations can take place within various spheres of life: social, economic, technological, institutional, and political. In order to transition to a low-carbon world, it is likely that a coordinated confluence of innovations from all such spheres will be required to produce deep behavioural, systemic, and structural change (see generally, SPREAD, 2011). This chapter focuses on the *socio-cultural* sphere. Without denying the importance of other spheres of transformative change, there are reasons to think the socio-cultural sphere may be of particular importance in driving the transition to a low-carbon world.

The socio-cultural domain may have special disruptive potential due to the fact that other spheres of innovation can be understood as *tools* or *means*, whereas the socio-cultural sphere can be understood to be the source of *goals* or *ends*. This difference is important because until there is a culture shaped by the values and vision of a low-carbon world, available tools or means for societal change (e.g., legislation, technology, capital, etc.) are likely to be misdirected, and perhaps even be employed in counter-productive ways. In much the same way as the tool of 'fire' can have a positive or negative impact on our lives, depending on how it is used and how much of it there is, the tools of technology, business, and politics can advance or inhibit the transition to a low-carbon society, depending on the social values and desires that shape their implementation and development. For these reasons, the socio-cultural sphere can be considered fundamental, in the sense that it provides the *ends* towards which available *means* are directed.

This point deserves some elaboration. The nature and develop-ment of technology in a society, for example, will take different forms depending on the social context and the dominant social values which drive innovation. If the primary *end* of 'research and development' is profit-maximisation, not necessarily the desire for a low-carbon world, it follows that technological innovations are just as likely to inhibit, rather than facilitate, a low-carbon transition (e.g., fracking technologies). A similar dynamic exists with respect to business and politics. Until there is a socio-cultural context that *incentivises* or *demands* economic or political change in the direction of a low-carbon world, the tools of business and public policy are unlikely to be sources of 'disruptive innovation', but at most sources of 'sustaining innovation'. More likely still, they will merely serve to reify and entrench the status quo.

Another way to think about the importance of the socio-cultural sphere is in terms of sequencing; that is, in terms of in what order various innovations may need to take place on the path to a low-carbon world. By the time business, politics, and technology are capable of 'disrupting' the status quo, it may be that a revolution in social values would need to have already taken place, in order to have driven such innovation in the first place and been receptive to it. After all, it is no good establishing an innovative bike-sharing business if few people are interested in cycling; just as an effective carbon policy will not be the foundation of a successful political campaign until the social conditions are ripe for its acceptance. Again, this is not meant to downplay the undeniable importance of technological, economic, and political innovations on the path to a low-carbon society. A coordinated, multi-faceted approach is both necessary and desirable. But insofar far as technology, business, and politics are a reflection of the culture in which they are situated, it would seem that disruptive innovation in the socio-cultural sphere may need to be the prime mover, so to speak, which would then enable or ignite further disruptive innovations in other spheres of life.

Significantly, the socio-cultural sphere is also the domain where individuals have most agency. We may not feel like we have much influence over the decisions of our members of parliament, or the decisions of big business or other global institutions, but within the structural constraints of any society there nevertheless resides a realm of freedom through which individuals and communities can resist and oppose the existing order and make their influence felt (Gibson-Graham, 2006; Holloway, 2010). However small those acts of opposition (or renewal) might seem in isolation, when they form part of a large social movement, their cumulative impact can reshape society 'from below' and ultimately form a tidal wave of revolutionary significance, washing away the old world, or aspects of it, and clearing space for the new. A brief glance at the history of social movements shows this to be true.

Of course, to suggest that technology, business, and politics are merely a reflection of culture is a contestable and, in many ways, an overly simplistic proposition. Public policy, for example, rather than always being shaped by culture in a uni-directional way, sometimes takes the *lead* in societal development and is influenced by forces *other* than culture. The same can be said of the spheres of business and technology, both of which *shape* culture as they are *shaped by* culture, in a dialectical fashion. Nevertheless, it would be fair to state that any transformative politics, technology, or business model needs to be complemented, and probably preceded by, a co-relative transformation in the socio-cultural sphere. This suggests that we must carefully consider not only what cultural or social conditions would best facilitate the realisation of a low-carbon world, but also what role social or cultural movements might have to play in producing those conditions.

The purpose of this chapter, then, is to review contenders, so to speak, for the category of most innovative social movements working toward a low-carbon world, movements which are potentially 'disruptive' in the sense outlined above. Admittedly, it is a difficult challenge indeed attempting to choose movements or innovations with genuinely disruptive potential. An element of arbitrariness is inevitable, especially since there is no 'criteria' as such by which they can be objectively ranked (see Science Communication Unit, 2014). Furthermore, the 'tipping points' of influential social movements in history have generally come as a surprise to the societies that they came to influence, due to the impossibility of anticipating the confluence of events and social conditions which were needed for them to flourish. Who anticipated the civil rights activist, Rosa Parks? Who could have foreseen that a simple act, such as not giving up one's seat on the bus, would give such momentum to the Civil Rights Movement? This calls for a healthy dose of humility in undertaking the current task.

It follows that different people would surely make different choices and see different degrees of potential in today's various social movements for a low-carbon world. Be that as it may, the movements reviewed below did seem to jump out somewhat as obvious contenders, not only for what they already are, but more importantly, what they are promising, or even threatening, to become (see also, Seyfang and Haxeltine, 2012; SPREAD, 2011; Seyfang *et al.,* 2010). It is an impossible calculation to know which of these are most likely to explode into the mainstream and 'change the world'. Perhaps none of them will; perhaps they may all play a part; or perhaps the change will be ignited by something else entirely. Fortunately, this very uncertainty comes with a silver lining – namely, that hope for a low-carbon world partly resides in the fact that the movement or movements that could spark the Great Transition beyond fossil fuels may, as yet, lie unimagined, or simply be dormant, awaiting ignition. For better or worse, a 'black swan' may lie around every bend in the river (Taleb, 2007).

As the philosopher Ludwig Wittgenstein once remarked about attempts to foresee the future (see Rorty, 1979, *xii*):

> When we think about the future of the world, we always have in mind its being at the place where it would be if it continued to move as we see it moving now. We do not realize that it moves not in a straight line, but in a curve, and that its direction constantly changes.

Bearing this message of caution and hope in mind, the following review will consider those social movements or social innovations that at least have the potential to change the current trajectory of history acutely in the direction of a low-carbon world.

2. Potential Contenders for Disruptive Social Innovation

2.1. *The fossil fuel 'divestment' campaign*

The analysis will begin with the fossil fuel 'divestment' campaign, which was initiated late in 2012 by climate activist, Bill McKibben, and his networking team at 350.org. In the 18 months since then this campaign has taken on a life of its own, as nascent social movements tend to do. The disruptive potential of this campaign lies in how directly it challenges the *financial foundations* of the fossil fuel industry, without which the industry could not support itself or develop new projects. Find a way to remove the financial lifeblood of the industry – that is, find a way to remove or minimise shareholder investment in fossil fuels – and the industry would inevitably wither away by the very same logic of capital that currently sustains it.

Motivated by this possibility, McKibben and his team organised a campaign for fossil fuel 'divestment', which calls on individuals, communities, institutions, and governments to withdraw or 'divest' their financial support from the fossil fuel industry with the ultimate aim of crippling it (see McKibben, 2012). Without investment, the fossil fuel industry cannot exist; without the fossil fuel industry, the primary cause of climate change is eliminated. The genius of this campaign lies both in its simplicity and its directness, and the movement seems to be growing in momentum.

In the US, 380 college campuses have committed to divestment (Conifeno, 2013), with successful divestment having already been achieved in nine universities and colleges, 22 cities, and 10 religious organisations, with further campaigns under way in Canada, the UK, Sweden, Finland, India, Bangladesh, as well as Australia and New Zealand (see Go Fossil Free, 2014a). While the campaign encourages individuals to divest wherever possible, the main focus is on larger institutions and organisations where the real financial power lies, especially banks, super schemes, universities, churches, and governments. A recent report from Oxford University concludes that this is the fastest growing divestment campaign in history (Ansar *et al.*, 2013).

Significantly, the transformative potential of divestment as a strategy for deep societal change is not without precedent. As the fossil fuel divestment website notes (Go Fossil Free, 2014b):

> There have been a handful of successful divestment campaigns in recent history, including Darfur, Tobacco and others, but the largest and most impactful one came to a head around the issue of South African Apartheid. By the mid-1980s, 155 campuses—including some of the most famous in the country—had divested from companies doing business in South Africa. 26 state governments, 22 counties, and 90 cities, including some of the nation's biggest, took their money from multinationals that did business in the country. The South African divestment campaign helped break the back of the Apartheid government, and usher in an era of democracy and equality.

One of the most interesting and promising elements to the fossil fuel divestment campaign is how it mixes financial self-interest with environmental and humanitarian ethics. The ethical side of the divestment campaign is obvious enough: fossil fuel emissions are the primary cause of climate change (IPCC, 2013), thus a moral case can easily be made that people and institutions should not be investing in, or profiting from, an industry that is in the process of destabilising the climate with potentially devastating social and environmental consequences (World Bank, 2012; Cristoff, 2013).

Just as it would be unethical to profit from the slave trade or from the sale of ivory, it is ethically dubious to profit from the cause of climate change. This argument is perhaps particularly relevant to universities, for there is a glaring moral and intellectual contradiction in funding the salaries of climate scientists with profits that flow, in part, from investments in the fossil fuel industry. Accordingly, divestment from the industry would seem to be a moral and intellectual imperative.

This ethical defence is arguably grounds enough for divesting from fossil fuels, but the fascinating thing about the 'divestment' campaign is how it frames a supplementary argument based on self-interest. Perhaps this is where the real revolutionary potential of the campaign lies. McKibben argues that people or institutions concerned about *their own financial assets* should immediately divest from fossil fuels because there is a 'carbon bubble' waiting to burst.

The 'carbon bubble' hypothesis is based on the notion of a 'carbon budget' (Carbon Tracker Initiative, 2011; IPCC, 2013), which represents the estimated amount of carbon emissions the atmosphere could safely absorb (where 'safely' means keeping temperatures under 2° from pre-industrial levels, which is the target internationally agreed to in the Copenhagen Accord of 2009). Put simply, McKibben and others argue that the 'carbon bubble' exists because the amount of fossil fuels already discovered far exceeds the world's carbon budget. More precisely, it is estimated that embedded carbon in existing global fossil fuel reserves lies in the vicinity of 2795Gt, but the world's carbon budget is only around 565Gt (Carbon Tracker Initiative, 2011). What this means is that, if the world is to stop temperatures rising above the threshold of 2°, around 80% of the fossil fuels already discovered simply cannot be burned and must remain in the ground.

A carbon bubble exists, therefore, because currently fossil fuel shares are priced on the assumption that *all reserves* will be produced. It follows that any serious response to climate change is going to burst the carbon bubble by turning a vast amount of fossil fuel reserves into 'stranded assets' of little or no value. The underlying threat of this approach arises out of the understanding that markets are notoriously whimsical, in the sense that they sometimes crash not because they necessarily have a reason to crash, but because a certain amount of people *think* that they might crash, leading to divestment. When a few sheep bolt, the rest tend to follow, if only because a few have bolted. Aware of this tendency, McKibben's divestment campaign is trying to shatter investor confidence in the fossil fuel industry and spark the initial capital flight, in the hope of opening the floodgates.

The divestment campaign is calling on people to recognise both the ethics and the economics of this situation, and withdraw their shares in the fossil fuel industry before the bubble bursts and the value of their shares implode. Not only do investors have a financial self-interest to do so, a broad-based divestment from fossil fuels could crash the industry by destroying its investment base, which, as noted, is a leading aim of the campaign.

Even if the campaign does not manage to bankrupt the industry economically, the campaign may nevertheless advance a critically important goal of 'stigmatising' the fossil fuel industry as a primary enemy of climate stabilisation, thereby bankrupting it politically and socially. Historically, stigmatisation has been an important function of divestment campaigns (see Ansar *et al.*, 2013).

While it could be argued that the 'divestment' campaign puts too much faith in market mechanisms as a means of responding to climate change, this potential indictment can easily be reconceived as a defence of the strategy: divestment uses the existing mechanisms of capitalism to undermine what is arguably capitalism's defining industry. If ever there was an "Achilles' Heel" to the fossil fuel industry, the divestment campaign just might be it.

Of course, it is not enough merely to 'divest' from the fossil fuel industry; it is equally important to 'reinvest' in a clean energy economy. This additional reinvestment strategy provides further grounds for thinking that the divestment campaign could be of transformative significance in bringing about a post-carbon or low-carbon world.

2.2. *Transition initiatives*

If the fossil fuel divestment campaign is one of the most promising social movements *opposing* and *undermining* the carbon-based society, the Transition Towns Movement is arguably one of the most promising and coherent social movements focused on *building the alternative* society (see Hopkins, 2008; Seyfang, 2009). This movement burst onto the scene in Ireland in 2005, and already there are more than 1000 Transition Towns around the world, in more than 40 countries. Given that this movement is explicitly seeking to mobilise communities for a low-carbon future, it is important to consider what exactly defines a Transition Town and evaluate the extent to which this movement has 'disruptive' potential.

The fundamental aims of the movement are to respond to the twin challenges of peak oil and climate change by decarbonising and relocalising the economy through a community-led model of change based on permaculture principles (Hopkins, 2008; Holmgren, 2002). In doing so, the movement runs counter to the dominant narrative of globalisation, and instead offers a positive, highly localised vision of a low-carbon future, as well as an evolving roadmap for getting there through grassroots activism. While this young and promising movement is not without its critics (e.g., James, 2010) there are some, such as Ted Trainer (2009: 11), who argue that if civilisation is to make it into the next half of the century in any desirable form, 'it will be via some kind of Transition Towns process'.

According to the movement's co-founder, Rob Hopkins, the strategy and vision of Transition is based on four key assumptions (Hopkins, 2008: 134):

(1) That life with dramatically lower energy consumption is inevitable, and that it's better to plan for it than to be taken by surprise;
(2) That our settlements and communities presently lack the resilience to enable them to weather the severe energy [and economic] shocks that will accompany peak oil [and climate change];
(3) That we have to act collectively, and we have to act now;
(4) That by unleashing the collective genius of those around us to creatively and proactively design our energy descent, we can build ways of living that are more connected, more enriching, and that recognise the biological limits of our planet.

The rationale for engaging in grassroots activity is that 'if we wait for governments, it'll be too little, too late. If we act as individuals, it'll be too little. But if we act as communities, it might just be enough, just in time' (Hopkins, 2013: 45). According to some commentators (Barry and Quilley, 2008: 2), this approach represents a 'pragmatic turn' insofar as it focuses on *doing* sustainability here and now. In other words, it is a form of 'DIY politics' (Barry and Quilley, 2009: 3), one that does not involve waiting for governments to provide solutions, but rather depends upon an actively engaged citizenry (Seyfang and Haxiltine, 2012; Seyfang *et al.*, 2010).

This approach is particularly relevant here in Australia, where the government is showing no signs of progressing the nation toward a low-carbon future, meaning that any movement toward such a future may have to be driven 'from below'. Therein lies the promise and coherency of the Transition Towns Movement: in an era of political paralysis, it seems that the *only* path beyond fossil fuels is one led by communities acting locally, and in that regard the

Transition Towns Movement is leading the way. Of course, whether grassroots movements for a low-carbon world ultimately march under the banner of 'transition' is of little importance; what is necessary and important is that people do not wait for governments to act or lead the way.

The paradigm shift of Transition is articulated around notions of 'decarbonisation' and 'relocalisation' of the economy. What this means in practice is complex, but the overarching idea is that decarbonisation is necessary and desirable for reasons of peak oil and climate change, and given how carbon-intensive global trade is, decarbonisation implies relocalising economic processes. As well as this, another central goal of the movement is to build community 'resilience', a term which can be broadly defined as the capacity of a community to withstand shocks and the ability to adapt after disturbances (Hopkins, 2008: Ch. 3; Barry, 2012).

Notably, crisis in the current system is presented not as a cause for despair but as a transformational opportunity, a change for the better that should be embraced rather than feared (Hopkins, 2011: 45). Consequently, the vision presented by the Transition Towns Movement is very positive, one that is 'full of hope' (Bunting, 2009: np) for a more 'nourishing and abundant future' (Hopkins, 2008: 5). Hopkins, who is by far the most prominent spokesperson for the movement, plays a crucial role in promoting such an optimistic message, while at the same time acknowledging the extent of the global problems and asserting that there is no guarantee of success (Hopkins, 2011: 17). By doing so, Hopkins skilfully walks a delicate line: he openly acknowledges the magnitude of the global predicament, but quickly proceeds to focus on positive, local responses and action. Whether his positivity is justifiable is an open question – some argue that it is not (Smith and Positano, 2010) – but it is nevertheless proving to be a means of inspiring and mobilising communities in ways that 'doomsayers' are unlikely to ever realise.

As promising as the Transition Towns Movement may be, there are crucial questions it needs to confront and reflect on if it wants to fully realise its potential for deep societal transformation. Firstly, some critics argue that the movement suffers, just as the broader environmental movement arguably suffers, from the inability to expand much beyond the usual middle-class, generally well-educated participants, who have the time, security, and privilege to engage in social and environmental activism. While the Transition Towns Movement is ostensibly 'inclusive', this self-image requires examination in order to assess whether it is as inclusive and as diverse as it claims to be, and what this might mean for the movement's prospects. Can it 'scale up' sufficiently? Secondly, there is the issue of whether a grassroots, community-led movement can change the macroeconomic and political structures of global capitalism 'from below' through re-localisation strategies, or whether the movement may need to engage in more conventional top-down political activity if it is to have any chance of achieving its ambitious goals (see, e.g., Sarkar, 1999). Other critics argue that the movement is insufficiently radical in its vision (Trainer, 2010). Does the movement need to engage more critically with the broader paradigm of capitalism, its growth imperative, and social norms and values that constrict the imagination? Is building local resilience within the existing system an adequate strategy? And does the movement recognise that decarbonisation almost certainly means giving up many aspects of affluent, consumer lifestyles? This is not the forum to offer answers to these probing questions (see Alloun and Alexander, 2014; Seyfang *et al.,* 2010; Seyfang, 2009), but engaging critically with these issues could advance the debate around a movement that may indeed hold some of the keys to transitioning to a just and sustainable, low-carbon world.

It may be that the practical reality of the Transition Towns Movement has been 'over-hyped' to some extent, but what seems clear is that a low-carbon world will never emerge unless there is an engaged citizenry that speaks up and gets active. Currently, the Transition Towns Movement is the most promising example of such a social movement, mobilising communities for a world beyond fossil fuels, and meeting with some real, albeit limited, success.

2.3. *Collaborative consumption and the sharing economy*

The term 'collaborative consumption' has emerged as one of the socio-economic buzzwords of recent times, with *Time* magazine (Walsh, 2011) listing it as one of the big ideas that will change the world. Surprisingly, perhaps, collaborative consumption is in many ways just a fancy name for 'sharing', although as the prime website dedicated to this concept notes, it is 'sharing reinvented through technology' (Collaborative Consumption, 2014). But if human beings have been sharing their wealth, possessions, and skills (to varying extents) throughout history, what role could collaborative consumption play in the transition to a low-carbon world? And to what extent could something as mundane-sounding as 'sharing' have disruptive potential?

While the term was coined decades ago (see Felson and Spaeth, 1978), collaborative consumption only began entering the popular lexicon over the last few years, primarily through the work of Rachel Botsman and Roo Rogers (2011: *xv*), who define this emerging practice as: 'Traditional sharing, bartering, lending, trading, renting, gifting, and swapping, redefined through technology and peer communities'. The innovation here is that people are using online forums and technologies to offer or acquire access to things without necessarily buying or selling them; instead, they often share, hire, or gift them in more or less informal ways – facilitated by online peer communities which make it easy to list or search for available goods and services. In economic parlance, the 'transaction costs' of sharing or trading are markedly reduced through the use of the internet, making it more efficient than ever to connect formal or informal sharers and traders.

Examples of collaborative consumption are many, varied, and expanding. A representative example is the upsurge in car-sharing businesses, which involve either a central business purchasing limited cars that are then used by a community of people (e.g., Zipcar, Flexicar, and GoGet), or alternatively, the central business can facilitate peer-to-peer car sharing (e.g., Car-Next-Door). The genius here was in recognising that many, if not most, cars sit idle for a huge portion of the day or week, opening up space to utilise them more efficiently through sharing access. If a person can easily hire a neighbour's car for an hour or two when needed, this means less need for a personal car. For the same reason, bike hire has also taken off in various cities around the world, often facilitated by local or national governments. Organisations like 'Lyft' facilitate ride-sharing, which portends a behavioral shift of paramount importance.

There is also a variety of websites that facilitate sharing with or without monetary exchanges, such as the Sharetribe, Streetbank, or Open Shed, which also function to make better use of existing resources. For example, if there are easy ways to facilitate sharing online, not everyone on the street needs a lawnmower or a jigsaw (since they tend to sit idle), thereby minimising the need for superfluous production and consumption. Other websites, such as Freecycle, rather than facilitating sharing or trading, simply facilitate the gifting of unwanted or superfluous things, thereby reducing the flow of waste to landfill. One of the real success stories of collaborative consumption has been Air BnB, which allows people to list a room or rooms in their home as short or long term accommodation for travellers, providing people with an alternative to hotels and backpacker accommodation.

What these examples show is that collaborative consumption is often more about *access* to goods and services than *ownership*. Botsman and Rogers argue that this 'new' form of consumption behaviour and entrepreneurship has the ability to radically transform business, cultures of consumption, and the environmental movement, with potentially deep implications on various aspects of life (Botsman and Rogers, 2011). This transformative potential remains even when the exchange of money is involved, as is the case with prominent websites such as Craigslist, Ebay, and Gumtree. These types of websites still provide an efficient means of allocating or reallocating goods and services beneath the surface of the traditional economy, even if these forms of exchange cannot be called 'sharing'. If a household finds itself with a surplus couch, table, or set of curtains, there are now numerous channels that are available to connect such goods with people who need them, through the click of a button. This highlights the point that collaborative consumption falls on a spectrum, with some practices taking the form of non-monetary 'sharing' or 'gift', and other forms sitting closer to conventional economic activity.

There are three broad categories of collaborative consumption: Product Service Systems, Redistribution Markets, and Collaborative Lifestyles (Botsman and Rogers, 2011):

- *Product Service Systems* refer to the switch from an ownership model of consumption toward a usage or access model (see Tischner, Ryan, and Vezzoli, 2009). Thus, people pay for, or get the benefit of a product, without owning it.[1]

- *Redistribution Markets* facilitate the redistribution of goods from where they are not needed to any place or person where they are needed. These markets have always existed, but current technologies, especially online social networks, are fuelling this type of collaborative consumption (Glind, 2013). These markets can either involve gifting, sharing, bartering, or more conventional trading, and they are challenging traditional business and consumption methods. According to Botsman and Rogers (2011) 'redistribution is the fifth 'R' - reduce, recycle, reuse, repair and redistribute'.[2]

- *Collaborative Lifestyles* are less about sharing tangible assets, and more about sharing things like time, space, and skills – again, facilitated by online forums.

---

[1] Note that not all product service systems should be considered collaborative consumption, because that would include the entire service economy. Instead, collaborative consumption in this context refers to the innovation of bringing *new* services into his category (e.g., car sharing or borrowing a neighbour's drill) through the use of technology, thus facilitating the sharing of resources that would otherwise have required individual ownership.

[2] Ibid. 73.

It is difficult to deny the potential of these types of collaborative exchange to challenge dominant cultures of wasteful and excessive consumption. Especially in affluent societies, where a vast amount of goods lie idle and unused, there seems to be huge potential for *avoiding further production of goods* by facilitating the *efficient reallocation of existing goods* through sharing, barter, and trade. Sharing and redistribution via these methods clearly provide a path to reduced carbon emissions, by minimising the need for continuous production, and they seem to have the added benefit of promoting community interaction at the nexus of social and economic life. Of course, there is the further incentive of self-interest: many people are drawn to collaborative consumption for the obvious reason that it can save money and hassle, or even make money.

Nevertheless, this potentially disruptive innovation has various risks that ought to be borne in mind too. For example, one of the obvious benefits for individuals who consume collaboratively is reduced costs; with less need to purchase a commodity, money is saved by hiring or borrowing only when needed. But this gives rise to a risk of a 'rebound effect' (see Herring and Sorrell, 2009). That is, if sharing saves an individual money, arguably that provides the person with increased funds to purchase *other* things, potentially negating the environmental benefits of collaborative consumption. Similarly, by providing cheaper access to goods and services, collaborative consumption could actually increase consumption. For example, the cheap accommodation provided through Air BnB could make carbon-intensive travel more financially affordable, again negating the potential environmental benefits of sharing. What this suggests is that, if collaborative consumption is to help catalyse the transition to a low-carbon world, these new mechanisms of exchange must be accompanied by an ethics of sufficiency (Princen, 2005), which is to say, an ethics that consciously uses collaborative consumption as a means of reducing the impact of one's consumption, rather than as a means of maximising consumption. Otherwise, collaborative consumption could just as easily promote rather than undermine consumerist cultures.

2.4. *Innovative approaches to renewable energy: Transcending political paralysis*

As the climate situation worsens, a louder chorus is forming amongst scientists, educators, and activists that an urgent top-down political response is needed to facilitate a rapid transition away from fossil fuels toward an economy based on renewables (see Wiseman *et al.*, 2013). Lester Brown (2011), among others, uses the metaphor of 'war time mobilisation' to signify the urgency needed. The US economy changed almost overnight with the bombing of Pearl Harbour in 1942, responding to an urgent security threat by refiguring, among other things, car factories to produce tanks, planes, and ammunition. In much the same way, the shrinking carbon budget suggests that some such mobilisation is needed again, this time to confront the threat of climate change, by mass producing solar panels, wind turbines, and other renewable technologies. Nevertheless, the failures at Copenhagen and later international climate-related conferences do not provide many grounds for hope that politicians are going to be the prime movers in the transition to a low-carbon society.

Fortunately, in recent years there has been a multitude of innovations in the socio-cultural sphere that suggest that, even in the absence of serious top-down political action, the transition to systems of renewable energy supply could be driven 'from below'. The preeminent example is Germany, which globally produces the most solar energy per capita. The interesting point about the example of Germany is not simply how much it is producing, but that approximately 65% of the renewable energy it produces is *owned by individuals and communities*, as opposed to being funded by the public purse (although attractive subsidies exist). This immediately suggests that there is an available escape from political paralysis, if only individuals and communities are prepared to fund the transition to renewables themselves. Beyond Germany, there are a growing number of inspiring examples – such as the Westmill Cooperative, in the UK, and Hepburn Wind, in Victoria, Australia – where communities, with less attractive subsidies, have still taken the transition to renewables into their own hands.

In order to make such a transition 'from below' as easy as possible, creative financing mechanisms and other innovations are being developed which have the potential to better enable individuals and communities to purchase renewable energy, with or without state support. Here are some promising examples:

- *Crowd-funding*: This refers to the collective effort of individuals and communities to pool their resources to support projects they believe in, usually facilitated and campaigned for through the internet. Small contributions from a large number of people are allowing innovators, entrepreneurs and businesses to utilise social networks to raise capital for all types of projects, including renewable energy projects, which do not receive any or sufficient governmental support. This innovation is putting both power and increased responsibility in the hands of grassroots movements, which now have a means of supporting renewable energy projects, if they are prepared to pay for them. Solar Mosaic, based in California, is one of the most prominent examples, with a similar organisation called Solar Share recently emerging in Canberra, Australia. Interestingly, as well as providing general ethical investment opportunities, these types of organisations also open up space for people to invest in renewable energy who may be unable to do so at the household level (e.g., due to a shaded roof or because they are living in a rental property).

- *Financing mechanisms from suppliers:* There have also been innovations in the way renewable energy can be financed, which is helping people overcome the barrier of upfront payment for renewables. As solar, especially, becomes more financially competitive with fossil energy, it is becoming economically more attractive to invest in solar panels, but some households struggle to afford the upfront cost of purchasing solar panels. That has prompted some energy companies, such as Vector in New Zealand, to offer solar panels to households with a relatively small upfront payment, supplemented by regular monthly payments for a period, rather than expecting a much larger – often prohibitively large – 'one off' payment upfront. Similarly, organisations like 'Every Rooftop' offer finance to people to lease or buy solar panels with little or no upfront payments. The moment solar becomes obviously cost competitive with traditional (fossil fuel) energy supply, these types of arrangements could facilitate a game-changing transition to renewables by nullifying financial barriers.

- *Environmental upgrade agreements:* These agreements refer to interesting new financing arrangements between private households, banks, and governments, whereby banks offer loans to households to 'retrofit' their houses to increase energy efficiency, expand water storage, or purchase solar. Instead of households paying the debt back directly to the bank, however, payments are made via local governments which draw the payments through a rates charge. This means that if the property is sold, the debt stays with the property, providing an incentive to retrofit one's house, even if one may sell the property in the foreseeable future. There are also means of splitting the repayments with tenants (if they consent, as they may do for self-interested reasons). This is another example of innovative financing mechanism reducing barriers to investments in renewable energy.

- *Social finance and self-managed super:* Other promising developments are taking place in the sphere of 'social' finance; that is, financial institutions that are explicitly motivated by the desire to help fund socially and environmentally beneficial projects. Australian institutions like BankMecu and Foresters are leading the way. There is also a huge sum of superannuation which private citizens around the world could access if they decided to 'self-manage' their own super and use it to invest in renewables.

All of these innovations are taking place in the context of increasing economic (and ecological!) incentives to invest in renewables. Significant advances are taking place, year on year, with respect to the price and efficiency of solar energy, wind energy, and battery storage. We can be sure the moment renewable energy is cheaper than fossil energy, we will see a truly disruptive change in a matter of years, and signs are emerging that such a transformation could be almost upon us, if it is not already (see, e.g., Parkinson, 2014a, 2014b). For example, the former head of the US's largest utility, Duke Energy, says traditional utilities will not change quickly enough in the face of advancements in solar energy, comparing those traditional utilities to frogs in warming water (see Parkinson, 2014c). More interestingly still, Goldman Sachs has recently announced that it is investing US$40 billion in renewable investments, which it regards as one of the most compelling and attractive markets. Stuart Bernstein, who heads the bank's clean-technology and renewables investment banking group, has recently claimed with respect to the renewable energy market: 'It is a transformational moment in time' (see Parkinson, 2014d).

2.5. *Reconstructing food systems from the ground up*

Transforming energy supply is perhaps the most direct path to a low-carbon world, but reconstructing food systems follows closely in terms of importance. Industrial methods of food production and distribution, and wasteful or high-impact consumption practices, make food a focal point for any transition to a low-carbon world.

Current practices are dominated by the use of carbon-intensive pesticides, fertilisers, oil-powered machinery, and plastic packaging, and the globalised food chain can mean that food often travels tens of thousands of kilometres to arrive on our plates. To make matters worse, it is estimated that, in Australia, more than $5 billion of food is thrown out every year (Baker, Fear, and Denniss, 2009). The result of all this is that food can be one of the most impactful aspects of modern life, with ecological footprint analyses estimating that food production and consumption accounts for around 28% of our ecological impact here in Victoria, Australia (EPA, 2008).

It follows that any transition to a sustainable society is going to require huge changes in our methods of food production and distribution, and our cultures of food consumption. Not only is food a critically important key to such a transition, it is often said that the way to a person's heart is through their stomach, suggesting that food may be an important way to engage people about broader issues of social and ecological concern. In the absence of progressive government action, however, it again seems likely that the driver for change may have to come from the socio-cultural sphere.

Community gardens are one example of where citizens are getting active in local food production. One must acknowledge, however, that these gardens presently produce only a tiny, often insignificant, percentage of a locality's food production. This is not to downplay the potential importance of community gardens as a mechanism for social change; they are arguably an important means of creating a social conversation about food, as well as creating social hubs and networks that promote community interaction and knowledge sharing. But currently community gardens are not really threatening to disrupt conventional, industrial food production.

Innovations with more disruptive potential involve new ways of connecting local people with local farmers. Food co-ops, local farmers' markets, Community Supported Agriculture (CSA), and farmer-direct veggie box schemes are increasingly providing urban and suburban people with access to locally grown food. Once more, online technologies are making it easier to connect local producers with local markets. One of the most promising innovations in this area is the Open Food Foundation (2014), which offers free software to support local food enterprises. For example, the 'Open Food Hub' software enables people to manage online ordering, multiple suppliers and products, and a range of distribution points; the 'Open Food Network' software is a free open source, scalable e-commerce marketplace and logistics platform that enables communities and producers to connect, trade, and coordinate movement of food. As the website explains, 'it's like a network of online farmers markets that enables everyone to participate.

Through peer-to-peer product traceability and transparency, it helps put control over food into the hands of farmers, eaters and local enterprises.' Although these types of open source innovations are in their infancy, their potential to empower communities to take control of their systems of food supply (and undermine the power of mega-supermarket chains) is evident. Watch this space.

Online networking groups like The Australian Food Sovereignty Alliance and the Australian City Farms and Community Gardens Network are also providing tools to connect what seems to be a growing movement of people determined to change the way food is produced and distributed in Australia. Similarly, organisations like Second Bite are dedicated to rescuing and reallocating fresh food to people in need across Australia. In 2012, Second Bite rescued 3 million kilograms of fresh food that would otherwise have gone to waste.

'Localising' food production, however, is only a relatively small part of the transformation needed. 'Food miles' is a concept that gets a significant amount of attention, but analyses suggest that the embedded carbon in the 'transporting' of food is only somewhere around 5-10% of the total emissions flowing from food. This is still a significant percentage, of course, and it suggests that localising food production can indeed reduce carbon emissions by reducing food miles (as well as build food resilience and security). But what it really shows is that the *way* food is produced (e.g., industrial vs. organic) and the *type* of foods produced and consumed (e.g., high meat vs. low meat diets), are more relevant to the carbon footprint of food than *where* food is produced (distant vs. local). Furthermore, 'food miles' can mislead insofar as different modes of transport change the carbon footprint. For example, transporting food by a truck can be 10 times more carbon intensive than using a train, so again, it is not simply about *where* food is produced, but *how* it is produced, *what* is produced, and *how* it is transported.

What, then, could provoke a radical change away from carbon-intensive methods of food production, distribution, and consumption? Rising energy costs – due to the peaking of oil production or by internalising the full costs of carbon (e.g., a carbon tax) – could be a significant means of changing the economics of the current system. Expensive energy would make organic and local production more economically competitive, and high meat consumption less affordable. In much the same way that we can expect a rapid transition to renewable energy the moment it is cheaper than fossil energy, so too could we expect a rapid transition to organic food production if high energy costs made industrial methods uneconomic. A third mode of transformation could be a culture shift away from high-impact diets, through which people choose to buy local and organic, and reduce meat consumption, due to *ethical* considerations more than *economic* ones. Ethical enlightenment, however, may not be a pathway to rely upon.

Whether a low-carbon system of food production is forced upon us or voluntarily chosen, the case of Cuba provides an inspiring example of what such a system might look like. With the collapse of the USSR, Cuba's oil imports were reduced significantly, forcing the nation, over a short time frame, to move away from oil-intensive, industrial methods of production to more local and organic systems of food production (see Freidrichs, 2013). In the early 90s, the urban landscape changed drastically, with all available growing spaces cultivated for organic production. Although the Cuban government played a role in this transition, the primary driving force came from people themselves, who just did what they needed to do to survive.

Could more urban centres adopt urban agriculture to the extent Cuba did during its oil crisis? Throughout the developed world and beyond, small but growing subcultures of food activists are experimenting with exciting methods of urban agriculture – food swaps, guerrilla gardening, home aquaponics, vertical gardens, green roofs, 'slow food' practices, community gardens, urban farms, etc. – but as yet, it must be admitted, these practices have been unable to 'scale up' sufficiently to threaten the existing system. But the case of Cuba presents one vision of urban agriculture's potential. It also demonstrates the speed at which food systems can change when ignited by some disruptive force.

2.6. *The Voluntary Simplicity Movement: Reimagining the good life*

Throughout history there have been individuals, communities, and subcultures that have expressed doubts about the ethics, and even the desirability, of materialistic lifestyles and value-orientations (Vanenbroeck, 1991; Kasser, 2002). However, in the present era of chronic environmental degradation, climate change, and burgeoning population, social movements exploring alternatives to Western-style consumer lifestyles are becoming increasingly relevant, insofar as they offer a direct and coherent response to such global problems. If the economy is in ecological overshoot, it follows that the global consumer class must reduce consumption; by doing so the wealthiest segments of the population also leave more resources for those living in destitution (Vale and Vale, 2013). Of course, reducing consumption at the personal or household level is unlikely to be a *sufficient* response to social and ecological problems, but many argue that a cultural rejection of high-impact consumer lifestyles is a *necessary part* of the transformation needed to achieve a just and sustainable world (Trainer, 2010; Alexander, 2012a; Burch, 2013).

Indeed, climate scientist Kevin Anderson (2012, 2013) has recently been receiving considerable attention for arguing that climate stabilisation requires that most people in the wealthier parts of the world must consume, not just differently and more efficiently; they must actually consume *less*. This is not a strategy or approach that many climate scientists or other sustainability advocates have either recognised or been brave enough to acknowledge publicly, but Anderson does not shy away from the radical implications of the numbers. It is worth unpacking Anderson's forceful emissions-based justification for consuming less, because this is a theoretical innovation with potentially 'disruptive' social and political implications.

Anderson's justification for reducing consumption can be summarised quite briefly. In the Copenhagen Accord of 2009, the international community agreed to take the actions necessary to stop temperatures rising 2° above pre-industrial levels. In order to meet this goal (and keep within the estimated 'carbon budget' that goal implies), Anderson shows that the wealthier nations will need to reduce their emissions by around 8-10% a year, if they are to leave the poorer parts of the world a fair share of the carbon budget (see Anderson, 2013; Anderson and Bows, 2011). The great challenge this presents, however, is that economists claim that emissions reductions above 3% or 4% p.a. are incompatible with economic growth (see, e.g., Stern, 2006). It follows that higher reductions of 8% or 10% p.a. will necessitate giving up economic growth as a national goal and embracing degrowth policies that deliberately initiate a process of 'planned economic contraction' (Alexander, 2012). In terms of lifestyle implications, this evidence-based response to climate change would mean that people in wealthy nations would have to 'cut back very significantly on consumption' (Anderson, 2012: np).

This argument is supported by the fact that it is likely to take much more than a decade to really scale up renewable energy and reduce emissions significantly through *energy supply* transitions (Anderson, 2011). While it is necessary, of course, to transition to renewable energy supply, Anderson (2013) concludes that the only way to reduce emissions sufficiently in the short-to-medium term is to greatly reduce *energy demand* by consuming and producing less goods and services. This is because decoupling of energy and economy is either not occurring, or not occurring fast enough or deeply enough (see Alexander, 2014). Anderson's position goes directly against other climate and broader environmental analyses, most of which continue to insist that increases in consumption and economic growth in the rich world are compatible with environmental health, climatic stability, and social justice (e.g., Grantham Institute, 2013; UN, 2012).

Against this backdrop, the significance and disruptive potential of the Voluntary Simplicity Movement becomes apparent. This movement can be understood broadly as a diverse and loosely-knit social movement made up of people who are resisting high consumption lifestyles and who are seeking, in various ways, a lower consumption but higher quality of life alternative (Grigsby, 2004; Alexander, 2009). In practice, this way of life might involve growing organic food or supporting local farmers' markets, harvesting rainwater, mending or making clothes, cycling or walking rather than driving, avoiding air flight, limiting work hours, co-housing, purchasing second-hand or 'fair trade', progressively reducing energy consumption, and generally minimising waste and all superfluous purchases. Although participants in this anti-consumerist movement find justification and motivation in a wide range of personal, social, ecological, economic, and even spiritual grounds (Burch, 2013), Anderson's new emissions-based case for consuming less arguably provides the movement with one of its most compelling and urgent justifications.

The largest empirical analysis of the Voluntary Simplicity Movement (Alexander and Ussher, 2012) shows that there could now be as many as 200 million people in the developed regions of the world exploring, to varying degrees, lifestyles of reduced and restrained consumption. This signifies an emerging social movement of potentially transformative significance, especially if it were ever to radicalise and organise itself with political intent. Notably, that same empirical study showed that the movement was developing both a 'group consciousness' and a 'political sensibility', features that are arguably necessary for any social movement to use its collective power in influential ways. As more people are exposed to the type of reasoning unpacked by Kevin Anderson – that is, as more people see that responding to climate change actually requires consuming less – the Voluntary Simplicity Movement could well grow in size and influence, perhaps with surprising speed.

Interestingly, the justification for embracing a lifestyle of voluntary simplicity does not begin and end with ecological or humanitarian arguments. In recent decades there has been a huge amount of literature exploring the relationship between income and subjective wellbeing (see Alexander, 2012b), and the results undermine the culturally entrenched assumption that 'money buys happiness'. Although the empirical debate is not over, the weight of evidence strongly suggests that money and material wealth is important at low levels of income, but once basic material needs for food, shelter, clothing, etc. have been met, money has fast diminishing marginal returns. In other words, beyond the basic needs threshold, the things that really contribute most to human wellbeing are not monetary or material, but instead things like socialising, creative activity, meaningful work, and other *non-material* sources of meaning and satisfaction. This literature is arguably a ticking time bomb for consumer culture, because if more people came to see that consumerist lifestyles are not a reliable path to a happy and meaningful existence, they would presumably give up the consumerist lifestyle and seek happiness and meaning in realms other than consumption. Although this culture shift might be motivated primarily by self-interest, clearly it would have beneficial social and ecological implications. The point is that a very strong case is developing for people to explore post-consumerist lifestyles of reduced or restrained consumption, suggesting that the conditions for a cultural revolution are ripe.

It is also worth acknowledging a new and controversial analysis presented by David Holmgren (2013), co-originator of the permaculture concept, which provides further grounds for thinking that the Voluntary Simplicity Movement could have disruptive potential. Voluntary simplicity has always been an *implicit* feature of the permaculture worldview, insofar as permaculture is about designing a way of life that minimises waste in order to work with nature rather than against nature (Holmgren, 2002). But Holmgren recently placed voluntary simplicity at the centre of his thinking, and arrived at a theory of change that has received a vast amount of online attention.

Always doubtful of the prospects of convincing politicians to lead the necessary transition to a low-carbon world, Holmgren has grown increasingly sceptical that any mass movement at the social level is going to produce significant change either. Accordingly, his pessimism has driven him to conclude that the best we can hope at this late stage is to deliberately 'crash' the existing fossil fuel-based system and build a permaculture alternative as the existing system deteriorates. His provocative theory, to oversimplify, is that if a new, relatively small social movement of anti-consumers were able to radically reduce their consumption, this reduction in demand for commodities could destabilise the global economy, which is already struggling. More precisely, Holmgren hypothesises that if merely 10% of people in a nation could reduce their consumption by 50%, this could signify a 5% reduction in total demand, which, although small, would likely cause havoc with any growth-based economy. It is important to emphasise that Holmgren does not romanticise the process of collapse; he acknowledges the worrying risks his strategy poses. First and foremost, it is unpredictable in its consequences. Nevertheless, he argues that whatever risks his strategy poses, there are greater risks – both socially and environmentally – in letting the existing system continue to degrade planetary ecosystems. What is most interesting about Holmgren's strategy is that it does not rely on a mass movement. He believes that a relatively small but radical anti-consumerist movement could be a truly disruptive force.

Whether one agrees with Holmgren's strategy or not, it provides further grounds for seeing the Voluntary Simplicity Movement as a social movement of potentially transformative significance. If growth-based economies require cultures of insatiable consumers to function, this suggests that such economies could be fundamentally transformed if enough people withdrew their support and instead embraced lifestyles of voluntary simplicity. Furthermore, it should be clear enough that any transition beyond fossil fuels is going to have hugely significant lifestyle implications, and voluntary simplicity – the idea of living more with less – is arguably the most coherent and attractive way of 'reimagining the good life' beyond a fossil-fuel-based economy. Indeed, one of the most radical acts of liberation and opposition in a consumer culture is the 'great refusal' to consume more than one needs. Admittedly, this is not an organised movement that draws attention to itself, and it is not attached to a 'buzz word' that excites much media attention. But it does seem to be bubbling under the surface of the dominant culture of consumption, threatening to expand.

2.7. Redefining 'progress' through alternative indicators to GDP

If social movements based on notions of transition, voluntary simplicity, collaborative consumption, permaculture, etc., provide coherent and attractive means of reconceptualising life at the personal, household, and community levels, the emergence of 'alternative indicators' to Gross Domestic Product (GDP) present themselves as an important way to reconceptualise the meaning of macroeconomic 'progress' on the path to a just and sustainable, low-carbon world. While this subject, at first instance, might seem to be more of an economic innovation than a socio-cultural innovation, the fact that these alternative indicators seem to be receiving increased socio-cultural attention and support is the 'movement' which it will be suggested has disruptive potential. As noted in the introduction, economic, political, and technological innovations are unlikely to be disruptive until there is a culture that desires them, or is at least receptive to them, and there are reasons to think that support for alternative indicators are on the rise. As leading advocates for alternative indicators have recently noted, 'The chance to dethrone GDP is now in sight' (Costanaza *et al.,* 2014: 283). In this section we explore why this might be significant.

Economic growth is conventionally defined as a rise in GDP. These national accounts first emerged in the 1930s with the onset of the Great Depression, and developed significantly during World War II to assist with planning. But it was really in the post-war era that GDP came to prominence, not only in the US but also increasingly around the world (Collins, 2000). Almost immediately international comparisons of GDP per capita were made as a way of assessing the relative 'progress' of nations (Purdey, 2010), and today almost all governments around the world consider growth in GDP to be their overriding objective (Hamilton, 2003). Not only is growth widely considered the best means of keeping unemployment at bay, growth is also considered the best means of providing individuals and governments with more economic power to purchase those things they need or desire most. The underlying assumption is that growth in GDP is always good, such that a bigger economy is always better.

The critical flaw in this macroeconomic paradigm lies in the fact that GDP is by no means a holistic measure of a nation's 'progress', a point made decades ago by pioneering ecological economists Herman Daly and John Cobb (Daly and Cobb, 1989). GDP is merely a measure of the total market activity of a nation over a given period – a measure that makes no distinction between market activity that contributes to wellbeing and activity that does not. For example, GDP treats market expenditure on guns, anti-depressants, and cleaning up oil spills no differently from expenditure on education, solar panels, and bicycles. All market activity is considered good. But obviously the *nature* of market activity influences a society's wellbeing, not just its extent, so GDP is a very crude measurement of progress, at best.

Furthermore, GDP says nothing at all about the level or nature of *non-market* activity in a society, such as community engagement, health, or the functioning of ecosystems; nor does GDP say anything about the distribution of wealth in a society (see also, Stiglitz, Sen, and Fitoussi, 2010). That last point on inequality is important in light of recent evidence showing that economies that have broader distributions of wealth do better on a whole host of social indicators (Wilkinson and Pickett, 2010). For present purposes, however, it is the absence of ecological factors within the GDP accounts that signify their greatest failing. It is no good having a growing, carbon-intensive economy if such growth undermines the ecosystems (including climate systems) upon which wellbeing fundamentally depends.

What all this means is that GDP should not be used as a proxy for national progress, because it totally overlooks these critically important factors. Indeed, as Robert Kennedy famously noted, GDP measures 'everything except that which makes life worthwhile' (as quoted in Costanza, 2014: 283). Furthermore, treating GDP as a proxy for progress obviously encourages governments to shape their policies to maximise GDP, even if that means degrading the environment, destroying communities, and increasing inequalities of wealth. In other words, fetishising GDP can lead nations to seek growth of the economy, even if that would have negative impacts on the overall wellbeing of a nation.

Wanting to provide much more nuanced and comprehensive indicators of the overall progress, Daly and Cobb (1989) pioneered the development of the Index of Sustainable Economic Welfare (ISEW). This index, and others like it – such as the Genuine Progress Indicator (GPI), the Happy Planet Index (HPI), and the Bhutanese notion of Gross National Happiness (GNH) – take into consideration important social and ecological factors that GDP simply does not reflect (e.g., Lawn, 2006; Lawn and Clarke, 2008). For example, the ISEW and GPI begin with total private consumption expenditure and then make deductions for such things as resource depletion, pollution, income inequalities, crime, loss of leisure, 'defensive expenditures', etc., and make additions for such things as public infrastructure, volunteering, and domestic work. The aim is to measure, as accurately as possible, the overall wellbeing of a nation, including its sustainability, not just its total market activity.

The results from such indexes tend to show that despite steady growth in GDP over recent decades, the genuine progress of many developed nations has been stagnant or even in decline (Kubiszewski et al., 2013). Put otherwise, the results indicate that growth has stopped contributing to wellbeing in most parts of the developed world and now may even be causing the very problems that growth is supposed to be solving, suggesting that many developed nations have entered a phase of 'uneconomic growth' (Daly, 1999). If this is so, it would mean that developed nations should stop treating GDP growth as the primary answer to societal problems and instead develop policies that more directly advance wellbeing. Such policies could include eliminating poverty, broadening the distribution of wealth, and protecting the environment, with GDP growth being a goal of lesser importance.

Importantly, some governments and institutions around the world are beginning to take these alternative indicators very seriously, led by the Bhutanese government, which has been shaping policy based on notions of Gross Domestic Happiness since 1972. During his presidency of France, Nicholas Sarkozy commissioned three prominent economists – Amartya Sen, Joseph Stiglitz, and Jean-Paul Fitoussi – to examine alternatives to GDP measures; the commission concluded that GDP was grossly inadequate as a measure of progress and that alternatives were necessary. In the past three years the US states of Vermont and Maryland have adopted the GPI as a measure of progress, and have implemented policies specifically aimed at improving it (see Costanza *et al.*, 2014). Even David Cameron has stated: 'It's time we admitted that there's more to life than money and it's time we focused not just on GDP but on GWB – general well-being' (see Stratton, 2010). Perhaps most significant of all, however, is the message flowing from the United Nations, which recently expressed the need for a new economic paradigm, convening an international conference on this theme in April 2012, tellingly hosted by the government of Bhutan (see Royal Government of Bhutan, 2012). These types of politico-economic developments have arguably been made possible by a growing cultural dissatisfaction with con-ventional measures of progress based on GDP, evidenced by the surge of interest in alternative indicators.

The disruptive potential of this shift in thinking lies in the fact that 'what we measure affects what we do' (Sen, Stiglitz, and Fitoussi, 2010: *xvii*). If alternative indicators continue to take root in the public consciousness, this may make it much easier to frame the transition to a low-carbon world as something that is genuinely in a nation's interest, even if it is not a policy that maximises GDP.

2.8. *Taking control: Direct action, political protest, and democratic awakening*

In any social context that is shaped by an apathetic citizenry, the decisions of government are more likely to be influenced by lobby groups and narrow, corporate interests, which will tend to privilege profits over people and planet. It follows that any transition beyond fossil fuels is going to depend not only on a citizenry that *wants* such a transition, but also on a citizenry that is prepared to *struggle* for it against such vested interests. Movements such as the divestment campaign and transition initiatives, especially, are examples of communities getting active in driving change in the socio-cultural sphere, attempting to undermine the status quo and build an alternative by participating in transformative, grassroots action. Promisingly, there also seem to be other signs of a renewed political sensibility that recognises the importance of participating, as far as possible, in the decisions that affect one's community, and actively resisting when the voices of ordinary people seem to be ignored. These political acts go beyond being merely transformative, and at times can be better characterised as transgressive.

One such example is the new 'Lock the Gate' movement in Australia. On its website (Lock the Gate, 2014), the movement defines itself as follows:

> Lock The Gate Alliance is a national coalition of community groups from across Australia who are uniting to protect our common heritage – our land, water and future – from reckless coal and gas expansions. In a David-and-Goliath struggle of farmers against mining giants, everyday citizens against global corporations, our communities are choosing grace under fire and displaying incredible courage, integrity and imagination.

Formed in 2010, this people's movement has grown to include thousands of participants and over 160 community action groups. The movement is mobilising against the fossil fuel industry, organising town meetings, and even engaging in acts of civil disobedience, in order to ensure that their voices are heard. More transgressive still is the relatively small but prominent activist group 'Quit Coal', who regularly employ peaceful acts of civil disobedience – such as scaling public buildings and locking themselves to industrial equipment – to bring public attention to climate-related issues in the hope of disrupting the expansion of the fossil fuel industry. As the climate situation worsens, it could be that more people are driven to what might seem, at first, like desperate acts of resistance. Desperate times arguably call for desperate measures.

Although these types of political resistance movements are focused directly on the fossil fuel industry, there are other movements, both in Australia and around world, which are similarly transgressive without being directly or exclusively focused on the fossil fuel industry. The relevance of these broader political movements to the present discussion lie in the fact that, while they may not be solely or even primarily defined by climate issues, they may contribute to the 'disruption' needed for our world to change course, through their direct confrontation with the power structures of global capitalism.

The Occupy Movement is one of the most prominent and 'disruptive' social uprisings of recent times, and deserves special note. Branded and organised by the anti-consumerist magazine *Adbusters*, the Occupy Movement was launched on 17 September 2011, when protesters set up a demonstration 'camp' in the Zuccotti Park, New York, situated symbolically close to the world's most significant financial base: Wall Street. Over coming months, similar occupations took place in over 951 cities, across 82 countries. This was an innovative form of political demonstration, which brought huge media attention to the issues of inequality and democracy that seemed to be the primary (though by no means the exclusive) motivations for the occupations. Media attention was heightened further when police forces around the world began forcefully removing the protesters from their places of occupation, often resulting in scenes of intense confrontation, sometimes violence. Although the movement has since lost momentum (and its media attention), Cornel West asserts that the Occupy Movement represents a 'democratic awakening', and the *Financial Times* states that the movement altered 'the terms of political debate'.

The expectation of further and more regular political demonstrations is not without grounds (irrespective of whether future demonstrations march under the banner of 'Occupy'). A recent report by the Initiative for Policy Dialogue (IPD) presents a comprehensive review of protests around the world between 2006 and 2013, and concludes that there has been 'a steady increase in the overall number of protests every year' (IPD, 2013: 5). Not only are protests becoming more regular, the number of people protesting is rising. The IPD report (2013: 6) states that 'Crowd estimates suggest that 37 protests had one million or more protesters; some of those may well be the largest protests in history (e.g., 100 million in India in 2013, 17 million in Egypt in 2013).'

And why shouldn't many citizens of the world feel aggrieved by the way their economies have distributed the product of decades of unprecedented economic growth? A recent report by Oxfam (Fuentes-Nieva and Galasso, 2014) shows that the 85 richest people now own the same as the poorest half of humanity (3.6 billion people); the richest 1% own 65 times more than the poorest 3.6 billion people; seven out of ten people live in countries where economic inequality has increased in the last 30 years. This extremely skewed, and indeed increasing, disparity of wealth is a result of political choices that have shaped property, market, and tax structures over many decades, and increasingly it seems that people are demanding that their governments reshape those structures to systematically broaden the distribution of wealth. This is part of a broader call for 'real democracy', which is reportedly the primary issue that has motivated political protests globally in recent years (IDP, 2013).[3] Similarly, from an environmental perspective, Naomi Klein (2013) argues that 'science is telling us all to revolt'.

---

[3] There have also been promising experiments in 'deliberative democracy' in various parts of the world, through which lay people are given responsibility

Another reason for thinking that political demonstrations could grow in number and intensity in coming years – potentially disrupting the status quo – is that the global economy continues to struggle and show signs of instability. When economies are doing well, keeping unemployment low and promising a rising living standard, people are less inclined to take to the streets in protest. A comfortable citizenry does not often call for a revolution. But what if historic rates of growth are coming to an end due to resource scarcity (Turner, 2012), the end of cheap energy (Heinberg, 2011), and/or further credit and debt crises (Tverberg, 2012)? What if more and more people find themselves without jobs, or with declining living standards, even as the world's richest get richer? Food crises and expensive energy have been widely cited as grounds for the revolutionary uprisings in Egypt in recent years, producing what is now referred to as the 'Arab Spring'. This is indicative of the type of dynamic being discussed – namely, that as life gets harder, eventually there comes a threshold point when civil discontent develops, sometimes explosively, into political resistance, sometimes with revolutionary intent. Bearing that in mind, it is worth noting that in the US, 95% of post-financial crisis growth went to the top 1%, with the bottom 90% getting poorer. How long this will be tolerated is an open question.

Again, the reason for discussing these issues is not because these forms of political protest are directly or exclusively related to climate issues. Sometimes climate has nothing to do with them. But if future civil discontent – locally, nationally, globally – manages to produce a different kind of political reality – something 'other' than capitalism as we know it, perhaps something 'other' than capitalism in any form – then it may be that whatever it is that existing capitalism is replaced with could advance the movement toward a low-carbon society. The reasoning here is that if escalating demonstrations of political resistance manage to create political systems that truly advance the common good, and respect the rights of future generations to a healthy planet, then one would think that such a system would recognise the risks of fossil fuels and initiate a rapid transition away from them.

---

for allocating funds to council. Interestingly, it seems that these modes of democracy produce more socially and environmentally conscious policies, suggesting that many politicians would make more progressive decisions if they truly represented their constituencies.

3. Conclusion

Any transition beyond fossil fuels is going to need a coordinated, multifaceted effort between various spheres of life: social, economic, technological, institutional, and political. This chapter has reviewed various innovations in the socio-cultural sphere – innovations that have the potential to 'disrupt' the current trajectory and rapidly reorient the world toward a low-carbon future. Just as the socio-cultural sphere will need the support of disruptive innovations in other spheres of life, it is also likely that even the innovations *within* the socio-cultural domain will need to be coordinated in order provide mutual support, if they are to fulfill their transformative potentials. Although this analysis has only skimmed the surface, the innovations, campaigns, movements, and strategies reviewed in this chapter can be summarised as follows:

- The divestment campaign has the potential to undermine the financial foundations of the fossil fuel industry and provide a huge amount of reinvestment capital to scale up renewable energy systems. As well as gaining increasing support from those motivated primarily by climate issues, the fear of 'stranded assets' could also mobilise large shareholders in the fossil fuel industry to divest for self-interested reasons. Whatever the motivation for divestment, the fossil fuel industry cannot exist without financial support from investors.

- The Transition Towns Movement could be the social movement which shows that communities have the power to lead the way to a low-carbon future. Through the strategy of relocalising the economy, Transition Initiatives are turning crises into opportunities for cultural renewal. In a time of widespread political paralysis, not waiting for governments to lead the way is a necessary strategic move.

- Collaborative consumption and the 'sharing economy' are providing ways to reduce fossil fuel-driven production through sharing existing goods, spaces, skills, etc. Online technologies are reducing the 'transaction costs' of sharing, creating innumerable new opportunities for collaborative consumption and threatening to undermine 'traditional' economic relationships and structures based on exclusive ownership.

- New community-based renewable energy projects are seeking to overcome political paralysis by side-stepping politics. While top-down support for renewable energy is still highly desirable, and perhaps necessary, energy and financing innovations in the socio-cultural domain are threatening to achieve what most of our political actors are refusing even to aim for.

- Community-driven urban agriculture projects are many and varied – as they should be. While each of them in isolation can seem insignificant, together they point to a growing social concern over where our food comes from and how it is produced. New open source innovations, such as Open Food Network, are connecting local farmers with urban markets, in ways that have the potential to fundamentally change how urban populations source food while radically reducing the carbon-intensity of food production and distribution.

- The Voluntary Simplicity Movement presents itself as the social movement that most coherently 'reimagines the good life' – directly challenging energy-intensive consumerist cultures by showing that lifestyles of reduced and restrained consumption can produce a high quality of life. If more people were to see the personal benefits, as well as environmental and social benefits, of embracing lifestyles of voluntary simplicity, then a new low-carbon culture of consumption could be born. David Holmgren argues a relatively small but radical anti-consumerist movement could disrupt the existing growth-based economy.

- By entering public consciousness, alternative indicators to GDP could fundamentally redefine what we mean by 'progress', providing measurement tools that highlight the social and ecological costs of narrowly economic conceptions of wellbeing, while opening up political space for bold policies seeking radical reductions in emissions.

- Direct forms of democracy and political protest seem to be on the rise, exemplified by movements such as 'Lock the Gate' and 'Occupy'. In good economic times, people are less likely to mobilise for political resistance. If it is the case, however, that historic rates of economic growth are being constrained by the biophysical limits to growth, then populations once pacified by the promise of increasing living standards might become increasingly agitated, especially if disparities of wealth remain so vast. While it is impossible to predict the ways in which such social agitation could transpire, political resistance to the status quo becomes more likely, in more places, as the steam of discontent builds pressure.

Could it be that the socio-cultural conditions for rapid transformation are almost here? While it remains difficult to be confident, this review suggests that it would be premature to despair.

References

Alexander, S. (ed.). 2009. *Voluntary simplicity: The poetic alternative to consumer culture*. Whanganui: Stead and Daughters.

Alexander, S. 2012a. 'Planned economic contraction: The emerging case for degrowth'. *Environmental Politics* 21(3): 349-368.

Alexander, S. 2012b. 'The optimal material threshold: Toward an economics of sufficiency'. *Real-World Economics Review* 61: 2-21.

Alexander, S. 2014. 'A critique of techno-optimism: Efficiency without sufficiency is lost'. *Melbourne Sustainable Society Institute Working Paper*. WP 1/14: January 2014.

Alexander, S. and Ussher, S. 2012. 'The voluntary simplicity movement: A multi-national survey analysis in theoretical context'. *Journal of Consumer Culture* 12(1): 66-86.

Alloun, E. and Alexander, S. 2014. 'The transition movement: Questions of diversity, power, and affluence'. *Simplicity Institute Report* (forthcoming).

Anderson, K. 2012. 'An interview with Kevin Anderson'. *Transition Culture*. 2 November 2012. Available at: http://transition culture.org/2012/11/02/an-interview-with-kevin-anderson-rapid-and-deep-emissions-reductions-may-not-be-easy-but-4c-to-6c-will-be-much-worse/ (accessed 20 February 2014).

Anderson, K. 2013. 'Avoiding dangerous climate change demands de-growth strategies from wealthier nations'. Available at: http://kevinanderson.info/blog/avoiding-dangerous-climate-change-demands-de-growth-strategies-from-wealthier-nations/ (accessed 1 February 2014).

Anderson, K. and Bows, A. 2011. 'Beyond "dangerous" climate change: Emission scenarios for a new world'. *Philosophical Transactions of the Royal Society* 369: 20-44.

Ansar, A., Caldecott, B., and Tilbury, J. 2013. 'Stranded assets and the fossil fuel divestment campaign: What does divestment mean for the valuation of fossil fuel assets'. Stranded Asset Programme, Oxford University, 2013. Available at: http://www.smithschool.ox.ac.uk/research/stranded-assets/SAP-divestment-report-final.pdf (accessed 1 February 2014).

Baker, D., Fear, J., and Denniss, R. 2009. 'What a waste: An analysis of household expenditure of food'. *The Australia Institute*. Policy Brief No. 6: 1-24.

Barry, J. 2012. *The politics of actually existing unsustainability*. Oxford: Oxford University Press.

Barry, J. and Quilley, S. 2008. 'Transition towns: "Survival", "resilience" and sustainable communities: outline of a research agenda'. *Advances in Ecopolitics* 2: 14-37.

Barry, J. and Quilley, S. 2009. 'The transition to sustainability: Transition towns and sustainable communities'. In *The transition to sustainable living and practice (Advances in ecopolitics Vol. 4)* John Barry and Liam Leonard (eds). Bingley: Emerald Publishing: 1-28.

Botsman, R. and Rogers, R. 2011. *What's mine is yours: The rise of collaborative consumption*. New York: HarperCollins.

Brown, L. 2011. *World on the edge: How to prevent environmental and economic collapse*. New York: W.W. Norton.

Bunting, M. 2009. 'Beyond Westminster's bankrupted practices, a new idealism is emerging'. *The Guardian*. 1 June 2009. Available at: http://www.theguardian.com/commentisfree/2009/may/31/reform-transition-a-new-politics (accessed 1 February 2014)

Burch, M. 2013. *The hidden door: Mindful sufficiency as an alternative to extinction*. Melbourne: Simplicity Institute.

Carbon Tracker Initiative. 2011. 'Unburnable carbon: Are the world's financial markets carrying a carbon bubble?' Available at: http://www.carbontracker.org/wp-content/uploads/downloads/2011/07/Unburnable-Carbon-Full-rev2.pdf (accessed 20 February 2014).

Christensen, C. 1997. *The innovator's dilemma: When new technologies cause great firms to fail*. Boston: Harvard Business Press.

Christoff, P. (ed.). 2013. *Four degrees of global warming*. London: Taylor and Francis.

Collaborative Consumption. 2014. Website available at: http://www.collaborativeconsumption.com/ (accessed 1 February 2014).

Collins, R. 2000. *More: The politics of economic growth in post-war America*. Oxford: Oxford University Press.

Conifino, J. 2013. 'Bill McKibben: Fossil fuel divestment campaign builds momentum'. *The Guardian*. 31 October, 2013. Available at: http://www.theguardian.com/sustainable-business/bill-mckibben-fossil-fuel-divestment-campaign-climate (accessed 1 February 2014).

Costanza, R. *et al.* 2014. 'Time to leave GDP behind'. *Nature* 505: 283-285.

Daly, H. 1999. 'Uneconomic growth in theory and fact'. The First Annual Feasta Lecture, 26 April, 1999. Available at: http://www.feasta.org/documents/feastareview/daly.htm (accessed 1 February 2014).

Daly, H. and Cobb, J. 1989. *For the common good: Redirecting the economy toward community, environment, and a sustainable future*. Boston: Beacon Press.

Environmental Protection Authority (EPA). 2008. 'Victoria's ecological footprint'. Available at: http://www.epa.vic.gov.au/~/media/Publications/1267.pdf (accessed 20 February 2014).

Felson, M. and Spaeth, J. 1978. 'Community structure and collaborative consumption: A routine activity approach'. *American Behavioural Scientist* 21: 614-24.

Friedrichs, J. 2013. *The future is not what it used to be: Climate change and energy scarcity*. Cambridge, MA: MIT Press.

Fuentes-Nieva, R. and Galasso, N. 2014. 'Working for the few: Political capture and economic inequality'. Oxfam Briefing Paper, 20 January 2014.

Gibson-Graham, J.K. 2006. *A post-capitalist politics*. London: University of Minnesota Press.

Glind, P. van de. 2013. 'The consumer potential of collaborative consumption. Master's thesis, Utrecht University, 2013. Available at: http://dspace.library.uu.nl/handle/1874/280661 (accessed 1 February 2014).

Go Fossil Free. 2014a. 'Commitments'. Available at: http://gofossilfree.org/commitments/ (accessed 1 February 2014).

Go Fossil Free. 2014b. 'Frequently asked questions'. Available at: http://gofossilfree.org/faq/ (accessed 1 February 2014).

Grantham Institute for Climate Change. 2013. 'Halving global CO2 by 2050: Technologies and costs' Available at: http://www3.imperial.ac.uk/climatechange/publications/collaborative/halving-global-co2-by-2050 (accessed 1 February 2014);

Grigsby, M. 2004. *Buying time and getting by: The voluntary simplicity movement*. Albany: State University of New York Press.

Hamilton, C. 2003. *Growth fetish*. Crows Nest, NSW: Allen & Unwin.

Heinberg, R. 2011. *The end of growth: Adapting to our new economic reality*. Gabriola Island: New Society Publishers.

Herring, H. and Sorrell, S. 2009. *Energy efficiency and sustainable consumption: The rebound effect*. London: Palgrave Macmillan.

Hopkins, R. 2008. *The transition handbook: From oil dependency to local resilience*. White River Junction, Vt: Chelsea Green Publishing.

Hopkins, R. 2011. *The transition companion: Making your community more resilient in uncertain times*. White River Junction, Vt: Chelsea Green Publishing.

Hopkins, R. 2013. *The power of just doing stuff: How local action can change the world*. Cambridge: UIT/Green Books.

Holloway, J. 2010. *Crack Capitalism*. New York: Pluto Press.

Holmgren, D. 2002. *Permaculture: Principles and pathways beyond sustainability*. Hepburn: Holmgren Design Services.

Holmgren, D. 2013. 'Crash on demand: Welcome to the brown-tech future'. *Simplicity Institute Report* 13c: 1-23.

Initiative for Policy Dialogue (IPD). 2013. 'World protests: 2006-2013'. Available at: http://policydialogue.org/files/publications/World_Protests_2006-2013-Final.pdf (accessed 20 February 2014).

Intergovernmental Panel on Climate Change (IPCC). 2013. 'Climate change 2013: The physical science basis'. The Fifth Assessment Report. Cambridge: Cambridge University Press.

James, C. 2010. 'Transition and raw resources'. *Arena Magazine* 104: 14-5.

Kasser, T. 2002. *The high price of materialism*. Cambridge, MA: MIT Press.

Klein, N. 2013. 'How science is telling us all to revolt'. *New Statesman*. 29 October, 2013. Available at: http://www.newstatesman.com/2013/10/science-says-revolt (accessed 24 February 2014).

Kubiszewski, I. *et al*. 'Beyond GDP: Measuring and achieving global genuine progress'. *Ecological Economics* 93: 57-68.

Lawn, P. 2006. *Sustainable development indicators in ecological economics*. Cheltenham: Edward Elgar Publishing.

Lawn, P. and Clarke, M. 2008. *Sustainable welfare in the Asia-Pacific: Studies using the genuine progress indicator*. Cheltenham: Edward Elgar Publishing.

Lock the Gate, 2014. Website available at: http://www.lockthegate.org.au/ (accessed 20 February 2014).

McKibben, B. 2012. 'Global warming's terrifying new math'. *Rolling Stone*. 19 July 2012. Available at: http://www.rollingstone.com/politics/news/global-warmings-terrifying-new-math-20120719 (accessed 1 February 2014).

Open Food Foundation. 2104. Website available at: http://openfoodweb.org/foundation/ofn/ (accessed 1 February 2014).

Parkinson, G. 2014a. 'Rooftop solar PV will soon be cheaper than coal'. *RenewEconomy*. 30 January 2014. Available at: http://reneweconomy.com.au/2014/wa-grid-may-become-first-big-victim-of-death-spiral-41428 (accessed 20 February 2014).

Parkinson, G. 2014b. 'WA grid may become first big victim of "death spiral"'. *RenewEconomy*. 30 January 2014. Available at: http://reneweconomy.com.au/2014/rooftop-solar-pv-will-soon-be-cheaper-than-coal-63562 (accessed 20 February 2014).

Parkinson, G. 2014c. 'Why traditional utilities are like frogs in warming water'. *RenewEconomy*. 31 January 2014. Available at: http://reneweconomy.com.au/2014/why-traditional-utilities-are-like-frogs-in-warming-water-58554 (accessed 20 February 2014).

Parkinson, G. 2014d. 'Goldman Sachs sees "transformational moment" in renewables investment'. *RenewEconomy*. 31 January 2014. Available at: http://reneweconomy.com.au/2014/goldman-sachs-sees-transformational-moment-in-renewables-investment-90317 (accessed 20 February 2014).

Princen, T. 2005. *The logic of sufficiency*. Cambridge, MA: MIT Press.

Purdey, S. 2010. *Economic growth, the environment, and international relations: The growth paradigm*. New York: Routledge.

Rorty, R. 1979. *Philosophy and the mirror of nature*. Princeton: Princeton University Press.

Royal Government of Bhutan. 2012. 'The Report of the High-Level Meeting on Wellbeing and Happiness: A New Economic Paradigm'. Available at: http://www.2apr.gov.bt/images/BhutanReport_WEB_F.pdf (accessed 14 December 2013).

Sarkar, S. 1999. *Eco-Socialism or Eco-Capitalism: A critical Analysis of Humanity's Fundamental Choices*. London: Zed books.

Science Communication Unit. 2009. *Social innovation and the environment*. Report produced for the European Commission DG Environment. Available at: http://ec.europa.eu/

environment/integration/research/newsalert/pdf/IR10.pdf (accessed 28 February 2014).

Seyfang, G. 2009. 'Green shoots of sustainability: The 2009 UK Transition movement survey'. Working Paper, University of East Anglia. Available at: http://www.uea.ac.uk/~e175/Seyfang/Publications_files/Transition%20Network%20 2009%20Survey%20Report.pdf (accessed 15 February 2012).

Seyfang, G. and Haxeltine, A. 2012. 'Growing grassroots innovations: Exploring the role of community-based initiatives in governing sustainable energy transitions'. *Environment and Planning C: Government and Policy* 30: 381-400.

Seyfang, G., Haxeltime, A., Hargreaves, T., and Longhurst, N. 2010. 'Energy and communities in transition – towards a new research agenda on agency and civil society in sustainability transitions'. *Centre for Social and Economic Research on the Global Environment*. Working paper EDM 10-13. Available at: http://www.econstor.eu/handle/10419/48803 (accessed 18 January 2013).

Smith, J. and Positano, S. 2010. *The self-destructive affluence of the first world: The coming crisis of global poverty and ecological collapse*. New York: Edwin Mellen.

SPREAD. 2011. 'Sustainable lifestyles: Today's facts and tomorrow's trends'. Centre for Sustainable Consumption and Production. Available at: http://www.sustainable-lifestyles.eu/fileadmin/ images/content/D1.1_Baseline_Report.pdf (accessed 20 February 2014).

Stern, N. 2007. *The economics of climate change*. Cambridge: Cambridge University Press.

Stiglitz, J., Sen, A., and Fitoussi, J.P. 2010. *Mis-measuring our lives: Why GDP doesn't add up*. New York: The News Press.

Stratton, A. 2010. 'Cameron aims to make happiness the new GDP'. *The Guardian*. 15 November, 2010. Available at: http://www. theguardian.com/politics/2010/nov/14/david-cameron-wellbeing-inquiry?intcmp=239 (accessed 15 December 2013).

Taleb, N. 2007. *The black swan: The impact of the highly improbable*. New York: Random House.

Tischner, U., Ryan, C., and Vezzoli, C. 2009. 'Product-service systems' in *Design for sustainability: A step-by-step approach*. Paris, United Nations Environmental Program. 95-103.

Trainer, T. 2009. 'Transitioning to where?' *Arena Magazine* 102: 11.

Trainer, T. 2010. *The transition to a sustainable and just world*. Sydney: Envirobook.

Turner, G. 2012. 'On the cusp of global collapse? Updated comparison of the *Limits to growth* with historical data'. *Gaia* 21(2): 116-124.

Tverberg, G., 2012. 'Oil supply limits and the continuing financial crisis'. *Energy* 37(1): 27-34.

United Nations. 2012. 'The future we want'. A/Res/66/88, 2012. Available at: http://daccess-dds-ny.un.org/doc/UNDOC/GEN/N11/476/10/PDF/N1147610.pdf?OpenElement (accessed 1 February 2014).

Vale, R. and Vale, B. 2013. *Living within a fair share ecological footprint*. London: Earthscan.

Vanenbroeck, G. (ed.). 1991. *Less is more: An anthology of ancient and modern voices raised in praise of simplicity*. Vermont: Inner Traditions.

Walsh, B. 2011. 'Today's Smart Choice: Don't Own. Share'. *Time*. 17 March 2011. Available at: http://content.time.com/time/specials/packages/article/0,28804,2059521 2059717 2059710,00.html (accessed 1 February 2014).

Wilkinson, R. and Pickett, K. 2010. *The spirit level: Why greater equality makes societies stronger*. London: Penguin.

Wiseman, J., Edwards, T., and Luckins, K. 2013. 'Post carbon pathways: Towards a just and resilient post carbon future'. CDP Discussion Paper. April 2013.

World Bank, 2012. 'Turn down the heat: Why a 4 degree warmer world must be avoided'. Washington: World Bank.

7

DEGROWTH AND THE CARBON BUDGET
Powerdown strategies for climate stability

Climate change is not 'a problem' waiting for 'a solution'. It is an environmental, cultural, and political phenomenon which is reshaping the way we think about ourselves, our societies and humanity's place on Earth.
                                                     – Mike Hulme

1. Introduction

In recent years the notion of a 'carbon budget' has entered the lexicon of climate science (e.g., IPCC, 2013; Meinshausen *et al.,* 2009). This concept refers to the estimated maximum amount of carbon emissions that can be released into the atmosphere in order to retain a reasonable chance of preventing global temperature levels from rising more than 2°C above pre-industrial levels. This is the global temperature threshold reaffirmed during the Copenhagen conference in 2009 but which many climate scientists argue should be revised downward (see, e.g., Jordan *et al.,* 2013). Although the science underpinning the carbon budget is increasingly robust (see Le Quere *et al.,* 2013), many scientists, politicians, and the broader public have been slow to recognise its radical socio-economic and political implications.

To have any hope of keeping within a 'safe' temperature threshold, deep and rapid decarbonisation is required, and yet existing trends show that global emissions are still growing rapidly. According to the recent IPCC report (2013), if the world is to have merely a 50% chance of keeping warming to less than 2°C, no more than 820-1445 billion tones of carbon dioxide and other greenhouse gases can be emitted during the rest of this century. Based on existing yearly emissions, and aiming for a 66% chance of success, this carbon budget is going to be used up by 2045. If existing trends of growth in emissions continue or accelerate, or if we demand a higher chance of success than 66%, that budget will be used up even sooner (see also, Carbon Tracker, 2013; Moriarty and Honnery, 2011). The consequences and risks of the current 'business as usual' scenario highlight the urgency with which deep decarbonisation must take place.

Given what is at stake here – the viability of the planet for human civilisation – carbon budget analyses need to become the basis for climate policies around the world, for they provide the most scientifically rigorous grounds for understanding the full extent of the climate challenge and what would constitute an appropriate response. The logic of the carbon budget numbers, however, leads to conclusions that most people, including most climate policy makers, refuse to accept, acknowledge, or understand. Most significantly, as outlined in this chapter, the carbon budget arithmetic indicates that rapid decarbonisation may well be incompatible with continuation of current global economic growth trends and paradigms. In fact, even more challengingly, carbon budget analysis seems to imply that in the most highly developed regions of the world, keeping within the carbon budget will require 'degrowth' strategies of significantly reduced energy and resource consumption. This broad line of argument has been made often by degrowth scholars in recent years, but the latest carbon budget analyses are providing the degrowth position with compelling new scientific support.

Degrowth has been defined as 'an equitable downscaling of production and consumption that increases human well-being and enhances ecological conditions' (Schneider *et al.,* 2010: 512). In a supplementary way, Serge Latouche (2014a: 211) has defined degrowth as

> a societal project of transforming industrial and market societies into socially and ecologically sustainable societies of frugal abundance. Its principle aim is to dismantle a widely shared belief in the productivist model of development – that is, the ideology of unlimited economic growth – and to reconstruct industrial societies according to the ideal of ecological democracy.

By emphasising the need for *contraction* of the economy in the most developed nations, degrowth can be understood as a transitional phase that would ultimately stabilise in a steady state economy that operates within the sustainable carrying capacity of the planet (see e.g., Daly and Farley, 2004). Within those ecological limits of significantly reduced energy and material throughput requirements, the art of living, of course, could forever improve and evolve.

Like the notion of a steady state economy, degrowth is not necessarily tied to notions of Gross Domestic Product (GDP) but is fundamentally a biophysical macroeconomic concept with profound socio-political implications, which leaves room for increased wellbeing even if GDP declines. Degrowth, therefore – which refers to *planned* economic contraction – must be distinguished from recession, which signifies *unplanned* economic contraction. From within a degrowth paradigm, there is no reason why planned reduction of energy and resource consumption cannot be associated with increased wellbeing, if the transition is negotiated wisely. This creates conceptual space for 'economic degrowth' to be contrasted with 'uneconomic growth' (see Alexander, 2012a; Kallis *et al.*, 2012; Kubiszewski, *et al.*, 2013), which is the space within which this chapter is situated.

This chapter begins by examining the key conclusions of the carbon budget research literature and unpacking some of the assumptions that frame the various decarbonisation scenarios. After doing so, the chapter builds on the work of climate scientists Kevin Anderson and Alice Bows, who have led the climate science analysis of the implications of carbon budgets on economic growth goals and policies. Although Anderson and Bows have been insightful enough to see (and brave enough to acknowledge) that meeting carbon budget targets implies a rapid shift to degrowth strategies, particularly in the most developed economies, they have not yet provided a detailed discussion of the ways in which degrowth strategies might be integrated with the broader decarbonisation policy agenda. In the final sections of this chapter, therefore, an attempt is made to contribute to this discussion by outlining the main elements of an integrated socio-economic and political strategy consistent with keeping emissions within the confines of the carbon budget.

2. The Foundations of Carbon Budget Analysis

The primary cause of greenhouse gas (GHG) emissions – especially CO_2 emissions – is burning fossil fuels. It is now scientifically accepted that when GHGs are released into the atmosphere they retain extra heat which has a warming effect on the planet (IPCC, 2013). This is the most important dynamic which explains climate change as it is unfolding today, although other factors are at play too, such as deforestation. It follows that as more GHGs are released into the atmosphere, more heat will be absorbed, leading to further rises in average global temperatures. As the scientific understanding of climatic systems has developed in recent decades, it has become possible to estimate with increasing confidence the climatic impacts of further GHG emissions. In other words, scientists are able to predict within a range of probabilities the likely temperature rise that would result from a certain amount of further GHG emissions. This is the foundation of 'carbon budget' analyses (see generally, Steffen and Hughes, 2013; Committee on Climate Change, 2013).

The size of the carbon budget depends on the parameters of the analysis. There are four main parameters that must be stipulated in order to arrive at a carbon budget: (1) the units of the analysis (i.e., what is being counted: just CO_2? Or all GHGs?); (2) the timeframe that defines the contours of the budget (i.e., from what date do we start counting emissions and what date defines the end point of the budget?); (3) what is the threshold temperature rise that we are trying to avoid? (e.g., 1°C, 1.5°C, 2°C, 4°C, etc.); and (4) what probability is considered acceptable for keeping to that temperature threshold? (e.g., 50%, 80%, 95% chance of success, etc.). Once those parameters are defined, the foundations of a carbon budget analysis are in place. (Note that the phrase 'carbon budget' is used for simplicity, but as stated above, some analyses are not limited solely to carbon dioxide emissions).

Although the parameters stated above are the main ones that shape a carbon budget, there are others that must also be considered. For example, aerosols (such as sulphur dioxide) have a cooling effect on the planet, so higher levels of aerosols (which may be harmful in other ways) have the potential to offset some of the warming effects of GHG emissions. Similarly, more CO_2 will be able to be burned if other GHG emissions are reduced faster than expected, so some informed assumptions have to be made about these relationships. Another unknown is the extent to which carbon sequestration techniques such as carbon capture and storage (CCS) will be able to reduce the level of emissions from burning fossil fuels entering the atmosphere.

As well as these issues, there are also complex questions surrounding climate sensitivity, changes in land use, and carbon cycle feedbacks, about which assumptions also have to be made, such as the extent to which emissions from CO_2 will be absorbed by the oceans or how long CO_2 will remain in the atmosphere (see Carbon Tracker and Grantham Institute, 2013). All these dynamics can increase or decrease the carbon budget, depending on the assumptions made.

Although increasing numbers of scientific articles and organisations have offered estimates of carbon budgets, the following review is limited, by way of example, to two of the most influential and frequently cited references. The first is the foundational publication by Meinshausen *et al.* (2009). This paper provides a comprehensive probabilistic analysis 'aimed at quantifying GHG emission budgets for the 2000-2050 period that would limit warming throughout the twenty-first century to below 2°C' (Meinshausen *et al.*, 2009: 1158). The authors conclude that limiting cumulative CO_2 emissions over 2000-2050 to 1000Gt of CO_2 yields a 25% probability of warming exceeding 2°C, and a limit of 1440Gt of CO_2 yields a 50% probability. Between 2000-2006 global CO_2 emissions were approximately 234Gt, which must be subtracted from those carbon budget estimates. Emissions since that time must also be subtracted. The authors note that keeping to these budgets would require leaving more than half of proven, economically recoverable fossil fuels in the ground (raising issues about 'stranded assets' to which I will return briefly later). If GHG emissions in 2020 are 25% above 2000 levels, then the analysis indicates that the probability of exceeding 2°C rises to 53-87%. We see here the types of frameworks and scenarios that can be discussed with the benefit of carbon budget analyses. It allows us to identify the level of emissions we are aiming to achieve at a particular time, and then back-cast scenarios in order to determine how to achieve the stated goal.

The more recent Carbon Tracker and the Grantham Institute analysis (2013) is based on the same models as Meinshausen *et al.* (2009) but explores some alternative assumptions. For example, this report assumes higher levels of aerosols in the atmosphere (which will offset some of the warming) and assumes greater reductions of non-CO_2 GHGs (which allows for higher CO_2 emissions but results in the same overall warming effect). Based on these alternative assumptions, the report then offers estimates of various carbon budgets for the period 2013-2049, with various temperature thresholds (1.5°, 2.5°, 3° and 4°) and two different probabilities (50% and 80%). The results are shown in Figure 1.

Maximum temperature rise (°C)	Fossil fuel carbon budget 2013-2049 (GtCO$_2$)	
Probability of not exceeding temperature threshold	50%	80%
1.5	525	-
2.0	1075	900
2.5	1275	1125
3.0	1425	1275

Figure 1: Carbon budgets for different temperature thresholds and probabilities (from Carbon Tracker and Grantham Institute, 2013: 10).

These two brief reviews of carbon budgets serve the purpose of outlining the nature of these analyses and their key conclusions. It is worth noting that this method of understanding the climate challenge has been given increased credibility in recent years with the IPCC (2013) and the International Energy Agency (2012a: 3) both now drawing on carbon budget methodologies as central tools in target-setting and policy formulation.

3. Normative Aspects of Carbon Budget Analysis

As noted above, setting different parameters to the analysis can produce higher or lower carbon budgets. The choice of different parameters, therefore, can have socio-economic and political implications, and this draws the scientific analyses into more normative, value-laden, or 'politicised' spaces. Indeed, even after a carbon budget has been determined, a critical normative question still remains about how that budget should be distributed between and within nations of the world, and what decarbonisation strategies should be adopted to keep emissions within the carbon budget. In the following sub-sections some of these normative questions are raised.

3.1. *Where should the temperature threshold be set?*

The temperature threshold is one of the most important questions to answer when framing a carbon budget analysis. The lower the threshold, the lower the carbon budget. As climate science and climate politics have developed over recent decades, a maximum 2°C temperature rise above pre-industrial levels has become entrenched in the political discourse as representing a relatively 'safe' threshold, beyond which humanity would enter increasingly 'dangerous' territory. In recent years this threshold has been continuously reaffirmed in high-level climate negotiations, including at Copenhagen (2009) and Cancun (2010). Because of this, many carbon budget analyses are framed by a 2°C temperature threshold to reflect the international consensus, such that it is.[1]

The 2°C threshold is, of course, a somewhat arbitrary threshold – why not 1.8°C or 2.2°C? It is an easily understood round number

---

[1] It should be noted that 2°C is not accepted as a safe threshold by many of the least developed countries or the Association of Small Island States who, at Copenhagen and elsewhere, have been pushing for reduced thresholds. See also, Spratt, 2014a; Spratt, 2014b; Spratt, 2015).

which may have served a useful political purpose when the framework for a global climate response was first being seriously negotiated in the mid-1990s. The most recent climate science evidence, however, suggests that i) many ecosystems are more sensitive to impacts at 2°C than was previously thought, and ii) many risks are self-reinforcing, threatening to produce cascading environmental impacts that would roll on to affect social systems (see Jordan *et al.*, 2013; Smith *et al.*, 2009; Mann, 2009; Lenton *et al.*, 2008). If current scientific knowledge was available in the mid-1990s, the threshold could well have been set at 1.5°C or below.

While some climate scientists, policy makers and activists argue that revising the temperature downward is a crucial step towards ensuring an appropriate alignment between scientific and policy objectives, others continue to argue that revising the threshold downward might have a negative effect if such a goal was widely perceived to be unattainable (see Jordan *et al.*, 2013). Whatever the case, if once it was thought that 2°C was the guard-rail keeping humanity 'safe', it may now be more accurate to say that it represents the bare minimum dividing line between 'dangerous' and 'extremely dangerous' climate change (Anderson, 2012; see also, Spratt, 2014a; Spratt, 2014b; Spratt, 2015).

3.2. *What probability of success should be assumed?*

Once a temperature threshold has been determined, a carbon budget must be framed in relation to a particular probability of success or failure. If climate systems were perfectly understood, this would be unnecessary, because scientists would be able to state with relative certainty that if x amount of CO_2 were released into the atmosphere then this would produce a temperature increase of precisely y. Needless to say, the complexity and interrelationships of climatic systems defy perfect understanding, so temperature effects from emissions can only ever be stated in terms of probability. This raises the normative question of what probability of avoiding dangerous climate change our species considers justified. The higher the probability of success, the lower the carbon budget.

In trying to arrive at an 'appropriate' probability, we need to situate this debate in the context of what is at stake if we fail. Emissions are already having an effect on climatic and broader environmental systems, with glaciers and ice caps melting, coral reefs eroding, the boundaries for vector-borne diseases expanding, and the frequency of extreme weather events increasing (see generally, IPCC, 2014). If these effects are occurring already, the question raised is: what effects will flow from a 2°C or 4°C or 6°C temperature rise? (see Potsdam, 2012; Christoff, 2013.) When the consequences of a course of action are small, the risk of failing to avoid those consequences is less important. But when consequences are potentially extremely dangerous, even catastrophic, then it is rational to expect a substantially higher probability of success (see generally, Gardiner, 2011).

The language used in the dominant political discourse about climate policy targets is quite clear. The Copenhagen Accord and Cancun Agreements both state categorically that the goal must be to 'hold the increase in global average temperature below 2°C, and to take action to meet this objective consistent with science and on the basis of equity' (UNFCCC, 2011). The European Commission (2007) is equally clear, affirming the need to '*ensure* that global average temperatures *do not* exceed preindustrial levels by more than 2°C' and states that we '*must* adopt the necessary domestic measures' to ensure this is the case (italics added). Similarly, the UK's Low Carbon Transition Plan (DECC, 2009: 5) states 'average global temperatures *must* rise no more than 2°C' (italics added; see also, Anderson, 2012).

The language does not talk of 'hoping' to avoid dangerous climate change, or that we should 'try' to avoid it, and it does not suggest that we should aim for a 50:50 chance of avoiding dangerous climate change. By using language such as 'ensure' and 'must' it can be assumed that, when framing a carbon budget analysis, the probabilities of avoiding climate change should be very high – arguably in the range of 80-95%, or higher. Not only should this follow from the scientific literature considering the potentially dire consequences of climate instability, it also follows from one of the underlying principles of the environmental movement – the 'precautionary principle'. In short, we should not gamble with the climate. This is especially so given that those who will be most affected by climate disorder – those in the poorest nations and future generations – have not been responsible for it. For these types of reasons, most carbon budget analyses have assumed a probability of success at 66% or higher, although other scenarios have explored probabilities of 50%. The choice of probability is a normative one that significantly influences any carbon budget analysis.

3.3. *How should the global carbon budget be distributed?*

Once a global carbon budget has been determined, there remains the critical question of how that budget should be distributed amongst (and within) nations. One seemingly objective and equitable way to distribute a carbon budget is to share it out equally on a per capita basis. While this approach has some intuitive plausibility, it ignores at least two critical issues. First, it ignores any 'differentiated responsibility' for the historic causes of climate change. A strong moral case can be made that those nations most responsible for historic emissions should bear the greatest responsibility for dealing with the effects of emissions, and if dealing with climate change implies hardship or burden, then again, those who caused the problem should shoulder that burden more than those least responsible. But even on this issue, we find the richest nations (which generally have the highest historic emissions) arguing that they should not be responsible for GHG emissions in historic eras when it was not understood that emissions warmed the planet. The date at which the science of climate change was sufficiently well established is a matter of some debate, although 1990 – the year the IPCC's First Assessment Report was published – is one reasonable option.

A second problem with sharing the carbon budget equally on a per capita basis flows from the fact that billions of people still live lives of material destitution. Cheap fossil fuels provide vast reserves of dense energy that could be directed toward eliminating such impoverishment. Given this humanitarian predicament – wanting to eliminate poverty but also wanting to minimise GHG emissions – a strong moral case can also be made that if the world is to continue burning fossil fuels for some time, the bulk of that fossil energy should be spent lifting the poorest people out of destitution rather than increasing the wealth of the most affluent societies. Part of the reasoning here is that energy consumption has diminishing marginal returns to wellbeing, which implies that increased energy consumption will produce more wellbeing in the poorest nations than in the richest nations (see Diffenbaugh, 2013).[2]

For these reasons, it follows that the apparent 'equity' of sharing a global carbon budget out equally on a per capita basis is in fact far from equitable. Instead, an equitable distribution would have to allow for more emissions from the poorer nations and those least responsible for historic causes of climate change, thus constraining the permissible emissions from the richest nations that are most responsible and most technologically and financially capable of dealing with the necessary societal transformation.

---

[2] However, as discussed briefly later in the chapter, it is critical that the carbon budget spent in the poorest nations, with the intent of lifting those nations out of poverty, avoids creating infrastructure that essentially locks them into decades of high-carbon living.

This general position, in fact, has been accepted in the international climate negotiations, which acknowledges the need for 'differentiated responsibility', even if the exact weighting of distribution remains highly contested. The Copenhagen Accord (UNFCCC, 2010) clearly distinguishes between Annex 1 nations (broadly the OECD nations) and non-Annex 1 nations (broadly the non-OECD nations), and calls for a response to climate change 'consistent with science and *on the basis of equity*' (italics added). More specifically, the Accord acknowledges that 'the time frame for peaking will be longer in developing countries' and, most significantly, that 'social and economic development and poverty eradication are the first and overriding priorities of developing countries'.

4. The Radical Implications of Carbon Budget Analysis

Having outlined the foundations of carbon budget analysis along with key parameters in relation to temperature thresholds, probabilities of success, and distributional issues, we are now in a position to unpack some of the implications by considering in more detail what these numbers actually mean for emissions reduction policies and strategies. In doing so, I draw primarily on the work of climate scientists Kevin Anderson and Alice Bows, who have published a number of rigorous and influential papers on the economic policy implications of carbon budget analysis (Anderson and Bows, 2008a; Anderson and Bows, 2011; Anderson, 2012; Anderson, 2013). Although their conclusions can be seen as confronting, they in fact argue their case based on robust premises which, in ways discussed below, are actually very conservative. The numbers, in short, speak for themselves, but many find the message confronting because the numbers show that keeping temperatures below 2°C will require Annex 1 nations to immediately initiate deliberate and planned 'degrowth' strategies of reduced consumption and economic contraction. The controversy this evidence-based conclusion has provoked has prompted Anderson (2013) to note that their critics 'don't so much disagree with our conclusion, but rather they simply dislike it'. In this section their arguments are outlined and analysed.

Anderson and Bows offer their analyses on the following explicit assumptions and parameters (see especially, Anderson and Bows, 2011; Anderson, 2013):

4.1 The world should aim to keep warming below 2°C

As discussed above, 2°C used to be considered the 'safe' threshold, but more recent evidence suggests that a 2°C rise would be 'dangerous', which is why increasing numbers of scientists are questioning the 2°C threshold and considering a reduced target of 1.5°C or less (see Jordan *et al.*, 2013; Sprat, 2014a; Spratt, 2014b). By staying with the 2°C threshold, Anderson and Bows are being conservative in their assumptions and keeping in line with the *agreed goal* of mainstream international climate discourse.

4.2 The probability of exceeding 2°C is set at 50%

Although Anderson and Bows offer various scenarios based on different probabilities of exceeding 2°C, for present purposes their argument that assumes a 50% probability of exceeding 2°C is being considered. As discussed above, given the grave consequences that are likely to flow from a 2°C temperature rise or more, a 50% probability of exceeding that threshold is an extremely conservative premise. Not only does the language of the international community reflect a far lower probability (arguably in the vicinity of 1-10%), the precautionary principle would imply that a 50% chance of failure is far too risky.

4. 3 Non-Annex 1 countries peak in emissions by 2025

In order to determine how much of the global carbon budget is left for Annex 1 nations, Anderson and Bows first determine how much of the carbon budget non-Annex 1 nations will need to minimally develop their economies on the basis of equity. In making this assessment, they make what they acknowledge are 'extremely ambitious' (Anderson, 2013) assumptions with respect to the anticipated emissions peak in non-Annex 1 countries and their post-peak decarbonisation trajectory (as outlined in Anderson and Bows, 2011; Anderson and Bows, 2008a). Specifically, they assume that the non-Annex 1 nations will peak in emissions by 2025 and thereafter reduce emissions at an unprecedented 7% p.a. Note, however, that these 'extremely ambitious' assumptions are, if anything, favourable to the Annex 1 nations, since they imply less of the carbon budget is used up by the non-Annex 1 nations, leaving as much as possible for the Annex 1 nations.[3]

---

[3] The other reason this premise can be considered 'favourable' to the Annex 1

4.4 Annex 1 nations must reduce emissions by 8-10% p.a

The Annex 1 carbon budget is determined by subtracting the non-Annex 1 emissions from the global carbon budget. Based on the above assumptions (all of which can be understood to leave a *favourable* carbon budget for Annex 1 nations), it follows that keeping to the carbon budget requires Annex 1 nations to decarbonise their economies by 8-10% p.a. over coming decades. Even that conclusion can be considered understated, given that the scenario was formulated in 2011 (Anderson and Bows, 2011), and since then carbon emissions globally have continued to rise (and indeed, at an increased rate). Every year emissions increase (or do not meet the 8-10% decarbonisation requirement) the decarbonisation strategies required to keep to the carbon budget become more stringent.

4.5 Emissions reductions of more than 3% or 4% p.a. are incompatible with a growing economy

Given that energy consumption and economic growth are intimately connected (Ayres and Warr, 2009), and that any significant transition to renewable and more efficient energy systems is going to take many years and probably decades to roll out (see Smil, 2014; Smil, 2010), it is widely accepted amongst orthodox economists that emissions reductions of more than 3% or 4% p.a. are incompatible with a growing economy. This view is supported by the pre-eminent climate change economist Nicholas Stern (2006), the UK's Committee on Climate Change and, as Anderson (2013) notes, 'virtually every 2°C emission scenario developed by "Integrated Assessment Modellers"'. Anderson (2013) also points out that 'if reductions of 4% each year are to occur in an economy growing at 2% each year, then the carbon intensity of the economy must continually improve at around 6% year on year'. Despite considerable engagement with the literature, Anderson admits that he has found no examples of economists suggesting that prolonged emissions reductions of 3% or 4% or more are compatible with a growing economy. On the contrary, Stern observes that annual reductions greater than 1% have 'been associated with economic

nations is because the calculations are based on 'production-based' accounting not 'consumption-based' accounting. Given that many of the emissions in the non-Annex 1 nations are used up producing things which are ultimately consumed in the Annex 1 nations, a 'consumption-based' accounting of emissions would leave less of the carbon budget for the Annex 1 nations.

recession or upheaval' (Stern, 2006: 204). Indeed, one of the only examples of deep and prolonged emissions reductions is during the collapse of the Soviet Union, when emissions fell by approximately 5% p.a. for ten years (Anderson, 2012: 25). As the Russian economy stabilised, however, and once more began to grow, emissions again began to rise. All this firmly suggests that decarbonising an economy by 8-10% p.a. is not something that can be achieved while growing the economy in conventional GDP terms.

Admittedly, this is a point that economists, including Stern, assert without a much elaboration. It is certainly a key issue that deserves more critical attention, and obviously *planning* for decarbonisation will involve different dynamics than decarbonisation through collapse or recession. All the same, the implicit reasoning seems relatively strong. Scaling up renewables takes many years, even decades, so does improving efficiency (Smil, 2010; Jackson, 2009). Even the theoretically 'ideal' scenarios for scaling up renewables and efficiency have to be placed in social and political context, where those 'ideal' scenarios will never be fully achieved. Therefore, one can conclude with some confidence that decarbonisation of 8-10% p.a. will never be achieved solely through a 'supply side' transition to renewables and more efficient production, especially in a growing economy. In order to achieve significant *absolute* reductions in emissions of 8-10%, the transition to renewables and more efficient processes must supplemented by planned 'demand side' reductions in energy consumption, and this energy descent requirement is what puts into question the continuation of economic growth (Ayres and Warr, 2009).

4.6 Therefore, the Annex 1 nations must initiate a 'degrowth' strategy.

If the Annex 1 nations must reduce emissions by 8-10% p.a. over coming decades in order to keep within their carbon budget; and, if emissions reductions of more than 3% or 4% are incompatible with economic growth, it follows, as Anderson and Bows conclude, that 'for a reasonable probability of avoiding the 2°C characterisation of dangerous climate change, the wealthier (Annex 1) nations need, temporarily, to adopt a degrowth strategy' (see Anderson, 2013). Although they have not provided much detail on what they mean by 'degrowth', the clear implication is that it means giving up the conventional pursuit of economic growth and deliberately seeking an equitable reduction of energy and resource consumption as necessary to meet their 8%-10% decarbonisation requirements. While this 'radical' conclusion flows logically from the conservative assumptions outlined above, it is a conclusion that contradicts most other large scale decarbonisation proposals, which almost always assume that maintaining a safe climate is consistent with continued economic growth in both developing and the developed nations (see, e.g., Grantham, 2013; SDSN and IDDRI, 2014).

Perhaps the most compelling aspect of the argument put forward by Anderson and Bows is the cautious and moderate way in which the underlying assumptions are framed. Each of the premises could in fact be justifiably more challenging. For example, if the temperature threshold were set at 1.5°C not 2°C; or if the probability of avoiding that threshold were raised to 80% or 90% not 50%; or if less ambitious figures were given for peak emissions and decarbonisation rates for the non-Annex 1 nations; and especially if *all* of those assumptions were not so moderately stated, then the available carbon budget left for the Annex 1 nations would be hugely reduced. This would demand significantly higher decarbonisation rates for Annex 1 nations, perhaps in the vicinity of 15% or 20% p.a. Accordingly, even if critics take issue with specific assumptions (e.g., argue that the temperature threshold should be 2.5°C or that decarbonisation at 6% p.a. is compatible with growth), this would not affect the overall conclusion that keeping to the carbon budget requires degrowth in the Annex 1 nations. Nevertheless, as noted, even some of the most promising climate policy documents of recent times (e.g., SDSN and IDDRI, 2014; Grantham Institute, 2013) steadfastly refuse to accept that an adequate response to climate might require rethinking the growth paradigm.[4]

While critics will doubtless continue to object to degrowth strategies on the basis of a range of other arguments (including both socio-economic outcomes and political efficacy), when the above figures of the carbon budget are taken seriously, the case for some

---

[4] Two other potential responses to the argument that some form of degrowth is necessary to achieve key carbon budget targets are to point to the contribution which 'carbon capture and storage' (CCS) and geo-engineering could make to addressing climate change risks. While a full review of the rapidly expanding literature on both these options is beyond the scope of this paper, I do note the extensive range of serious ethical, governance, and technical questions which have been raised about geo-engineering (see, e.g., Hamilton, 2013). As for CCS, this, indeed, may need to play a role in reducing emissions, but the technology at present is highly undeveloped, especially in the context of a decarbonisation requirement of 8-10% p.a. that must start immediately. Even when, or if, it becomes ready, implementation will take many years, probably decades, so it is not something that affects the necessity for exploring and implementing more immediate decarbonisation strategies.

form of degrowth strategy is extremely strong on scientific grounds. In this sense the onus is on critics of the Anderson and Bows proposition to demonstrate any fundamental flaws in the key assumptions or logic of the argument. In fact, critics really need to respond to the degrowth argument based on more challenging premises and even higher decarbonisation requirements (see Spratt, 2015), given that the argument from Anderson and Bows is really too moderately stated (e.g., the probability of success should be far higher than 50%).

It should be noted also that although this argument for degrowth is based solely on carbon budget analysis, it finds much support in more general 'limits to growth' literature (see generally, Meadows *et al.,* 2004; Rockstrom *et al.,* 2009; Trainer, 2010; Turner, 2012; Hopkins and Miller, 2012; Alexander, 2014a) and, more specifically, the emerging degrowth literature (see Latouche, 2009; Latouche, 2014b; Kallis, 2011; Alexander, 2012a; Victor, 2012). These literatures argue that the developed nations (in particular) must give up the growth paradigm for various ecological and social reasons, of which climate change is only one.

5. Powerdown: Degrowth Strategies for Climate Stability

While Anderson and Bows (2011) have presented a robust case for degrowth based on climate science, the challenge that flows from this is to begin to outline the overall shape of an integrated decarbonisation policy framework consistent with the scale and speed required to stay within the constraints of carbon budget targets, and consistent with democracy, political and social stability, and equity. The following sub-sections aim to contribute to that enormous task, while acknowledging that this preliminary discussion is likely to raise as many questions as it answers.

5.1. *Strengthening public understanding of the full implications of carbon budget analysis*

In order to fully understand the necessary scale and speed of action required to significantly reduce climate change risks, citizens and governments must first understand the full extent and implications of the carbon budget challenge. This includes broadening the recognition that, even if most existing decarbonisation policies and plans were immediately implemented, they would still fail to sufficiently address the core problem (i.e., they would not keep us within the carbon budget). The economic growth implications of carbon budget analysis therefore need to become a central element in informed public debate about climate change solutions and strategies.

5.2. Identify and adopt 'post-growth' macroeconomic indicators as a key step toward the implementation of post-growth economic paradigms and policies

Once the case for degrowth is understood (both in terms of carbon budget analysis and the more general 'limits to growth' critique), it follows that different macroeconomic indicators will be required. Currently, growth in GDP is the most widely used measure of politico-economic success, but for decades scholars (especially ecological economists) have shown that GDP is a fundamentally inadequate measure of genuine progress (see generally, Daly and Cobb, 1989; Daly and Farley, 2004; Lawn, 2005; Stiglitz, Sen, and Fitoussi, 2010; Kubiszewski, et al., 2013). GDP measures the benefits of economic activity in monetary terms, but does not account for most social and ecological costs (it even treats those costs as benefits!). This can lead to 'growth' that is 'uneconomic', in the sense that the overall costs of growth outweigh the benefits (see Daly, 1999). What are needed are macroeconomic indicators such as the Genuine Progress Indicator that better account for the full social and ecological costs of economic activity. This will help explain and communicate why a post-capitalist degrowth, far from being a retrograde strategy, is actually what 'genuine progress' now looks like, at least in the most developed nations of the world. Assessing degrowth policies through the conventional lens of GDP will look absurd, whereas those same policies when seen through more inclusive indicators will look necessary and sensible, while uneconomic growth will look absurd. Although far from being a sufficient public policy innovation, post-growth indicators of progress will be a necessary part of the macroeconomic paradigm shift required.

5.3. Introduce an appropriately robust price on carbon

According to neoclassical economic theory, for a market economy to function in a roughly 'optimal' way, the full costs of productive activity need to be 'internalised' to the productive process, not 'externalised' to society as a whole (see generally, Clarke, 2011). While this is extremely hard to do (providing grounds for doubting purely 'economic' solutions to social or ecological problems), it makes good sense to try to ensure prices accurately reflect full social and ecological costs (including the full, long term costs of climate change and of not staying within the carbon budget). Given that currently the costs of climate change are widely 'externalised', it follows that a part of the response to climate change requires putting an appropriate price on carbon (see generally, Tietenberg, 2013). There are two main ways to do this: either through a Pigouvian 'carbon tax' or through an emissions trading scheme (ETS).[5]

The great advantage of a carbon tax is that it is relatively simple and direct, even if it is also something of a blunt instrument. By taxing emissions, the price of carbon goes up for producers, a cost that is then passed on to consumers, thus incentivising businesses and individuals to reduce carbon consumption and invest in efficiency improvements (see Meltzer, 2014). Furthermore, as noted above, by making fossil energy more expensive, renewable energy sources become more price-competitive, which would encourage fossil energy being replaced with renewable sources. The revenue from taxing 'bads' (fossil energy) can also be used to fund 'goods' (renewable energy, efficiency improvements, or assistance for low-income households).

The alleged advantage of an ETS is that it would achieve the same ends as a carbon tax, but at a reduced socio-economic cost (see generally, Betsill and Hoffmann, 2011). In theory that might be true, but the realities of ETSs have been that they are very complicated to design and operate successfully, creating much room for the schemes being abused. They can also create counter-productive incentives, as reductions in one area of society can be increased elsewhere. While a carbon tax is arguably the better mode of pricing carbon, due to its relative simplicity and directness, the main point for present purposes is that carbon has to be priced appropriately *somehow* if economies are to have price signals that incentivise reduced carbon consumption. Currently, fossil fuels are artificially cheap (due to their costs being externalised), thus leading to their overconsumption and producing a grossly sub-optimal economy. Indeed, climate change is fairly characterised as the global economy's greatest 'market failure'.

While pricing carbon is a necessary part of the preliminary transition to a low-carbon economy, it must not be assumed that it

---

[5] Note that calling the former policy a carbon 'tax' is actually a misuse of the term, since it is really just internalising an externality. We do not, for example, say that a company is being 'taxed' when we expect it to clean up the river it polluted. We will, however, defer to convention and use the term carbon tax to differentiate this form of pricing carbon from an emissions trading scheme.

is a sufficient policy. Both carbon taxes and ETSs are market-based mechanisms that seek to achieve decarbonisation through the incremental effects of prices. But such incremental mechanisms will be insufficient to produce deep and rapid decarbonisation of 8-10% p.a. Pricing carbon must therefore be deemed only one string on the bow of broader decarbonisation and degrowth strategies, initiating a transition that must eventually replace the destructive market forces of capitalism with an economy that exists safely within the biocapacity of the planet. Detailing the nature of that post-capitalist society is a task for another time. Presently, the focus is on some initial, although bold, policy options that can get the transition underway.

5.4. Abolish fossil fuel subsidies and divest from the fossil fuel industry

How we spend our private and public money is akin to voting for what kind of world we want to live in. Accordingly, if we seriously seek a low-carbon economy we must stop 'voting' for a carbon-intensive economy, and this means stopping subsidising and investing in the fossil fuel industry. The IEA (2013b: 1) notes that the 'global cost of fossil-fuel subsidies expanded to $544 billion in 2012 despite efforts at reform', adding that 'financial support to renewable sources of energy totalled $101 billion'. These figures alone show how misguided the existing climate response is. Abolishing subsidies would help 'price' fossil fuels more accurately, meaning that the price of fossil energy would increase. It would also incentivise reduced consumption (through efficiency gains and the substitution effect) and make renewables more price competitive, encouraging an investment switch. As well as abolishing subsidies, individuals, communities, financial institutions, and governments should be encouraged to progressively 'divest' their existing financial support from the fossil fuel industry and refuse to provide financial support, permits, or a 'social license', for new fossil fuel projects and infrastructure.

Promisingly, an international 'divestment' campaign is currently under way, led by 350.org (McKibben 2012) and other activist organisations (see generally, Alexander, Nicholson, and Wiseman, 2014). Notably, the fossil fuel divestment movement is founded, in large part, upon carbon budget analysis. Participants in the movement argue that approximately 80% of fossil fuels must remain in the ground if the world is to keep within the 2°C temperature threshold (similar conclusions have been reached by the IEA) (IEA, 2012a). Since all fossil fuels are currently valued as if they will all be burned, this suggests that there is a vast 'carbon bubble' which is at risk of popping and rendering most fossil fuel resource 'stranded assets' of 'unburnable carbon' (see Carbon Tracker and Grantham Institute, 2013). This provides an additional more self-interested, financial argument for divestment, adding further weight to the already compelling scientific and moral case.[6]

5.5. *Rapidly accelerate a comprehensive switch to renewable energy*

The most important corollary of the moral and financial arguments against subsidising and investing in fossil fuels is to shift that financial support toward renewable energy systems and other low-carbon technologies. Existing subsidies for fossil fuels provide significant funds to get this transformation of energy systems underway. This spending shift could be achieved without finding new investment funds, although significant additional investment funds (both public and private) will need to be reprioritised in order to fully implement the switch to renewable energy (see Wiseman, Edwards, and Luckins, 2013). It is imperative to point out, however, that renewable energy systems are not on their own a climate change silver bullet. While they are, of course, a necessary part – indeed, the foundation – of any transition to a low-carbon economy, it is a mistake to think that the world can just transition to renewable energy systems and otherwise carry on within the same growth-based, industrial paradigm.

First of all, climate change is only one environmental problem among a whole host, so decarbonising the existing economy without otherwise changing its nature would leave other significant ecological problems, such as the profound threats to biodiversity,

---

[6] In an important aside, if the world decided to take climate change seriously, one of the first investment changes necessary would be to stop financing new or existing infrastructure projects aimed at producing unconventional shale oil and the tar sands, as these oils are significantly more carbon-intensive than conventional oil (Hansen and Kharecha, 2008). Nevertheless, stopping production of unconventional oils would mean global liquid fuel production would immediately peak or even be in decline, despite demand growing, which would inevitably mean significantly higher oil prices (which are already at historically high trend levels). The further challenge this would raise, however, is that expensive oil has a suffocating effect on oil-dependent economies, inhibiting growth (see Alexander, 2014b). This is not an argument in support of unconventional oil, of course; it simply provides further grounds for decarbonising our economies and moving toward a post-growth macroeconomic paradigm that is far less dependent on oil.

unresolved (see generally, Turner, 2012). Secondly, when a full lifecycle analysis of solar and wind is undertaken, they often are shown to have far lower energy returns on investment (EROIs) than previously thought (see, e.g., Pietro and Hall, 2013; Palmer, 2013), suggesting that it will be extremely difficult to run a growth-orientated industrial civilisation on renewable energy. Finally, the intermittency of most renewable energy sources means that huge amounts of expensive storage or redundant plant would be required to cover the base loads of a growing, globalised industrial economy (see Trainer, 2013a; Trainer, 2013b; Honnery and Moriarty, 2012).

Even if electricity could be provided by 100% renewable energy (or even nuclear), electricity only constitutes around 18% of global final energy consumption (IEA, 2012b: 28), leaving unresolved (among other things) the problem of replacing liquid fuels for transport and machinery, especially. This is perhaps the largest challenge to decarbonisation. While electric vehicles may go some way to mitigating this problem, the fact that there are currently about one billion fossil fuel-powered vehicles on the road suggests that any transition to an electric fleet is going to be slow, exceedingly expensive, and resource intensive. The solution, I suggest, lies not so much in running a globalised transport system on biofuels or electricity, but in driving less and in other ways reducing oil dependency (e.g., growing food organically and localising production). In short, the challenge of rapid decarbonisation cannot be solved purely from the 'supply side' (i.e., transitioning to renewable energy systems), partly because such a transition will inevitably be slow (requiring a decade or two, at least), even if undertaken with 'war mobilisation' urgency (Smil, 2010; Smil, 2014). More specifically, Annex 1 nations could not decarbonise at 8-10% p.a. purely by transitioning to renewables. In order to transition rapidly to a low-carbon economy, we must decarbonise from the 'demand side' as well, by increasing efficiency and, most importantly, by simply consuming less energy and less energy-intensive products and services. This means that any degrowth transition to a low-carbon economy means adjusting to a prolonged period of planned 'energy descent' and creatively adapting to post-consumerist, moderate-energy lifestyles (Alexander, 2013).

5.6. *Greatly increase efficiency through incentives, subsidies, regulation, and education*

There is enormous scope for significantly decarbonising and dematerialising our economies through efficiency gains (see, e.g.,

Weizsacker *et al.*, 2009). By exploiting the best low-carbon technologies and designs, human beings will be able to lead high quality lives at a fraction of the carbon intensity of lifestyles in developed nations today (see, e.g., Druckman and Jackson, 2010). Efficiency can be promoted through incentives (such as a carbon tax); subsidies (for such things as energy efficient fridges or bicycles); regulation (such as minimum standards for products, especially energy consuming products); and education (showing individuals and businesses the easiest ways to lower their carbon footprints). While some will argue that this process should be left to the market, given the urgency of the challenge, government policies can also play a crucial role in driving efficiency improvements. In China, for example, the government has enforced efficiency improvements in 1000 of its state-owned enterprises, contributing to a 20% improvement in efficiency in the last five years. According to *The Economist* (2013), this is 'arguably the single most important climate policy in the world'.

Once again, however, the risk of promoting efficiency as a stand-alone solution is that people can assume that efficiency will be enough to decarbonise at 8-10%p.a., without requiring deeper changes to the way we live. Efficiency gains will never decarbonise or dematerialise economic activity enough for a global population to be able to live affluent, consumer lifestyles in a growing economy (particularly an economy operating in ways consistent with carbon budget constraints). This means efficiency gains have to be complemented by lifestyle and structural changes that significantly reduce energy and resource demands compared to levels prevalent in 'developed' economies.

5.7. Introduce diminishing resource and energy caps to contain the 'rebound effect'

Although efficiency gains are a necessary part of any transition to a low-carbon economy, there is great risk that all or some of those efficiency gains will be lost to the 'rebound effect' unless measures are taken to contain that phenomenon (Herring and Sorrell, 2009). When efficiency is increased, this can provide more income or productive capacity that can easily be redirected back into energy or resource intensive consumption or production. In fact, as W.S. Jevons (1865) argued long ago, efficiency can actually increase overall resource or energy consumption, by making certain products cheaper and therefore more available or affordable to a wider group of people. In order to contain this well documented phenomenon, diminishing resource and energy caps – or 'impact caps' – should be introduced to ensure that efficiency gains are directed into *reducing* resource and energy consumption, not directed into consuming more stuff with the same amount of (or even increased) resources or energy (Alcott, 2010). In an age of gross ecological overshoot, what are needed are absolute energy/resource reductions (absolute decoupling), not merely decreased energy/resource costs per unit (relative decoupling) (see Jackson, 2009: Ch. 4). This could be achieved either (1) through Pigouvian taxes (such as the carbon tax discussed above), which would make carbon sufficiently expensive that sustainable levels would not be exceeded; or (2) through direct regulation, which would legally prohibit more than a set amount of fossil fuels being produced each year (Alcott, 2010). By capping impact, the rebound effect would be avoided. Whichever approach is taken, it could be introduced over a specific timeframe (say, over 10 years) to allow markets and culture to adjust, although the detailed institutional design of such policies requires careful consideration (Kallis and Martinez-Alier, 2010).

5.8. *Rethink budget spending to facilitate low-carbon infrastructure*

If governments decide to take climate change seriously, this will require a huge investment in low-carbon technologies (especially renewable energy systems), but it will also require huge investment in 'greening' the infrastructure of our carbon-intensive urban centres. This point highlights the fact that our consumption practices do not take place in a vacuum. They take place within structures of constraint, and those structures make some lifestyle options easy or necessary, and other lifestyle options difficult or impossible. Currently many people find themselves 'locked in' to high consumption lifestyles due to the structures within which they live their lives (see Sanne, 2002). To provide one example: it is very difficult to escape a culture of driving if there is poor public transport or no bike lanes. Change the infrastructure, however, and new lifestyles would be more easily embraced. New infrastructure and systems are required to make low-impact lives easier. Given that public funding is far from limitless, this will require a significant revision of conventional spending patterns for most societies. Treating climate change as a 'security threat' and, on that basis, taking a significant portion of military spending is one path to funding low-carbon infrastructure, but deeper revisions may be needed in other places in order to fund these projects. There is no universally applicable method for determining how best to do this, and each national or local government will have to address the question in relation to their unique contexts and financial capacity. But the longer we wait before beginning this task, the harder and more urgent it becomes (see Murphy, 2012).

5.9. *Ensure an equitable pathway to global decarbonisation by resourcing transfer technologies and climate resilience strategies in non-Annex 1 nations*

While the Annex 1 developed economies must take responsibility for the majority of historic emissions it is also the case that future projections show that non-Annex 1 nations are set to become the highest overall emitters in the foreseeable future. What is necessary is that those non-Annex 1 nations are given increased support to create low-carbon economies *now*, rather than have them follow the conventional, industrialised development path which is at real risk of creating infrastructure and cultures that essentially 'lock' societies into decades of high-carbon living. Exactly how to do this, of course, is an extremely complex issue which cannot be addressed here, but one way to assist in this post-industrial development is for the Annex 1 nations to freely share their technological know-how and design methods with the non-Annex 1 nations to help them 'leap frog' an industrial phase of development and move more directly to an economy that meets basic needs for all with low-carbon emissions. This is one way the Annex 1 nations can pay back some of their 'ecological debt' (Simms, 2005) to the non-Annex 1 nations, to be supplemented by direct financial aid. A significant transfer of resources from developed to developing economies to support climate adaptation and resilience initiatives will be essential.

5.10 *Reimagine and reinvent the 'good life' beyond consumer culture*

Reimagining and reinventing the 'good life' lies at the heart of any degrowth transition to a low-carbon economy. High-consumption lifestyles simply cannot be universalised to seven, or nine, or ten billion people, while keeping within a carbon budget (to say nothing of the other limits to growth). Therefore, any sufficient response to climate change and other ecological limits requires a cultural paradigm shift that involves a significant shift away from high-consumption lifestyles toward ways of life informed by principles and practices of material sufficiency.

The 'degrowth' principles of increased frugality, moderation, and sufficiency need not necessarily be seen as principles of hardship or deprivation. A strong socio-psychological case can be made that income has diminishing marginal returns, meaning that income is very important at low levels of income, but once basic material needs have been met, priorities other than income become increasingly important (e.g., social engagement, more meaningful employment, more time for private passions). In fact, the evidence suggests that high consumption societies are widely mis-consuming, in the sense that many people could actually reduce their consumption while also increasing their wellbeing (see Alexander, 2012b; Bilancini and D'Alessandro, 2012). In this context, degrowth can be understood to mean trying to find that 'optimal' material/energy threshold.

In much the same way that carbon budget analysis must be the basis of a pro-active education campaign, so too should support for the goal of 'voluntary simplicity' be built as an attractive alternative to consumer lifestyles. Such a campaign may need to begin at the grassroots level, where a cultural shift is initiated as more individuals and communities provide real-world examples of low consumption, high quality living. This cultural transformation also highlights the point made above: that decarbonisation cannot be achieved simply from the 'supply side' but actually requires people to reduce the consumption of resources and energy from the 'demand side' too. This might mean driving less and cycling more; growing local organic food; putting on woollen clothing rather than always turning on the heater; taking shorter showers; flying less or not at all; making and mending things rather than buying new; and in countless other ways rethinking lifestyles in ways that reduce energy and resource burdens. This is an immensely creative challenge, which finds promising movements already underway based on notions of voluntary simplicity (Alexander, 2009), permaculture (Holmgren, 2002), and Transition Towns (Hopkins, 2008). It is highly likely that these types of social movements will need to expand if the policies outlined above are to find broad social support. Indeed, to the extent that governments refuse to act decisively, it follows that the transition to a low-carbon, post-growth economy will need to be driven 'from below', without much state support (see generally, Trainer, 2010).

It is also necessary to acknowledge, in closing, that the above proposals, bold though they are, would not, in themselves, be enough to produce a just and resilient degrowth economy (Trainer, 2012). The proposals above are focused primarily on the question of decarbonisation, but given how fundamental the transition to a low-carbon economy is, a wide range of broader social, economic, and political changes will also be required. For example, a degrowth economy will require new banking and financial systems that are not so dependent on debt or the expansion of the money supply through interest-bearing loans. Similarly, providing access to cheap and affordable housing, or sufficient job security, in a degrowth economy may require a fundamental restructure of existing property and tax systems (see Alexander, 2011; Kallis *et al.,* 2012). Land use patterns will need to be revised in order to assist with decarbonisation too. This chapter has not attempted to address these or other remaining complex issues, but I note them here as issues deserving of more attention by those who see the transition to a post-growth economic paradigm as a necessary part of any low-carbon transformation. Whether 'degrowth' is the best term to describe this necessary societal transformation remains open to question. But that terminological debate is less important than the fact that this debate is occurring in recognition of the radical implications of carbon budget analysis and the broader limits to growth critique.

6. Conclusion

In order to have a reasonable chance of staying within carbon budget constraints and therefore of avoiding the most extreme global warming scenarios, this chapter has argued that an integrated matrix of decarbonisation initiatives must be implemented that aim to initiate a rapid transition to a degrowth economy. In the Annex 1 nations, this would require a systematic, planned reduction in the consumption of energy and resources. The rapid and deep reductions in emissions required if the Annex 1 nations are to decarbonise at 8-10% over coming decades cannot be achieved merely with a 'supply side' transition to renewable energy, necessary though that transition is. It must also be supplemented by a 'demand side' reduction in carbon-intensive consumption and production. That means creating a fundamentally different kind of economy – one not based on limitless growth – and embracing ways of living far less impactful than high consumption lifestyles.

While I am fully conscious of the challenges involved in building broad public support for this argument, I hope that the analysis presented here can contribute to a more informed public debate about the crucial contribution which the transition to a post-growth economic paradigm will need to make in achieving climate stability and a just and resilient future. After all, as Winston Churchill once noted: 'It is no use saying, "We are doing our best". You have got to succeed in doing what is necessary.'

References

Alcott, B. 2010. 'Impact caps: Why population, affluence, and technology strategies should be abandoned'. *Ecological Economics* 18: 552-560.

Alexander, S. 2009. *Voluntary simplicity: The poetic alternative to consumer culture.* Whanganui: Stead and Daughters.

Alexander, S., 2011. *Property beyond growth: Toward a politics of voluntary simplicity.* Doctoral thesis, Melbourne Law School. Available at: http://papers.ssrn.com/sol3/papers.cfm?abstract_id=1941069 [accessed 10 September 2013].

Alexander, S. 2012a. 'Planned economic contraction: The emerging case for degrowth'. *Environmental Politics* 21(3): 349-368.

Alexander, S. 2012b. 'The optimal material threshold: Toward an economics of sufficiency'. *Real-World Economics Review* 61: 2-21.

Alexander, S. 2013. *Entropia: Life beyond industrial civilisation.* Melbourne: Simplicity Institute.

Alexander, S. 2014a. 'Post-growth economics: A paradigm shift in progress'. Post Carbon Pathways. Working Paper, 2/14, February, 2014. 1-24.

Alexander, S. 2014b. 'The new economics of oil'. MSSI Issues Paper No. 2, March 2014. 1-14.

Alexander, S. Nicholson, K., and Wiseman, J. 2014. 'Divest/Invest: The initial development and significance of the fossil fuel divestment movement'. MSSI Issues Paper, 2014.

Anderson, K. 2012. 'Climate change going beyond dangerous – Brutal numbers and tenuous hope'. *Development Dialogue* 61: 16-40.

Anderson, K. 2013. 'Avoiding dangerous climate change demands de-growth strategies from wealthier nations'. Available at www.kevinanderson.info (accessed 15 July 2014).

Anderson, K. and Bows, A. 2008a. 'Reframing the climate change challenge in light of post-2000 emissions trends'. *Philosophical Transactions of the Royal Society* 366: 3863-3882.

Anderson, K. and Bows, A. 2008b. 'Contraction and convergence: An assessment of the *COOptions* model'. *Climatic Change* 91: 275-290.

Anderson, K. and Bows, A. 2011. 'Beyond "dangerous" climate change: Emission scenarios for a new world'. *Philosophical Transitions of the Royal Society* 369: 2-44.

Anderson, K. and Bows, A. 2012. 'A new paradigm for climate change'. *Nature Climate Change* 2: 639-640.

Ayres, R. and Warr, B. 2009. *The economic growth engine: How energy and work drive material prosperity.* Cheltenham: Edward Elgar Publishing.

Betsill, M. and Hoffman, M. 2011. 'The contours of "cap and trade": The evolution of emissions trading systems for greenhouse gases'. *Review of Policy Research* 28(1): 83-106.

Bilancini, E. and D'Alessandro, S. 2012. 'Long-run welfare under externalities in consumption, leisure, and production: A case for happy degrowth vs. unhappy growth'. *Ecological Economics* 84: 194-205.

Carbon Tracker Initiative and Grantham Research Institute, 2013. 'Unburnable carbon 2013: Wasted capital and stranded assets'. Available at: http://carbontracker.live.kiln.it/Unburnable-Carbon-2-Web-Version.pdf (accessed 15 July 2014).

Christoff, P. (ed.). 2013. *Four degrees of global warming.* London: Taylor and Francis.

Clarke, H. 2011. 'Some basic economics of carbon taxes'. *Australian Economic Review* 44(2) 123-36.

Cobb, J. and Daly, H. 1989. *For the common good: Redirecting the economy toward community, the environment, and a sustainable future.* Boston: Beacon Press.

Committee on Climate Change. 2013. 'The Fourth Carbon Budget Review – Part 1'. Available at: http://www.theccc.org.uk/publication/fourth-carbon-budget-review-part-1/ (accessed 15 July 2013).

Daly, H., 1999. 'Uneconomic growth in theory and fact'. In *The First Annual Feasta Lecture.* 16 April, 1999. Available at: http://www.feasta.org/documents/feastareview/daly.htm (accessed 10 April 2010).

Daly, H. and Farley, J. 2004. *Ecological Economics: Principles and Applications.* Washington: Island Press.

Diffenbaugh, N. 2013. 'Human well-being, the global emissions debt, and climate change commitment'. *Sustainability Science* 8: 135-141.

Department of Energy and Climate Change (DECC). 2009. 'UK Low Carbon Emissions Plan'. Available at: https://www.gov.uk/government/uploads/system/uploads/attachment_data/file/228752/9780108508394.pdf (accessed 1 July 2014).

Druckman, A. and Jackson, T. 2010. 'The bare necessities: How much household carbon do we really need?' *Ecological Economics* 69: 1794-1804.

Economist, The. 'The East is grey'. *The Economist.* 10 August 2013.

European Commission. 2007. *Limiting global climate change to 2 degrees Celsius: The way ahead for 2020 and beyond.* Brussels, Belgium.

Gardiner, S. 2011. *The perfect moral storm: The ethical tragedy of climate change*. Oxford: Oxford University Press.

Grantham Institute for Climate Change. 2013. 'Halving global CO2 by 2050: Technologies and costs'. Available at: http://www3.imperial.ac.uk/climatechange/publications/collaborative/halving-global-co2-by-2050 (accessed 10 October 2013).

Hansen, J. and Kharecha, P. 2008. 'The implications of "peak oil" for atmospheric CO2 and climate'. *Global Biochemical Cycles* 22: GB3012, 1-10.

Hamilton, C. 2013. *Earthmasters: The dawn of the age of climate engineering*. New Haven: Yale University Press.

Herring, H. and Sorrell, S. 2009. *Energy efficiency and sustainable consumption: The rebound effect*. London: Palgrave Macmillan.

Holmgren, D. 2002. *Permaculture: Principles and Pathways beyond Sustainability*. Hepburn: Holmgren Design Services.

Hopkins, R. 2008. *The transition handbook: From oil dependency to local resilience*. Totnes, Devon: Green Books.

Hopkins, R. and Miller, A. 2012. 'Climate after growth: Why environmentalists must embrace post-growth economics and community resilience'. *Post-Carbon Institute Report* 1-28.

Honnery, D. and Moriarty, P. 2012. 'What is the global potential for renewable energy'. *Renewable and Sustainable Energy Reviews* 16: 244-252.

Hunt, C. 2013 'Illustrated implications of the terrifying new math of Meinshausen and McKibben'. *Economic Analysis and Policy* 43(3): 235-246.

Intergovernmental Panel on Climate Change (IPCC). 2013. 'Climate Change 2013: The physical science basis (Fifth Assessment Report). Available at: http://www.ipcc.ch/report/ar5/wg1/ (accessed 1 August 2014).

Intergovernmental Panel on Climate Change (IPCC). 2014. 'Climate Change 2014: Impacts, adaptations, and vulnerability (Fifth Assessment Report). Available at: http://www.ipcc.ch/report/ar5/wg2/ (accessed 1 August 2014).

International Energy Agency (IEA). 2012a. *World Energy Outlook 2012 (Executive Summary)*. Available at: http://www.worldenergyoutlook.org/publications/weo-2012/ (accessed 1 July 2014).

International Energy Agency (IEA) 2012b. *Key World Energy Statistics 2012*. Available at: http://www.iea.org/publications/freepublications/publication/kwes.pdf (accessed 1 July 2014).

International Energy Agency (IEA) 2013a. *World Energy Outlook 2013*. Available at: http://www.iea.org/Textbase/npsum/WEO2013SUM.pdf (accessed 25 November 2013).

International Energy Agency (IEA) 2013b. *World Energy Outlook 2013 Factsheet.* Available at: http://www.iea.org/media/files/WEO2013_factsheets.pdf (accessed 1 July 2014).

Jackson, T. 2009. *Prosperity without growth: Economics for a finite planet.* London: Earthscan.

Jevons, W.S. 1865. *The coal question: An inquiry concerning the progress of the nation and the probable exhaustion of our coal-mines.* MacMillan: London.

Jordan, A., Rayner, T., and Schroeder, H. *et al.* 2013. 'Going beyond two degrees? The risks and opportunities of alternative options'. *Climate Policy* 13(6): 751-769.

Kallis, G. 2011. 'In Defence of Degrowth'. *Ecological Economics* 70: 873-80.

Kallis, G. and Martinez-Alier, J. 2010. 'Caps yes, but how? A response to Alcott'. *Journal of Cleaner Production* 18: 1570-1573.

Kallis, G., Kerschner, C., Martinez-Alier, J. 2012. 'The economics of degrowth'. *Ecological Economics* 84: 172-180.

Kanitkar, T., Jayaraman, T., D'Souza, M., and Purkayastha, P. 'Carbon budgets for climate change mitigation – a GAMS-based emissions model'. *Current Science* 104(9): 1200-1206.

Klein, N. 2013. 'Science says: Revolt!'. *New Statesman.* October 2013: 35-37.

Kubiszewski, I. *et al.* 2013. 'Beyond GDP: Measuring and achieving global genuine progress'. *Ecological Economics* 93: 57-68.

Latouche, S. 2009. *Farewell to Growth.* Cambridge: Polity Press.

Latouche, S. 2010. 'Degrowth' *Journal of Cleaner Production* 18: 519-522.

Latouche, S. 2014a. 'Degrowth'. In Alexander, S. and McLeod, A. 2014. *Simple living in history: Pioneers of the deep future.* Melbourne: Simplicity Institute.

Latouche, S. 2014b. 'Essays on frugal abundance: Degrowth – misinterpretations and controversies'. *Simplicity Institute Reports* 14c, 14d, 14e and 14f.

Lawn, P. 2006. *Sustainable development indicators in ecological economics.* Cheltenham: Edward Elgar Publishing.

Lenton, T.M. *et al.* 2008. 'Tipping elements in the Earth's climate system'. *Proceedings of the National Academy of Sciences of the United States of America* 105(6): 1786-1793.

Le Quere, C., Peters, G.P., Andres, R.J. *et al.* 2013. 'Global carbon budget 2013'. *Earth Systems Science Data* 6: 689-670.

Macintosh, A. 2010. 'Keeping warming within the 2C limit after Copenhagen'. *Energy Policy* 38: 2964-2975.

Mann, M. E. 2009. 'Defining dangerous anthropogenic interference'. *Proceedings of the National Academy of Science USA* 106: 4065-4066.

McKibben, B. 2012. 'Global warming's terrifying new math'. *Rolling Stone.* 19 July, 2012.

Meadows, D., Randers, J., and Meadows, D. 2004. *Limits to growth: The 30-year update.* White River Junction, Vt: Chelsea Green Publishing.

Meinshausen, M. *et al.* 2009. 'Greenhouse-gas emission targets for limiting global warming to 2-degrees'. *Nature* 458: 1158-1162.

Meltzer, J. 2014. 'A carbon tax as a driver of green technology innovation and the implications for international trade'. *Energy Law Journal* 35: 45-69.

Messner, D., Schellnhuber, J., Rahmstorf, S., and Klingenfeld, D. 'The budget approach: A framework for a global transformation toward a low-carbon economy'. *Journal of Renewable and Sustainable Energy* 2: 1-14.

Murphy, T. 2011. 'The Energy Trap', available at 'Do the math': http://physics.ucsd.edu/do-the-math/2011/10/the-energy-trap/ (accessed 1 July 2014)

Odum, H. and Odum, E. 2001. *A prosperous way down: Principles and policies.* Colorado: University of Colorado Press.

Palmer, G. 2013. 'Household solar voltaics: Supplier of marginal abatement, or primary source of low-emissions power?' *Sustainability* 5(4): 1406-1442.

Pearce, J. 2008. 'Thermodynamic limitations to nuclear energy deployment as a greehouse gas mitigation technology'. *International Journal of Nuclear Governance, Economy, and Ecology* 2(1): 113.

Potsdam Institute, 2012. *Turn down the heat: Why a 4° warmer world must be avoided.* Published by the World Bank, available at: http://documents.worldbank.org/curated/en/2012/11/17097815/turn-down-heat-4%C2%B0c-warmer-world-must-avoided (accessed 15 July 2014).

Prieto, P. and Hall, C. 2013. *Spain's photovoltaic revolution: The energy return on investment.* New York: Springer.

Rezai, A., Taylor, L., Mechler, R. 2013. 'Ecological macroeconomics: An application to climate change'. *Ecological Economics* 85: 69-76.

Rockstrom, J. *et al.* 2009. 'A safe operating space for humanity'. *Nature* 461: 471-475.

Sanne, C. 2002. 'Willing consumers – or locked in? Polices for a sustainable consumption'. *Ecological Economics* 42: 273.

Schneider, F., Kallis, G., and Martinez-Alier, J. 2010. 'Crisis or opportunity? Economic degrowth for social equity and ecological sustainability'. *Journal of Cleaner Production* 18(6) 511-18.

Simms, A. 2005. *Ecological debt: The health of the planet and the wealth of nations.* London: Pluto.

Smil, V. 2010. *Energy transitions: History, requirements, prospects.* Westport: Praeger.

Smil, V. 2014. 'The long, slow rise of solar and wind'. *Scientific American 310:* 52-57.

Smith, J.B. *et al.* 2009. 'Assessing dangerous climate change through an update of the Intergovernmental Panel on Climate Change (IPCC) "reasons for concern"'. *Proceedings of the National Academy of Science USA* 106: 4133-4137.

Spratt, D. 2014a. 'The real budgetary emergency and the myth of "burnable carbon"'. *Climate Code Red*, published 22 May 2014. Available at: http://www.climatecodered.org/2014/05/the-real-budgetary-emergency-burnable.html (accessed 28 July 2014)

Spratt, D. 2014b. 'Carbon budgets, climate sensitivity, and the myth of burnable carbon'. *Climate Code Red*, published 8 June 2014. Available at: http://www.climatecodered.org/2014/06/carbon-budgets-climate-sensitivity-and.html (accessed 28 July 2014).

Spratt, D. 2015. 'Recount: It's time to "do the math" again'. *Breakthrough Discussion Series Report.* April 2015. Available at: http://media.wix.com/ugd/148cb0_bb2e61584dbb403e8e33fd65b1c48e30.pdf (accessed 10 May 2015).

Steffen, W. and Huges, L. 2013. 'The Critical Decade 2013: Climate change science, risks, and responses'. *Climate Commission* available at: http://www.climatecouncil.org.au/uploads/b7e53b20a7d6573e1ab269d36bb9b07c.pdf (accessed 15 July 2013).

Stern, N. 2006. *Stern review on the economics of climate change.* Her Majesty's Treasury. Cambridge: Cambridge University Press.

Stiglitz, J., Sen, A., and Fitoussi, J.P. 2010. *Mis-measuring our lives: Why GDP doesn't add up.* New York: The New Press.

Sustainable Development Solutions Network (SDSN) and Institute for Sustainable Development and International Relations (IDDRI). 2014. 'Pathways to deep decarbonisation: interim 2014 report'. Published by the SDSN and IDDRI. July 2014.

Tietenberg, T. 2013. 'Reflections – carbon pricing in practice'. *Review of Environmental Economics and Policy* 7(2): 313-329.

Trainer, T. 2010. *Transition to a sustainable and just world.* Sydney: Envirobook.

Trainer, T. 2012. 'Degrowth – do you realise what it means?' *Futures* 44: 590-599.

Trainer, T. 2013a. 'Can Europe run on renewable energy? A Negative Case'. *Energy Policy* 63: 845-850.

Trainer, T. 2013b. 'Can the world run on renewable energy'. *Humanomics* 29(2): 88-104.

Turner, G. 2012. 'Are we on the cusp of collapse? Updated comparison of the *Limits to growth* with historical data'. *Gaia* 21(2): 116-124.

UNFCCC, 2010. *Report of the conference of the parties on its fifteenth session, held in Copenhagen from 7-19 December 2009.* Available at: http://unfccc.int/resource/docs/2009/cop15/eng/11a01.pdf (accessed 1 July 2014).

UNFCCC, 2011. *The Cancun Agreements.* Available at: http://unfccc.int/resource/docs/2010/cop16/eng/07a01.pdf#page=2 (accessed 1 July, 2014).

Victor, P. 2012. 'Growth, degrowth, and climate change: A scenario analysis'. *Ecological Economics* 84: 206-212.

Weizsacker, E.U. von, Hargroves, C., Smith, M.H., Desha, C., and Stasinopoulos, P. 2009. *Factor five: Transforming the global economy through 80% improvements in resource productivity.* London: Routledge.

Wiseman, J., Edwards, T., and Luckins, K. 2013. *Post carbon pathways: Toward a just and resilience post carbon future.* CDP Discussion Paper, April 2013. Available at: http://www.postcarbonpathways.net.au/wp-content/uploads/2013/05/Post-Carbon-Pathways-Report-2013 Final-V.pdf (accessed 1 July 2014).

8

VOLUNTARY SIMPLICITY AND THE SOCIAL RECONSTRUCTION OF LAW
Degrowth from the grassroots up

The inner crisis of our civilisation must be resolved if the outer crisis is to be effectively met.
– Lewis Mumford

1. Introduction

Degrowth scholars and other growth sceptics have done a considerable amount of important work exposing the many defects inherent to the dominant macroeconomics of growth (Kallis, 2011; Latouche 2009; Jackson 2009; Victor 2008; Daly 1996). In recent years a growing body of literature has also emerged exploring what structural changes could be undertaken to facilitate the emergence of a degrowth or steady state economy (Alexander 2011a, Jackson 2009; Hamilton 2003). Very little has been written, however, on what role social or cultural evolution may need to play in providing the necessary *preconditions* for such structural change. The neglect of this issue is problematic for two main reasons. First, it seems highly unlikely that a degrowth or steady state economy will ever arise voluntarily within cultures generally comprised of individuals seeking ever-higher levels of income and consumption (Hamilton and Denniss, 2005). Accordingly, before growth economics can be overcome, this significant cultural obstacle must be acknowledged, confronted, and somehow transcended. Secondly, even if notions of degrowth or steady state economics were to gain widespread acceptance within a culture, it seems highly unlikely that a degrowth or steady state economy would arise voluntarily unless people had some idea of what needed to be done at the personal and community levels to bring about such an economy (Trainer, 2010; Hopkins, 2008). In other words, it is not enough merely to offer a critique of existing *structures* of growth; it is equally important to explore the question of *how one ought to live* in opposition to those structures. This chapter engages some aspects of these complex issues by looking into what role social movements may have to play in creating the preconditions needed for a degrowth or steady state economy to materialise. More specifically, this chapter examines the potential of the Voluntary Simplicity Movement to socially reconstruct law to that end.

1.1. *The Voluntary Simplicity Movement in geographical and theoretical context*

The Voluntary Simplicity Movement (hereafter, the Simplicity Movement) can be understood broadly as a diverse social movement made up of people who are resisting high consumption lifestyles and who are seeking, in various ways, a lower consumption but higher quality of life alternative (Alexander, 2011b; Grigsby, 2004). Participants in this movement generally seek to 'downshift' the level and impacts of their material consumption, while at the same time aiming to create for themselves an alternative conception of 'the good life' in opposition to the Western-style consumerist ideal. This living strategy typically involves transferring progressively more of one's time and energy away from materialistic sources of satisfaction (e.g., money, assets, possessions, etc.) toward non-materialistic or post-consumerist sources of satisfaction (e.g., social relations, community engagement, creative activity, home-based production, self-development, spiritual exploration, relaxation, etc.). Because this lifestyle implies the privilege of choosing one's standard of living, the Simplicity Movement arises, by and large, within the affluent Western nations where such a choice is most widely available, and those are the broad geographic locations toward which the analysis in this chapter is directed.

While the practice and values of voluntary simplicity take many forms, and are always context-dependent and evolving, prominent simplicity theorist David Shi (2007: 3), has suggested that some of the primary attributes of the Simplicity Movement include: thoughtful frugality; minimising expenditure on consumer goods and services; a reverence and respect for nature (and its limits); a desire for self-sufficiency; a commitment to conscientious rather than conspicuous consumption; a privileging of creativity and contemplation over possessions; an aesthetic preference for minimalism and functionality; and a sense of responsibility for the just uses of the world's resources. More concisely, Shi defines voluntary simplicity as 'enlightened material restraint' (2007: 131). Variously defended by its advocates and practitioners on personal, communitarian, humanitarian, and ecological grounds, the Simplicity Movement seems to be predicated on the assumption that human beings can live meaningful, free, happy, and infinitely diverse lives, while consuming no more than an equitable share of nature (Alexander, 2009).

It is difficult to establish precisely the size of this movement, however the largest empirical study in this area (Alexander and Ussher, 2012) has presented a case that as many as 200 million people in the developed world could be embracing lifestyles of voluntary simplicity. This study does acknowledge, however, that there will be a wide diversity of lifestyles within this large group, with some participants taking relatively minor steps to downshift and others taking more radical steps. Nevertheless, if these people are connected by their attempt to reduce or restrain their consumption – and if they also *feel* connected – then together they are a social movement of considerable collective power and political import, potentially, at least (see also, Holmgren, 2013).

The central argument of this chapter is that the Simplicity Movement (or something like it) will almost certainly need to expand, organise, radicalise, and politicise, if anything resembling a degrowth or steady state economy is to emerge in law through democratic processes. That is the 'grassroots' or bottom-up theory of structural transformation that will be expounded and defended in this chapter. The essential reasoning here is that legal, political, and economic structures will never reflect a post-growth ethics of macroeconomic sufficiency until a post-consumerist ethics of microeconomic sufficiency is embraced and mainstreamed at the cultural level. Conversely, a microeconomics of 'more' will always generate, or try to generate, a macroeconomics of 'growth'.

Law was chosen as the site of engagement for this chapter, not because it is the only place where a 'politics of simplicity' could emerge, but because it is a site of particular importance. Our consumption decisions do not take place in a vacuum. Rather, they take place within *structures of constraint*, and those structures make some lifestyle decisions easy and others difficult or impossible. To provide but two examples: it is very difficult to escape car culture in the absence of good public transport or safe bike lanes; and it is very difficult to 'vote with your dollar' in the absence of laws that require adequate product labelling. The point is that if we were to change the structures, different lifestyle options would emerge, and legal change is obviously one very powerful means of changing social, political, and economic structures.

Politicising voluntary simplicity through legal change, however, might strike some as paradoxical, in the sense that anything mandated by law does not sound very 'voluntary'. The argument being presented, however, is not that simplicity of living should be *imposed* on people, but that simplicity, rather than consumerism, should be systematically privileged, supported, and encouraged when making decisions about how to structure society (see also, Alexander, 2011b).

The background theoretical framework within which this chapter is situated is that of 'social constructionism', a position, or variety of positions, which holds that the meaning of concepts, including legal concepts, is the product of evolving social practices and values rather than a reflection of an unchanging, objective reality (Wittgenstein, 1953; Berger and Luckman, 1966; Barnet, 1993). While there are highly abstract philosophical issues surrounding social constructionism (Fish, 1989; Rorty, 1979), the analysis of this chapter begins by questioning how and why, as a practical matter, socially constructed legal concepts acquire meaning, and how and why those meanings change. In examining these issues the analysis looks to the emerging scholarship surrounding law and social movements (McCann, 2006a). In various ways this socio-legal literature explores how social movements in any given society have impacted or could impact on the legal system to bring about structural change. Drawing on that literature and developing it, the preliminary argument of this chapter is that law can be understood, to a large extent, as a reflection of social values and assumptions, such that social or cultural evolution tends to induce legal evolution. (I will use the terms 'social' and 'cultural' interchangeably in this chapter to refer broadly to the aggregation of personal values, behaviours, and relationships in a society.) In more theoretical terms, the basic argument is that if legal concepts are 'social constructs', then social movements can be understood as a mechanism through which legal concepts are socially constructed and reconstructed. As critical jurist Roberto Unger (2001) has argued, any transformative politics of law needs to be complemented, if it is to succeed, by a cultural revolution in personal and social relations. This conclusion, so far as it is true, suggests that legal, political, and economic reformers – including, or especially, radical reformers – should carefully consider not only what cultural conditions would best facilitate the realisation of their transformative programmes, but also what role social or cultural movements might have to play in producing those conditions (see Alexander, 2014).

Before beginning the substantive analysis, there are two terminological issues that require clarification in order for this chapter to be correctly understood. The first concerns the term 'reform', which I use to refer to deep structural change, not merely 'tinkering' with the existing system. That is, I am interested in exploring how the Simplicity Movement could radically reshape the structures of a growth-orientated, consumer society, not merely soften the edges. The second terminological issue concerns the word 'law', which I ask readers to interpret broadly. While my primary focus in this chapter is on the conventional understanding of 'law' as referring to rules produced by the judicial, legislative, or executive branches of government, I feel much of the analysis could also apply to social rules and customs more generally, as they also have a structuring role in how we live. So even an anarchist, for example, who rejects the strategy of seeking 'top down' transformations facilitated by the state, can still read this analysis as arguing that the restructuring of society by local, self-governing communities will still depend on a culture that wants such restructuring. In other words, even the 'laws' or 'social rules' of a self-governing anarchist community will inevitably be shaped by its culture, and that relationship between culture and structure is the central theme of this chapter.

2. Law and Social Movements

'This abstraction called Law,' Justice Oliver Wendell Holmes, Jr. once observed, 'is a magic mirror, [wherein] we see reflected, not only our own lives, but the lives of all men that have been!' (Holmes, 1891: 17.) Building upon this insight, celebrated legal historian, Kermit Hall, developed a conception of law as a 'magic mirror', that is, as a reflection of culture that offers historians an opportunity to explore the social choices and moral imperatives of previous generations (Hall, 2009). Consistent with social constructionist theory, though without being framed in such terms, Hall (2009: 2) argued that law 'is indeed a cultural artefact, a moral deposit of society. Because its life stretches beyond that of a single individual, its meaning reaches the values of society'. Although Hall correctly acknowledged that law both affects and is affected by the social order – indeed, that law can both change and reinforce the social order – his theory of law is characterised predominately by how it describes 'the rapidity with which changes in the general culture penetrated the legal system' (Hall, 2009: 341). Meticulously researched and robustly argued, Hall's primary conclusion is that a legal system 'is more like a river than a rock, more the product of social and cultural change than the molder of social development'

(2009: 383). This chapter builds upon Hall's thesis that law is more the product of social and cultural change than the reverse.

It should be acknowledged from the outset, however, that 'law reflects culture' is a contestable and, in many ways, overly simplistic proposition, especially when stated so bluntly. Law, rather than being shaped by culture in a unidirectional way, sometimes takes the *lead* in social development and is influenced by forces *other* than cultural values (Sarat, 2004). Nevertheless, for reasons to be explained, lawmakers (whether judges or politicians) have little option but to respond to significant changes in cultural values, and on that basis it will be argued that cultural forces (including social movements), while not the exclusive source of law, are indeed one of its primary sources (Rosen, 2006). This is especially so in democratic societies where, in ways elaborated on below, political parties have a powerful incentive to follow shifts in culture so as not to alienate the voting citizenry upon whose support their power and legitimacy depends.

Hall's conception of law and legal history is of interest not so much for its historical component but for what it implies about law today and in the future. If Hall is correct that the substance and structure of legal systems have changed over time, 'reflecting the values and assumptions of past generations' (2009: 379), it would seem to follow that the future of law depends upon the values and assumptions of present and future generations. Within this framework, today's growth-based economies can be understood as a reflection of the dominant values and assumptions of today's consumerist culture (Schor, 2000). That is, if most individuals in advanced capitalist societies want 'more' then, naturally, those legal systems will tend to be structured to 'grow' (Alexander, 2011a). Hall's theory implies, however, that if those cultural values and assumptions were to change, this would likely induce changes to law. Put otherwise, the idea is that changes in cultural values will tend to precipitate the emergence of new laws and the application of existing laws in new ways to new contexts. This is because social movements are part of what creates social meaning, and socially constructed understandings of the world inevitably become reflected in the technical construction and application of law's commands (Torres, 2009).

This close relationship between law and culture is why I maintain that the Simplicity Movement will need to enter the cultural mainstream and radicalise to some significant extent if there is to be any hope of a degrowth or steady state economy being realised (or reflected) in law. In other words, the legal structure of a 'macroeconomics of sufficiency' depends for its realisation upon the cultural embrace of a 'microeconomics of sufficiency.' Accordingly, I put forward the Simplicity Movement as a social movement of fundamental importance to the related projects of degrowth and steady state economics. For reasons to be canvassed below, however, the Simplicity Movement does not fit neatly into the existing literature on law and social movements and, therefore, in many ways it needs to be considered in its own light.

2.1. What is a social movement? Sketching the boundaries of an idea

Before going any further it is worth clarifying the term 'social movement', which scholars have defined in various, often overlapping, ways. An exact definition is not necessary for present purposes, but some clarification is needed for the discussion to proceed. Sidney Tarrow's oft-cited definition holds that social movements are 'groups possessing a purposive organisation, whose leaders identify their goals with the preferences of an unmobilised constituency which they attempt to mobilise in direct action in relation to a target of influence in the political system' (Tarrow, 1983: 7). Charles Tilly, a political scientist, adds to this understanding, proposing that a social movement is a sustained series of interactions between power-holders and persons speaking on behalf of a constituency that lacks formal representation, 'in the course of which those persons make publicly visible demands for changes in the distribution or exercise of power, and back those demands with public demonstrations of support' (Tilly, 1984: 306). More recently, another helpful definition has been provided by socio-legal theorist Cary Coglianese (2001: 85), who writes:

> A social movement is a broad set of sustained organizational efforts to change the structure of society or the distribution of society's resources. Within social movements, law reformers typically view law as a resource or strategy to achieve desired social change. Since social change is the purpose of a social movement, law reform generally is taken to provide a means of realizing that goal.

Finally, for present purposes, there is the further clarification provided by Michael McCann, who states that 'social movements aim for a broader scope of social and political transformation than do more conventional political activities. While social movements may press for tangible, short-term goals within the existing structure of relations, they are animated by more radical aspirational visions of a different, better society' (McCann, 2006a: xiv). McCann (1998) also claims that social movements tend to develop through four broad phases, namely: (1) initial group identity formation, consciousness raising, and movement organising; (2) early battles to win recognition by dominant groups or to get on the public agenda; (3) struggles of policy development and implementation; (4) eventual movement decline, trans-formation, 'hibernation', or rebirth.

It is suggested that the development of the Simplicity Movement is at most in transition between phases (1) and (2), although the extensive multi-national study noted above has shown that there are signs of a heightened political sensibility and 'group consciousness' developing within the movement (Alexander and Ussher, 2012). This development could prove to be self-propelling and draw more people into its current, as most people seem to place considerable importance on being socially accepted, as being 'normal' and 'part of the group', rather than being seen as 'abnormal', 'radical', or 'pathological.' If the Simplicity Movement continues to expand, therefore, more people will come to see that voluntary simplicity lifestyles are increasingly an accepted lifestyle within the mainstream. Consequently, any prejudice that the Simplicity Movement is 'just for hippies' should fade, as would the very distinction between this counter-culture and mainstream culture.

2.2. Social movements and the mobilisation of law

Social movements often employ a wide range of tactics to advance their causes, including public education, media campaigns, and social networking, as well as disruptive 'symbolic' tactics which are intended to halt or upset social practices, such as protests, marches, strikes, and the like (McCann, 2006a: xiv). As the definitions above outlined, however, more developed social movements generally seek to make an impact not only in the social sphere but also a structural impact in the political and legal spheres, and such structural impact depends in a large part on being able to mobilise law for the movement's causes. This is not always (or ever) a unidirectional process, however, but a dialectical one, in the sense that social movements affect law while law can also affect social movements. On this point Susan Coutin has argued that social movements 'shape (or attempt to shape) the path of law, even as such pathmaking can redefine social reality in ways that, in turn, redefine causes and reshape activism' (Coutin, 2001: 101).

It is also important to recognise that law and legal institutions can cut both ways, serving as resources both to challenge the existing order and to fortify the status quo against challenges

(McCann, 2006a: xx). Law has long been recognised as having a legitimising or mystifying effect on the existing order (Marx, 1983; Balkin, 2008), colouring it at times with what Roberto Unger (2001) aptly terms 'false necessity'. Just as clearly, though, legal history is replete with examples of social movements having successfully used law as a tool to generate genuinely revolutionary reform – at times, even, over a relatively short timeframe. Joel Handler, in his pioneering text *Social Movements and the Legal System: A Theory of Law Reform and Social Change*, discusses the social movements associated with environmentalism, consumer protection, civil rights, and social welfare (Handler, 1978). All these areas featured social movements that included, as a central aspect of their programme, the creation of new laws or the reform of existing ones. The US Civil Rights Movement, in particular, provides one of the clearest and most striking case studies on this subject, since it had both judicial effects (e.g., *Brown v Board of Education*) and legislative effects (e.g., Civil Rights Act 1964) of arguably unprecedented proportions. It is all the more striking since the massive legal restructuring generated by this particular social movement was ignited by seemingly inconsequential acts in the social sphere, such as when Rosa Parks refused to give up her seat on the bus.[1]

Participants in social movements are correct to perceive the judicial process as one of the main mechanisms for legal reform. As Justice Sackville of the Australian Federal Court puts it, 'Courts, like all institutions of government, have no option but to respond to social change.... Changes in community values... quickly permeate legal doctrine' (Sackville, 2005: 375). Indirectly, social movements can affect how judges decide cases simply through the fact that social movements are a part of what constitutes and shapes culture, and judges themselves are inevitably shaped and influenced by the culture in which they adjudicate. Put otherwise, even if law is not directly mobilised by a social movement, arguments that may have been persuasive in court in the past (e.g., arguments based on race, gender, or sexual orientation, etc.) may not be so persuasive today as a result of social movements impacting on culture, including legal

---

[1] Of course, one must be wary of exaggerating the significance of the role Rosa Parks, as an individual, played in the Civil Rights Movement; but the point remains that it was an act of opposition in the social sphere – an example of innumerable acts, really – that helped spark the Civil Rights revolution in legal relations. It is also worth acknowledging the role that cases such as *Brown* played as a catalyst for social changes which, in turn, led to further legal changes.

culture. In this way, as Edwin Rubin argues, 'the social sphere is... an important source of law' (Rubin, 2001: 11).

In a more direct fashion, however, social movements can influence law and the judicial process by proactively initiating legal proceedings themselves and forcing the judiciary to reconsider or take a stand on issues that may otherwise have been left sleeping. As Justice Sackville, again, notes, 'social change generates new legal issues requiring resolution by the courts' (Sackville, 2005: 375). This more direct mode of influence has been the primary interest of current literature on law and social movements, which has focused on the role activist attorneys or 'cause lawyers' play in furthering the interests of social movements (Sarat and Scheingold, 2006). Since law is notoriously comprised of indeterminate concepts and often contradictory principles (Singer, 1988), cause lawyers acting in the name of social movements can initiate judicial proceedings to challenge existing interpretations of legal principles or concepts in order to redefine entitlements and formulate new aspirations for collective living. Although this approach has very real limitations and constraints, it is a matter of historical fact that 'law can serve as a useful site for articulating and advancing alternative visions of the good' (Sarat and Scheingold, 2006: 9).

As well as mobilising the judicial process, social movements can also seek to mobilise the legislative process to advance their alternative visions of the good (Hutton and Connors, 1999; Dalton, 1994). The reasoning here, as outlined by Kristian Ekeli, is quite simple: 'Political parties will in many cases have a strong incentive not to take a position that deviates too much from the preferences of their voters, in order not to be punished during the elections' (Ekeli, 2005: 431). It follows that if those social preferences change and/or their advocates become more vocal and influential, the prospect of mobilising the legislature increases, since politicians will have an incentive to reconsider the priorities of their constituencies and act accordingly, or else risk losing office. In this way, as other scholars have correctly noted, '[t]he law's power depends on the values, beliefs, and behaviour of individuals' (Marshall and Barkley, 2003: 622). Since social movements are made up of innumerable, seemingly insignificant acts of individuals, those individual acts can be understood to socially construct law on account of their cumulative politico-juridical influence. This expands conventional ideas about where the authoritative commands we call 'law' originate (Torres, 2009). What this expanded perspective suggests is that social movements and other cultural forces play a larger role in the construction of law than is acknowledged by those who conceive of law merely as a politico-juridical construction promulgated from 'the top down'. To understand the process of radical law reform, therefore – and to be able to develop effective strategies for law reform – attention must be paid to the influential (but often unnoticed) forces that shape law from the bottom up.

While no socio-legal theorists suggest that social movements are the *only* forces that shape law, those cited above are surely correct to insist that their powerful influence and impact cannot be denied. What Rubin, Hall, Coglianese, and other theorists argue is that 'changes in society's values and public opinion can feed back into the legal system and affect the prospects for law reform and enhance the effective implementation of legislation' (Coglianese, 2001: 86). Not only that, 'law reform efforts themselves may have an impact on public opinion, with action by courts and other legal institutions sometimes lending legitimacy to the claims advanced by social movements' (Coglianese, 2001: 86). The legal system, therefore, can be used both to enlarge opportunities for grassroots collective action and to consolidate any achievements. In these ways law reform efforts by social movements can function both as a club and a catalyst for structural transformation.

3. Uniqueness of the Simplicity Movement and the Implications for Structural Change

It was noted earlier that the Simplicity Movement does not fit neatly into the conceptual frameworks commonly used for thinking about law and social movements. One reason for this is that social movements tend to be conceptualised (often with every just-ification) as subordinate or excluded groups in society seeking increased empowerment, recognition, and respect through social struggle. Obvious examples, particularly in the US, are the Civil Rights, Women's Rights, and Gay Rights movements. The Simplicity Movement, however, cannot be placed coherently into this category, since the very act of voluntarily reducing consumption and production generally implies a certain position of privilege and material security in society, which subordinate or excluded groups typically (though not necessarily) lack. As David Shi remarks, 'By its very nature... voluntary simplicity has been and remains an ethic professed and practiced by those free to choose their standard of living' (Shi, 2007: 7).

It is not clear, however, exactly what implications this may have for any law reform efforts arising out of the Simplicity Movement. One negative implication might be a relatively diminished sense of social solidarity within the Simplicity Movement, at least in the sense that participants may not be driven together by a deep and immediate sense of personal or social injustice which historically gave intense motivational fire to other movements, such as Civil Rights, Women's Rights, and Gay Rights (Capeheart and Milovanovic, 2007). Indeed, one criticism levelled at the Simplicity Movement has been its tendency, historically, at least, to be apolitical (in the narrow sense of not engaging significantly in top-down reform activity). A lack of passionate solidarity among participants might explain this, however it would be wrong to jump to conclusions here. After all, the various strains of the Environmental Movement (Doherty and Doyle, 2008) do not fit obviously into the category of subordinate/excluded groups – many of the participants are well educated and middle-class (even if the environmental 'cause' itself remains subordinate) – and yet environmental activists are notoriously as passionate, driven, and committed as any (Wall, 2005; Manes, 1990). In fact, the environmentalist sensibility within the Simplicity Movement may provide it with all the motivational intensity it needs, since the various ecological crises are arguably the greatest challenges humanity has ever faced (Hansen, 2011; Heinberg and Lerch, 2010). Looking at the uniqueness of the Simplicity Movement from a very different and more positive perspective, however, the fact that the movement arises out of relatively privileged socio-economic circumstances may actually prove to be to its advantage, in that there may be fewer hurdles to overcome should it seek to access or influence legal and political processes for the purposes of structural reform.

These points suggest that the social movement which most closely resembles the Simplicity Movement, and which might shed some light on it, is the Environmental Movement (Rootes, 1999). This heterogeneous movement has contributed to considerable changes in law and social values over the last few decades, as Coglianese (2001: 109) writes: 'Legal reform, if it is to have an enduring impact, needs to be accompanied by a genuine change in public values. Broad public support for the environment has helped to sustain the nation's basic institutional commitment to the environment as reflected in contemporary law.' Furthermore, he adds, '[j]ust as the legal system helps sustain environmentalism during periods of public inattention, the system of environmental law is itself sustained by a broad social consensus in favour of environmental protection and by a latent environmentalism that stands ready to be activated by environmental groups' (Coglianese, 2001: 116). He sums up his central conclusion neatly in the following passage:

[L]aw reform is not simply a tool for changing society; rather, law reform is itself affected by society and its nonlegal norms and values. To be successful, social movement reformers need not only seek changes in the law but changes in public values too. In the absence of direct changes to society's values, law reform efforts could prove at worst vacuous or at best vulnerable to counterattack or atrophy over time (Coglianese, 2001: 116).

In the context of this chapter, the significance of this conclusion lies in how it exposes the need for law reformers to pay attention to social values as a necessary part of law reform efforts. Social movements clearly need law reform to help achieve their goals of social change, but 'law reform itself needs a supportive social and political climate if it is to maintain its viability and effectiveness over time' (Coglianese, 2001: 116). This point draws attention to the 'reactive' rather than 'proactive' nature of liberal democracies, as the following passage explains (also in the context of the Environmental Movement): 'Political parties are just a reflection of their society... Political parties will only behave in a more environmental fashion from the moment that the average citizen will do so and not in the reverse order' (De Geus, 2003: 25, quoting Dick Tommel). This is no doubt the kind of reasoning which led Robyn Ekersley (1992: 17) to assert that 'the environmental problematic is a crisis of culture and character'. More generally, the various problems of growth economics could be characterised in much the same way, suggesting that the cause of and the solution to those problems may lie primarily – at least, initially – in the social sphere. This is not to deny, of course, the necessary role law will need to play in any transformative politics; it is only to propose that transformative change in the legal, political, and macroeconomic spheres will depend, ultimately, on a social sphere that deems such change necessary and legitimate.

A second factor that distinguishes the Simplicity Movement from most literature on law and social movements is that it does not imply – at least, not obviously – a political agenda. It may be obvious that it *needs* a political agenda, but even if that is so it is much less obvious what such an agenda would look like. Contrast this with other movements. The politics of the early Women's Rights movement, for example, obviously called for such structural changes as the right to vote; the Civil Rights Movement obviously called for desegregation, among other things; the Gay Rights Movement obviously called for the decriminalisation of homosexuality, etc (Rodrigues and Loenen, 1999). Although it can be argued that deeper and less apparent structural biases did and still do discriminate unjustly against these groups, the present point is that as those groups were forming into social movements there were at least some political changes to focus on that were quite clearly implied from the outset by the nature of the movements themselves.

As noted above, however, it is not immediately obvious what transformative politics is implied by the Simplicity Movement. I would suggest that this is primarily due to the highly problematic nature of one of the Simplicity Movement's defining concerns, namely, reducing and changing consumption habits in affluent societies (Segal, 1999). As Albert Lin notes, '[t]ackling the problems posed by consumption quickly entangles one in questions of lifestyle choices and equity' (Lin, 2008: 476). According to liberal theory and neoclassical economics, consumption is generally conceived of as a matter of 'private preference', an area of life in which individuals make their own decisions in the marketplace free from politico-juridical mandates. As Tim Jackson (2003: 64) observes:

> There has been a tendency in conventional policy to assume that government should play as little role as possible in regulating or intervening in consumer choice. The doctrine of consumer sovereignty has dominated both economics and politics for several decades.

From that liberal/economic perspective, reducing or changing consumption habits may or may not be a requirement of morality or ethics, but it is certainly not an area that should be governed by law. In other words, the mainstream liberal/economic position is that lawmakers should not seek to shape or govern private preferences as expressed in the market; rather, lawmakers should be neutral in regard to consumption by taking private preferences as 'given'. That conception of market consumption may well need to be rethought if there is ever to be a politics of voluntary simplicity, a politics of consumption.

Fortunately, some of the background analysis on this point has been canvassed elsewhere, by theorists who have argued at length that law (including property and market structures) cannot be neutral, as such, but are always and necessarily value-laden (Singer, 2000; Robertson, 1997). On that basis I would argue that the prospect of a politics of voluntary simplicity should not be dismissed in advance simply on the grounds that it would be non-neutral with respect to its effects on consumption habits (since every legal regime is non-neutral). But even if that theoretical point is accepted, that does not say anything about what concrete politics of consumption is actually implied by the Simplicity Movement. Once again, this lack of clarity distinguishes the Simplicity Movement from those other social movements which seemed to have at least a preliminary political agenda implicit in their very natures. For these reasons I contend that the Simplicity Movement should dedicate much more attention to formulating a coherent political agenda, partly as a means of fostering increased 'group consciousness' and partly as a means of amplifying the movement's political sensibility. That task of formulating a politics of voluntary simplicity is explicitly taken up elsewhere (Alexander, 2011a), where the radical transformation of private property/market systems is explored with the aim of outlining a transition by way of degrowth to steady state economy. That vast subject cannot be explored in detail here, however, although it is touched on in the conclusion. In what remains of this chapter I present a more detailed statement of the relationship between the Simplicity Movement and a degrowth or steady state economy, for the central argument being advanced in this chapter is that the Simplicity Movement will need to expand and organise at the social level if any such economy is to emerge.

4. Degrowth from the Grassroots Up: The Promise and Potential of the Simplicity Movement

This chapter began by arguing that law is a social construct. It did so in the context of law and social movement literature with the aim of showing how and why changes in a society's culture quite directly lead to changes in law, and in ways that are not always obvious or widely acknowledged. From the premise that 'law reflects culture' it is only a small step further to see that culturally induced changes in law inevitably impact on political and economic structures too, given that those structures have legal foundations, or, at least, are framed and secured by the force of law (Kennedy, 1991; Kennedy, 1984). These issues deserve attention because if the relationship between law and culture is not understood, precious time, energy, and resources can be easily wasted on ineffectual or misguided strategies of transformation. The motivating concern of this chapter was to draw more attention to what role cultural evolution might need to play in providing the necessary *preconditions* for a degrowth or steady state economy.

Having outlined the socially constructed nature of law and legal reform, the underlying argument of this chapter can now be restated: A degrowth or steady state economy will depend for its realisation on the emergence of a post-consumerist culture, one that understands and embraces 'sufficiency' in consumption (Princen, 2005). Those who question the soundness of this thesis need only try to imagine a voluntary transition to a degrowth or steady state economy occurring within a culture generally comprised of individuals who seek ever-higher levels of income and consumption.

It is impossible to imagine, I would suggest, because it entails a fundamental contradiction in economic trajectory. Therefore, with respect to the affluent societies, at least, degrowth depends on voluntary simplicity. The analysis above aimed to expose the theoretical foundations of that relationship of dependence by outlining the close but often obscure relationship between law and culture.

This argument, however, must not be misunderstood. The argument is not that personal or grassroots action can 'change the world' without any need for significant structural transformation – far from it. The pro-growth structures of advanced capitalist societies (Purdey, 2010) make transitioning to a simpler lifestyle of reduced consumption very challenging, and to some extent, in certain ways, almost impossible (Alexander, 2011b). For example, people might find it extremely hard to escape 'car culture' at the personal level without safe and accessible bike paths. This is one of countless structural obstacles lying in the path of 'simpler lifestyles', and often top-down transformative reform and investment is needed for such obstacles to be transcended. Personal action alone, therefore, will never be enough.

The limitations of personal action alone, however, are not simply due to current structures opposing lifestyles of voluntary simplicity. It may also be the case that the initial ecological benefits of reduced consumption are quickly eliminated by the 'sufficiency rebound effect', which Blake Alcott (2008: 775) describes as follows: 'some of what was "saved" through non-consumption is consumed after all – merely by others'. So far as this rebound effect exists, simple living is unlikely to be an effective response to the ecological problems of overconsumption in the absence of structural change. Accordingly, there is little doubt that structural change by way of legal, political, and economic reform is a *necessary* part of any transition beyond growth capitalism.

The point I am arguing – and it is a point that theorists like Alcott (2008) seemingly fail to appreciate – is that such structural change will almost certainly not eventuate unless it is accompanied and probably preceded by a widespread cultural shift in attitudes toward consumption, such as that being advocated and explored in practice by the Simplicity Movement today. For even if the 'sufficiency rebound effect' exists to some extent, this would not mean people should not seek to live simpler lives of reduced consumption. To adopt a lifestyle of voluntary simplicity is to live in opposition to the cultures of consumption that give shape (and are shaped by) the pro-growth structures of advanced capitalism. Only by changing those cultures of consumption, I conclude, is there any hope of transcending and socially reconstructing those pro-growth structures.

Any such process of social reconstruction will need to entail innumerable personal acts of 'material simplification' or 'downshifting', acts which might seem insignificant in isolation but which cumulatively have the potential to be of revolutionary import. The primary justification for such personal acts, I wish to emphasise, is not due to the immediate good such downshifting may produce. Rather, the importance of a culture of downshifting lies in how such a culture is a precondition for the deep restructuring of society that is necessary. Transgressive, personal acts must become the building blocks of a strong counterculture – a counterculture that votes consistently with its time and money, and which also sends clear messages through the ballot box. Should this grassroots uprising enter the mainstream, including the political mainstream, it will inevitably put increasing amounts of pressure on the structures of growth capitalism. Over time, I contend, those pro-growth structures will end up so thoroughly disfigured, weakened, dismantled, reshaped, and reconstructed that something very different – something much better, more resilient, and more beautiful – will come to stand in its place. That, at least, is a future one might dare to hope for when enjoying the respite of an optimistic mood (Alexander, 2011c).

4.1. Globalisation, resistance, and the problem of 'Empire'

There is one final point that deserves some comment, even if space does not permit a detailed examination. The age of globalisation is upon us, and it could be that any attempt to realise a degrowth or steady state economy will face forms of resistance today that may not have been faced as recently as 50 years ago. We could call this the problem of 'Empire' (Hardt and Negri, 2000). Not only are nation-states today constrained by numerous international trade agreements and influenced by powerful global institutions, but the free flow of capital around the globe has given new power to transnational corporations which can now move their financial resources from country to country with unprecedented ease (Stiglitz, 2002). A strong case can be made that this has led to economic forces becoming more autonomous from political controls, and consequently that political sovereignty has declined (Sassen, 1996). But as Hardt and Negri (2000: xi) have argued, *'The decline in sovereignty of nation-states... does not mean that sovereignty as such has declined.'* Sovereignty, they argue, has just taken on a new, globalised form – the form of 'Empire' – which can be understood as a decentralising and deterritorialising apparatus of power which is 'composed of a series of national and supranational organisms united under a single logic of rule' (Hardt and Negri, 2000: xii). The logic of rule to which they refer, of course, is the globalised logic of profit maximisation.

Could it be that the materialisation of 'Empire' means that it would be impossible for one nation-state to transition to a degrowth or steady state economy without either violating international trade agreements or inducing, almost instantaneously, the mass exodus of capital? (Victor, 2008: 221-2). Although I cannot respond to the problems of Empire in any detail, I can indicate a response, and it is a response that returns us to the central normative ideas of this chapter, namely, voluntary simplicity and the grassroots theory of structural transformation. If indeed it is so that Empire is slowly but steadily emasculating the nation-state, such that it is becoming progressively less likely that post-growth structural transformation will ever originate from the top down, then it follows, perhaps necessarily, that true opposition to Empire and the forces of globalisation may only be possible today if it is driven from the grassroots up (Lindholm and Zuquete, 2010; Curran, 2007). What could defy the profit-maximising logic of Empire more funda-mentally than a large, oppositional social movement based on the living strategy of voluntary simplicity? What could challenge the rule of capital more directly than thousands upon millions of people militantly embracing, yet at the same time celebrating, the tantalising paradox that less is more?

Although still in their infancy, the fast-expanding Transition Initiatives associated with Rob Hopkins (2008) are perhaps the most notable contemporary example of this type of grassroots action. These initiatives are primarily a response to the dual crises of peak oil and climate change (Heinberg and Lerch, 2010), but obviously there is much overlap here with the Simplicity Movement's primary concern with overconsumption. Furthermore, the Transition Initiatives exemplify quite well the power dynamics between personal change, social change, and structural change that this chapter has been considering. Those involved in Transition Initiatives often find themselves drawn into community engagement by their own sense that things must change, and by joining such initiatives the individual strengthens the social current, and in turn this draws others in too, which strengthens the current further, and thus a 'snowball effect' is created. Rather than waiting for the state to act, however, Transition Initiatives just get to work, decarbon-ising their own economies by relocalising them. Community gardens are often one of the first community projects undertaken by such initiatives, and such projects might involve resisting development projects that were intended, say, to turn a vacant plot of land into a new mall. In ways such as this, Transition Initiatives engage with structure, and to the extent they succeed their impact on structures can resonate beyond immediate intentions – for example, by weakening the economic might of agri-business, opening up further space for individual and social change, or by making farmers' markets more competitive, which can then produce further structural change, and so forth. Deserving of more attention by critical scholars and activists alike, these power dynamics are complex and always dialectical, but they are suggestive of ways that current structures can be resisted, destabilised, and overcome from the grassroots up.

Although framed in different terms, this is an approach that Hardt and Negri, the pre-eminent theorists of Empire, make themselves:

> Militancy today is a positive, constructive, and innovative activity. This is the form in which we and all those who revolt against the rule of capital recognize ourselves as militants today.... This militancy makes resistance into counterpower and makes rebellion into a project of love (Hardt and Negri, 2000: 413).

Significantly, it is in the life of St Francis of Assisi – one of the most radical and inspirational figures in the history of voluntary simplicity – where Hardt and Negri (2000: 413) discover 'the ontological power of a new society.' They conclude their text with a message both of hope and opposition – or rather, hope *in* opposition – a message which is reproduced here in sympathy: 'Once again in postmodernity we find ourselves in Francis's situation, posing against the misery of power the joy of being. This is a revolution that no power will control...' (Hardt and Negri, 2000: 413).

While the problem of 'Empire', then, must be recognised as a real one, there is a sense in which the very nature of the problem provides further validation for the defining commitment of this chapter to a grassroots theory of legal transformation based on the oppositional living strategy of voluntary simplicity. The logic of justification here is quite simple, even if its implications are not: so far as the power of one's political representatives is taken away (or misused), one's individual political responsibility increases. As Hardt and Negri suggest, this may be the only logic more powerful than the profit-maximising logic of capital.

It was Victor Hugo who once said, 'There is nothing more powerful than an idea whose time has come' (as quoted in Schultz, 1971: ix).

While there are no grounds for complacency, just perhaps voluntary simplicity is such an idea.

5. Conclusion

The grassroots or bottom-up theory of legal transformation outlined in this chapter would benefit from a more detailed and nuanced explication in the future. Assuming, however, that the general approach is sound – that the social sphere is an important source of law – one area in particular that needs more development is the *specific actions* that the Simplicity Movement could take in attempting to socially reconstruct law. This chapter framed the Simplicity Movement in the context of law and social movement scholarship, indicating that social movements can shape or mobilise law in three main ways: (1) by influencing the culture within which judges adjudicate and thereby change what is considered a legitimate interpretation of law; (2) by more directly engaging with the judicial process by initiating legal proceedings in an attempt to challenge existing interpretations of law; and (3) by using electoral votes and cultural influence to mobilise the legislative process. But although this framework for understanding the social reconstruction of law was described, a detailed programme for grassroots action was not provided, partly because any such programme would require a substantial work in its own right (Hopkins, 2008); and partly because such a programme – if it is indeed to be grassroots – needs to be locally organised and context-specific (as well as jurisdiction-specific), a task which in many ways resists any general or universalising pronouncement. Nevertheless, if the Simplicity Movement is to 'politicise' – with the aim, for example, of transitioning by way of degrowth to a steady state economy – then the question of how the movement can become a more significant oppositional force needs to be given much more attention by activists, educators, and scholars. The maintenance and protection of ecological integrity, on the one hand, and the redistribution of wealth and work to lessen inequalities and eliminate poverty, are some of the central policy objectives which seem to be implied by the idea of a degrowth transition to a steady state economy (Alexander, 2012). Another key policy objective (which amounts in many ways to the same thing) would be to systematically resist the uptake high consumption lifestyles and systematically encourage lifestyles of voluntary simplicity. If, for present purposes, these objectives are assumed to be the most coherent framework for a 'politics of simplicity', then the potential areas to promote are obviously many and diverse. Some proposals to explore might include: (1) Establishing a Basic Income Guarantee or a Negative Income Tax in order to provide every permanent resident with a minimal though dignified standard of economic security; (2) Initiating a massive investment in renewable energy, public transport, bike lanes, energy efficiency improvements, and urban farms; (3) Funding such investments through significant inheritance taxes plus a system of progressive income or consumption taxation that culminates in a maximum wage; (4) Explicitly adopting post-growth measures of wellbeing (such as an Index for Sustainable Economic Welfare or the Genuine Progress Indicator) for the purpose of opening up space for top-down reforms that contribute to 'genuine wellbeing' even if they would lead to a phase of degrowth; (5) Regulating advertising more strictly; (6) Mandating better product labelling to allow people to 'vote with their money' more effectively; and (7) Restructuring the labour market to facilitate systematically the exchange of money for time; and so forth (Alexander, 2011a; 2012a). It is suggested that the mainstreaming of the Simplicity Movement might provide the cultural preconditions needed for this kind of structural reform to materialise. Perhaps the most important effect of such structural reform, however, is that it might open up new space to allow communities to govern themselves more directly, and build the new society within the shell of the old. That is, the primary purpose of such structural change may not be to actually drive the transition to a new society, but to liberate individuals and communities so that they can more easily drive the transition themselves, 'from below'. This again points to the complex and dialectical relationship between culture and structure. While the short list of proposals above makes absolutely no claim to being exhaustive or uncontroversial – and no doubt it raises more questions than it answers – it is hoped, nevertheless, that this chapter as a whole is received by interested parties as an invitation to explore some of these issues in more detail.

References

Alcott, B. 2008. 'The sufficiency strategy: Would rich-world frugality lower environmental impact?' *Ecological Economics* 64(4): 770-86.

Alexander, S. (ed.). 2009. *Voluntary simplicity: The poetic alternative to consumer culture*. Whanganui: Stead & Daughters.

Alexander, S. 2011a. *Property beyond growth: Toward a politics of voluntary simplicity.* Ph. D. Thesis, Melbourne Law School, University of Melbourne. http://papers.ssrn.com/sol3/papers.cfm?abstract_id=19410 69 (accessed 5 May 2011).

Alexander, S. 2011b. 'Degrowth implies voluntary simplicity: Overcoming barriers to sustainable consumption'. *Simplicity Institute Report* 12b: 1-17.

Alexander, S. 2011c. 'Looking backward from the year 2099: Ecozoic reflections on the future'. *Earth Jurisprudence and Environmental Justice Journal* 1(1): 25-59.

Alexander, S. 2012a. 'Planned economic contraction: The emerging case for degrowth'. *Environmental Politics* 21 (3): 349-368.

Alexander, S. 2014. 'Disruptive Social Innovation for a Low-Carbon World'. In David Humphreys and Spencer Stober (eds). 2014. *Transitions to sustainability: Theoretical debates for a changing planet.* Ch. 19: 296-315

Alexander, S. and Ussher, S. 2012. 'The voluntary simplicity movement: A multi-national survey analysis in theoretical context'. *Journal of Consumer Culture* 12 (1): 66-86.

Balkin, J. 2008. 'Critical legal theory today'. In Mootz, F. (ed.). *On philosophy in American law.* Cambridge: Cambridge University Press.

Barnett, L. 1993. *Legal construct, social concept: A macrosociological perspective on law.* New York: A. de Gruyter.

Berger, P. and Luckman, T. 1966. *The social construction of reality: A treatise in the sociology of knowledge.* Garden City, NY: Doubleday.

Capeheart, L. and Milovanovic, D. 2007. *Social justice: Theories, issues, and movements.* New Brunswick, NJ: Rutgers University Press.

Coglianese, C. 2001. 'Social movements, law, and society: The institutionalization of the environmental movement'. *University of Pennsylvania Law Review* 150: 85.

Coutin, S. 'Moving law on behalf of central American refugees'. In Sarat, A. and Scheingold, S. 2006. *Cause lawyers and social movements.* Stanford, Calif., Stanford Law and Politics.

Curran, G. 2007. *21st Century dissent: Anarchism, anti-globalization, and environmentalism.* New York: Palgrave MacMillan.

Dalton, R. 1994. *The green rainbow: Environmental groups in Western Europe.* New Haven: Yale University Press.

Daly, H. 1996, *Beyond growth: The economics of sustainable development.* Boston: Beacon Press.

De Geus, M. 2003. *The end of over-consumption: Towards a lifestyle of moderation and self-restraint.* Utrecht: International Books.

Doherty, B. and Doyle, T. (eds). 2008. *Beyond borders: Environmental movements and transnational politics.* Oxon: Routledge.

Ekeli, K. 2005. 'Giving a voice to posterity: Deliberative democracy and representation of future people. *Journal of Agricultural and Environmental Ethics,* 18: 429-450.

Eckersley, R. 1992. *Environmentalism and political theory: Toward an ecocentric approach.* Albany: State University of New York Press.

Fish, S. 1989. *Doing what comes naturally: Change, rhetoric, and the practice of theory in literary and legal studies.* Durham, NC: Duke University Press.

Gibson-Graham, J.K. 2006. *A postcapitalist politics.* Minneapolis: University of Minnesota Press.

Grigsby, M. 2004. *Buying time and getting by: The voluntary simplicity movement.* Albany: State University of New York Press.

Hall, K. 2009 (revised edn). *The magic mirror: Law in American history.* New York: Oxford University Press.

Hamilton, C. 2003, *Growth fetish.* Crows Nest, NSW: Allen & Unwin.

Hamilton, C. and Denniss, R. 2005. *Affluenza: When too much is never enough.* Crows Nest, NSW: Allen & Unwin.

Handler, J. 1978. *Social movements and the legal system: A theory of law reform and social change.* New York: Academic Press.

Hansen, James, 2011. *Storms of my grandchildren.* London: Bloomsbury.

Hardt, M. and Negri, A. 2000. *Empire.* Cambridge, Mass; London: Harvard University Press.

Heinberg, R., and Lerch, D. (eds). 2010. *The post carbon reader managing the 21st century's sustainability crises.* Healdsburg: Watershed Media.

Holmes, O.W. Jr. 1891. *The speeches of Oliver Wendell Holmes, Jr.* Boston: Little, Brown.

Holmgren, D. 2013. 'Crash on demand: Welcome to the brown tech future'. *Simplicity Institute Report* 13c: 1-23.

Hopkins, R. 2008. *The transition handbook: From oil dependency to local resilience.* Totnes, Devon: Green Books.

Hutton, D. and Connors, L. 1999. *A history of the Australian environment movement.* Cambridge; Melbourne: Cambridge University Press.

Jackson, T. 2003. 'Policies for sustainable consumption'. *A report to the sustainable development commission* 1-77. Available at: <http://www.sd-commission.org.uk/file_download.php?target=/publications/downloads/030917%20Policies%20for%20sustainable%20consumption%20_SDC%20report_.pdf> (accessed at 15 December 2010).

Jackson, T. 2009. *Prosperity without growth: Economics for a finite planet.* London: Earthscan.

Kallis, G. 2011. 'In defence of degrowth'. *Ecological Economics* 70: 873.

Kennedy, D. 1984. 'Role of law in economic thought: Essays on the fetishism of commodities'. *American University Law Review* 34: 939.

Kennedy, D. 1991. 'The stakes of law, or Hale and Foucault!' *Legal Studies Forum* 15: 327.

Latouche, S. 2009. *Farewell to growth.*, Cambridge: Polity Press.

Lin A. 2008. 'Virtual consumption: A second life for Earth,' *Brigham Young University Law Review* 2008: 47.

Marx, K. 1983. 'The German ideology'. In Kamenka, E. (ed.). *The portable Marx.* New York: Penguin.

Manes, C. 1990. *Green rage: Radical environmentalism and the unmaking of civilization.* Boston: Little, Brown.

Marshall, A.-M. and Barclay, S. 2003. 'In their own words: How ordinary people construct the legal world'. *Law & Social Inquiry* 28: 617.

McCann, M. 1998. 'How does law matter for social movements?' In Garth, B. and Sarat, A. (eds). *How does law matter?* Evanston, IL: Northwest University Press.

McCann, M. 2004. 'Law and social movements'. In Sarat, A. (ed.). *The Blackwell companion to law and society.* Malden, MA: Blackwell.

McCann, M. (ed.). 2006a. *Law and social movements.* Ashgate: Aldershot.

McCann, M. 2006b. 'Law and social movements: Contemporary perspectives'. *Annual Review Law and Social Science* 2: 17-38.

Merry, S. 1985. 'Concepts of law and justice among working-class Americans: Ideology as culture'. *Legal Studies Forum* 9: 59.

Princen, T. 2005. *The logic of sufficiency.* Cambridge, Mass: MIT Press.

Purdey, S. 2010. *Economic growth, the environment and international relations: The growth paradigm.* London: Routledge.

Robertson, M. 1997. 'Reconceiving private property'. *Journal of Law and Society* 24: 465.

Rodrigues, P. and Loenen, T. 1999. *Non-discrimination law: Comparative perspectives.* The Hague; Boston: Kluwer Law International.

Rootes, C. 1999. *Environmental movements: Local, national, and global.* London: Frank Cass.

Rorty, R. 1979. *Philosophy and the mirror of nature.* Princeton: Princeton University Press.

Rosen, L. 2006. *Law as culture: An invitation.* Princeton: Princeton University Press.

Rubin, E. 2001. 'Passing through the door: Social movement literature and legal scholarship'. *University of Pennsylvania Law Review,* 150: 1.

Sackville, J.R. 2005. 'Courts and social change'. *Federal Law Review* 33: 373.

Sarat, A. (ed.). 2004. *The Blackwell companion to law and society.* Malden, MA: Blackwell.

Sarat, A. and Scheingold, S. 2006. *Cause lawyers and social movements.* Stanford, Calif., Stanford Law and Politics.

Sassen, S. 1996. *Losing control? Sovereignty in an age of globalization.* New York: Columbia University Press.

Schor, J. and Holt, D. 2000. *The consumer society reader.* New York, NY: New Press.

Schultz, 1971. *English liberalism and the state.* Lexington, Mass: Heath.

Segal, J. 1999. *Graceful simplicity: Toward a philosophy and politics of the alternative American dream.* New York: H. Holt & Co.

Shi, D. 2007 (revised edn). *The simple life: Plain living and high thinking in American culture.* Athens: University of Georgia Press.

Singer, J. 1988. 'Legal realism now'. *California Law Review* 76: 467.

Singer, J. 2000. *Entitlement: The paradoxes of property.* New Haven: Yale University Press.

Stiglitz, J. 2002. *Globalization and its discontents.* New York: Penguin.

Tarrow, S. 1983. *Struggling to reform: Social movements and policy change during cycles of protest.* Ithaca, NY: Center for International Studies, Cornell University.

Tilly, C. 1984. 'Social movements and national politics'. In Bright, C. and Harding, S. (eds). *Statemaking and social movements.* Ann Arbor: University of Michigan Press.

Torres, G. 2009. 'Social movements and the ethical construction of law'. *Capital University Law Review* 37: 535.

Trainer, T. 2010. *The transition to a sustainable and just world.* Canterbury, NSW: Envirobook.

Unger, R. 2001. *False necessity: Anti-necessitarian social theory in the service of radical democracy.* London; New York: Verso.

Victor, P. 2008. *Managing without growth: Slower by design, not disaster.* Cheltenham: Edward Elgar Publishing.

Wall, D. 2005. *Babylon and beyond: The economics of anti-capitalist, anti-globalist, and radical green movements.* London: Pluto.

Wittgenstein, L. 1953. *Philosophical investigations.* New York: Macmillan.

9

WILD LAW FROM BELOW
Examining the anarchist challenge to
Earth Jurisprudence

Our struggle is to open every moment and fill it with an activity
that does not contribute to the reproduction of capital. Stop
making capitalism and do something else, something sensible,
something beautiful and enjoyable. Stop creating the system that
is destroying us. We only live once: why use our time to destroy
our own existence? Surely we can do something better with our
lives.
    – John Holloway

1. Introduction

At least since Marx there has been a line of critical theory that
conceptualises the capitalist state as merely a tool for advancing and
entrenching the narrow economic interests of the rich and powerful,
to the detriment of wider society (Marx 1983). A broader critique
has arisen more recently that holds that governments across the
political spectrum have developed a 'growth fetish' (Hamilton
2003), through which all societal goals, including or especially
environmental ones, are subordinated to the overarching aim of
maximising economic growth. These critical perspectives raise
challenging issues for progressive legal theorists and activists who
seek to advance their social or environmental causes by way of 'top
down' legal change. Given that Earth Jurisprudence can be
understood, first and foremost, as a movement that treats ecological
sustainability as a fundamental legal principle (Berry 1999;
Bosselmann 2008) – more fundamental even than the growth
imperative (Alexander 2011a; 2011b) – the question of whether law

227

will ever accept such a principle in a growth-orientated world is a confronting question that ought not to be avoided. After all, what if the institutions of law are so compromised by growth fetishism and corporate interests that the changes needed to create a sustainable and just society will never be generated from the top down? Put otherwise, what if asking law to produce a sustainable and just society is like asking a zebra to change its stripes? We may desire the zebra to do so, and it may tell us it will change, but all history suggests that by nature it will not.

Furthermore, if the changes needed to produce a sustainable and just society will never be driven from the top down, but could only arise through social movements from below (Trainer 2010), what are the implications of this for Earth Jurisprudence, which to date has been characterised almost exclusively by the attempt to formulate and justify top-down legal approaches to environmental law? Is Wild Law a coherent category if the society it vaguely implies is something that could only be created at the grassroots by social movements, as opposed to something that could be produced by the legislature or the judiciary? These are some of the issues I wish to examine in this chapter, although my purpose is to raise questions rather than to lay down answers or provide solutions. I confess that the sands of my own thinking are shifting with uncertainty beneath my feet as I write, owing in part to the complexity of the issues involved (see Bollier and Weston 2013; Healy *et al.*, 2012). Nevertheless, what I am convinced of is that the importance of the questions posed justifies the attempt to grapple with them, so I ask that this exploratory essay be treated merely as an 'invitation to discuss'.

The central issue I would like to raise for Earth jurists, and for oppositional lawyers more generally, is the question of 'strategy'. That is to say, I would like to raise the question of how best to direct our limited energies and resources, for if change is truly what we desire, our energies and resources must be used to their fullest practical effect. Earth Jurisprudence, after all, is not an intellectual game we play to amuse ourselves. It is a framework for deep societal transition, and if we truly believe in the 'ends' for which we ostensibly struggle, then surely we must take care that the 'means' we employ are the best we have available.

To be clear, I do not seek to question the 'ends' or 'principles' of Earth Jurisprudence, with which I am deeply sympathetic (Burdon 2011a). Rather, this chapter seeks to evaluate the 'means' which Earth jurists (including myself) have generally taken up to try to achieve or realise those 'ends'. More directly, I want to ask the question of whether top-down change is really where we should be directing our energies, and to suggest that perhaps we should be directing more of our energies toward building the new society at a grassroots level; building it beneath the legal structures of the existing society with the aim that one day new societal structures will emerge 'from below' to replace the outdated forms we know today. In this way, it could be said, I am presenting an 'anarchist' challenge to Earth Jurisprudence, in the limited sense, at least, that I am proposing that we consider ignoring the state rather than trying to use the state to advance 'deep green' causes which it seems wholly uninterested in supporting.

I feel this perspective could be easily misunderstood, so before developing my line of reasoning a word of clarification is immediately in order. I do not wish to suggest that strong top-down environmental laws, such as those proposed by Earth jurists, are not desirable. On the contrary, it is perfectly clear to me that the judiciary and especially parliament could do many things to protect and conserve Earth's ecosystems (see Bollier and Weston, 2013), and over the last decade or so Earth Jurisprudence has been, and continues to be, a rich source of inspiration for what an eco-centric legal system might look like (Burdon 2011a). My tentative thesis, however, is that growth fetishism has such a strong hold on the branches of government that efforts directed toward producing strong top-down environmental law will essentially be ignored by lawmakers, and thus those efforts for progressive top-down change could well be wasted. We do not, of course, have a surplus of oppositional energy or resources to waste or misdirect, so if it is the case that the zebra of law will not change its stripes, it arguably follows that we should not dedicate our efforts toward convincing it to do so, no matter how desirable that top-down change may be. Rather, we should dedicate our efforts toward areas with the greatest leverage – with the greatest potential to effect positive change – and I have come to suspect that the areas that have the greatest leverage lie amongst the grassroots of social movements and culture, not parliament or the courts.

I do not pretend to be able to do this line of thinking justice in the space available; nor could I expect to convince the reader of its veracity, since I have already implied that in my eyes its veracity remains an open question. All I hope to do is raise the question of 'strategy' – the question of how best to direct our limited energies and resources – and if I can do that successfully I feel the essay should serve a worthwhile purpose. I begin unpacking these ideas in the next section by describing briefly how the growth model of progress has come to shape law. I proceed to outline ways that law has attempted (without success) to deal with the ecological impacts of growth and how Earth Jurisprudence opens up space for an alternative, post-growth approach to legal governance. Insofar as it confronts growth, however, Earth Jurisprudence arguably renders itself politically unpalatable, and so I conclude by delving deeper into the question of strategy in order to explore the prospects or even the possibility of a Wild Law 'from below'.

2. Law and the Growth Model of Progress

With the development of the steam engine in the early decades of the 18th century, for the first time humankind was able to harness the vast stores of energy embodied in fossil fuels – coal, at first, and later oil and gas. This led to the industrialisation of economies around the world, a process that is still continuing to this day. Not since the Agricultural Revolution around 10,000 years earlier had there been such a radical change in the way human beings lived on Earth. The productive capacity of industrialising nations grew at exponential rates, driven onward by the seemingly endless supply of cheap and abundant energy, and this growth of production and trade provided industrialising nations and their inhabitants with what seemed like an endless supply of resources with which to meet their every desire. As a result, economic growth became the overriding objective of governments – the solution to all problems – especially in the Western world but increasingly elsewhere (Purdey 2010). Indeed, growth of the global economy seems to have become synonymous with 'progress' itself, and today this remains the dominant paradigm or lens through which social, economic, and political success is judged.

Unsurprisingly, perhaps, this growth paradigm also came to shape legal systems around the world, such that law, in many jurisdictions, can be seen to have developed a pro-growth structure (Alexander 2011a). The dynamics at play here are relatively straightforward: when economic growth, as measured by increases in GDP, is considered synonymous with national progress, laws that foster economic growth are presumptively justified, while laws that inhibit, slow, or reduce economic growth are presumptively unjustified. Over time this 'normative filter' has given legal systems their pro-growth structures, and while one could point to exceptions to this general statement (e.g., Filgueira and Mason, 2011), they are just that, exceptions within a growth paradigm that marginalise them.

Economic growth has brought with it many social benefits, of course, lifting millions of people out of poverty and providing many with a high material standard of living that would have been unimaginable only a few generations earlier. When focusing only on these types of material provision, the growth paradigm has some initial plausibility, especially since there are billions of people on the planet who clearly still need to develop their economic capacities in some form, just to provide for their most basic material needs. At first consideration, then, it is quite understandable why economic growth is widely considered to be an appropriate, even necessary, social goal. It is arguably a goal that not only *does* but also *should* shape our social, economic, and political structures, including our legal systems.

Economic growth, however, is a two-edged sword, one that produces both benefits and costs, especially ecological costs. Vast bodies of rigorous scientific evidence now indicate that today the size of the global economy exceeds, by some way, the sustainable carrying capacity of the planet (see, e.g., Vale and Vale, 2013). Furthermore, despite extraordinary technological advances in recent decades – advances that were supposed to solve the ecological crises – the overall impacts of economic activity continue to grow and intensify, not decline (Jackson, 2009). These facts radically call into question the legitimacy of the growth paradigm, at least in the most developed parts of the world, for if there is to be any 'ecological room' for an expanding human population to live at a dignified material standard of living, the richest societies must not continue increasing their material demands on a finite planet (Meadows *et al.*, 2004). Rather than rethink the growth paradigm, however, the international community has fudged the issue by talking of 'sustainable development,' which sounds lovely but has been rendered meaningless by decades of greenwash. Today, sustainable development has come to signify the attempt to produce and consume more sustainably, *provided this does not interfere with continued economic growth.* This description might sound cynical, but even a glance at reality will testify to its accuracy (Worldwatch Institute, 2013). As the global economy struggles to emerge from the global financial crisis, it is clear that 'growth fetishism' is alive and well – growth appears more important now than ever, the environment be damned – and this paradigm continues to provide a normative filter that determines which environmental laws are allowed to pass through the institutions of capitalism. It is at least arguable, then, that any approach to environmental law that seriously challenges the growth paradigm will never make it through this normative filter, and it is now worth taking a closer look at the various approaches to environmental law in order to better understand the forces that are at play here.

3. Three Broad Approaches to Environmental Law

In the legal sphere it could be said that there are three broad approaches to dealing with the environmental impacts of economic activity: 'market-based' approaches; 'command-and-control' app-roaches; and the 'deep green' approach of Earth Jurisprudence. I will now briefly outline these three approaches and emphasise the relationship of each approach to the growth paradigm.

3.1 'Free market' environmentalism

Within advanced capitalist societies today, the dominant approach to environmental law is based on neoclassical economics, exemplified most clearly by law-and-economics scholarship but which also has a much broader influence (Posner 1986). This approach (which comes in many varieties) assumes that the best way to maximise utility in a society, over the long term, is to create a well-functioning 'free market' economy. To oversimplify, this broadly involves the state protecting private property rights and enforcing contracts, but otherwise generally 'staying out' of the economy. In such an economy it is assumed that there will be price incentives in place to ensure that natural resources are exploited to an 'optimal' degree, but not further. If natural resources are overexploited in such a way as to engender sustainability concerns, this can only be because the costs of production are not fully internalised, often because the degradation of common resources is not being built into the price of the commodities produced, leading to overconsumption (i.e., a 'market failure'). Accordingly, within this model, environmental law aims to internalise any externalities, and privatise common resources, but otherwise let prices and market mechanisms determine how the economy functions in relation to the natural environment.

Without going further into the details of this complex theory of law, the point to emphasise presently is how easily this approach to environmental law sits within the growth model. Far from challenging growth, the neoclassical approach to environmental law assumes that the common good will be advanced most efficiently if individuals, businesses, and governments seek to maximise profits and grow the economy. Growth provides money, after all, and money provides individuals and governments with power to satisfy their desires, including environmental desires. The role of law is simply to create structures to ensure that markets function in an 'optimal' way. From this view, environmental problems are not due to economic growth, as such, but due to imperfect structures within which economic activity occurs. Accordingly, growth itself is not questioned.[1]

3.2 'Command-and-control' environmentalism

The free market approach to environmental law might work nicely in theory, but its relationship with reality has proven to be tenuous indeed. An alternative approach can broadly be called 'command-and-control' environmentalism, which arose due to the failures of free market environmentalism to protect nature. The command-and-control approach (which also comes in many varieties) does not accept that market mechanisms will ever be sufficient, own their own, to adequately protect planetary ecosystems. Rather, this broad school holds that more direct regulation of the economy is needed. While the command-and-control approach might accept that internalising externalities is an important step in the right direction, it nevertheless insists that 'market failures' are so pervasive, and ultimately unavoidable to some degree, that direct governmental involvement is required, at least to address the most egregious environmental harms. Advocates of the free market respond arguing that such paternalism is an inefficient mode of governance, and that the same ends can be achieved more efficiently via market mechanisms. However, advocates of the command-and-control approach typically consider certain inefficiencies an acceptable price to pay for the more direct environmental regulation.

Again, the many nuances of this approach, and the intricate debate between approaches, cannot be unpacked further here (see Godden and Peel 2010). For present purposes, the point to note is that, like the free market approach, the command-and-control approach does not question the growth paradigm, but rather tries to better regulate economic activity in order to diminish the ecological costs of growth. The more direct regulation may, at times, slow growth to some extent, but this is considered an unfortunate side effect of environmental protection, not one of its aims. The underlying aim remains growth, although it is usually softened by such terms as 'green growth', 'smart growth', or that now dangerous

---

[1] It is worth noting, however, that if all environmental externalities were actually internalised this might so radically change the nature of economic activity that something very different from a growth economy might arise. In fact, neoclassicism could well be its own worst enemy, in the sense that the only reason neoclassicists promote growth is because they do not understand the radical implications of their own theory (see Alexander, 2011a: 245-6).

euphemism, 'sustainable development' (Worldwatch Institute 2013).

3.3 Earth Jurisprudence

When one asks advocates of free market or command-and-control environmentalism why the overall ecological impacts of economic activity are still increasing, both parties will claim that it is because their own systems of governance have not yet been fully or properly implemented. Advocates of the free market will insist that with a bit more deregulation and some tweaking of prices here and there, the 'invisible hand' will ensure that both growth and sustainability are achieved as a natural result of market forces. Advocates of command-and-control will argue that with some stricter regulation of the growth economy, the ecological costs of growth can be reduced within safe boundaries. But there is another reason for why both approaches have failed to produce sustainability, and I would argue that it is because neither approach questions the growth paradigm (Alexander, 2012a; 2012b). By assuming the legitimacy and desirability of growth, the mainstream approaches to environmental law outlined above formulate strategies for environmental protection within a macroeconomic framework that is inherently unsustainable. It should come as no surprise, therefore, that those strategies fail. In order for environmental law to have any chance of being effective, what is needed, first and foremost, is a jurisprudence 'beyond growth', and I have argued elsewhere that Earth Jurisprudence is the most promising place for such a jurisprudence to take hold (Alexander, 2011b).

Earth Jurisprudence is far from being a homogenous body of literature (Burdon, 2011a), but there do seem to be threads of commonality that unite the various forms. First among them is the idea that nature – the life-support system upon which the entire community of life depends – is more than a 'resource' to be exploited for human gratification. Nature is something that should not be, and indeed, cannot be understood merely in economic terms. An old growth forest or a marsh, for example, should be valued not merely (or at all) in terms of dollars, or treated as resources to be developed in ways that maximise profits, but primarily in terms of the role they play in maintaining the health and integrity of planetary ecosystems. In this sense Earth Jurisprudence treats ecological sustainability as fundamental, and accordingly seeks ways to construct legal systems in order to achieve that defining goal. If this approach interferes with economic development, then it is 'development' that must be reconsidered, not the 'principle of sustainability' (Bosselman 2008). From this view, then, law should seek to facilitate the creation of 'post-growth economies' that sit safely within ecological limits, rather than trying to make 'growth economies' sustainable, as mainstream environmentalism tries to do, without success. Earth Jurisprudence must hack at the roots of unsustainability, not merely the branches, and I believe that this means operating beyond the growth paradigm.

As noted earlier, it is not the purpose of this chapter to unpack the details of what an Earth-centred jurisprudence would look like or how it might function. Those issues have been taken up with rigour in other chapters of this book, and elsewhere (Burdon, 2011a). Nor have I attempted to present the case against growth in any detail, a critique that has been made many times before (e.g., Meadows *et al.*, 2004; Jackson, 2009). Instead, the present analysis seeks to evaluate the prospects of a post-growth Earth Jurisprudence in a growth-orientated world, and, in particular, to consider whether top-down change is a strategy that Earth jurists should be focusing on. I am now in a position to consider these issues in a little more detail and bring my argument to a head.

4. Three Strategies for Change: Democratic, Socialist, Anarchist

My analysis so far has been based on the following two premises: (1) that the growth paradigm acts as a normative filter which over time has given law a pro-growth structure; and (2) that the growth paradigm is inherently unsustainable. Upon those premises I argued that environmental laws that do not question the growth paradigm have failed and will always fail to achieve sustainability, and that Earth Jurisprudence must therefore be a post-growth jurisprudence if it is to succeed where free market and command-and-control environmentalism have failed. The issue I will now address is the question of what strategies could or should be taken if the aim is to create an Earth Jurisprudence beyond growth.

The strategy that Earth jurists (including myself) have generally taken up to advance their causes is what can be called the 'democratic' strategy. This essentially involves formulating and defending top-down legal proposals that embody the principles and values of Earth Jurisprudence. This strategy trusts that when the majority see the desirability of developing an eco-centric legal system, that sentiment will filter upward and eventually manifest in law. With particular reference to the legislature, the democratic strategy expects that when there is a culture that wants Earth

Jurisprudence, those cultural values will be embraced by representative politicians and used to shape public policy in order to win or maintain office (Alexander, 2013).

This strategy is perfectly coherent in theory, but it assumes that representative democracies are functioning well, and a strong case can be made that many so-called democracies are under the undue influence of corporate interests (e.g., Tham, 2010). If that is so, even a culture shift in favour of Earth Jurisprudence would not necessarily bring about the required top-down structural change, because we can be sure that the corporate interests influencing public policies are not interested in Earth Jurisprudence, certainly not an Earth Jurisprudence beyond growth. In the Australian context, a disheartening example of corporate influence in politics occurred in 2010 when then Prime Minister, Kevin Rudd, sought to impose a relatively small tax on the mining industry, only to be subjected to a multi-million dollar, corporate-funded scare campaign that ultimately resulted in Rudd being booted out of office and replaced with a more 'moderate', more corporate-friendly Prime Minister. The most worrying aspect to this political event was the fact that the tax being proposed was hardly radical, and yet corporate interests shut down even this moderate legal reform. On a global scale, the same point could be made with respect to how the state responded to the Occupy Movement. As soon as the movement looked like it could potentially develop some real momentum, the state bore down with the full force of executive power and ensured that this fundamentally anti-capitalist political demonstration was nipped at the bud.

These are but particularly explicit examples of what is generally a more insidious process of control. Arguably the deeper forms of undemocratic influence come from political parties' dependence on corporations for political campaign funding, or from privately owned media conglomerates feeding the public only or mainly what is in the corporate interest, thereby 'manufacturing consent' and keeping politicians in line (Chomsky and Herman, 1994). Of course, culture often puts pressure on politicians to act this way or that, and sometimes, in accordance with democratic theory, the politicians are forced to abide or lose office. Fragments of an Earth Jurisprudence might even slip through law's normative filter (e.g., Filgueira and Mason, 2011), as might some advances in social justice. But as soon as politicians, or the culture which those politicians are supposed to represent, seriously threaten to confront corporate power, it seems that a sophisticated political and ideological process is set in motion that functions to maintain, more or less, the existing order of things. In such circumstances, what hope is there for a top-down Earth Jurisprudence beyond growth?

Empire, we can be sure, will not contemplate self-annihilation (Hardt and Negri, 2000); it will struggle for existence all the way down.

Marxists essentially accept this critical view of representative democracy, arguing that, indeed, the capitalist state is merely a tool for maintaining the status quo and furthering the narrow interests of economic elites. From this perspective, the deep changes that are arguably needed for Earth Jurisprudence depend not on the citizenry putting upward pressure on representative politicians, but on the citizenry taking control of the state more directly in order to advance the common good by way of state socialism. Since the economic elites will never voluntarily give up their hold on power, it follows that the Marxist or socialist revolution must be a violent revolution. In theory, at least, state socialism presents Earth Jurisprudence with a second strategy for achieving its environmental goals.

The problem with this strategy for societal change, however – aside from the acceptance of violence which seems fundamentally contrary to the ethics of Earth Jurisprudence – is that Marxism, and socialism more generally, have almost without exception remained embedded within the growth paradigm that I have argued Earth Jurisprudence must reject. In other words, state socialists have tended to seek state power, not to use that power to move away from the growth economy, but to facilitate continued growth only in more socially just ways and with a broader distribution of wealth. The same could be said of social democrats. While it is possible to imagine an eco-socialist Earth Jurisprudence – certainly it is easier than imagining a state capitalist Earth Jurisprudence! – there arguably remains the concern that states of *any type* – whether capitalist, socialist, or some other variety – are in and of themselves structurally inclined to be pro-growth. The basic critique here, which I cannot detail presently, is that all states are dependent for their existence on a taxable economy, and the larger the tax-base, the more funds the state can draw from to carry out its policies. This is the basic incentive structure that makes governments of any variety inclined toward growth.

This line of reasoning leads to a third, broad vision of social change, arising out of the anarchist tradition – the environmental anarchists, in particular, such as Murray Bookchin (1990) and Ted Trainer (2010). Although these theorists have their important differences, they essentially agree with Marxists that state capitalism is unjustifiable on the grounds that it is being used unjustly as a tool to maintain the existing order. But unlike Marxists, they do not think the solution is taking control of the state. They think the solution is building the new society at the local, grassroots level, where communities create self-governing, localised, participatory democracies. Part of the disagreement with Marxists here is because these 'deep green' anarchists think that the state is inextricably intertwined with economic violence against nature, and so from this perspective, no state, not even state eco-socialism, is going to lead to sustainability. But even if there were hope of a green state, these theorists would not advocate that people direct their energies toward top-down change, because they think that state governance is an unjustifiable form of hierarchy and rule, no matter how 'green' it might be. Accordingly, they believe that if a just and sustainable society is to emerge, it has to be built without help from the state (and probably with a lot of resistance). Far from giving up on democracy, however, these theorists are demanding it – in the most direct form possible.

While this brief review does a disservice to the richness of the ideas and thinkers discussed, it does serve the purpose of raising questions about how any transition to a sustainable way of life could unfold. Would it (or could it) be somehow voted in through the mechanisms of parliamentary democracy? Would it require a political revolution and the introduction of some form of eco-socialism? Or would it require grassroots movements to essentially do it mostly themselves, building the new economy underneath the existing economy, without state assistance? I have tentatively argued that efforts to convince or pressure the state to adopt a post-growth Earth Jurisprudence might be an exercise in futility, on the basis that governments seem to be fundamentally committed to growth economics. Not only can the argument be made that governments are effectively tools used for securing and advancing the narrow interests of economic elites, as Marxists have long asserted, but a broader critique suggests that governments across the political spectrum, whether capitalist or socialist, are in the grip of a 'growth fetish' (Hamilton, 2003). If either or both of these diagnoses are correct, then this raises challenging questions about how and where Earth jurists should be directing their efforts. I have come to think that a post-growth Earth Jurisprudence is, and for the foreseeable future will be, politically unpalatable, and this suggests to me that, as a matter of strategy, Earth jurists should be dedicating more of their efforts toward building the Earth-centred society at the grassroots level, where – if you will excuse the metaphor – we are likely to get a better 'return on investment'. Strategy will always be a context-dependent issue, of course, and there may be times when attempting to push on governments might be the best strategic use of our efforts. That is for each of us to assess as individual agents embedded in unique contexts. But given the limits of oppositional energy at our disposal, it is important that not one joule of it is wasted, and saying that 'top down' change is *desirable* is not a sufficient excuse for misdirecting that energy. Of course top-down change is desirable! But the question I have posed in this chapter is the question of how to achieve the 'ends' of Earth Jurisprudence *most effectively*, and the tentative thesis I have presented is that this might involve working toward a Wild Law 'from below'.

5. Wild Law from Below: A Coherent Legal Category?

Before closing I would like to offer a word about whether it is appropriate to speak of Wild Law if the changes aimed for are brought about from below rather than from the top down. After all, conventional use of the word 'law' implies a rule or body of rules emanating from parliament or the courts, and indeed Earth jurists accept that 'In Earth Jurisprudence, "human law" is the essence of what is meant by the term law. It's meaning is largely consistent with orthodox theory' (Burdon 2011b: 67). This raises the question of whether Wild Law is even a coherent category if it were something that could only emerge in the social sphere, beneath parliament and the courts. Perhaps 'law' is not the right word for the mode of governance to which I refer?

If 'law' were interpreted narrowly as meaning the rules emanating from parliament and the courts, then it would follow that Wild Law from below is not a coherent category on the grounds that it is not law, proper. However, this conventional understanding of law is arguably unduly narrow, evidenced by the fact that jurists have long accepted 'customary law' to be a legitimate form of law, despite in such cases there being an absence of conventional lawmaking institutions, such as parliament or courts as we know them today (Bollier and Weston, 2013). The customary laws of many indigenous communities are a case in point, where cultures were governed, and to some extent still are, by sets of knowable and enforceable rules that arose from elders, myth, and tradition – from customs – rather than from parliament or courts. As Ng'ang'a Thiong'o writes of Earth Jurisprudence in an African context:

> In Africa, wilderness, or what you call 'wild law,' is the great source of law, not written common law. In fact, our traditional law is oral and is passed from one generation to another orally, through music, art, dance, drumming, and through the "do's and don'ts" of the community (Ng'ang'a Thiong'o 2011: 183).

While I am not arguing that systems of common law or civil law should adopt African customary law, I am suggesting that there could be space, even in the West, for a customary Wild Law to develop beneath conventional lawmaking institutions (see also Bollier and Weston, 2013: Chs 4 and 8 especially). This would depend, however, on a cultural revolution of sorts, through which the values and principles of Earth Jurisprudence become broadly accepted and acted upon at the community level, irrespective of, and perhaps in defiance of, state-based law. 'The force behind customary law,' Thiong'o (2011: 175) writes, 'is that legitimisation comes from the community,' and that 'It is important to see [customary law] as a way of life, rather than hard, cold, legal norms imposed from elsewhere' (Thiong'o 2011: 174). Could it not be, then, that over time a Wild Law from below could develop at the community level, changing the structures of society, not as a result of new statutes or case law, but as a result of new social and economic customs based on principles of ecological sustainability? That is indeed the possibility I have tried to raise in this chapter. Having only sketched out a skeletal framework, however, it follows these bones must await another occasion to be fleshed out.

6. Conclusion

An objection that is likely to be levelled at the thesis presented in this chapter is that I have unwisely or inappropriately privileged one mode of transition (grassroots social movements) above another (top-down legal change), when both modes are equally necessary to create a sustainable society and thus both modes should be pursued. It is important that this objection and my response to it are understood, otherwise it could be very easy for my argument to be misunderstood. My argument has not been that top-down legal change could not help facilitate the transition to a sustainable society. Obviously there is much that parliament and the courts could and should do to help in such a transition (see, e.g., Bollier and Weston, 2013), and for many years Earth jurists, among others, have been explicating some of the laws and legal principles upon which such a transition could be based. Rather, my argument has been that the formal institutions of law may be so compromised by the growth paradigm that expecting those institutions to produce a fundamentally Earth-centred legal system, at the expense of growth, is akin to expecting a zebra to change its stripes. I do not claim to have established this thesis to any level of certainty. My aim has simply been to bring this issue to the surface, because if my tentative thesis that 'law is a growth-orientated zebra' were more or less correct, this has significant implications on how and where oppositional lawyers (and activists more generally) should direct their energies and resources. More specifically, it suggests that trying to convince a growth-orientated state to use the vehicle of law to create a post-growth society might be futile, a waste of our efforts. If that were so, it would seem to be more fruitful for oppositional lawyers to dedicate their energies and resources toward advancing their causes at the grassroots level and attempting to build the new society from below, rather than trying to bring it about from the top down. Put otherwise, I am suggesting, as an Earth jurist, that we consider ignoring the state that is almost certainly going to ignore us, and instead attempt to create eco-centric customs of Wild Law among the grassroots of our local communities. How we might do that, and what it might look like, are subjects for another occasion.

References

Alexander, S. 2011a. *Property beyond growth: Toward a politics of voluntary simplicity*. Doctoral thesis, Melbourne University. Available at: http://papers.ssrn.com/sol3/papers.cfm?abstract id=1941069 (accessed 10 September, 2013).

Alexander, S. 2011b. 'Earth jurisprudence and the ecological case for degrowth'. In P. Burdon (ed.). *Exploring wild law: The philosophy of earth jurisprudence*. Kent Town, SA: Wakefield Press.

Alexander, S. 2012a. 'Planned economic contraction: The emerging case for degrowth'. *Environmental Politics* 21(3): 349-68.

Alexander, S. 2012b. 'Peak oil and the twilight of growth'. *Alternative Law Journal* 37(2): 86-90.

Alexander, S. 2013. 'Voluntary simplicity and the social reconstruction of law: Degrowth from the grassroots up'. *Environmental Values* 22(2) 287-308.

Berry, T. 1999. *The great work: Our way into the future*. New York: Bell Tower.

Bollier, D. and Weston, B. H. *Green governance: Ecological survival, human rights, and the law of the commons*. Cambridge: Cambridge University Press.

Bookchin, M. 1990. *Remaking society: Pathways to a green future*. Cambridge, MA: South End Press.

Bosselmann, K. 2008. *The principle of sustainability*. Burlington: Ashgate Publishing.

Burdon, P. (ed.) 2011a. *Exploring wild law: The philosophy of earth jurisprudence*. Kent Town, SA: Wakefield Press.

Burdon, P. 2011b. 'The great jurisprudence'. In Burdon, P. (ed.). *Exploring wild law: The philosophy of Earth Jurisprudence.* Kent Town, SA: Wakefield Press.

Chomsky, N. and Herman, E. 1994. *Manufacturing consent: The political economy of mass media.* London: Vintage.

Filgueira, B. and Mason, I. 2011. 'Is there any evidence of earth jurisprudence in existing law?' In P. Burdon (ed.) *Exploring wild law: The philosophy of earth jurisprudence,* Kent Town, SA: Wakefield Press.

Godden, L. and Peel, J. 2010. *Environmental law: Scientific, policy, and regulatory dimensions.* London: Oxford University Press.

Hamilton, C. 2003. *Growth fetish.* Crows Nest, NSW: Allen & Unwin.

Hardt, M. and Negri, A. 2000. *Empire.* London: Harvard University Press.

Healy, H., Martinez-Alier, J., Temper, L., Walter, M., Gerber, J-F. 2012. *Ecological economics from the ground up.* London: Routledge.

Jackson, T. 2009. *Prosperity without growth: Economics for a finite planet.* London: Earthscan.

Marx, K. 1983. *The portable Marx.* In Kamenka, E. (ed.). London: Penguin.

Meadows, D. Randers, J. and Meadows, D. 2004. *Limits to growth: The 30-year update.* White River Junction, Vt: Chelsea Green Publishing.

Posner, R. 1986. *Economic analysis of law.* Boston: Little Brown.

Purdey, S. 2010. *Economic growth, the environment, and international relations: The growth paradigm.* New York: Routledge.

Tham, J.C. 2010. *Money and politics: The democracy we can't afford.* Sydney: University of New South Wales Press.

Trainer, T. 2010. *The transition to a sustainable and just world.* Sydney: Envirobook.

Thiong'o, N. 2011. 'Earth jurisprudence in the African context'. In Burdon, P. (ed.) *Exploring wild law: The philosophy of earth jurisprudence.* Kent Town, SA: Wakefield Press.

Vale, R., and Vale, B. 2013. *Living within a fair share ecological footprint.* London: Earthscan.

Worldwatch Institute, 2013. *Is sustainability still possible?* State of the World 2013 London: Island Press.

10

THE DEEP GREEN ALTERNATIVE
Debating strategies of transition

We don't have a right to ask whether we're going to succeed or not. The only question we have a right to ask is 'what's the right thing to do'?
– Wendell Berry

1. Introduction[1]

Evidence continues to mount that industrial civilisation, driven by a destructive and insatiable growth imperative, is chronically unsustainable, as well as grossly unjust. The global economy is in ecological overshoot, currently consuming resources and emitting waste at rates the planet cannot possibly sustain (Global Footprint Network, 2013). Peak oil is but the most prominent example of a more general situation of looming resource scarcity (Klare, 2012), with high oil prices having a debilitating effect on the oil-dependent economies which are seemingly dependent on cheap oil to maintain historic rates of growth (Heinberg, 2011). At the same time, great multitudes around the globe live lives of material destitution, representing a vast, marginalised segment of humanity that justifiably seeks to expand its economic capacities in some form (World Bank, 2008). Biodiversity continues to be devastated by deforestation and other forms of habitat destruction (United Nations, 2010), while the global development agenda seems to be aiming to provide an expanding global population with the high-impact material affluence enjoyed by the richest parts of the world

---

[1] This chapter is a lightly revised version of *Simplicity Institute Report 14a* (2015), co-authored by Samuel Alexander and Jonathan Rutherford.

(Hamilton, 2003). This is despite evidence crying out that the universalisation of affluence is environmentally unsupportable (Smith and Positano, 2010; Turner, 2012) and not even a reliable path to happiness (Lane, 2001; Alexander, 2012a). Most worrying of all, perhaps, is the increasingly robust body of climate science indicating the magnitude of the global predicament (IPCC, 2013). According to the Climate Tracker Initiative (2013: 4), the world could exceed its 'carbon budget' in around 18 years, essentially locking us into a future that is at least 2° warmer, and threatening us with 4° or more. It is unclear to what extent civilisation as we know it is compatible with runaway climate change. And still, almost without exception, all nations on the planet – including or especially the richest ones – continue to seek GDP growth without limit, as if the cause of these problems could somehow provide the solution. If once it was hoped that technology and science were going to be able to decouple economic activity from ecological impact, such a position is no longer credible (Huesemann and Huesemann, 2011). Technology simply cannot provide any escape from the fact that there are biophysical limits to growth. Despite decades of extraordinary technological advance, which it was promised would lighten the ecological burden of our economies, global energy and resource consumption continue to grow, exacerbated by a growing population, but are primarily a function of the growth-orientated values that lie at the heart of global capitalism (Turner, 2012).

Against this admittedly gloomy backdrop lies a heterogeneous tradition of critical theorists and activists promoting what could be called a 'deep green' alternative to the growth-orientated, industrial economy. Ranging from the radical simplicity of Henry Thoreau (1983), to the post-growth economics of the Club of Rome (Meadows *et al.,* 1972; 2004), and developing into contemporary expressions of radical reformism (Latouche, 2009; Heinberg, 2011; Jackson, 2009), eco-socialism (Sarkar, 1999; Smith, 2010), and eco-anarchism (Bookchin, 1989; Holmgren, 2002; Trainer, 2010a), this extremely diverse tradition nevertheless agrees that the nature of the existing system is inherently unsustainable. Tinkering with or softening its margins – that is, any attempt to give capitalism a 'human face' – is not going to come close to addressing the problems we, the human species, are confronted with. What is needed, this tradition variously maintains, is a radical alternative way of living on the Earth – something 'wholly other' to the ways of industrialisation, consumerism, and limitless growth. However idealistic or utopian their arguments might seem, the basic reasoning is that the nature of any solutions to current problems must honestly confront the magnitude of the overlapping crises, or else one risks serving the destructive forces one ostensibly opposes.

In this chapter we do not seek to defend, as such, the 'deep green' alternative, but rather analyse the most prominent strategies that have been put forth to bring it into existence. In other words, we take the vision outlined below for granted – we assume a deep green alternative is necessary – and critically analyse how such an alternative may be realised. We begin in the next section by outlining the deep green vision with a very broad brush, in order to give the more critical and substantive sections some context. It seems to us that there is some interesting and heartening overlap with respect to the envisioned 'end state' of the deep green school, and yet there is fierce debate over how to get there. Our primary interest in this chapter, therefore, is to examine these various theories of transition or transformation – ranging from parliament-arianism to socialism to anarchism – in order to highlight the most important factors at play, and hopefully shed some light on the question of strategy. While we do not expect or even intend to provide answers to this thorny question, the chapter should serve a worthwhile purpose if it helps clarify the debate and bring more attention to the issues under consideration.

2. The Deep Green Alternative

It is somewhat misleading, of course, to talk of *the* deep green alternative, or *the* deep green school, when in fact there are really a multitude of deep green alternatives, each of which acknowledges the context-dependency of any form of life. Nevertheless, despite this diversity, there is, as implied above, a significant degree of overlap within the body of radical literature we are examining concerning the desired 'end state'. For present purposes it is the general agreement that interests us, rather than the matters of detail or substance about which disagreement does, and forever may, exist. On that basis, we will now briefly sketch one vision of the deep green alternative, leaving the disagreement over 'how to get there' for examination in forthcoming sections.

At the heart of the deep green alternative is the recognition that a just and sustainable way of life, on a finite planet, must be based on material sufficiency and frugality, not material affluence (Alexander, 2013a). High-consumption lifestyles can never be universalised, even if the global economy were to transition to renewable systems of energy (Trainer, 2012). Steb Fisher (2013) has recently estimated that affluent countries such as Australia must reduce energy and material consumption to 6% of current levels in order to end the holocaust of species extinction and for humanity to have a good chance of long-term survival. Even allowing for some uncertainty in such estimates, the sheer scale of overshoot suggests that sustainability is not simply about people in consumer societies taking shorter showers, turning off the lights, and composting, necessary though those practices may be. Nor is it simply about transitioning to renewable energy. True sustainability – deep green sustainability – implies embracing a lifestyle of radical simplicity, which exemplifies extremely frugal but sufficient ways of living (Trainer, 2010a). Yes, it is imperative to transition rapidly to economic systems that run entirely or almost entirely on renewable energy. But this means living with much less energy than is typical in developed nations (Trainer, 2012), although most simplicity advocates also highlight the many benefits that could flow from living in less energy and resource intensive ways (Alexander, 2012a). That is, generally it is argued that the radical changes that are required for sustainability would actually be in our interests, if only we were to negotiate the transition wisely, and be open to living very differently than is customary in consumer societies today.

It must also be acknowledged, however, that this vision does not imagine that flourishing lifestyles of radical simplicity could easily arise within existing economic, political, and social structures. Not at all. In order for a sufficiency-based economy to function in desirable ways, a fundamental reevaluation of existing systems and structures is required. Primarily, this involves moving away from a growth-orientated economy and embracing a zero-growth economy which operates within the sustainable carrying capacity of local and global ecosystems. In the over-developed nations of the so-called 'first world', this would first involve moving through a phase of planned economic contraction – or degrowth – before stabilising in an economy that had 'zero growth' in resource and energy consumption. In the poorer parts of the world, this would involve developing or growing economic capacities until basic needs for all were met, and then those economies too would need to transition to a zero-growth model (Lawn and Clarke, 2010).

What would life look like in a zero-growth economy based on material sufficiency? Obviously, this question would have to be answered depending on context, but some broad comments can be made for present purposes. As much food as possible would be produced locally and organically, in order to minimise or eliminate fossil fuel dependency and build resilience and self-reliance (Hopkins, 2010). This would involve a vast increase in urban agriculture throughout the suburbs, with all growing spaces cultivated, as well as the development of farms on the urban periphery. Another means of reducing fossil fuel dependency would be to localise most production of goods, and transporting them, when necessary, via electric trains or vehicles, or even returning to the horse and cart in some situations. Walking or cycling would become the dominant mode of transport. Presumably some international trade and travel would still occur, as would some factory production, although the extent of such activities would have to be drastically reduced. Home production and self-sufficiency would inevitably increase. Many industries in existence today would become redundant, such as the fashion and marketing industries, for they would be superfluous in a world not driven by profit-maximisation. Other industries, such as solar and wind energy, would need to expand tremendously and urgently (a manufacturing process which, currently at least, depends on fossil fuels). Houses would be retrofitted to increase energy efficiency, and new houses would be built using mostly local resources, with housing density increasing in preference to further urban sprawl. A significant degree of re-ruralisation may also be required in some contexts. Clothes would first be mended rather than replaced, and necessary tools would be built to last. A great deal more sharing and barter would have to occur to mitigate the challenges of having much less stuff. Reuse, recycling, and conservation would be vigilantly embraced, and in many cases people would just have to do without many comforts and conveniences. But according to this deep green vision, basic material needs would be met, even if people did not have access to much beyond that threshold. Whether it would be necessary to live as simply as the Amish remains an open question, but that type of material culture provides a touchstone for understanding the radical simplicity that may indeed be required for genuinely sustainable living, especially in a world with seven billion people and counting. An Amish material standard of living, of course, need not necessitate an Amish culture or religion. As J.S. Mill (2004[1848]) noted long ago, a 'stationary state' economy need not imply a stationary state in culture or human improvement. While this brief outline probably raises as many questions as it answers, it is hoped that it nevertheless provides some insight into the deep green vision of life under consideration.

3. Debating Strategies of Transition: Five Pathways

Having outlined a general vision of the deep green alternative, we now wish to look more closely at the question of transition; that is, at the question of how to realise the alternative outlined. For it is not enough, of course, to be able to describe the nature of a just and sustainable society. It is equally necessary to consider strategic issues about how to mobilise communities and destabilise existing power structures for the purpose of bringing such a society into existence. In the following sections we critically examine five theories of transition: (1) the radical-reformism strategy; (2) the eco-socialist strategy; (3) the eco-anarchist strategy; (4) the deep green resistance strategy; and finally (5) a pathway defined more by 'crisis and response' than any deliberate strategy for change. Naturally, our examination of these large themes cannot be comprehensive, so readers should treat the analysis as merely an invitation to discuss.

2.1 *Radical reformism*

> Our economic and financial system... is a tool that we have developed and that reflects our goals and values. People do not worry about the future, but only about their current problems... And when for many people the future does not matter, they will create an economic and financial system that destroys the future. You can tweak this system as long as you want. As long as you do not change the values of the people, it will continue. If you give someone a hammer in his hand and he uses it, and it kills his neighbor, it helps nothing to change the hammer. Even if you take away the hammer, it remains a potential killer (Meadows, 2013).

In what follows we use the term 'radical reformism' neutrally, neither as a term of criticism nor praise, but merely to signify a strategy that is based on radical change brought about through radical parliamentary reform. This approach to transition is currently dominant in green circles. As the term suggests, there are two defining elements. It is 'reformist' because it does not seek to overturn or replace the basic structure of a market economy[2] or the centralised democratic state. Implicitly or explicitly, this position holds that the deep green transition required could be achieved in

---

[2] In what follows, much reference will be made to capitalism and the market system. These terms will refer to a system in which a) there is private ownership of most means of production; and b) a market system through which fundamental economic outcomes (that is *what*, *how*, and *for whom* to produce and allocate) are determined via price signals and exchange, rather than through deliberate social or governmental planning (Fotopoulos, 1997: 5). For a discussion of the blurry lines between market economies and socially planned economies, see Samuel Alexander, 'Property beyond growth: Toward a politics of voluntary simplicity'. Doctoral thesis, Melbourne Law School. Ch. 2.

and through these institutions that, today, dominate the globe (Fotopoulos, 1997; Harvey, 2005; Robinson, 2011). Often there is little focus on class or elite power, as barriers to transition. Instead, it is believed that, in principle, a peaceful transition to a sustainable world can be achieved by winning political support across the social hierarchy. Commonly there is a call to do away with outdated 'left' and 'right' distinctions, in order to forge a new form of progressive green politics (Sutton, 2013; Mcknight, 2005). In short, the basic aim, as Terry Leahy argues, 'is to effect a transition to sustainability without class conflict or a change in the mode of production' (Leahy, 2013: 13). Nevertheless, the strategy is certainly 'radical' in that, of necessity, it seeks a massive shift in the *modus operandi* of today's globalised neo-liberal capitalism and at all levels of society. As one of the leading advocates of radical reformism, Tim Jackson has put it, paraphrasing Spock from *Star Trek*, 'It's capitalism, Jim. But not as we know it' (Jackson 2009: 202).

One of the central underlying beliefs of radical reformism is what Marxists would critically call 'idealism'. This is the belief 'that reality is constituted by ideas, not material conditions' (Keith *et al.,* 2011: 217). According to this view, ideas and values shape and mold social structures, rather than the other way around. Thus, economic growth is explained in terms of ideology. It is likened to a religion or addiction and consumerism is characterised as a disease of 'affluenza' (Hamilton and Denniss, 2005). In the epigraph to this section, Dennis Meadow, one the original authors of *Limits to Growth* (1972), provides an example of this view. Here is another example from Paul Gilding:

> Our addiction to growth is a complex phenomenon, one that can't be blamed on a single economic model or philosophy. It is not the fault of capitalism or Western democracy, and it is not a conspiracy of the global corporate sector or the rich ... Growth goes to the core of the society we have built because it is the result of who we are and what we have decided to value (Gilding, 2011: 66).

According to Gilding, economic growth and the debt crisis are not, ultimately, due to the systemic working of capitalism but rather, the values and ideas that citizens have chosen to adopt. It follows that the central task for transition is a cultural revolution – an over-turning of presently dominant competitive and individualistic values and ideas – to be replaced by a culture that fosters healthy relationships, community building, and rewards altruism and simple living (Latouche, 2009: 34). This in turn will pressure governments to make the radical policy shifts required for the deep green vision to be realised (assuming democracies are functioning sufficiently well).

Moves toward shaping this new culture require efforts at all levels of civil society, as well as within business and government. At the household level, individuals and families are encouraged to downshift and simplify lifestyles. There is evidence this process has begun with nationwide surveys indicating a quarter of Australian and British middle-aged adults downshifting in the 10 years prior to 2001 (Hamilton and Breakspear, 2003a; Hamilton and Breakspear, 2003b). In the largest empirical study of the Voluntary Simplicity Movement, it has been estimated that as many as 200 million people, to varying degrees, have begun exploring lifestyles of reduced and restrained consumption (Alexander and Ussher, 2012). This signifies a movement of potentially transformative significance if it ever radicalised and organised itself with political intent (see also, Holmgren, 2013).

At the local, community level, radical reformists promote the expansion of existing social movements such as slow food, permaculture, eco-villages and Transition Towns (Holmgren, 2002; Hopkins, 2008; Gilding, 2010; Heinberg, 2011). Together these movements are beginning the process of re-localising food, decarbonising energy production, and developing the embryo of a new informal economy based on sharing and gifting within neighborhoods, suburbs, and towns. Examples include community gardens, farmers' markets, local currencies, co-housing projects, recycling schemes, and skill sharing networks. Radical reformists generally believe these grassroots initiatives, in addition to building local resilience, can help to generate the values and ideas needed to win support for radical political reforms at all levels of government (Gilding, 2011; Heinberg, 2011).

Within the Transition Towns Movement in particular there is a strong emphasis on not being too prescriptive. Though the transition 'handbook' outlines 12 steps to transition, the focus is to provide guidance on the initial setting up and building of a movement. There is minimal direction given on the actual projects that should be attempted and in what order. Though this has been the subject of criticism (Trainer, 2010a), the movement founders consider it to be a virtue. It allows local manifestations of transition the flexibility to respond to the felt needs and interests of participants, according to context and circumstance. The overall focus is on encouraging ordinary people to take initiative and 'just do stuff' in order to make their communities more sustainable (Hopkins, 2013).

Many radical reformists have begun to think through how grassroots action could influence public policy more decisively. The

Australian-based climate activist Phil Sutton, for example, has drawn up an approach to strategy aimed at winning support for a 'climate emergency' policy but which, arguably, could be applied to the broader task of achieving a deep green society (Sutton, 2013). Initially efforts should be made to target local councils, which sometimes have a strong base of green support. The electoral results of Green parties could be used as a rough indicator. In these green-friendly zones, activists should make sustained efforts to win over both local residents and council workers to a climate emergency agenda of rapid decarbonisation, while building social support amongst civil society. Even if only one council adopts this position, they can act as 'champions... beyond their border, and across the country' (Sutton, 2013: 24). Eventually, it is argued, this could have a decisive influence on state and federal policy making. In the future, it is thought this same approach could also apply at the global level; coalitions of radical 'green' states could influence the outcome of international environmental negotiations (Sutton, 2013: 24).

Eventually, most radical reformists believe state and federal government will need to pursue radical policy change. Here, the ecological economist Herman Daly has been influential. To achieve the necessary 'degrowth' in resource and energy consumption,[3] a comprehensive Cap-Auction-Trade system is advocated (Daly, 2013). This would work in a similar way to the Australian Labor Party's recently implemented (yet soon to be abolished) carbon scheme, though obviously much more comprehensive and with far deeper cuts. Legally binding resource quotas would be placed on resources across the entire economy (Alcott, 2008). The quotas would be 'owned' by the government, which would then auction them to firms throughout the economy, giving them a financial incentive to make the most 'efficient' resource reductions without

---

[3] Some critics point out that we can make a distinction between physical growth and GDP growth. Physical growth refers to an increase in energy and material inputs into the economy, whereas GDP refers to total monetary value of production and consumption. Some believe GDP growth can be 'decoupled' from physical inputs through technological change and efficiency improvements (Sutton, 2013). However, given the historically tight relationship between GDP and resource/energy inputs, as well as the deep cuts required in the latter, maintaining GDP growth while initiating degrowth in resource/energy throughput will prove extremely challenging. Nevertheless, degrowth advocates do tend to argue that their agenda for change will be in people's self-interest (as well as in social and environmental interests), so in this sense degrowth can be considered 'economic', even if it implies a contraction of GDP (see Alexander, 2012b).

requiring the state to 'pick winners'. This overarching policy goal is then supported by additional policy reforms (Daly, 2013; Terry Leahy, 2013; Heinberg, 2011; Jackson, 2009; Hamilton, 2003). There is disagreement and debate among reformists but some of the most commonly proposed policies include:

- Redistribution of wealth via taxation;
- Trade protections to promote 'green' industries and regulate damaging industries;
- Reform of International Institutions such WTO, IMF, World Bank;
- Provision of a guaranteed adequate income for all citizens;
- Reduced working hours in exchange for high consumption;
- Banking reforms (e.g., an end to fractional reserve banking and predatory lending);
- Population policies and targets;
- Direct investment in renewables (including subsidies) and 'green' jobs;
- Promotion of cooperative businesses and ethical investment.

Reformists are aware that these proposals would require almost unprecedented levels of government regulation – a far cry from today's globalised neo-liberalism. Gilding, for example, sees a need to go far beyond carbon trading or taxes to reduce carbon emissions as quickly and deeply as the science requires (Gilding, 2011). He calls for a government-mandated phase-down of the coal industry and a 'massive' programme of direct investment in renewables (Gilding, 2011: 136-7). Jackson and Heinberg also foresee the need for nationalisation of 'strategic firms', particularly the banking sector, so that debt can be cancelled and government can take back control of money creation. Terry Leahy (2013), in a critical review of radical reformism, goes further and argues the above proposals would, in practice, require levels of government control, regulation, and planning that would make it virtually indistinguishable from heavy state-socialism. But on this point radical reformists are likely to disagree. They remain confident that their goals can be achieved, albeit within a heavily moderated 'market economy' framework. They explicitly argue that the economy should, to the largest extent possible, remain in private hands with competitive markets determining the allocation of resources (Heinberg, 2011; Daly, 1991). Thus, for Herman Daly, the above measures 'are based on the impeccably conservative institutions of private property and decentralised market allocation' (Daly, 2013). Likewise Paul Gilding (2011) is clear that more revolutionary changes are not required:

> Is the end of growth the end of markets? The end of capitalism? Most definitely not. We will still need competition, we will still want ideas and innovation to flourish and we will want capital allocated as efficiently as possible. Markets are good at all those things.

Again this is because, for radical reformists, the core problem does not lie *inherently* within the market economy and private production. Rather, the core problem is the culture in which these institutions are embedded. If radical cultural change can be achieved – including among the 'power elite' (Gilding, 2011) – then transition will occur, without the need to consider more revolutionary change.

A major attraction of reformism is its non-revolutionary approach. Though within the political class the above policy reforms would be considered 'extreme', the adoption of a reformed capitalism nevertheless opens up the possibility of working with business, government, and civil society groups, in order to build support for radical policy shifts. It is, obviously, easier to build mass support for such a vision than try to build support for the even more radical proposals considered below. This is particularly the case with localised movements such as Transition Towns, slow-food and permaculture. These initiatives currently thrive, at least in part, because they offer participants a positive, flexible, and *relatively* non-confrontational approach to achieving the transition.

That said, if a radical reformist movement were ever to build serious momentum and influence, conflict and hostility would seem inevitable. It would be naïve to think governments, corporations, and wealthy citizens would willingly accept the above policy proposals, particularly the imposition of a national 'degrowth' policy. Such measures will almost certainly be vigorously opposed, ideologically and by force if necessary, by elite groups and most governments. 'How,' asks Leahy, 'could we possibly suppose that the capitalist class would not resist radical reformism when it is intended to attack every part of their current power base?' (Leahy, 2013: 21). In Australia, one only needs to look at the ferocious corporate opposition to even mild carbon and mining taxes, to see evidence of what one could expect. Global responses to the Occupy Movement provide another telling example. Confrontation and conflict will therefore be an inevitable part of the transition.

More challengingly, eco-socialists and eco-anarchists, as we will now see, argue that reformism – even if it were vigorously pursued – is inherently incapable of achieving the transition to a deep green society. The eco-socialists and eco-anarchists offer differing reasons for this view. Let us first consider the eco-socialists.

2.2 *The eco-socialist strategy*

> Millions of people must realize that overcoming the crises and,
> in the end, ensuring the survival of mankind, are not possible as
> long as capitalism continues to exist. People have to be
> convinced of the necessity of a newly conceived socialism
> (Sarkar, 2008: 5).

Socialists tend to share a common desire to see a society 'based upon the common ownership and democratic control of the means and instruments for producing and distributing wealth by and in the interest of the whole community' (Pepper *et al.*, 2010: 33). At present, however, very few socialists – even among those who are concerned about the environmental crises – have adopted the deep green vision. But there are now a growing number of eco-socialists, such as Saral Sarkar (1999), Richard Smith (2010), and John Bellamy Foster (2010), who recognise that today any socialism worthy of the name will inevitably require a challenge to current levels of industrialism and affluence. The work of Saral Sarkar, in particular, is worth highlighting. He is very clearly and boldly expressing the need for a re-conceived eco-socialism that incorporates the essential elements of the deep green vision, such as decentralisation, localism, and simplified living. His ideas will therefore be the prime focus in this section.

All eco-socialists argue that market-capitalism is fundamentally irreconcilable with ecological sustainability (Smith, 2010; Sarkar, 1999;). Capitalist firms enter the market in order to sell commodities in competition with other firms. Thus, to remain viable all firms must constantly re-invest their profits in order to maximise economic expansion. They can do this, for example, by investing in labour-saving technologies, exploiting cheap labour and resources, maximising the sales effort through marketing, and increasing the scale of production, in order to benefit from economies of scale (Smith, 2010). They *must*, in other words, enhance the forces of production. And, unless regulations prevent them, they must do this regardless of any social and environmental 'externalities' created in the process. As a result, eco-socialists argue, there is a 'grow or die' dynamic built into the foundations of the capitalist-market system.

In normal times, growth at the micro level of the firm results in growth across the entire economy. But, as Smith points out, when it does not there will be a recession. And, he notes, 'it's not a pretty sight: capital destruction, mass unemployment, devastated communities, foreclosures, spreading poverty and homelessness, school closures, and environmental considerations shunted aside in the all-out effort to restore growth' (Smith, 2010: 14). We witnessed this very clearly in the wake of the global financial crisis when governments, of every stripe, used emergency fiscal and monetary action to 'stimulate' their economies.[4] Richard Smith concludes that 'the growth imperative is virtually a law of nature built-into in any conceivable capitalism' (Smith, 2010, 10; cf. Lawn, 2011). Eco-socialists therefore contend that a capitalist framework cannot be made compatible with a 'steady state' economy, let alone a process of degrowth, as required by the deep green vision.

To be clear, most, though not all eco-socialists would see some place for 'markets' – in the sense of trade and exchange – particularly among the self-employed, family businesses, and worker cooperatives (Sarkar, 1999). However, these 'markets' would have to work under firm regulations and guidelines set by democratically developed local and regional planes and guidelines (Smith, 2010; Sarkar, 1999; Trainer, 2010a). Critics of socialism, of course, would question whether such a non-market economy could in fact be compatible with a truly democratic state (Friedman, 1982).

On the question of what activists should be doing *right now*, however, radical reformists and eco-socialists have much in common. Sarkar suggests that a primary initial task is to build a 'simple-lifestyle' campaign to create within growing numbers of people a 'readiness to sacrifice luxury and comfort' (Sarkar, 1999: 229). The campaign must be one that is 'based on ecological arguments, [and] appeals to people's sense of equality, justice and solidarity with the third world and the interests of the future generations' (Sarkar, 1999: 229). Eco-socialists therefore agree, up to a point, that achieving a radical shift in values among ordinary people is necessary. For this revolution, Sarkar argues, 'moral progress is a precondition of success' (Sarkar, 1999: 266).[5]

---

[4] Though, as many have pointed out, governments frequently did this in ways which primarily benefitted the large banks and corporations – i.e., by bailing them out or granting loans. The Australian Government was a partial exception, in that their stimulus package gave money directly to ordinary people to spend into circulation.

[5] This, of course, is a significant departure from the theoretical assumption of traditional Marxist 'historical materialism'. Marxists always believed that a 'new man' was required for socialism, however it was thought this would develop *after* the revolution. New revolutionary ideas and values could not become hegemonic *prior* to the revolution because, according to historical materialism, material conditions determine consciousness. This meant socialist property relations had to be achieved before a culture of solidarity and co-operation could become widespread. Moreover, a change in the *relations of production* (i.e., socialist property relations) could not be achieved until the *forces of production* (i.e., technical advance) had been built up. But, as Sarkar

Some eco-socialists would also agree with reformists that, in the short term, liberal-democratic governments must be pressured into making radical reforms. Eco-socialists John Bellamy Foster and Fred Magdoff, for example, propose a long list of reforms, similar to those listed previously, which should form the basis of green campaigns (Foster and Magdoff, 2011: 126-130). They argue that making such demands will push capitalism to its limits, leading to tension and conflict and eventually raising consciousness on the need for more far-reaching change in terms of the underlying property system (Foster & Magdoff, 2011). For these reasons there is a strong basis for reformist and socialist activists to work together on environmental and social campaigns, even if significant differences exist about the ultimate nature of the alternative society, including the nature of transformation.

In the long term eco-socialists believe the deep green vision can only finally be achieved through a socialist revolution. They disagree with reformists that a revolution in values and ideas, coupled with parliamentary reform, will be sufficient; systemic economic change away from the fundamental structures of market capitalism is also required. Before this is possible, there will have to be a sustained effort to achieve 'cultural hegemony' – that is, an intellectual acceptance throughout civil society – for an eco-socialist perspective. This must begin firstly with a widespread attempt, using all means possible, to de-legitimise capitalism (Sarkar and Bruno, 2008). Sarkar does not believe, at this stage, the priority should be on forming an eco-socialist party. However, if one is started 'its task should be to strengthen the movement' (Sarkar, 1999: 228) rather than contest for power. The attempt to gain short-term electoral respectability frequently results in watering down the political agenda. This has been the broad experience of the Greens, with the classic example being the German Greens. In that case, after a long internal struggle, the more pragmatic 'realos' won out

---

points out, all this has to be rethought in light of the limits to growth. An *eco-socialist* revolution, today, cannot be based on the further development of productive forces: '...on the contrary, moral progress is necessary to stop the development of productive forces!' (Sarkar, 1999: 266). A willingness to accept this will have to become widespread among people in the first world, *prior* to any revolution. But Sarkar does not reject historical materialism entirely; he agrees that the 'new man' will not be achieved before the revolution. Instead, he hedges his bets: '...the new man will develop in the process of developing the new society' (Sarkar, 1999: 266). But for Sarkar, unlike eco-anarchists (see below), a vital part of this process will involve taking state power.

over the 'fundis' who wanted the party to remain true to its founding values and principles (Biehl, 1993). But, Sarkar argues, compromising to achieve power makes no sense if the central goal of the party, in the long term, is to help build cultural hegemony for an eco-socialist vision. As such, if the party takes part in elections 'it must be prepared, for many years to come, to be rejected by the vast majority of voters' (Sarkar, 1999: 228). Only when widespread cultural influence had been attained could a serious attempt be made by an eco-socialist party to win democratic elections. Obviously, we are far from such a situation today.

The difficulties would not end there. Most eco-socialists think the movement will have to be *internationalist* from the outset. This would be particularly necessary given today's high levels of global economic integration. According to many theorists, globalisation has resulted in the emergence of a global capitalist class, with immense ideological, political, and economic power (Robinson, 2011; Fotopoulos, 2005; Hardt and Negri, 2000). If an eco-socialist party in one isolated country made an attempt on power, it would be highly vulnerable to economic attacks in the form of embargoes, boycotts, and capital flight. Sarkar therefore recommends withholding attempts to win power until 'the pressure for change in the direction of eco-socialism ha[s] built up in several countries' (Sarkar, 1999: 230).

A crucial question that arises is who or what would be the agent of this 'newly conceived socialism'? Which class or group within society can be expected to lead the fight? Traditionally socialists have placed their hopes in the organised working class. But, as Sarkar makes clear, eco-socialism can no longer promise the working class, at least in affluent societies, increased shares of wealth and income, which has, historically, been the raison d'être of the union movement. On the contrary, this revolution involves reductions in income and material wealth – though not necessarily quality of life – for first-world workers. Sarkar therefore does not think the working class will play a unique or pivotal role, though of course, like everyone else, they must eventually be won over. He quotes, instead, Erich Fromm: 'today there are only two camps, those who care and those who don't' (quoted in Sarkar, 1999: 230). The ranks of those 'who care' could come from all levels of society, apart from private entrepreneurs, perhaps, who must endorse the growth imperative in order to remain competitive.

This view on the working class is hotly contested among eco-socialists. Traditionally, the socialist movement has placed its hope in the working class, as the only social agency with both the *interest* and the potential *power*, to end capitalist exploitation and create a classless society. Ellen Meiskins Wood is typically emphatic: 'Unless the class-interests of the working class themselves direct them into political struggle and to the transformation of the mode of production, the socialist project must remain an empty and utopian aspiration' (Wood, 2012: 319). And, for this same reason, most eco-socialists cannot stomach Sarkar's strategic ambivalence toward the working class. John Bellamy Foster is among the many who are putting their hopes in a new 'environmental working class' that would forge alliances with other oppressed groups in response to environmental degradation (Foster, 2013). But even if one is convinced of the strategic importance of the working class, it cannot be denied that for this revolution – the deep green revolution – class *interests* are going to have to be radically redefined. Perhaps, eco-socialists could press the union movement to focus on meaningful and secure work, full employment, and democratic control of the workplace. None of these are secured by today's neo-liberal capitalism, and they are consistent with a viable eco-socialism. But eco-socialism cannot be achieved without material sacrifice. As Sarkar notes, in this revolution first world workers 'have more than their chains to lose, they have their prosperity' (Sarkar, 1999:237).

A consolation, of sorts, is that the case for eco-socialism is most compelling when one considers how an orderly economic contraction or 'degrowth' may be achieved. As we saw above, radical reformists advocate for a gradual reduction in resource and energy consumption through the imposition of steadily lowering resource caps, while allowing markets to continue to determine resource allocation. Eco-socialists point out major difficulties with this scenario (Smith, 2010; Sarkar, 1999). A contraction of materials and energy would almost certainly lead to diminishing profits for firms and therefore reduced per-capita income alongside rising levels of bankruptcy and unemployment. If allocation were left to market forces, lower income groups and unskilled workers would also be hit hardest by rising costs of food and other basic living items. Furthermore, as Richard Smith (2010) points out, environmental and social outcomes, if left to the market, would not necessarily be equitable. The profit-driven growth compulsion would still be operative and, as such, firms would continue to produce 'goods and services we don't need, or goods designed to wear out, or goods designed to become obsolete as fast as possible' (Smith, 2010: 41). This would become intolerable in a context of rising scarcity. In short, a contraction within a capitalist framework would be 'a recipe for chaos and social unrest' (Sarkar, 1999: 219).

Eco-socialists argue this type of transition could never win broad-based political support, particularly among workers. This would only be conceivable if the burden and sacrifices were shared out equally among all, and nobody was left without economic security. This would require rationing of goods and services, deliberate planning of investment and employment, and price controls. Eco-socialists do not shirk from drawing the politically unfashionable conclusion: the only way to humanely contract the economy is for the democratic state to take ownership of, at least, all large enterprises and comprehensively plan an orderly contraction of the economy (Sarkar, 1999: Ch 6; Smith, 2010).

Sarkar distinguishes between this transition phase and the future eco-socialist society. During the transition, the state, though democratically elected, will necessarily require tough action to push through policies in the face of 'strong opposition of those who have much to lose' (Sarkar, 1999: 214). Once the contraction has occurred, however, the new decentralised and simplified eco-socialist economy will be more amenable to extensive democratic input from the broader population, both within firms and local community planning bodies. And people will have a strong incentive to become involved. Everyone will understand that his or her own economic welfare, and local reputation, would depend on making a valued contribution. Ideally, this local dependency will also increase the efficiency of a planned economy and help to avoid the corruption and inefficiency that stifled previous attempts (Sarkar, 1999, Ch. 6).

There are several weaknesses within the eco-socialist strategy. The most obvious is that, after the disappointments of 'actually existing socialism' and the rise of post-modern identity politics, the socialist 'brand' has taken a battering. In most affluent countries socialist organisations have small numbers and minor influence. And this is the case despite the fact that very few socialists have incorporated the limits to growth into their politics. Sandy Irvine rightly points out that a glance at far left literature 'suggests that, so far, any greening has been rather skin deep' (Irvine, 2001: 8). If they did incorporate the limits to growth, in the short term at least, their popularity – particularly within unions – is likely to sink further. In addition, as Pepper points out, there has been a long-running rift, both practical and theoretical, between socialism and the ecology movement that will prove difficult to overcome (Pepper, 1994). Though they are often unaware of it, the ideas, values, and tactics of modern greens, have their roots in the anarchist tradition more than Marxian socialism (Pepper, 1994: 4). As we will see below, contemporary eco-anarchists raise further objections to the eco-socialist transition strategy.

Eco-socialists can point to positive indicators. Recent polls in the US, for example, indicate high levels of support for socialism among the young, increasing significantly since the 2008 global financial crisis.[6] In Germany, polling suggests over half the population believes socialism is a good idea, but its implementation has failed in the past (Sarkar, 1999: 218). Socialists are also encouraged by the turn to the left across Latin America in countries such as Venezuela, Bolivia, Ecuador, Brazil, and Nicaragua. This new brand of socialism articulates a strong concern for the environment, as evidenced by the 'Rights of Mother Earth' statement that was issued at the World People's Conference on Climate Change in Bolivia in 2010 (Foster and Magdoff, 2011). But, while hopeful, none of these trends provide evidence that many socialists have embraced the deep green vision. Still, there is no doubt eco-socialism offers a forthright challenge to deep greens of all varieties: a fair and orderly transition to a sustainable society, they argue, can only be achieved within a state-driven socialist framework. It is a claim that needs to be taken seriously by all those who recognise the extent and urgency of the unfolding crises the world is currently facing.

3.3 *The eco-anarchist strategy*

> The only realistic approach in creating a new society beyond the market economy and the nation-state... is a political strategy that comprises the gradual involvement of increasing numbers of people in a new kind of politics and the parallel shifting of economic resources (labor, land, capital) away from the market economy. The aim of such a transitional strategy should be to create changes in the institutional framework and value systems that, after a period of tension between the new institutions and the state, would, at some stage, replace the market economy and statist democracy (Fotopoulos, 1997: 282).

Eco-anarchism is one current within the broad school of anarchism. For the purposes of this chapter it refers to those anarchist thinkers who adopt core elements of the deep green vision. Eco-anarchists share much in common with eco-socialists in terms of their critique of capitalism. In most cases they agree that capitalism cannot be reconciled with sustainability. A socialised, planned economy is therefore usually endorsed, though there is considerable debate on the degree to which private property, markets, and money, should be part of a desirable future economy (Trainer, 2010a; Fotopoulos, 1997; Nelson and Timmerman, 2011; Leahy, 2013).

---

[6] See http://www.huffingtonpost.com/2011/12/29/young-people-socialism_n_ 1175218.html

Eco-anarchists, however, share a different *ultimate goal* to eco-socialists in that they want to end, or at least minimise, political hierarchy; that is, the situation in which some have greater power over political decisions than others. This, among other things, leads to their rejection of the centralised state, even in the form of representative democracy. They point to the failure of state socialism as evidence of the inevitable corruption that takes place when political and economic power is concentrated in the hands of a centralised state bureaucracy. Furthermore, power, according to anarchists, not only corrupts those who monopolise it; it demoralises those without it. As Ted Trainer stresses, 'Humans will not have reached social maturity until they have learned to govern themselves' (Trainer, 2010a: 153). In place of the state, anarchists want a *self-governing* society. This would still involve collective laws, rules, and regulations. However, it would be ordinary people themselves who *directly* determine the key economic and political decisions that affect their lives, through neighbourhood and town assemblies and local committees. Local assemblies should then be federated at the regional and national level where delegates, subject to regular rotation and recall, would be charged with responsibility for representing the wishes of their local assemblies. In other words, anarchists want a *participatory* democracy as opposed to all other forms of 'statist' society, whether democratic, authoritarian, or totalitarian. It can also be argued that governments have an inherent bias toward growth, insofar as policies depend on taxation. With a larger economy, therefore, there is a larger tax base to fund government policies, making it difficult for governments to promote post-growth economics, especially a policy of degrowth.

But apart from ideological opposition to the state, eco-anarchists offer practical reasons why the centralised state, by its very nature, will be unable to run decentralised and localised economies, which will be non-negotiable elements of deep green society from an eco-anarchist perspective (Trainer, 2010a). These economies will require a high degree of self-sufficiency, using local resources to meet local needs. This will involve a great deal of variation from locality to locality, resulting in a diverse range of rules, procedures, and arrangements. In these novel circumstances, Trainer argues, it will only be ordinary people, at the local level, who will be capable of satisfactorily running their own local economies. Only they 'will know the situation, the soils, the history, the likes and the dislikes, what will and won't work there' (Trainer, 2010a: 153). Distant bureaucrats will not have the knowledge or expertise to do this well, and the 'one-size-fits-all' approach of a centralised state will not suit the diverse circumstances of different localities.

Neither, argues Trainer, will it be ideal for these new local economies to be run by a few representatives or powerful rulers (Trainer, 2010a: Ch. 6). In conditions of resource and energy scarcity only a society based on high levels of cooperation and collectivism will result in rules and procedures that work out well for all. But, of course, cooperation and collectivism depend on at least the majority of people being content with the running of their locality. This, in turn, will require that everyone has a say over the decisions that impact him or her. Without an inclusive democratic approach, town morale will rapidly decline. 'Resentful people who don't own the decisions,' Trainer quips, 'are not going to turn up well to the working bees to implement them' (Trainer, 2010a: 154). According to eco-anarchists, in other words, a truly ecological society will have to be a self-governing society. It will not be run well by powerful representatives, either at the national or local level.

We must, however, separate out the eco-anarchist *goal* of radical self-government – which many today would see as unfeasible – from the eco-anarchist perspective on *transition*. Their ideas on transition are extremely important for all deep greens to consider, regardless of whether the ultimate goal is adopted. The core point made by eco-anarchists – in contrast to the previous two approaches – is that they do not believe it makes sense to take state power, *as a means* of achieving the transition. Even if one thinks the democratic state will have a major role to play in the new society, it will surely be incapable or unwilling to carry *the transition* unless and until a critical mass of citizens have *first* come to support the necessary changes. Moreover, eco-anarchists argue, this will only happen after growing numbers of people have developed the skills and experienced the benefits of self-government, cooperation, sharing, living simply and frugally. This is thought to be the only way political support could be developed for laws and regulations enabling greater household self-sufficiency, the re-zoning of suburbs, development of commons, and, at the national/state level, the necessary planning and contraction of the economy. In other words, if the movement does end up taking state power via elections this will only be as a *consequence* of a long grassroots process of radical change.

For all the above reasons, eco-anarchists advocate a strategy based on 'pre-figuring' the new society inside the old. Rather than wait for the revolution to be pushed through by the state, the idea is to start building elements of the new society here and now. Leahy, for example, talks about creating hybrids of the new anarchist 'gift economy' that will co-exist alongside contemporary capitalism (Leahy, 2011: 132). Of course, most eco-anarchists are realistic enough to recognise that this process will, inevitably, involve lobbying councils or NGOs and, eventually, states in order to change legislation and perhaps provide needed funding for local projects. Obviously, no large structural changes could occur without this. But these efforts should be engaged in only in so far as they support *citizens themselves* in creating new local economies, settlements, governing structures, and cultures. The hope is that the new formations will grow and, through a long process, eventually challenge the institutions and values of present-day consumer-capitalism. That is to say, radical change in values and institutions must occur *concurrently*, via the grassroots building of the new society.

Eco-anarchists usually offer specific suggestions on the type of local initiatives that make most sense. Trainer believes the focus should be on the creation of Community Development Co-operatives (CDCs) within towns and suburbs (Trainer, 2010a: Ch 14). The CDCs will attempt to create a new 'Economy B' existing beneath the present market economy. Trainer spells out the difference between these economies in stark terms:

> We have to build a local economy, not a national or globalised economy; an economy designed to meet needs, not to maximise profits; an economy under participatory social control and not driven by corporate profit; and one guided by rational planning as distinct from leaving everything to the market. This is the antithesis of capitalism, markets, profit motivation and corp-orate control. Nothing could be more revolutionary. If we don't plunge into building such an economy we will probably not survive in the coming age of scarcity (Trainer, 2010b).

How could local communities possibly begin to achieve such a momentous and radical change? Eco-anarchists understand that this will take decades of work. The CDCs will be tiny at first, seeking to undertake small, seemingly insignificant, projects. The CDCs could begin by growing food in a community garden, creating tool-sharing systems, baking bread, or repairing old furniture, bicycles, and appliances. Unemployed, elderly, and disadvantaged people would be ideal participants to engage in these activities, as they would have the most to gain and time to offer. The economic activity thus generated could then be linked to a new local currency, with participants earning a share of the produce according to the hours they contributed. Labour credit schemes like this have been used, very successfully, for many years at the egalitarian commune in Twin Oaks, Virginia (Nelson and Timmerman, 2011: Ch 9). Eventually the new economy could use their new currency to begin trading with local businesses within the town or suburb. Trainer wants to stress that the most important function of the CDCs is not the actual building of alternative ways, at least at first. Rather, projects like these will put activists in the best position to raise awareness on the urgent need for radical change toward a deep green society.

Another eco-anarchist, Takis Fotopoulos, while endorsing such local initiatives, puts far more emphasis on engaging with local politics (Fotopoulos, 1997: Ch. 7). According to Fotopoulos, after a long period of spreading radical ideas, efforts should be made to win local council or municipal elections. If successful, the winning candidate would then rescind and devolve power to local citizen assemblies. The assemblies would then be in a position to give decisive support to a new model of economic development that breaks with the market economy and its growth dynamic. Fotopoulos hopes that such local formations could, eventually, confederate and 'create the conditions for the establishment of a new society' (Fotopoulos, 1997: 283).

At this point, one may ask, how does this 'pre-figuring' strategy differ, in practice, from the local projects promoted by reformists, such as Transition Towns, LETS, and permaculture? Currently there may be little *practical* difference. Eco-anarchists are supportive of these types of initiatives (Trainer, 2010a; Fotopoulos, 1997, Leahy, 2013; Nelson and Timmerman, 2011). They would have no issue with current attempts to build community gardens, develop co-housing arrangements, initiate sharing and gifting economies and, indeed, for individuals and families to downshift. However, for eco-anarchists, these initiatives will only be of long-term value if they eventually form part of a larger movement for radical change. Presently this is rarely the case. These initiatives are usually only aimed, at least explicitly, at making improvements or adjustments *within* capitalist society, rather than openly seeking to replace such a society. If not set within such a radical vision and programme (i.e., for a deep green society) such initiatives, it is argued, will be easily accommodated by consumer capitalism and will constitute no threat to it (Trainer, 2010a).

Eco-anarchists believe these local initiatives must eventually become part of a global revolutionary movement – though everywhere acting locally – aimed at the achievement of a zero-growth economy embedded within new self-governing and highly self-sufficient communities and economies, emerging from within present-day towns and suburbs. As David Pepper argues, localisation movements and projects for building ecological aware-ness are valuable but only if 'set within a culture of non-capitalist values and a clearly radical social change agenda' (Pepper, 2010: 43). Trainer encourages activists to get involved with local initiatives, but with this bigger picture in mind. They should attempt to persuade their fellow participants that these projects must form part of a larger revolutionary project (Trainer, 2010a).

It is important to point out, finally, that eco-anarchists are not so naïve as to think this grassroots renewal will occur, on a large scale, simply through a voluntary retreat from consumer society. The vast majority of people will only start to look for alternatives when financial difficulties begin to impact on them directly. But when this happens, people will increasingly be searching for alternatives and a radical local movement must be ready to fill the vacuum in order to have a decisive influence over the course of events. Only if a *pre-emptive* radical economy and culture has been developed, argue eco-anarchists, can we have reasonable hope of avoiding chaotic breakdown and descent into a new dark age.

There are several major criticisms that have been levelled at the eco-anarchist strategy. Many would view the vision for a self-governing non-hierarchical society as hopelessly impracticable and unworkable. Almost all hitherto societies have had a degree of hierarchy and domination, suggesting that this is a deeply entrenched – perhaps unavoidable – element of any 'complex' society, whether desirable or not. Many would believe that some kind of coercive state apparatus is necessary to maintain social order. One might accept, for example, the beauty of the anarchist vision of self-government, but have deep doubts about how such a system could prevent anti-social individuals or groups from imposing themselves on society in oppressive or violent ways. The management of regional and national systems, let alone global negotiations, is also frequently argued to require representatives with the power to make decisions, unencumbered by the narrow concerns of local assemblies (Pepper, 1994).

With respect to transition, for reformists, adopting radical 'anti-capitalist' and 'anarchist' positions will only alienate people who are joining the Transition Towns and related movements. In a debate with Trainer, Rob Hopkins (2009) expressed concern that framing the transition in such terms would put every constituency, including business, government, and workers, offside. The result would be marginalisation and impotence for the movement, which would then achieve nothing of significance. Brian Davey (2009) worries that such a radical agenda risks overwhelming activists, many of whom are struggling to establish small-scale initiatives that, presently at least, seem anything but revolutionary. These less ambitious projects are undertaken in order to achieve something rather than nothing (Alexander, 2013b).

Both reformists and eco-socialists would criticise eco-anarchists for underestimating the importance of the state in an effective transition. This is not just a matter of logistics or the required political authority. For them, the problems are far too urgent to wait until the unlikely time when a grassroots anarchist movement seriously challenges the cultural, economic, and political landscape. For a crisis of this scale, it is argued, the centralised state – and indeed global institutions – will be necessary to push things through, sadly, often against the will of many. Marxist socialists would raise a concern of the opposite variety. For them such 'pre-figuring' strategies are bound to fail because if they ever grew to be a threat to capitalism, the state would use its ideological, economic, and, if needed, military power to crush these movements before they posed a major threat. It would also siphon energy and effort away from the revolutionary project and potentially even weaken the resolve of sections of the community by providing a non-revolutionary outlet. From this view, only a revolution backed by the majority of the working class can hope to succeed.

For eco-anarchists, regardless of whether a radical grassroots transition is likely, it offers us our best chance in a bad situation. And this remains the case regardless of whether one sees a vital role for a centralised state. In their view, the question of taking state power, or indeed campaigning and building political parties, is irrelevant both now and for the foreseeable future. Transition to a deep green society can and will only take place *after* a grassroots process of radical economic, political, and cultural change has gathered momentum. It is only through this type of process that the 'political will' could be developed that would persuade the state to pass the laws and enact regulations required for a zero-growth economy, and the radical localisation of the economy. In this sense, the Transition Towns and related movements, whether intentionally or not, are adopting the anarchists' approach to transition. But, for eco-anarchists, these movements will have to radicalise their goals and vision if they are to play a decisive role when consumer-capitalism begins to break down.

3.4 *The 'deep green resistance' strategy*

> Our actionists are not trying to change consciousness. They're not trying to get press. They're not after a new government or a seat at the political table. They are trying to stop the burning of fossil fuels and industrial-scale destruction of the life support systems of their planet (Keith, 2011: 499).

The Deep Green Resistance (DGR) has been a controversial movement arising out of the US and headed by key thinkers such as Aric McBay, Lierre Keith, and Derrick Jensen (Jensen *et al.*, 2011). In terms of political outlook, DGR would share much in common with the eco-anarchists, though the movement has been criticised by many anarchists.[7] The key difference, and the focus of this section, is their preparedness to advocate for industrial sabotage, in order to 'bring down industrial civilization' (Jensen *et al.*, 2011: 109). This is obviously highly controversial terrain and some readers may feel concerned it is being discussed. However, we feel it is important to do so, because advocacy of a more 'militant' response is likely to be common when people come to appreciate the gravity of today's ecological crisis and see the state of political and cultural paralysis.

The fundamental belief underlying the DGR strategy is that there is neither the time nor the will, amongst the vast majority of the population, for a mass movement. Grassroots sustainability initiatives, in the DGR view, will therefore never be enough to stop the ongoing ecological calamity. Lierre Kieth makes no attempt to hide her exasperation with the masses: 'The vast majority of the population will do nothing unless they are led, cajoled, or forced... there will be no mass movement, not in time to save this planet, our home' (Kieth, 2011: 26). Arguably, elitist statements such as this profoundly shape the transition strategy adopted.

Throughout the DGR literature, there is also a strong sense of urgency. Waiting for an impending calamity is unacceptable. This will only prolong the inevitable collapse, which will be worse the longer it is drawn out. The desire to stop the ongoing mass extinction of species provides another critical moral incentive for DGR activists. Their clear admonition is to act decisively *now*.

Much of DGR's pessimism derives from what they see as the liberal assumptions underpinning the environmental movement (Jensen *et al.*, 2011: Ch 3). In the liberal worldview the individual is the focus of transformative action. Social change is believed to come about through a process of rational argument and education, persuading individuals to adopt green lifestyles or campaign for sensible government policy. DGR contrasts this approach with 'radicalism', which begins with the group as the basic social unit, into which individuals are socialised. Society is made up of various groups based on class, gender, race, or ethnicity and these are frequently defined by *conflicting* relationships of power and oppression. Of course, as liberals point out, much oppression seems to be voluntarily accepted by the oppressed. But, according to DGR, this is just the perverse logic of oppression; the oppressed psychologically acquiesce in their oppression through denial, accommodation, and consent. Dominating groups use their power – political, ideological, and physical – to oppress, divide and mislead

---

[7] See, for example, http://www.anarchistnews.org/content/deep-green-resistance-book-review.

subordinate groups. Thus, for radicals, *real* social change can only come through organised political resistance, which challenges the power of dominant groups.

DGR believes green activists need to focus on building a 'culture of resistance' which, while friendly and supportive, has as its central aim the confrontation and dismantling of 'systems of power' which, for them, are the central causes driving today's ecological crisis (Jensen *et al.*, 2011: Ch 2). No amount of awareness-raising or inspiring examples of sustainable living can take the place of a culture which is systematically focused on resisting the plans and projects of the powerful. But, although building such a culture will be necessary for success, they hold out no hope of more than a small minority of today's affluent citizens joining.

The movement should be divided into two components: 'above-ground' and 'below-ground' activists (Jensen *et al.*, 2011: Ch 8). Above-ground activists are to engage in many of the same activities promoted in the previous sections. There is a strong focus on engaging in acts of non-violent direct action, such as blockades, protests, and demonstrations. Importantly they also strongly support the work that has begun, by Transition Towns and others, to build 'strong local communities that embrace direct democracy, economies of support, universal human rights and the rights of nature' (Jensen *et al.*, 2011: 500).

However, for DGR these 'above-ground' activists are not enough to avert the destruction of the planet in a palatable timeframe. A more militant secretive underground wing is needed, to carry out illegal acts of strategic sabotage against industrial infrastructure, with a particular focus on the fossil fuel industry and transnational mega-corporations. It is pointed out that industrial society is heavily dependent on 'very fragile infrastructure' such as the fossil fuel, electricity, internet, and global financial systems (Jensen *et al.*, 2011: 108). Given this dependence, industrial society is very vulnerable to well-targeted attacks – what they call 'Decisive Ecological Warfare' (DEW). The authors make clear that they would prefer to disrupt these systems through non-violent direct action. However, given their pessimism about winning recruits – and the moral imperative to act now – militant measures are often advocated. They claim that, even if it were possible, the purpose of these actions is *not* to single-handedly bring down industrial civilisation. Rather they want to create enough disruption to awaken the affluent from their present slumber:

> DEW will give the global rich an opportunity to realize the vulnerability inherent in their dependence on industrial

civilization and start rebuilding the resilient communities that is the core project of the Transition Towns Movement (Jensen *et al.*, 2011: 503).

The DGR strategy has strong critics. Most obviously, many would be deeply concerned about the potential direct and indirect harm caused by militant attacks on infrastructure. Apart from the direct harm, the consequences of such action are totally unpredictable, and potentially devastating. Whether DGR activists like it or not, today, most people depend on industrial society for their livelihood, and even mild disruption could have unforeseeable consequences. Implicit in the strategy is a questionable presumption that forcing disruption will jolt people to move in a desirable direction. But given presently dominant individualistic and competitive systems and values – and the fact that even most transitioners remain heavily dependent on the global economy – a rapid descent into chaos and conflict may seem more likely. This is particularly so given DGR activists have given up all hope of building a mass movement that could act as a counter-veiling force against the dominant culture.

In response, some DGR activists would insist that the moral imperative is not to build (an unlikely) mass movement, but to bring down our destructive civilisation as soon as possible. One might, therefore, ask whether there is a moral contradiction built into the DGR strategy. Does it make sense to use violence as a *means* of ending the systemic violence inflicted by industrial-capitalism? Even if such a strategy could be 'successful', should we morally endorse it? Can the admirable ends (e.g., preservation of nature) ever justify the destructive means? Maybe they can, but surely there is a threshold, a point at which the chosen methods simply seem too dangerous, too fraught with risk, too ethically dubious, to seriously contemplate? Is not the 'precautionary principle' foundational to green politics? This kind of moral reflection seems dangerously lacking in the DGR literature. That said, these theorists and activists would doubtless argue that *not* resisting carries its consequences too.

The eco-socialist Ian Angus argues that recent history suggests militant tactics are unlikely to succeed. The attacks on property carried out by groups such as Earth Liberation Front, Earth First!, and Animal Liberation Front, have failed to further green politics in any positive way. Such tactics are, in general, counter-productive, particularly when they are used in isolation from a mass base of popular support. This is certainly the case with deep greens that, today, certainly cannot claim mass support for dismantling consumer-capitalist society. Angus makes a persuasive prediction about the likely outcome of DGR tactics:

Long before the underground groups achieve any significant size or ability to act, they are infiltrated by police spies and provocateurs and disrupted by arrests. Key activists are imprisoned for years; many more are isolated and demoralized (Angus, 2012).

For all that, DGR does offer a welcome level of urgency and anger to the deep green camp. They remind us that the fate of not just humans but innumerable species rests on whether we can make a relatively rapid transition to a new type of society. They force us to consider the lengths we are prepared to go to, in order to turn the situation around. What will be our commitment? Where is our threshold point for action? Where should we put our energies? One may disagree strongly with the chosen means of DGR, but there is still room to admire their commitment to the cause.

3.5 The muddy pathway of crisis, shock, and response

The first three strategies discussed above could be called 'ideal' theories of strategy, which posit transition pathways based on particular political philosophies – democratic, socialist, and anarchist, respectively – and which outline how an ideal transition to a deep green alternative either should or will need to transpire. Such idealised perspectives are supposed to guide action, even though an 'ideal' transition is rarely if ever expected to occur. The fourth strategy – based on Deep Green Resistance – could be called a 'non-ideal' theory of change, insofar as the actions DGR engage in are a result of the perceived failure of all other strategies for change (coupled with the expectation that those strategies will continue to fail). For present purposes, a final transition pathway to consider is also a 'non-ideal' pathway, and could be called the pathway of crisis, shock, and response.

In many ways this final 'pathway' could be built into all of the previous perspectives, because none of the theorists considered above (especially the DGR camp) would think that the transition to a deep green alternative could ever be smooth, rational, or painless. Even many radical reformers, whose strategy involves working *within* the institutions of liberal democracy rather than *subverting* or *ignoring* them, clearly expect political conflict and economic difficulties to shape the pathway to the desired alternative (Gilding, 2011). Nevertheless, for those who are deeply pessimistic about the likelihood of any of the previous strategies actually giving rise to a deep green alternative (however coherent or well justified they may be), there remains the possibility that some such alternative could arise not by design so much as by disaster. In other words, it is worth considering whether a crisis situation – or a series of crises – could either (i) *force* an alternative way of life upon us; or (ii) be the *provocation* needed for cultures or politicians to take radical alternatives seriously. Those two possibilities will now be considered briefly, in turn.

As industrial civilisation continues its global expansion and pursues growth without apparent limit, the possibility of economic, political, or ecological crises forcing an alternative way of life upon humanity seems to be growing in likelihood (Ehrlich and Ehrlich, 2013). That is, if the existing model of global development is not stopped via one of the pathways reviewed above, or some other strategy, then it seems clear enough that at some point in the future, industrial civilisation will grow itself to death (Turner, 2012). Whether 'collapse' is initiated by an ecological tipping point, a financial breakdown of an overly indebted economy, a geopolitical disruption, an oil crisis, or some confluence of such forces, the possibility of collapse or deep global crisis can no longer be dismissed merely as the intellectual playground for 'doomsayers' with curdled imaginations. Collapse is a prospect that ought to be taken seriously based on the logic of limitless growth on a finite planet, as well as the evidence of existing economic, ecological, or more specifically climatic instability. As Paul Gilding (2011) has suggested, perhaps it is already too late to avoid some form of 'great disruption'.

Could collapse or deep crisis be the most likely pathway to an alternative way of life? If it is, such a scenario must not be idealised or romanticised. Fundamental change through crisis would almost certainly involve great suffering for many, and quite possibly significant population decline through starvation, disease, or war. It is also possible that the 'alternative system' that a crisis produces is equally or even more undesirable than the existing system. Nevertheless, it may be that this is the only way a post-growth or post-industrial way of life will ever arise. The Cuban oil crisis, prompted by the collapse of the USSR, provides one such example of a deep societal transition that arose not from a political or social movement, but from sheer force of circumstances (Piercy *et al.,* 2010). Almost overnight Cuba had a large proportion of its oil supply cut off, forcing the nation to move away from oil-dependent, industrialised modes of food production and instead take up local and organic systems – or perish. David Holmgren (2013) published a deep and provocative essay, 'Crash on Demand', exploring the idea that a relatively small anti-consumerist movement could be enough to destabilise the global economy, which is already struggling. This presents one means of bringing an end to the status quo by inducing a voluntary crisis, without relying on a mass movement. Needless to say, should people adopt such a strategy, it would be imperative to 'prefigure' the alternative society as far as possible too, not merely withdraw support from the existing society.

Again, one must not romanticise such theories or transitions. The Cuban crisis, for example, entailed much hardship. But it does expose the mechanisms by which crisis can induce significant societal change in ways that, in the end, are not always negative. In the face of a *global* crisis or breakdown, therefore, it could be that elements of the deep green vision (such as organic agriculture, frugal living, sharing, radical recycling, post-oil transportation, etc.) come to be forced upon humanity, in which case the question of strategy has less to do with avoiding a deep crisis or collapse (which may be inevitable) and more to do with negotiating the descent as wisely as possible. This is hardly a reliable path to the deep green alternative, but it presents itself as a possible path.

Perhaps a more reliable path could be based on the possibility that, rather than *imposing* an alternative way of life on a society through sudden collapse, a deep crisis could *provoke* a social or political revolution in consciousness that opens up space for the deep green vision to be embraced and implemented as some form of crisis management strategy. Currently, there is insufficient social or political support for such an alternative, but perhaps a deep crisis will shake the world awake. Indeed, perhaps that is the *only* way to create the necessary mindset. After all, today we are hardly lacking in evidence of the need for radical change (Turner, 2012), suggesting that shock and response may be the form the transition takes, rather than it being induced through orderly, rational planning, whether from 'top down' or 'from below'. Again, this 'non-ideal' pathway to a post-growth or post-industrial society could be built into the other strategies discussed above, adding some realism to strategies that might otherwise appear too utopian. That is to say, it may be that only deep crisis will create the social support or political will needed for radical reformism, eco-socialism, or eco-anarchism to emerge as social or political movements capable of rapid transformation. Furthermore, it would be wise to keep an open and evolving mind regarding the best strategy to adopt, because the relative effectiveness of various strategies may change over time, depending on how forthcoming crises unfold.

It was Milton Friedman (1982: *ix*) who once wrote: 'Only a crisis – actual or perceived – produces real change. When that crisis occurs, the actions that are taken depend on the ideas that are lying around.' What this 'collapse' or 'crisis' theory of change suggests, as a matter of strategy, is that deep green social and political movements should be doing all they can to mainstream the practices and values of their alternative vision. By doing so they would be aiming to 'prefigure' the deep green social, economic, and political structures, so far as that it is possible, in the hope that deep green ideas and systems are alive and available when the crises hit. Although Friedman obviously had a very different notion of what ideas should be 'lying around', the relevance of his point to this discussion is that in times of crisis, the politically or socially impossible can become politically or socially inevitable (Friedman, 1982: ix); or, one might say, if not inevitable, then perhaps much more likely.

It is sometimes stated that every crisis is an opportunity – from which the optimist infers that the more crises there are, the more opportunities there are. This may encapsulate one of the most realistic forms of hope we have left.

4. Conclusion

This chapter began by sketching the contours of a 'deep green' vision of the alternative society, and then – after assuming the validity of that basic vision – explored various strategies that have been proposed about how such a vision could be realised. While it was not our purpose to defend one strategy over another, it is hoped that the analysis will provoke more debate about which strategy is most likely to succeed. After all, the deep green camp hardly has energy or resources to waste, so it is important that those who broadly agree with the deep green vision think very carefully about how and where to direct their energies. We hope this essay provides some provocation to continue this critical exploration of the question of strategy. There is much to lose and even more to gain.

Despite the often heated disagreements between the various schools of thought reviewed above, we have seen that there is considerable strategic overlap with respect to what actions should be undertaken *in the short term* (with the exception of deep green resistance). Whether one's long-term vision is radical reformist, eco-socialist, or eco-anarchist, it seems that the most important activities the deep green school should be undertaking today are: (i) attempting to prefigure the deep green alternative in local communities; (ii) educating about the gross unsustainability of limitless growth on a finite planet and the need for a post-growth macroeconomics; (iii) joining with other green/red groups to resist and oppose various forms of unsustainable development; and (iv) showing in theory and practice that lifestyles based on material sufficiency and frugality are both a necessary and a desirable part of any just and sustainable future for humanity. Whatever form the required revolution ultimately takes, it will only transpire after many more people are involved in such activities. This suggests that a deep green alliance should be formed to facilitate these activities and build upon areas of commonality, rather than factions within the deep green school getting too caught up in their differences about longer-term strategy. In the short term, the deep green school should try to act as one body, and that is the strategic point this chapter leaves readers to ponder.

References

Alcott, B. 2008. 'The sufficiency strategy: Would rich-world frugality lower environmental impact?' *Ecological Economics* 64: 770-86.

Alexander, S. 2012a. 'The optimal material threshold: Toward an economics of sufficiency'. *Real-World Economics Review* 61: 2-21.

Alexander, S. 2012b. 'Planned economic contraction: The emerging case for degrowth'. *Environmental Politics* 21(3): 349-368.

Alexander, S. 2013a. *Entropia: Life beyond industrial civilisation.* Melbourne: Simplicity Institute Publishing.

Alexander, S. 2013b. 'Ted Trainer and the simpler way: A sympathetic critique'. *Capitalism Nature Socialism* (in press).

Alexander, S. and Ussher, S. 2012. 'The voluntary simplicity movement: A multi-national survey analysis in theoretical context'. *Journal of Consumer Culture* 12(1): 66-86.

Angus, I. 2012. 'Deep green resistance: How not to build a movement'. *Green Left Weekly.* Available at https://www.greenleft.org.au/node/51600 (accessed 17 October 2013).

Biehl, J. 1993. 'From movement to parliamentary party: Notes on several European green movements'. *Society and Nature* 1(3). Available at http://democracynature.org/vol1/biehl_movement.htm (accessed 17 October 2013).

Breakspear, C. and Hamilton, C. 2003. 'Getting a life understanding the downshifting phenomenon in Australia'. *The Australia Institute*, Discussion paper No. 62.

Climate Tracker Initiative. 2013. 'Things to look out for when using carbon budgets'. Available at: http://www.carbontracker.org/wp-content/uploads/2013/11/Carbon-budget-checklist-FINAL.pdf (accessed 22 November 2013).

Daly, H. 2013. 'Top 10 policies for a steady-state economy'. Available at *Resilience* website http://www.resilience.org/

stories/2013-10-29/top-10-policies-for-a-steady-state-economy (accessed 2 November 2013)

Davey, B. 2009. 'Brian Davey responds to Ted Trainer'. Available at http://transitionculture.org/2009/12/03/brian-davey-responds-to-ted-trainer/ (accessed 31 March 2012).

Fisher, S. 2013. 'Our sustainability crisis didn't start and doesn't stop at climate change'. Available at: *http://theconversation. com/our-sustainability-crisis-didnt-start-and-doesnt-stop-at-climate-change* (accessed 13 October 2013).

Foster, J. and Magdoff, F. 2011. *What every environmentalist needs to know about capitalism*. New York: Monthly Review Press.

Foster, J. 2013. 'The epochal crisis'. In *Monthly Review* vol. 65, issue 05 (October). Available at: http://monthlyreview.org /2013/10/01/epochal-crisis (accessed October 13 2013).

Fotopoulos, T. 1997. *Towards an inclusive democracy: The crisis of the growth economy and the need for a new liberatory project*. London & New York: Cassell.

Friedman, M. 2002. *Capitalism and freedom*. Chicago: Chicago University Press.

Gilding, P. 2011. *The great disruption: How the climate crisis will transform the global economy*. London: Bloomsbury.

Global Footprint Network. 2012. Reports available at http://www. footprintnetwork.org/en/index.php/gfn/page/world_footprint / (acessed 10 February 2012).

Greer, J.M. 2008. *The long descent*. Gabriola Island: New Society Publishers.

Hall, C. and Murphy, D. 2011. 'Energy return on investment, peak oil, and the end of economic growth'. *Annals of the New York Academy of Sciences* 1219: 52.

Hamilton, C. 2003a. *Growth fetish*. Crows Nest, NSW: Allen & Unwin.

Hamilton, C. 2003b. 'Downshifting in Britain: A sea change in the pursuit of happiness'. Australia Institute Discussion Paper No. 58.

Hamilton and Denniss. 2005. *Affluenza: When too much is never enough*. Crows Nest, NSW: Allen & Unwin.

Hansen, J. 2011. *Storms of my grandchildren*. London: Bloomsbury.

Hansen, J. et al., 2008. 'Target atmospheric CO_2: Where should humanity aim?' Available at: http://www.columbia.edu/~jeh1/2008/TargetCO2_20080407.pdf [Accessed 31 March 2012].

Hardt, M. and Negri, A. 2000. *Empire*. London: Harvard University Press.

Harvey, D. 2005. *A brief history of neo-liberalism*. New York: Oxford University Press.

Heinberg, R. 2011. *The end of growth: Adapting to our new economic reality*. Gabriola Island: New Society Publishers.

Holmgren, D. 2002. *Permaculture: Principles and pathways beyond sustainability*. Hepburn: Holmgren Design Services.

Holmgren, D. 2013. 'Crash on demand: Welcome to the brown tech future'. *Simplicity Institute Report* 13c: 1-23.

Hopkins, R. 2008. *The transition handbook: From oil dependency to local resilience*. Totnes, Devon: Green Books.

Hopkins, R. 2009. 'Responding to Ted Trainer's friendly criticism of transition'. Available at: http://transitionculture.org/2009/09/08/responding-to-ted-trainers-friendly-criticism-of-transition/ (accessed 24 October 2013).

Hopkins, R. 2013. *The power of just doing stuff*. Cambridge: Cambridge UIT.

Huesemann, M. and Huesemann, J. 2011. *Techno-fix: Why technology won't save us or the environment*. Gabriola Island: New Society Publishers.

Intergovernmental Panel on Climate Change (IPCC). 2013. Climate change 2013: The physical science basis (fifth assessment report). Available at: http://www.ipcc.ch/report/ar5/wg1/#.Uk6k-CjqMRw (accessed 4 October 2013).

Irvine, S. 2001. 'Review of eco-socialism or eco-capitalism'. Available at: http://www.sandyirvine.pwp.blueyonder.co.uk/PDFs/Review%20of%20Eco-Socialism%20or%20Eco-Capitalism%20by%20Sarkar.pdf (accessed 26 October 2013).

Jackson, T. 2009. *Prosperity with growth: Economics for a finite planet*. London: Earthscan.

Jensen, D., Mcbay, A., and Kieth, L. 2011. *Deep green resistance: Strategy to save the planet*. New York: Seven Stories Press.

Latouche, S. 2009. *Farewell to growth*. Cambridge, UK: Polity Press.

Lawn, P. 2011. 'Is steady-state capitalism viable? A review of the issues and an answer in the affirmative'. In Costanza, R. *et al.* (ed.). *Ecological Economics Reviews*. Annals of the New York Academy of Sciences 1219: 1-25.

Leahy, T. 2013. 'The new environmentalism and its critics'. Available at: http://www.gifteconomy.org.au/page180.html (accessed 14 October 2013).

Meadows, D. 2013. 'There is nothing we can do – Meadows'. Available at http://damnthematrix.wordpress.com/?s=dennis+meadows (accessed 15 October 2013).

Mcknight, D. 2005. *Beyond right and left: New politics and the culture wars*. Crows Nest, NSW: Allen & Unwin.

Mill, J.S. 2004 [1848]. *Principles of political economy: With some of their applications to social philosophy*. New York: Prometheus Books.

Nelson, A. and Timmerman, F. (eds). 2011. *Life without money: Building fair and sustainable economies*. London: Pluto Press.

Piercy, E., Granger, R., and Goodler, C. 2010. 'Planning for peak oil: Learning from Cuba's "Special Period"'. *Urban Design and Planning* 4(1): 169-176.

Pepper, D. 1994. *Eco-socialism: From deep ecology to social justice*. London & New York: Routledge.

Sarkar, S. 1999. *Eco-socialism or eco-capitalism: A critical analysis of humanity's fundamental choices*. London: Zed Books.

Sarkar, S. and Bruno, K. 2008. 'Eco-socialism or barbarism: An up-to-date critique of capitalism'. Initiative Eco-Socialism. Available at: http://www.oekosozialismus.net/en_oekosoz_en_rz.pdf (accessed 5 November 2013).

Smith, R. 2010. 'Beyond growth or beyond capitalism'. *Institute for Policy Research & Development*. Available at: http://iprd.org.uk/wp-content/uploads/2011/02/Beyond-Growth-or-Beyond-Capitalism-by-Richard-Smith-2011.pdf (accessed 16 October 2013.

Sutton, P. 2013. 'The Darebin climate emergency plan'. Available at http://www.voteplanet.net/uploads/1/2/7/5/12758111/darebin-climate-emergency-plan-v4.pdf (accessed 15 October 2013.

Trainer, T. 2010a. *The transition to a sustainable and just world*. Sydney: Envirobook,

Trainer, T. 2010b. 'The transition towns movement: Its huge significance and a friendly criticism'. Available at: http://www.resilience.org/stories/2010-02-17/transition-towns-movement-its-huge-significance-and-friendly-criticism (accessed 28 October 2013).

Trainer, T. 2012. 'Can renewable energy sustain consumer societies? A negative case'. *Simplicity Institute Report* 12e.

Turner, G. M. 2012. 'On the cusp of global collapse? Updated comparison of the *Limits to growth* with historical data'. *Gaia* 21(2): 116-124.

United Nations (UN). 2010. *Global biodiversity outlook 3*. Available at: http://www.cbd.int/doc/publications/gbo/gbo3-final-en.pdf [accessed 20 December 2013].

11

THE TRANSITION MOVEMENT
Questions of diversity, power, and affluence

1. Introduction[1]

As the global economy continues to degrade planetary ecosystems (Rockstrom *et al.,* 2009); as biodiversity continues to decline (United Nations, 2010); as climate scientists offer increasingly confident and dire warnings (IPCC, 2013); as peak oil arrives (Miller and Sorrell, 2014; Brecha, 2013); as fresh water and other key resources become scarcer (Brown, 2011) while population continues to grow (UNDSEA, 2012); and as financial systems continue to show signs of instability (Tverberg, 2012), the question of how nations around the world are going to 'transition' to a stable, just, and sustainable society is more pressing than ever. Things seem to be getting worse, not better, which calls for new thinking and new action, both at the personal and social levels, but also at the macroeconomic and political levels. If early in the environmental movement it was assumed that buying 'green' products, switching to energy efficient light bulbs, and taking shorter showers were the 'lifestyle' solutions to environmental problems, more recent evidence firmly indicates that such measures are not working or are not going to be anywhere near sufficient, necessary though they may be. The extent of ecological overshoot is too great (Global Footprint Network, 2013). Furthermore, many promised efficiency gains that were supposed to flow from technological advances seem to be getting lost to the Jevons Paradox and rebound effects (Herring and Sorrell, 2009; Polimeni *et al.,* 2009), meaning that technology – the

---

[1] This chapter is a lightly revised version of *Simplicity Institute Report 14g,* co-authored by Samuel Alexander and Esther Alloun.

great hope of Ecological Modernisation – will not lead to environmental rejuvenation unless technological advances are governed by an ethics of sufficiency, not a growth imperative. Efficiency without sufficiency is lost (Alexander, 2014). But just as the planet seems to be reaching the 'limits to growth' that were anticipated long ago (Mill, 1848; Meadow et al., 1972; Meadow et al., 2004; Heinberg, 2011; Turner, 2012), governments and institutions around the world seem to be more focused than ever on 'going for growth' (OECD, 2013). This is the great contradiction underlying the attempt to achieve sustainable development by way of 'greening' capitalism: evidence is mounting that economies must give up the limitless pursuit of growth, but growth-based economies dare not consider this policy option, let alone implement it.

All this may tempt some to despair, but as Bertrand Russell (2009: 45) once stated: 'Gloom is a useless emotion'. This mood of defiant positivity is in fact a defining characteristic of the Transition Towns Movement, which is one of the more promising social movements to emerge during the last decade in response to the overlapping problems outlined above. Since its inception in 2005 (see Hopkins, 2008), the Transition Towns Movement has spread to many countries around the world (Bailey et al., 2010: 602-3), and is gaining increased attention from academics, politicians, and media. Defined further below, its fundamental aims are to respond to the twin challenges of peak oil and climate change by decarbonising and relocalising the economy through a community-led model of change based on permaculture principles (Holmgren, 2002). In doing so, the movement runs counter to the dominant narrative of globalisation and economic growth, and instead offers a positive, highly localised vision of a low-carbon future, as well as an evolving roadmap for getting there through grassroots activism. While this young and promising movement is not without its critics (e.g., James, 2010) there are some, such as Ted Trainer (2009: 11), who argue that if civilisation is to make it into the next half of the century in any desirable form, 'it will be via some kind of Transition Towns process'.

As promising as the Transition Towns Movement may be, there are crucial questions it needs to confront and reflect on if it wants to fully realise its potential for deep societal transformation. Firstly, critics argue that the movement suffers, just as the broader Environmental movement arguably suffers, from the inability to expand much beyond the usual middle-class, well-educated participants, who have the time and privilege to engage in social and environmental activism (see James 2009a; James 2009b; Connors and McDonald, 2010). While the Transition Towns Movement is ostensibly 'inclusive', in this chapter we examine this self-image in order to assess whether it is as inclusive and as diverse as it claims to be, and what this might mean for the movement's prospects. Secondly, we consider the issue of whether a grassroots, community-led movement can change the macroeconomic and political structures of global capitalism 'from below' through (re)localisation, or whether the movement may need to engage in more conventional 'top down' political activity if it is to have any chance of achieving its ambitious goals. Finally, we raise the question of whether the movement is sufficiently radical in its vision. Does it need to engage more critically with the broader paradigm of consumer capitalism, its growth imperative, and social norms and values? Is building local resilience within this paradigm an adequate strategy? And does the movement recognise that decarbonisation almost certainly means giving up many aspects of affluent, consumer lifestyles? We do not expect to be able to offer complete answers to these probing questions, but by engaging critically with these issues we hope to advance the debate around a movement that may indeed hold some of the keys to transitioning to a just and sustainable world.

The analysis begins with a brief literature review, through which we offer a more extensive definition and history of the movement. After outlining some the movement's defining activities and most attractive features, we offer a sympathetic critique of the movement along the lines outlined above, raising questions about the movement's diversity, its relationship to power structures, and the nature of its underlying vision. Our analysis draws from the academic and generalist literature, but it is also shaped inevitably by our involvement in and connection with Transition Coburg, a 'transition initiative' based in an inner suburb of Melbourne, Australia. All researchers have potential biases that may result from studying a subject from a particular viewpoint, but we feel that one means of being reflexive and transparent in this regard is for us to state our relationship with the movement from the outset. That is to say, we are sympathetic critics looking at things 'from the inside'.

2. Overview of the Transition Towns Movement

The concept of a 'Transition Town' originated in Kinsale, Ireland, in 2005, where Rob Hopkins, one of the founders of the movement and a permaculture teacher at the time, developed an 'Energy Descent Action Plan' with his former students from the Kinsale Further Education College (Hopkins, 2011: 20). The plan outlined strategies to respond and adapt to peak oil and resource scarcity in various sectors, such as food and agriculture, technology, energy production, transport, economics, and livelihoods. The idea of planning for energy descent at the community level was explored and developed further in the market town of Totnes (Devon, UK) and soon after in Lewes (East Sussex, UK), where Hopkins, in collaboration with Naresh Giangrande, fleshed out the Transition Towns model and implemented it on the ground. The model spread to other parts of the UK and the world, and the notion of a 'transition town' was soon renamed a 'transition initiative' to reflect the diversity of places involved in the movement – not just 'towns' but also cities, neighbourhoods, suburbs, villages, schools, etc. (Hopkins, 2008: 136).

The Transition Network was founded in 2006 to 'inspire, encourage, connect, support and train communities' on their 'transition' (see Transition Network, 2013a). It reinforces the idea of self-organisation (Hopkins and Lipman, 2009), as its objective is not to centralise decision-making but to connect diverse initiatives in order to share experiences, knowledge, skills, and ideas on best practice. As of September 2013, the network comprises 462 official initiatives and 654 non-official initiatives ('mullers') in over 43 countries (Transition Network, 2013b). According to Rob Hopkins, the Transition Towns Movement is based on four key assumptions (Hopkins, 2008: 134):

(1)   That life with dramatically lower energy consumption is inevitable, and that it's better to plan for it than to be taken by surprise; [2]
(2)   That our settlements and communities presently lack the resilience to enable them to weather the severe energy [and economic] shocks that will accompany peak oil [and climate change];
(3)   That we have to act collectively, and we have to act now;

---

[2] Within the Transition movement the inevitability of 'energy descent' is based on the general acceptance that fossil fuels will eventually peak and decline; that climate change requires giving up fossil fuels; and that renewable energy systems, while necessary, are unlikely to be able to replace fully the net energy production of the current fossil fuel industry. There also seems to be deep scepticism with respect to nuclear energy, or at least a pragmatic realisation that, especially since Fukushima, nuclear is likely to contribute a smaller, not a larger, part of global energy supply in the future. For these reasons combined, Transition envisions and plans for a world with less energy production and consumption, not more, which is another one of its defining characteristics (see generally, Hopkins, 2011; Heinberg, 2011; Trainer, 2013a; Trainer, 2013b).

(4)   That by unleashing the collective genius of those around us to creatively and proactively design our energy descent, we can build ways of living that are more connected, more enriching, and that recognise the biological limits of our planet.

One of the primary goals of the Transition Towns Movement, therefore, is to catalyse localised, grassroots responses to peak oil (or the end of cheap oil) and climate change. More recently, the theme of economic instability is being introduced more prominently into the debate (Hopkins, 2011), adding to the original concerns about peak oil and climate change. The rationale for grassroots activity is that 'if we wait for governments, it'll be too little, too late. If we act as individuals, it'll be too little. But if we act as communities, it might just be enough, just in time' (Hopkins, 2013: 45). According to some commentators (Barry and Quilley, 2008: 2), this approach represents a 'pragmatic turn' insofar as it focuses on *doing* sustainability here and now. In other words, it is a form of 'DIY politics' (Barry and Quilley, 2009: 3), one that does not involve waiting for governments to provide solutions (Seyfang *et al.,* 2010), but rather depends upon an actively engaged citizenry.

The paradigm shift of Transition is articulated around notions of 'decarbonisation' and 'relocalisation' of production and consumption. What this means in practice will be unpacked further below, but the basic dynamic is that decarbonisation is necessary and desirable for reasons of peak oil and climate change, and given how carbon-intensive global trade is, decarbonisation implies relocalising economic processes. As well as this, a central goal of the movement is to build community 'resilience', a term which can be broadly defined as the capacity to withstand shocks and the ability to adapt after disturbances (Hopkins, 2008: Ch. 3; Barry, 2012). Notably, crisis in the current system is presented not as a cause for despair but as a transformational opportunity, a change for the better that should be embraced rather than feared (Hopkins, 2011: 45). Consequently, the vision presented by the Transition Towns Movement is very positive, one that is 'full of hope' (Bunting, 2009: np) for a more 'nourishing and abundant future' (Hopkins, 2008: 5). Hopkins, who is by far the most prominent spokesperson for the movement, plays a crucial role in promoting such an optimistic message, while at the same time acknowledging the extent of the global problems and asserting there is no guarantee of success (Hopkins, 2011: 17). By doing so, Hopkins skilfully walks a delicate line: he openly acknowledges the magnitude of the global predicament, but quickly proceeds to focus on positive, local responses and action. Whether his positivity is justifiable is an open question – some argue that it is not (Smith and Positano, 2010) – but it is nevertheless proving to be a means of inspiring and mobilising communities in ways that 'doomsayers' are unlikely to ever realise.

Many issues are included under the banners of relocalisation, decarbonisation, and resilience, which helps broaden the movement's appeal (Bailey *et al.*, 2010: 602). Indeed, 'the Transition Network has sought to fashion energy scarcity into a general metaphor for ruptures between the spatially-joined but issue-disconnected world of globalisation' (Bailey *et al.*, 2010: 3). This turns energy descent into a springboard for the broader critique of globalisation and economic growth, both of which are arguably unsustainable in their current form and which oil scarcity may make 'irrelevant' (Bailey *et al.*, 2010: 598; Hopkins, 2011: 33-34; Heinberg, 2011; Rubin, 2012). Through the lens of energy – which remains its focus – the Transition model nevertheless attempts to engage broader issues of power imbalances 'associated with corporate globalism' (Mason and Whitehead, 2012: 496), as well as issues such as individualism, atomisation of social relationships, social justice concerns about poverty and inequality, boom-and-bust economic cycles, financial crises leading to economic instability, and increased living costs and unemployment. Beyond climate change and peak oil, therefore, these issues are being used 'as a way to open up discussion over scarcity and community economic resilience' (Barr and Wright, 2012: 530), and positions the Transition Towns Movement as not merely an 'environmental' movement, but a movement that encompasses broader societal concerns. How successfully the movement takes on these broader issues is a question to be considered in more detail below.

When it comes to applying these broad ideas and concerns in practice, Hopkins (2008) outlines a 12-step roadmap that is intended to help communities start, grow, and run a localised 'transition initiative'. These steps involve setting up a steering group, raising awareness about critical issues, developing visible practical projects, organising activities to 're-skill' the community, and formulating an Energy Descent Action Plan. These steps, it should be noted, are fairly generic and demonstrate that the Transition Towns Movement does not propose 'prescriptive solutions' (Hopkins, 2008: 137) or a 'one-size fits all' approach, but rather constitutes an 'open-ended experiment' (Barry, 2012: 114) and a broad rethinking of 'how local economies feed, house, and power themselves' (Hopkins, 2012: 74-75). Hopkins' *Transition Handbook*, published in 2008 (with a second Australian and New Zealand edition in 2009), was a milestone for the movement and provides some strategies on how to operationalise the Transition model. This text is supplemented in helpful ways by his *Transition Companion* (Hopkins, 2011) and *The Power of Just Doing Stuff* (Hopkins, 2013), both of which offer deeper insight into the achievements and challenges of the movement during its relatively short lifetime. While the apparently non-prescriptive nature of these texts can be considered one of their more attractive features, it could be argued that prescription certainly exists in these texts, only in implicit ways. Others (Trainer, 2009) argue that transition initiatives need to be provided with *more* guidance on the best strategies to adopt, not less, and that the questionable attempt to avoid prescription is actually harming the movement. Debates such as these are to be expected in any new social movement, and indeed we would suggest that such debates are both healthy and vital.

2.1. *Head, heart, and hands: Three dimensions of the Transition model*

As Hopkins (2011: 72-76) emphasises, 'transitioning' is both an inner and outer process. Change is needed not only in the external physical structures, institutions, and organisations upon which societies rest, but also in our worldviews, norms, attitudes, and values. In recognition of this, the Transition model of change attempts to weave together the power of imagination, visioning, and storytelling, with the practical manifestation of these alternative narratives, through the engagement of the head, the heart, and the hands (Hopkins, 2008). Below we explore these dimensions in more detail, as they are central to understanding the movement.

First, the psychology of change underpinning the movement is worth highlighting, as well as the way the movement conceptualises and articulates inner change as an enabler for long-term outer change (Hopkins, 2011: 75). Transition recognises that the challenges of peak oil, climate change, and the shocks they are likely to bring can seem confronting and even overwhelming. However, in contrast to some prominent approaches in the traditional environmental movement, Hopkins contends that negative feelings like anger and guilt, or focusing on 'doom and gloom', do not foster change (Hopkins, 2011: 78; Hopkins, 2013: 41). Rather, the Transition Towns Movement draws on psychotherapy and psychology (including eco-psychology) to describe, understand, and support incremental inner change in people and communities, with the intention of leading to enduring behaviour change. For example, different communication strategies and activities are used at different stages, from raising awareness to taking action (Hopkins,

2011: 124). The movement also uses insights from Eastern religions and traditions around mindfulness, meditation, and the 'transformation of consciousness' (Prentice in Hopkins, 2011: 141) to learn how to deal with change in a positive way. These 'inner' efforts are part of the development of 'different self-understandings' and 'new subjectivities' that are required for the transition to a radically different society based on low-carbon living (Seyfang *et al.*, 2010: 14-15; Barry, 2012: 99; Bay 2013: 180-190).

Second, Transition relies on 'unleashing' powerful 'expression[s] of imagination' (Sharp, 2009: 35) through positive visioning and storytelling. This is one of the defining approaches of the movement. As Chamberlin (2009) outlines, collective or cultural narratives shape our understanding of the world and our place in it, and in order to transition to a post-petroleum, localised society where 'small is beautiful', we need very different narratives and imaginaries than the one(s) we have now (see also, Barry, 2012: 99). Furthermore, as Pelling and Navarrete (2011) note, there are many elements in the current system that inhibit the process of 'conscientisation' and reinforce the 'institutionalised status quo' by 'closing down imagination and discussion of alternative values and organisation' (2011: np). In this context, different collective narratives can play a role in 'questioning the inevitability of the neoliberal model' (Amin, 2013: 142) and opening up space for alternatives. This is what Transition does, or aims to do, by opening up new possibilities and story-lines in various ways, including sharing stories and experiences; developing 'Transition Tales' (a programme based in Totnes for secondary students, Hopkins, 2011: 229-230); drafting articles, ads, and cartoons for the newspapers of the future (see Hopkins, 2008; 2011), and visioning exercises such as 'what will the town/neighbourhood look like in 2030?' (Hopkins, 2011: 114-116). This promotes a holistic and 'whole of system' approach to the issues, while always focusing on local action, responses, and solutions. These initiatives tell the story of a future that will be highly local and situated, and speaks to 'a desire to reconnect with a lost sense of the importance of the place itself' (Cato, 2008: 92). But these stories are also about people and an 'untheorised sense of the goodness of humanity' (Sharp, 2009: 35), a sense of community, and social solidarity. In these ways, Transition is attempting to shift the current social framework, cultivating different cultural values and identities, and creating microcosms of hope and sustainability (Greene, 2010). Storytelling in transition is therefore about the 'possibility of change' (Cato and Hillier, 2010: 877) and transforming the stories communities tell themselves about where they are and where they want to go.

Third, in addition to providing a space for reworking, negotiating, and assembling stories, identities and values, the Transition Towns Movement aspires to lead by 'practical example' (Hopkins, 2011: 73) and puts into action some of the stories and ideas coming out of the community. Hopkins emphasises that the Transition Towns Movement should not be 'just a talking shop' and that 'practical manifestations' (Hopkins, 2011: 146) of relocalisation are essential to create momentum. As he notes, 'a transition initiative with dirt under its fingernails will gain credibility' and thereby attract new people (Hopkins, 2011: 146). These projects also offer an opportunity for experiential and social learning, connecting or reconnecting with nature, as well as acquiring new skills. This 'Great reskilling', as Hopkins (2011: 152-154) calls it, is an essential aspect of resilience building and developing local adaptive capacities. As a practical matter, food usually appears as an early focal point of Transition Initiatives, and many initiatives offer training in permaculture and organic gardening, and cooking and preserving food (Hopkins *et al.,* 2009; Pinkerton and Hopkins, 2009; Bay, 2013). Collective initiatives are also put together to encourage local food provisioning, with the aim of 'delinking food and fossil fuels' (Heinberg and Bomford, in Hopkins, 2011: 56) and promoting bioregionalism. For example, many Transition Initiatives try to set up a community garden/allotment or a veggie box scheme, organise an urban farmers' market, as well as fruit tree and nut tree planting days, seed banks, and seed swap days. These are merely illustrations of the broader attempt to build resilience and decarbonise the economy by relocalising it. Other transition activities include: establishing local currencies (Longhurst, 2012) and community owned renewable energy companies; organising carpooling schemes, car-free days, educational films nights, bicycle or sewing workshops and cooperatives, and workshops on energy efficiency in the home and workplace (Hopkins, 2011; 2013). According to the transition literature, these projects and the process involved should be fun, enjoyable, convivial, 'playful and unthreatening' (Hopkins, 2011: 149). This relentlessly positive discourse may be problematic given the extent of change needed and the likely resistance of existing organisations and powers in place, but as a definitional matter, positivity in the face of challenges is a central characteristic of the movement.

Overall, the Transition Towns Movement aims to catalyse deep societal change through envisioning a different, post-carbon collective story for a community and taking steps toward realising it. To the extent that the movement attempts to create new meanings, identities, and subjectivities beyond the dominant socio-cultural paradigm, it fits within the conceptualisation of new social movements (Barry and Quilley, 2008: 21-24; Seyfang *et al.*, 2010: 14-15) and given that it is a prominent and promising social movement in response to peak oil and climate change, it deserves critical attention. As noted in the introduction, there are obstacles and limitations to the Transition model and they should not be underestimated. The movement is still relatively small and young and, according to some commentators, Transition Initiatives mainly attract the usual suspects (see an example of this in Smith, 2011) who have 'the resources and leisure to be open to radical thinking' (Cato, 2008: 95). Furthermore, 'doing' Transition often turns out to be more difficult than expected for various reasons, including lack of funding (hence the reliance on volunteers), difficulty mobilising people and building momentum for action (Seyfang, 2009; Seyfang and Haxeltine, 2012), and adapting the model to larger scales and urban settings (see Taylor, 2012; North and Longhurst, 2013, Hopkins, 2013: 74-75 addressing the issue of scale). In the remainder of this chapter we explore some of these issues from a more critical perspective.

3. Diversity and Inclusion: Transition for whom? By whom?

The Transition Towns Movement explicitly advocates collective, community-based action and an inclusive approach to building resilience. Inclusion is the second 'principle' of Transition (see Hopkins, 2009: 144). Diversity is one of the key characteristics of resilience (Walker and Salt 2006) and permaculture ('use and value diversity', Hopkins, 2009: 142), both of which are major underpinnings of the movement. The rhetoric of community in social movements is not new, but there have long been criticisms that the environmental movement, in particular, has not lived up to that rhetoric and that it has instead been somewhat insular and 'middle-class'. The suggestion is that caring for the environment is a privilege that generally only arises once the struggle for basic necessities has been won. Whether that is a valid characterisation of the broader environmental movement is a question we leave to one side (Martinez-Alier, 1995), but we do wish to explore the question of whether the Transition Towns Movement is just another 'pleasurable, leisure based community movement' (James, 2009a: 19) and an expression of 'bourgeois community resilience' (James, 2009b: 15), as some of its critics, often from the political left, assert (see Trapese Collective, 2008). We contend that the reality of what Mason and Whitehead (2012: 511) call 'inclusive localism' is more complex than that, although the danger is real that the Transition

Towns Movement may end up as little more than an exclusive middle-class club for nice, comfortable people who already have the resources and options to adapt. Empirically, little research has been conducted on the demographics of the Transition Towns Movement, with some notable exceptions. For example, the surveys of Transition coordinators and participants conducted by Seyfang (2009) and Seyfang and Haxeltine (2012: 388) confirm the stereotypes of primarily white, highly educated 'postmaterialists' who already are environmentally conscious. If this is so, what are the implications of this? And what, if anything, can the movement do about expanding its demographic reach?

It is worth noting that the movement is demonstrating a level of transparency and reflexivity around this issue, and its 'leaders' have acknowledged the challenge of 'extending the transition movement's outreach beyond the demographic silo of middle-class pro-environmentalists' (Bailey, Hopkins, and Wilson, 2010: 601). They have started addressing it through the appointment of a 'diversity coordinator' in 2010 and the launch of a 'diversity plan' and a 'diversity and social justice newsletter', and while this initiative ended in 2011 because of a lack of funding (Transition Network, 2011), these themes remain present. Additionally, there has been some discussion around what the right means of communication and marketing should be in order to target as many people as possible. This is reflected in the shift of rhetoric in the *Transition Companion* (Hopkins, 2011) and *the Power of Just Doing Stuff* (Hopkins, 2013) that both emphasise economic instability and crisis a lot more than the original *Handbook* (Hopkins, 2008). The intended message is sufficiently clear: getting involved in transition is fun, and should lessen impact on the environment, but it will also save you money (through growing more food, recycling and re-using, DIY skills such as sewing, preserving, brewing beer, etc.). Some academics close to the movement have similarly argued that 'the doing of community-based activities which offer immediate benefits (cost savings, pleasure, sociability, sense of achievement, community self-expression)' (Seyfang and Haxeltine, 2012: 394-395) should take precedence over the more abstract/intellectual awareness raising and education focused activities (which constitute the first steps prescribed by the *Transition Handbook*'s roadmap).

Rather than condemning the movement for its perceived lack of openness or elitism, it may be more constructive to investigate the barriers that prevent the Transition Towns Movement from 'responding to a diversity of needs using a diversity of strengths' (Pickering, diversity coordinator in Transition Network 2011). After all, the authenticity of the movement's desire for inclusivity is not in doubt; we only seek to inquire into the realisation of that desire. In her thesis, Danielle Cohen (2010) explores the issue of diversity in an inner-city London area and notes that Transition is not 'explicitly concerned with social justice' (Cohen 2010, 3). That may have been true at the time, or in that particular initiative, but the transition discourse seems to have shifted in the last couple of years and now explicitly engages with issues of social justice, albeit still usually only in passing (Hopkins, 2013: 67).

Nevertheless, Cohen fairly points out that the Transition model is generally based on specific participative methods such as Open Space technology (or world cafe), 'a method of creating participant-led events [which] exemplifies self-organisation, stressing individual responsibility for learning and contribution' (Cohen, 2010: 44; see also Aiken, 2012: 95). So while valuing inclusion, Transition's focus on 'catalysing people to generate their own solutions' to promote 'empowered individualism' [as the basis for community building] in itself influences who shows up (Cohen, 2010: 44). Some people might not feel conformable or 'expert enough' to turn up and the focus on individualism 'is associated with a middle-class way of life, where the inner self is often highlighted' (Cohen, 2010: 10) The fact that a pass to the yearly Transition Network Conference in the UK costs £100 with few concession tickets available, does not help diversity either (see Cutler and Chatterton, 2009).

Cohen (2010) and others (e.g., Trapese Collective, 2008: 34; James, 2009a) also highlight that Transition Towns seems to be insufficiently attentive of the power differential and dynamics within communities and the way ethnicity, gender and socio-economic background play a role in shaping community relationships. In this context, inclusion arguably means 'assimilating others to our way' of thinking about the world (Cohen, 2010: 45). The challenge, therefore, is to find a way of being open and encouraging diversity without 'othering', 'perpetuating social stratification, denying inequality or claiming superiority' (Cohen, 2010: 51). This challenge is not unique to the Transition Towns Movement but one of the ways to overcome it may be to embrace the particular context and cultures of individual transition initiatives instead of strictly following the 12 steps and the movement's 'Bible', that is, the *Transition Handbook* and its grand narrative, which some argue can lead to 'cultural blindness' (Connors and MacDonald, 2010: 570). The top-down 'steering' of the Transition Network and 'brand management' (Seyfang and Haxeltine, 2012: 391) by the founders in England (e.g., through the accreditation process to become an 'official' transition town) has been perceived as running counter to the bottom-up grassroots 'creativity [and diversity] the movement seeks to embody' (Smith, 2011: 102, see also Trapese Collective, 2008: 26; Cato and Hillier,

2010: 877; Connors and MacDonald, 2010: 569). This may involve re-thinking the way the movement is organised (to push for more non-hierarchical structures – see an example in Australia in Bay, 2013) or doing away with the prescriptive 12 steps and the 'managerialist approach' (Smith, 2011: 102). On the other hand, perhaps some level of 'brand management' is useful or important to preserve the cohesion or coherence of the movement and possibly contribute to making Transition Initiatives more recognisable by mainstream organisations like local governments and funding bodies (Smith, 2011: 102). Again, this is unlikely to be an issue that will reach a consensus any time soon, but arguably the movement will be stronger for continuing to debate it.

Looking at the issue from a different perspective, by pushing a very inclusive agenda, the movement is arguably 'bound to disappoint its adherents' (Connors and McDonald, 2010: 561) because it cannot possibly satisfy everybody. The inclusivity and diversity within the movement creates 'latent tensions in relation to the geographical form and ideals of the movement' (Mason and Whitehead, 2012: 497), potentially resulting in significant delays, conflict, division, and 'lack of focus' (Smith, 2011: 102). For example, food can be a thorny issue: since meat is a high-impact food, should Transition Towns more clearly advocate a low or no-meat diet through its literature and activities, or would that alienate too many people? A similar issue arises in terms of consumption: should the movement highlight the significant lifestyle implications of post-carbon living, or would that also alienate too many people? Overall, if inclusion means going for the lowest common denominator, it may lead to 'little meaningful change' (Connors and McDonald, 2010: 560) or worse 'a bland local consensus of inaction' (Mason and Whitehead, 2012: 511).

The movement has also been criticised for its 'political naivety and absence of an analysis of power' (Cato and Hillier, 2010: 871; see also, Cato, 2008 and North, 2010) and we now turn to this question.

4. Transition, Politics, and Power: Angles of Political Critique

4.1 Reflecting on Transition strategies for change

As mentioned in the previous section, the Transition Towns Movement presents itself as very positive, fun, and non-confrontational. Indeed, in its rhetoric, the movement in general and Hopkins in particular are, in many ways, non-political or apolitical, in the sense that they generally pitch the movement against 'protesting', 'campaigning', 'rocking the boat', conventional political activism, parliamentarianism, etc. By aiming to be as accessible and inclusive as possible, some argue that the movement 'does not support particular campaigns but rather develops a model that forms around what many different people have in common. It's a model about positive responses and not something that takes positions against institutions or projects' (Trapese Collective, 2008: 5-6; see also Bay, 2013: 182-183 for a practical example of this). In the words of Richard Heinberg, the movement is 'more like a party than a protest march' (see foreword to Hopkins, 2008: 10). This makes sense in light of the 'inclusive' goal of the movement and the psychology of change it deploys. After all, talking openly about radical opposition to consumer capitalism, protesting, civil disobedience, and direct action may not appeal to a broad range of people and it may be that the more political and 'radical' issues are not explicitly discussed for strategic reasons (see Alexander, 2012a: 9-10). Yet, as Cutler and Chatterton (2009) point out, the dichotomy between 'positive alternative building activism' and negative 'radical left activism' (as Hopkins calls it) is artificial because a lot of groups and individuals can and often do engage in both strategies. Stereotyping 'good' and 'bad' activists who are essentially motivated by very similar concerns for environmental and social justice may not be very constructive in the long term either. At the same time, it is essential that the movement is self-reflective about its strategies for change, because it hardly has energy and resources to waste. This is particularly important because some argue that de-politicised or post-political discourse can serve conservative or neoliberal agendas by framing an issue as one that can be solved with 'consensual' knowledge or 'neutral' expertise, hence 'diverting attention from [or even rendering invisible] questions of power, justice, or the types of (socio-natural) future that can be envisaged' (Welsh, 2013: 7; see also James, 2009a: 19).

This raises the question: To what extent can the Transition Towns Movement avoid the pain, hardship, and conflict historically associated with significant social movements (e.g., Civil Rights, Women's Rights, Gay Rights, etc.)? After all, vested interests in the status quo are almost certainly going to try to maintain the status quo, suggesting that the ambitious goals of the Transition Towns Movement (including decarbonisation, relocalisation, and building a new economy) are probably going to confront, or are confronting, hard political opposition from enormously powerful political and economic forces. For this reason, we would argue that pain and conflict cannot be sidestepped on the path of 'transition', while at the same time acknowledging that activists and participants in the movement may well find the struggle meaningful and worthwhile, no matter how difficult the path turns out to be. To paraphrase Friedrich Nietzsche: They who have a *why* to live, can bear almost any *how*.

As well as the possibility of having to engage in old-fashioned political struggle, as opposed to building the alternative 'beyond politics', there are also questions about how the impacts of peak oil and climate change are going to play out, and the political implications of this (see Bettini and Karaliotas, 2013 for a critical analysis of the peak oil discourse in the Transition Towns Movement and other red-green groups). It is almost certain that peak oil and climate change are going have varying impacts depending on space, time, and class, and this suggests that the ideal of relocalisation may not be directly or equally applicable to everyone (Bailey *et al.,* 2010: 598; North, 2010). According to some critics, the implicit assumption of the Transition Towns Movement is that 'localisation will be capable of solving political as well as environmental problems. This suggests an inadequate consideration of the aspect of change that is about power rather than place' (Cato, 2008: 96). Indeed, it is becoming increasingly evident that some places and people will be more affected than others and more or less capable of adapting (Paavola and Adger, 2006; Barnett and Campbell, 2010). In this sense, the transition away from cheap oil, for example, is likely to be 'politically troublesome and highly divisive' (Dennis and Urry, 2009 in Barr and Wright, 2012: 530) because relocalisation is a highly 'subversive project in relation to neoliberal globalisation' (Cavanagh and Mander, 2004 in North, 2010: 591). As Barr and Wright (2012: 531) put it, in 20 years time, 'there is likely to be a diverse geography of resilience within and between communities that map onto existing social, economic and political systems and inequalities'. Therefore, the movement needs to address these more political and social justice questions or it runs the risk of becoming another form of 'gated community' or 'bunker' sheltering the powerful from 'environmental terror' (Duffield, 2011: 19; see also James, 2009a and 2009b on the survivalist drift within the movement). Or, as Trainer (2009: 11) puts it, the movement may become 'a Not-In-My-Backyard phenomenon, with towns trying to insulate themselves from the coming scarcities and troubles'.

The issue or issues here can be put more directly: can a social movement, such as the Transition Towns Movement, achieve fundamental change without engaging in top-down political action? And is grassroots localism the best way, or even an effective way, to change 'the system'? Traditional 'leftists' and eco-socialists answer these questions in the negative (e.g., Sarkar, 1999). A number of critiques have focused critical attention on the 'small step' bottom-up approach used by the Transition Towns Movement, as well as its emphasis on localisation. The central question is 'whether small acts of resistance and micro-transformation can destabilise macro-systems and effect transformation of the system as a whole' (Cato and Hillier, 2010: 880). More specifically, if the movement grows enough food itself and sets up farmers' markets and community gardens, can it eventually undermine industrial agriculture? If the movement develops alternative currencies, can it undermine global finance? If it creates more cooperative business ventures, can it undermine corporate capitalism? If it creates more decentralised, small, local-scale renewable energy projects, can it make coal companies irrelevant and change energy planning and policy? Is localisation of production and consumption the best way to achieve a more sustainable and equitable future? Or, on the other hand, does the movement need to take state power, or more directly challenge state power, through civil disobedience, parliamentarian lobbying, progressive voting, or even violent revolution? These are very complex issues, and opinions differ vastly on the question. We do not pretend to have the 'right' answer, but these tensions in the Transition Towns Movement are worth examining further.

4.2 Problematising relocalisation: Strengths and weaknesses as a political strategy

People in Transition tend to argue that actions to build resilience and increase local provisioning from the bottom up is the 'right' way to go about changing the system. Much can be said in support of this approach. In a neoliberal era, waiting for governments to do something may not be useful (perhaps even wasteful or harmful), so a case can be made that communities should do things themselves and lead by practical example using the resources they have at the local scale. Once a Transition Initiative is relatively well established, Hopkins (2008: 170) argues that transitioners should 'build a bridge to Local Government' and seek 'alliances and coalitions of the willingly local' (Barry, 2012: 108) for funding and other forms of support. Researchers and academics have even called for more external networking with governments at the local and national level (Bailey *et al.*, 2010: 603; Seyfang *et al.*, 2010: 12; Seyfang and Haxeltine, 2012: 391-394; Bay, 2013: 182); for example, by providing *evidence* of the impacts of the transition activities through a managerial performance-based approach (using the 'measure-ment' language of corporate actors with proxies, quantitative aggregations, etc; see Merritt and Stubbs' (2012) proposal for a Local Sustainability Index). For many, this 'politics of engagement' therefore has the potential to develop into a 'productive sub-politics' to shake up local administrations (North and Longhurst, 2013: 1426). From a bottom-up localisation perspective, these series of small steps at the individual and community levels could have a cumulative effect and lead to bigger structural change (Alexander, 2013). This approach is similar to what Handmer and Dovers (1996) call 'type 2 resilience' or 'change at the margins', an approach which argues that 'gradual nondisruptive change is the only realistic option' (Handmer and Dovers, 1996: 500). However coherent this strategy may be, there are also potentially significant limitations with this as a theory of change.

To begin with, there is arguably no 'causal relationship' between 'environmental improvements in a *place* and environmental improvements to a *system*' (Trapese Collective, 2008: 33). Similarly, there is no guarantee that building resilience to shocks like climate change, peak oil, and economic crisis at a small scale will create similar resilience at a bigger scale (James, 2009a: 18). In fact, looking at the literature on resilience, this assumption does not seem warranted, since complex adaptive systems like most socio-ecological landscapes tend to function in a non-linear and unpredictable fashion (see Holling *et al.,* 1998; Folke, 2006; Walker and Salt, 2006; Miller *et al.,* 2010).

The 'local' is also a problematic notion and needs to be qualified further. The local can often be reified and romanticised; it can be a way to construct places in an isolationist way, as if they could be cut off from the rest of the world. In this case, the local can become synonymous of autarky and protectionism leading to practices of exclusion (Mason and Whitehead, 2012). This conceptualisation of the local often goes hand in hand with the assumption that local communities are homogenous and free of conflict or inequalities, which is problematic (Featherstone *et al.,* 2012). Consequently, localisation can potentially turn into little more than 'middle-class voluntarism' (Featherstone *et al.,* 2012: 178). Furthermore, critiques of localisation as a strategy, particularly from the political left, maintain that localisation is too often associated with 'backwards, constraining, authoritarian and parochial' ideas and practices (North, 2010: 592; see also, James, 2009b; Aiken, 2012). Others argue that localisation, rather than enhancing human welfare and wellbeing, leads to 'retrograde balkanisation' (North, 2010: 592).

However, we would argue that these features do not flow *necessarily* from localisation as a strategy for change. An 'inclusive' (Mason and Whitehead, 2012), 'intentional' (North, 2010), or 'progressive form of localism' (Mackinnon and Derickson, 2012: 266) is possible if the local is understood as 'open and relational' (Mackinnon and Derickson, 2012: 264) in terms of linking with other places, other groups, and other movements grappling with the consequences of globalisation, climate change, or resource scarcity. The local can become a powerful tool of mobilisation because it is where people live and experience the world, and therefore constitute 'socio-ecological memory' (Bathel *et al.*, 2010: 255). In this sense, the local has been and can continue to be a 'moral starting point and a locus of ecological concern' (Tomaney, 2013: 1) where (impacting) change is more likely to be within reach (Hopkins, 2013).

The Transition Towns Movement, however, still has some way to go to reach more progressive forms of localism. While the *Transition Companion* spells out that localisation is not self-sufficiency, insularity, or dominance by local powerful actors (Hopkins, 2011:48), a concern (beyond lip service) for inequalities within and between communities and places remains largely absent from the strategies proposed by the movement. For example, Transition's vision of a new localised resilient economy (Hopkins 2013: 27) does not seem to recognise the differential patterns of (socio-economic) vulnerability and capacities that exist within communities of places (i.e., the barriers that prevent people from engaging in Transition Initiatives like lack of time, social or economic capital). It generally ignores conflict that inevitably arises between different interests within communities (e.g., capital and labour, environmentalists and sceptics, libertarian and egalitarian versions of democracy) and also presumes that everybody will benefit from increased resilience (Fainstein, 2013: 15).

Another key issue with localisation as a political strategy is that the local does not necessarily constitute the most effective scale to tackle climate change, peak oil or economic instability given how multi-scalar these phenomena are (North, 2010: 587) and how globalised and interconnected the current system is. Arguably, even the most successful relocalised communities in the Transition Towns Movement like Totnes are 'still embedded within the global capitalist system through their dependencies on jobs, pensions [...] and economic exchanges with often global customers' (Wilson, 2012: 1229).

Lastly, from a left-leaning political economy perspective, issues of 'social justice at a distance' (Mason and Whitehead, 2012: 507) in terms of North/South development and relationships also need careful consideration. If bottom-up localisation means severing most trade relations with the developing South, it may result in leaving the poor fending for themselves 'with nothing other than their own wiles and materials they can temporarily muster' (Amin, 2012: 152); if that is indeed a consequence of relocalisation, it is an ethically dubious option, so this aspect of transition also needs to be negotiated carefully. Admittedly, the movement is again showing some reflexivity around this issue. North and Scott-Cato (2012: 104), who are both engaged in Transition Initiatives, note that 'It would be important from a progressive standpoint to maintain the benefits of fair trade and of international connection, if transport could be justified within ecological limits.' Hopkins (2011:52) also talks about the need for 'fair trade'. It would be fair to say, however, that this aspect of the movement is under-theorised.

4.3 The problem of power, politics, and structure

As the previous section suggests, localisation has many positive features but it is not without its challenges and limitations, and alone it is unlikely to bring about the changes required. It would be naïve to think that existing structures, organisations, and powerful (public and private) players will just crumble away and be made irrelevant by climate change and the end of cheap oil (Connors and MacDonald, 2010, 560; Seyfang and Haxeltine, 2012: 394). As some Marxist critics maintain, 'uneven access to material resources and the levers of social change must be redressed' as well (MacKinnon and Derickson, 2012: 255). This would involve re-centring the political and questioning what sorts of community and socio-ecological relations we want to see in the future. From the perspective of the orthodox political left, finding ways to change individual behaviour and reduce personal consumption is not enough, and *real* transition means 'taking on power and those who hold wealth and influence' and who continue to push 'business-as-usual scenarios' (Trapese Collective, 2008: 7). In other words, some argue that more direct, anti-systemic challenge is needed; in particular, some political theorists hold that nothing less than taking control of the state for structural transformation and fundamentally changing the rules of the game will get us there in the time frame available. Eco-socialist approaches, such as those defended by Sarkar (1999), advocate this. Without having to go as far as revolution, there are clear risks in adopting a reformist approach that is mostly apolitical and brushes aside or gives insufficient attention to sensitive questions of power, state, and structure.

Indeed, as with most reformist, non-confrontational approaches, by the time the movement creates enough change to become noticeable, the existing system may already have had time to adapt and simply adjust to that change, or at least give the appearance that it has by adopting particular rhetoric or discourses. This has little impact on actual policy and leaves underlying structure, unequal social relations, and hierarchies intact (Handmer and Dovers, 1996: 501; Smith, 2011: 102). In other words, reformist movements are easily co-opted into the political mainstream and the Transition Towns Movement is no exception, especially because it seems to neglect or underestimate the adaptive capacities of the current system (Trapese Collective, 2008: 27-32; Trainer, 2009). Politically charged projects or those disturbing economic activity can be hindered (or blocked) by technical and administrative strategies and inertia from governments. Overall, the often subtle and insidious resistance from governments reflects the broader legal, economic, social, and structural constraints that potentially 'lock in' people in unsustainable behaviours and high-consumption lifestyles. These lifestyle and political decisions are not made in a vacuum; rather, they are influenced by laws and policies and not addressing those top-down state structures may ensure that the Transition Towns Movement remains incidental, marginal, and dependent on the very systems it ostensibly opposes.

This leads us to think that the Transition Towns Movement needs a stronger political dimension *in addition* to generating knowledge and practices about how to deal with climate change and peak oil at the community level. While the project of formulating a coherent and detailed 'politics of transition' lies well beyond the scope of this chapter, the movement may eventually need to engage more directly with political and structural issues. This may take the form of more participants in the movement standing for local government or actively lobbying councillors and parliamentarians; or it may require formulating a strategy that falls within the eco-socialist tradition that works on replacing capitalism with something 'wholly other'.

Ted Trainer (2010a), on the other hand, envisions a political solution to our current dilemma through anarchism or, using a less loaded term, through grassroots self-organisation and radical, participative democracy. Trainer places no hope in the existing political system because he argues that the state will never voluntarily dissolve the structures of growth that drive ecological degradation, therefore individual citizens and communities need to build cultural, social, and economic alternatives themselves underneath the current model. For Trainer, capitalism cannot be reformed, it has to be replaced, not with a centralised eco-socialism, but with self-governing communities who essentially set out to ignore capitalism to death by building the new economy within the shell of the old (see also, Holmgren, 2013).

Overall, there are no silver bullets or miracle recipes to tackle climate change and peak oil but there are synergies between the different approaches which should be recognised and fostered further. The strength of the Transition Towns Movement lies with its ability to generate a change of mentalities, and to start to put into practice other ways of living, working, producing, and consuming in a post-oil community (rather than in 'its ability to make the necessary changes alone', North and Scott Cato, 2012: 99). The grassroots relocalisation of Transition can be 'extended as part of alternative political projects', whether it is anarchist, eco-socialist, or some expression of radical democracy (Featherstone *et al.*, 2012: 180) to tackle systemic issues such as exclusion, inequalities in resources and power, and the economic and political factors that keep supporting business-as-usual. Obstacles (structural or otherwise) that still prevent parts of the community from participating in and benefiting from Transition Initiatives also need to be spelt out and tackled. As mentioned earlier, a starting point could be bridging with other places and groups to feed into broader socio/ecological/political movements, standing in solidarity with nearby communities and groups in resistance, getting involved in non-violent direct action, divestment campaigns, etc. There is no doubt that individual Transition members are already doing some of this (see North, 2011; North and Scott Cato, 2012, for experiences in Liverpool and Stroud) and they should be encouraged to do so.

In the last section, we turn to the question of whether Transition Towns is radical enough. We articulate our critique around two key aspects: the resilience discourse used by the movement and the often timid engagement with consumerism and the macroeconomics of growth.

5. Challenging consumption, capitalism, and growth

5.1 Is resilience enough?

The Transition Towns Movement's discourse and vision is underpinned by resilience thinking, arguably the new 'pervasive idiom of global governance' (Walker and Cooper, 2011: 144). Indeed, if sustainability and sustainable development were the buzzwords of the 20th century, resilience has imposed itself as the dominant discourse when it comes to risk management and change management in the 21st century (Walker and Cooper, 2011; Zolli and Healy, 2013). There is a very large number of definitions and conceptualisations of resilience in the academic literature (Walker *et al.*, 2004; Brand and Jax, 2007; Miller *et al.*, 2010; Davoudi, 2012). Nevertheless, the central feature of resilience relates to adapting to change and disturbances while maintaining a system's integrity and basic functions, and factors that generate this sort of resilience include diversity, modularity (system elements are distributed and loosely connected, independent but overlapping in some ways), and tight feedback loops (consequences of actions are felt quickly in social and ecological systems allowing people to recognise thresholds and tipping points) (Hopkins, 2013 and Miller and Hopkins, 2013 define resilience in a similar way). Just like sustainability, resilience is a 'boundary object used as a comm-unication tool' across different communities of knowledge and practice (Brand and Jax, 2007: np). In other words, the concept is vague and stretchable enough that it can attract a very large and diverse audience of people with different aims and interests (the survey conducted by Seyfang [2009: 5] confirmed that 'building self-reliance', a concept often associated with resilience, is the main priority for participants in Transition Initiatives). The purposeful vagueness embedded in resilience constitutes the 'primary appeal of the movement and its central weakness' (Cato, 2008: 96) because it 'hides conflicts and power relations' (Brand and Jax, 2007: np) and also avoids or conceals the more normative questions of 'whose resilience we are concerned with and to what end' (Cote and Nightingale, 2012: 482); put differently, transition to what or where, by whom and for whom? There is no a-political consensus on these questions and the distributional and asymmetrical consequences of these decisions (particularly across places like developed and developing countries) need to be considered (Hornborg, 2009; Beymer-Farris *et al.*, 2012). This is a common theme found in the literature on transition in terms of what a resilient community might look like, how is power distributed politically and/or otherwise, who is included, etc (see e.g., Smith 2011; Barr and Wright, 2012: 530). Resilience theory does not provide a clear answer to this.

Another issue with resilience discourse is exemplified by the *New York Times* article 'Forget sustainability, it's about resilience' (Zolli, 2012). The piece's sub heading is 'Learning to bounce back' and this is precisely the sort of message that is associated with resilience in mainstream culture – bouncing back to where you were before the shock, the resistance and robustness of your system (i.e., engineering resilience, see Davoudi, 2012). Mainstream resilience discourses use the same 'feel-good rhetoric characteristic of discussions of sustainability' (Fainstein, 2013: 15) and remain within stability framings (i.e., the status quo); this is why resilience (not revolution) has become the 'rallying-cry of the early 21st century' (Hornborg, 2009: 252). Within this particular framing, resilience does not necessarily encourage the sort of regime shift, transformation, and social learning required to transition to the low-carbon economy Transition Towns envisions (Welsh, 2013: 8); nor, some argue, does it 'provide the basis for the mobilisation that can ultimately change the boundaries of the politically possible' (Fainstein, 2013: 15).

In addition, resilience has become instrumental to the neoliberal agenda of many Western governments (certainly in the UK, US, and Australia) and has been 'mobilised to facilitate archetypal governmental technologies of neoliberalism; government at a distance, technologies of responsibilisation' (Welsh, 2013: 2). Amin (2013) among others (Fainstein, 2013; Welsh, 2013) sees the widespread use of resilience discourses as a neoliberal push to move away from 'an all-protections and state-dependant culture of risk management on ideological grounds' (Amin, 2013: 140); the new UK Conservative's policy 'Big Society', which is accompanied by drastic cuts to the public service, exemplifies this 'latest mutation of neoliberalism' (Featherstone *et al.,* 2012: 178). In this sense, resilience discourse fits the bill quite well: it shifts the responsibility for action in the face of crisis (climate change or peak oil) from the state to local communities and individuals (without providing funding or support) who need to become active/autonomous subjects and vigilant citizens, responsible for their own protection in a context of increased uncertainty. Resilience discourses also act as means of systematically lowering public expectations by putting a lot of emphasis on 'adversity as only partially preventable' and almost necessary (Amin, 2013: 150), thereby sending the message that we cannot expect to be protected against everything and that we certainly cannot rely on the state for it. By presenting crisis as opportunity, resilience thinking is also self-referential and makes itself immune to critique (Walker and Cooper, 2011). Resilience becomes the measure, not of one's fitness to live, but of one's 'fitness to survive' (Welsh, 2013: 4) in an evolutionary and deterministic sense. Put differently, when used in a particular way (especially by government and the private sector), resilience is not about altruistic, ecocentric concern for 'global environmental change' but rather it focuses on 'the pragmatism of greater self-interest and survivability' (Barr and Wright, 2012: 525). Resilience rhetoric therefore potentially undermines 'a regime of worth with universalist protections' and the 'cross-societal commitment' to protect those without means (Amin, 2013: 142). By using resilience thinking and principles, the Transition Towns Movement may become an inadvertent ally of this sort of politics and again only engage those who can afford it.

Overall, resilience does not tend to address normative questions (of power, inequalities, distribution of resources and culture) and big-picture issues associated with risk and socio-ecological change; thus it can be argued that it implicitly maintains the 'social-ecological relations of capitalist resource extraction'

(Nadasdy, 2007: 217–18, quoted in Hornborg, 2009: 255). Because of its affinity with neoliberal economics and governance, the risk of co-option is high and to an extent already on the way. While some acknowledge the limits of resilience and argue that it's the best we can aim for at the moment (Alexander, 2012b), others warn that the type of resilience embedded in Transition (change at the margin) will lead us on the same road to nowhere as did sustainability and sustainable development (Handmer and Dovers, 1996: 501).

5.2 Challenging consumer capitalism and growth

Mackinnon and Derickson (2012) argue convincingly that 'the processes which shape resilience operate primarily at the scale of capitalist social relations' (255), so capitalism and the growth paradigm are unavoidable questions for a social movement like Transition Towns. Consumer capitalism is one of the root causes of our current predicament and often, it is also the big elephant in the room. Trainer (2009, 2010) and others (Alexander, 2012a; Latouche, 2010) have championed this type of critique and it is worth reiterating and developing. Currently, the Transition Towns Movement is not 'motivated by the clear and explicit goal of replacing the core institutions of consumer-capitalist society' (Trainer, 2010b: np). Rather, its 'targets' are more 'abstract' and 'diffuse' like climate change vulnerability and socio-economic instability (Barry and Quilley, 2009: 11), and the movement prefers a consensual positive approach as highlighted earlier. Yet, it is arguably impossible to 'decouple economic growth from carbon emissions' (Trapese Collective, 2008: 11) and it is partly the 'exploitative dynamic of capitalism' (Hornborg, 2009: 255) that got us in trouble in the first place. The current rate of resource consumption and GHG emissions is driven by the obsession for economic growth and it cannot be ignored (Latouche, 2010). To put it directly, the low-carbon society envisioned by many in the Transition Towns Movement arguably cannot be a capitalist society or a growth-based society, because that may just produce more of the same, i.e., environmental destruction and blatant social inequalities. It cannot be a society that measures social wellbeing and human happiness with GDP (see Jackson, 2009).

Interestingly, recently there have been some developments on this front in the 'official' transition literature. In the *Transition Companion*, economic growth starts to be addressed through the central theme of energy (that is, cheap energy is one of the foundations of economic growth, Hopkins, 2011: 33) and economic instability (Hopkins, 2011: 34-35). In the *Power of Just Doing Stuff*,

Hopkins (2013: 13) asserts that 'relentless growth in GDP is no longer an appropriate or desirable idea' and should be replaced 'with a goal of well-being, of happiness, of community, and connectedness' (Hopkins, 2013: 31). He challenges the mainstream 'growth-at-all-costs agenda' (Hopkins, 2013: 27) and starts to explicitly talk about the fact that 'we need to live within certain constraints' and to build a 'post-growth economy' (Hopkins, 2013:30; see also, Miller and Hopkins, 2013). These are positive steps but it still shies away from specifically addressing 'capitalism' and from spelling out what the consequences of degrowth may be (Trainer, 2012). Obviously, Hopkins may find it difficult to talk openly about radical change because of the movement's demographics and there is evidence that this type of message does not sit easily with people's lifestyles and everyday realities even in Transition communities (Bailey *et al.*, 2010; Wilson 2012). The current economic context, particularly in Europe, also makes it hard to talk about degrowth and capitalism since economic growth is heralded as *the solution* to our problems, i.e., what will bring back prosperity and jobs.

Consumption is another thorny issue because to challenge those pro-growth structures, we need 'a radical change in cultural attitudes towards consumption' (Alexander, 2012a: 7) and this represents one of the biggest challenges for the movement at the moment. The lack of clear communication on this topic may partially explain why Transition Initiatives have been portrayed as bourgeois and middle-class since they (implicitly or indirectly) convey the idea that you can transition to something better – environmentally and ethically – without having to downsize your material standard of living and consumption levels. In practice, despite the discourse around resilience, connection to nature, and inner transformation in the Transition Towns Movement, for the majority of people this 'plays second fiddle to the everyday acts of consumption that define us as practicing, mainstream members of a high-consumption society' (Barr and Wright, 2012: 530).[3] Obviously this is a difficult issue, not least because historically 'no one has ever rioted for austerity, people have taken to the streets in the past because they want to consume more of things, not because they want to consume less' (Monbiot 2005, in Barry and Quilley, 2009:

---

[3] Although there has not been specific study on consumption levels in Transition, Pir's (2009) study on resilient food systems in one of the historical and most established initiatives in Totnes shows that despite people being aware of the problems associated with large scale industrial food production, they still shop primarily at the supermarket (because of cost and convenience, choice and variety offered by big retailers, and lack of social cohesion).

7). In addition, consumption touches on lifestyle choices and
individual liberty as well as deeply engrained norms and values. So
getting the message across that a life based on 'far simpler material
living standards' and 'frugal self-sufficient collectivism' would be a
good life is not an easy task. Yet, transitioning to low-consumption
lifestyle is indispensable for both pragmatic and symbolic reasons
within the Transition movement. First, consumption is part of what
drives the growth engine (and the widespread ecological degradation that goes with it) so it needs to be addressed if we want a
fighting chance to curb/slow the effects of climate change and
biodiversity loss. Second, if the Transition Towns Movement is ever
to grow to a significant size, people will need to be able to dedicate
more time to building the movement and a new society, instead of
being locked into long working hours just to provide for high-
consumption lifestyles. Lastly and more symbolically, if the frame of
reference and measure of success remains individual income and
ever-expanding material possession and consumption, and
Transition Towns does not challenge it, the movement will not be
able to influence social practices around consumption because they
are shaped by individual decisions but also by the broader context,
narrative, and 'lifeworld' people are in (see Spaargaren, 2003).
Transition 'from the grassroots up' (Alexander, 2013) needs to
involve a move away from growth-orientated capitalism – or
perhaps capitalism altogether – which itself implies overcoming the
cultures of competition and overconsumption that are so deeply
entrenched in modern life.

5. Conclusion

The Transition Towns Movement is a nascent movement that aims
to tackle some of the biggest challenges of our times. It makes the
case that the transition to a localised economy and a low-carbon
lifestyle can be fun, and that the transition will benefit the
community and the environment. It argues that an incremental
approach to building community resilience 'can add up to
something big and extraordinary' (Hopkins, 2013: 132). The
movement aims to create a different vision for where we want to go
and provides ideas and techniques to get us there collectively.
Questions remain around how inclusive the movement really is and
whether local initiatives can have enough influence and/or build
enough momentum to lead to a transformation of the current
growth-based consumerist capitalist system. Transition will most
likely not be able to achieve this alone and it could benefit from
collaborating with dissident and defiant groups that challenge

consumerism, capitalism, and the actors that support/generate our 'unsustainable, ecocidal economic system' (North and Scott Cato, 2012: 110). On a global scale, the movement is still small, but so were the Civil Rights, the Women's Rights, sexual liberation, LGBTI movements once; they looked too small to effect change. But tipping points arrive, often unexpectedly. It could be that we are at the pre-tipping-point stage with Transition and the potential is definitely there. But it needs a spark of some sort for that potential to be unleashed.

References

Aiken, G. 2012. 'Community transitions to low carbon futures in the Transitions Towns Network (TTN)'. *Geography Compass* 6(2): 89-99.

Alexander, S. 2012a. 'Ted Trainer and the Simpler Way'. *Simplicity Institute Report* 12d: 1-19.

Alexander, S. 2012b. 'Resilience through simplification: Revisiting Tainter's theory of collapse'. *Simplicity Institute Report* 12h: 1-20.

Alexander, S. 2013. 'Voluntary simplicity and the social reconstruction of the law: Degrowth from the grassroots up'. *Environmental Values* 22: 287-308.

Alexander, S. 2014. 'A critique of techno-optimism: Efficiency without sufficiency is lost'. *MSSI Working Paper* (WP/1, January 2014): 1-21.

Amin, A. 2012. *Land of strangers*. Cambridge: Polity Press.

Amin, A. 2013. 'Surviving the turbulent future'. *Environment and Planning D: Society and space* 31: 140-156.

Bailey, I., Hopkins, R., and Wilson, G. 2010. 'Some things old, some things new: The spatial representations and politics of change of the peak oil relocalisation movement'. *Geoforum* 41: 595-605.

Barnett, J. and Campbell, J. 2010. 'Climate change and small island states: Power, knowledge and the South Pacific'. London: Earthscan.

Barr, S. and Wright, P.D. 2012. 'Resilient communities: Sustainabilities in transition'. *Local Environment* 17(5): 525-532.

Barry, J. 2012. *The politics of actually existing unsustainability*. Oxford: Oxford University Press.

Barry, J. and Quilley, S. 2008. 'Transition towns: "Survival", "resilience" and sustainable communities – Outline of a research agenda'. *Advances in Ecopolitics* 2: 14-37.

Barry, J. and Quilley, S. 2009. 'The transition to sustainability: Transition towns and sustainable communities'. In Leonard, L. and Barry, J. (eds), Ch 1. *The transition to sustainable living and practice (Advances in Ecopolitics vol. 4)*. Emerald Group Publishing Limited: 1-28.

Bathel, S., Folke, C., Colding, J. 2010. 'Social-ecological memory in urban gardens: Retaining the capacity for management of ecosystem services'. *Global Environmental Change* 20(2): 255-265.

Bay, U. 2013. 'Transition town initiatives promoting transformational community change in tackling peak oil and climate change challenges'. *Australian Social Work* 66(2): 171-186.

Bettini, G. and Karaliotas, L. 2013. 'Exploring the limits of peak oil: Naturalising the political, de-politicising energy'. *The Geographical Journal* 179(4): 331-341.

Beymer-Farris, B.A., Bassett, T.J., and Bryceson, I. 2012. 'Promises and pitfalls of adaptive management in resilience thinking: The lens of political ecology'. In Plieninger, T. and Bieling, C. (eds). *Resilience and the cultural landscape*. Cambridge: Cambridge University Press: 283-299.

Brand, F.S. and Jax, K. 2007. 'Focusing the meaning(s) of resilience: Resilience as a descriptive concept and a boundary object'. *Ecology and Society* 12(1) Available at: http://www.ecologyandsociety.org/vol12/iss1/art23/ (accessed 29 July 2013).

Brecha, R. 2013. 'Ten reasons to take peak oil seriously'. *Sustainability* 5(2): 664-694.

Brown, L. 2011. *World on the edge: How to prevent environmental and economic collapse*. New York: W.W. Norton and Co.

Bunting, M. 2009. 'Beyond Westminster's bankrupted practices, a new idealism is emerging'. *The Guardian,* May 2009. Available at: www.guardian.co.uk/commentisfree/2009/may/31/reform-transition-a-new-politics/ (accessed 18 January 2013).

Cato, M. 2008. 'Reviews: Weighing transition towns in the carbon balance'. *Soundings* 40: 92-97.

Cato, M. and Hillier, J. 2010. 'How could we study climate-related social innovation? Applying Deleuzian philosophy to Transition Towns'. *Environmental Politics* 19(6): 869-887.

Chamberlin, S. 2009. 'The transition timeline: For a local, resilient future'. White River Junction, Vt: Chelsea Green Publishing.

Cohen, D.K.M. 2010. 'Reaching out for resilience: Exploring approaches to inclusion and diversity in the Transition movement'. Unpublished Thesis, Master of Science in Human Ecology, University of Strathclyde, Glasgow. Available at: http://transitionculture.org/wp-content/uploads/Danielle Cohen-MSc-HE-Thesis.pdf (accessed 17 February 2013).

Connors, P. and McDonald, P. 2010. 'Transitioning communities: Community participation and the Transition Town movement'. *Community Development Journal* 46(4): 558-572.

Cote, M. and Nightingdale, A.J. 2012. 'Resilience thinking meets social theory: Situating social change in socio-ecological systems (SES) research'. *Progress in Human Geography* 36(4): 475-489.

Cutler, A. and Chatterton, P. 2009. 'New preface to "The rocky road to transition"'. Trapese Collective. Available at: http://www.paulchatterton.com/2009/08/17/the-rocky-road-to-a-real-transition-reprinted-with-new-preface/ (accessed 18 January 2013).

Davoudi, S. 2012. 'Resilience: A bridging concept or a dead end?' *Planning Theory and Practice* 13(2): 299-233.

Duffield, M. 2011. 'Environmental terror: Uncertainty, resilience and the bunker'. *Global Insecurities Centre*, University of Bristol, Working paper no.06-11. Available at: http://www.bris.ac.uk/spais/research/workingpapers/wpspaisfiles/duffield-0611.pdf (accessed 10 October 2013).

Fainstein, S. 2013. 'Resilience and Justice'. *Melbourne Sustainable Society Institute*, research paper no.2. Available at: http://www.sustainable.unimelb.edu.au/files/mssi/MSSI-ResearchPaper-02_Fainstein_Resilience-Justice_2013.pdf (accessed 21 October 2013).

Featherstone, D., Ince, A., Mackinnon, D., Strauss, K., and Cumbers, A. 2012. 'Progressive localism and the construction of political alternatives'. *Transactions of the Institute of British Geographers* 37: 177-182.

Folke, C. 2006. 'Resilience: The emergence of a perspective for social-ecological systems analyses'. *Global Environmental Change* 16: 253-267.

Global Footprint Network, 2013. Reports available at http://www.footprintnetwork.org/en/index.php/gfn/page/world_footprint/ (accessed 10 February 2012).

Greene, M. 2010. 'Microcosms of sustainability: A critical cultural analysis of the Transition movement'. Unpublished Thesis, Master of Environment, Science and Society, University College London. Available at: http://www.transitionnetwork.org/resources/microcosms-sustainability-critical-cultural-analysis-transition-town-movement (accessed 18 March 2013).

Handmer, J.W. and Dovers, S.R. 1996. 'A typology of resilience: Rethinking institutions for sustainable development'. *Organization and Environment* 9(4):482-511.

Heinberg, R. 2011. *The end of growth: Adapting to our new economic reality.* Gabriola Island: New Society Publishers.

Herring, H. and Sorrell, S. 2009. *Energy efficiency and sustainable consumption: The rebound effect.* London: Palgrave Macmillan.

Holling, C.S., Berkes, F., and Folke, C. 1998. 'Science, sustainability and resource management'. In Berkes, F. and Folke, C. (eds). *Linking social and ecological systems: Management practices and social mechanisms for building resilience.* Cambridge: Cambridge University Press: 342-362.

Holmgren, D. 2002. *Permaculture: Principles and pathways beyond sustainability.* Hepburn: Holmgren Design Services.

Holmgren, D. 2013. 'Crash on Demand: Welcome to the brown tech future'. *Simplicity Institute Report* 13c: 1-23.

Hopkins, R. 2008. *The transition handbook: From oil dependency to local resilience.* White River Junction, Vt: Chelsea Green Publishing.

Hopkins, R. 2009. *The transition handbook: Creating local sustainable communities beyond oil dependency (Australian and New Zealand Edition).* Lane Cove: Finch Publishing.

Hopkins, R. 2011. *The transition companion: Making your community more resilient in uncertain time.* White River Junction, Vt: Chelsea Green Publishing.

Hopkins, R. 2012. 'Peak oil and transition towns'. *Architectural Design* 82(4): 72-77.

Hopkins, R. 2013. 'The power of just doing stuff: how local action can change the world'. Cambridge: UIT/Green Books.

Hopkins, R. and Lipman, P. 2009. 'Who we are and what we do'. Version 1.0, transition network.org. Available at: http://transitionculture.org/wp-content/uploads/who_we_are_high.pdf (accessed 10 March 2013).

Hopkins, R., Thurstain-Goodwin, M., and Fairlie, S. 2009. 'Can Totnes feed itself? Exploring the practicalities of food relocalisation'. Version 1.0, Transition Network and Transition Town Totnes. Available at: http://transitionculture.org/wp-content/uploads/Can-Totnes-Feed-Itselfarticle-revised-Sept-09.pdf (accessed 22 February 2013).

Hornborg, A. 2009. 'Zero-sum world: Challenges in conceptualising environmental load displacement and ecologically unequal exchange in the world system'. *International Journal of Comparative Sociology* 50: 237-263.

Intergovernmental Panel on Climate Change (IPCC), 2013. 'Climate Change 2013: The Physical Science Basis (Fifth Assessment Report)'. Available at: http://www.ipcc.ch/report/ar5/wg1/#.Uk6k-CjqMRw (accessed 4 October 2013).

Jackson, T. 2009. *Prosperity without growth: Economics for a finite planet*. London: Earthscan.

James, C. 2009a. 'The politics of transition'. *Arena Magazine* 101: 18-19.

James, C. 2009b. 'Transition and the revitalisation of the middle class'. *Arena Magazine* 103: 14-15.

James, C. 2010. 'Transition and raw resources'. *Arena Magazine* 104: 14-15.

Latouche, S. 2010. 'Le pari de la décroissance' (2ème édition). Paris: Librairie Arthème Fayard.

Longhurst, N. 2012. 'The Totnes pound: A grassroots technological niche'. In Davies, A. (ed.), Ch. 9. *Enterprising communities: Grassroots sustainability innovations (Advances in ecopolitics, Volume 9)*. Emerald Group Publishing Limited: 163-188.

MacKinnon, D. and Derickson, K.D. 2012. 'From resilience to resourcefulness: A critique of resilience policy and activism'. *Progress in Human Geography* 37(2): 253-270.

Martinez-Alier, J. 1995. 'The environment as a luxury good or "too poor to be green"'? *Ecological Economics* 13(1): 1-10.

Mason, K. and Whitehead, M. 2012. 'Transition urbanism and the contested politics of ethical place making'. *Antipode* 44(2): 493-516.

Meadows, D., Randers, J., and Meadows, D., 1972. *Limits to growth*. New York: New American Library.

Meadows, D., Randers, J., and Meadows, D. 2004. *Limits to growth: The 30-year update*. White River Junction, Vt: Chelsea Green Publishing.

Merritt, A. and Stubbs, T. 2012. 'Incentives to promote green citizenship in UK Transition Towns'. *Development* 55(1): 96-103.

Mill, J.S. 2004 [1848]. *Principles of political economy: With some of their applications to social philosophy*. New York: Prometheus Books.

Miller, A. and Hopkins, R. 2013. 'Climate after growth: Why environmentalists must embrace post-growth economics and community resilience'. *Post Carbon Institute and Transition Network*. Available at: http://www.postcarbon.org/reports/Climate-After-Growth.pdf (accessed 2 December 2013).

Miller, F. *et al.,* 2010. 'Resilience and vulnerability: complementary or conflicting concepts?' *Ecology and Society* 15(3) Available at: http://www.ecologyandsociety.org/vol15/iss3/art11/ (accessed 29 July 2013).

Miller, R. and Sorrel, S. (2014) 'The future of oil supply'. *Philosophical Transactions of the Royal Society A* 372, 20130179: 1-27.

North, P. 2010. 'Eco-localisation as a progressive response to peak oil and climate change: A sympathetic critique. *Geoforum* 41: 585-594.

North, P. 2011. 'The politics of climate activism in the UK: A social movement analysis'. *Environment and Planning A* 43(7): 1581-1598.

North, P. and Scott Cato, M. 2012. 'A suitable climate for political action? A sympathetic review of the politics of transition'. In Pelling, M., Manuel-Navarrete, D., and Redclift, M. (eds). *Climate change and the crisis of capitalism: A chance to reclaim self, society and nature*. London: Routledge: 99–113.

North, P. and Longhurst, N. 2013. 'Grassroots localisation? The scalar potential of and limits of the "Transition" approach to climate change and resource constraint'. *Urban Studies* 50(7): 1423-1438.

OECD, 2013. 'Economic policy reforms: Going for growth'. Available at: http://www.keepeek.com/Digital-Asset-Management/oecd/economics/economic-policy-reforms-2013 growth-2013-en#page1 (accessed 20 December 2013).

Paavola, J. and Adger, N.W. 2006. 'Fair adaptation to climate change'. *Ecological Economics* 56(4): 594-609.

Pelling, M. and Navarrete, D.M. 2011. 'From resilience to transformation: The adaptive cycle in two Mexican urban centers'. *Ecology and Society* 16 (2) Available at: http://www.ecologyandsociety.org/vol16/iss2/art11/ (accessed 15 January 2013).

Pinkerton, T. and Hopkins, R. 2009. *Local food: How to make it happen in your community*. Totnes, Devon: Green Books.

Pir, A.L.P. 2009. 'In search of a resilient food system: A qualitative study of the transition town Totnes food group'. Unpublished thesis, Master of Philosophy, Centre for Development and the Environment, University of Oslo. Available at: http://transitionculture.org/wp-content/uploads/aLp-Thesis 13.1.2010-1.pdf (accessed 18 January 2013).

Polimeni, J. *et al.* 2009. *The myth of resource efficiency: The Jevons paradox*. London: Earthscan.

Rockstrom, J. *et al.* 2009. 'Planetary boundaries: Exploring the safe operating space for humanity'. *Ecology and Society* 14(2): Article 32.

Rubin, J. 2012. *The end of growth: But is that all bad?* Toronto: Random House.

Russell, B. 2009. *Russell: The basic writings of Bertrand Russell.* Routledge: London.

Sarkar, S. 1999. *Eco-socialism or eco-capitalism: A critical analysis of humanity's fundamental choices.* London: Zed Books.

Seyfang, G. 2009. 'Green shoots of sustainability: The 2009 UK transition movement survey'. University of East Anglia. Available at: http://www.uea.ac.uk/~e175/Seyfang/Publications_files/Transition%20Network%202009%20Survey%20Report.pdf (accessed 15 February 2012).

Seyfang, G., Haxeltime, A., Hargreaves, T., and Longhurst, N. 2010. Energy and communities in transition – towards a new research agenda on agency and civil society in sustainability transitions. *Centre for Social and Economic Research on the Global Environment*, Working paper EDM 10-13. Available at: http://www.econstor.eu/handle/10419/48803 (accessed 18 January 2013).

Seyfang, G. and Haxeltine, A. 2012. Growing grassroots innovations: Exploring the role of community-based initiatives in governing sustainable energy transitions. *Environment and Planning C: Government and Policy* 30: 381-400.

Sharp, N. 2009. Listening to voices that touch the heart. *Arena Magazine* 100: 32-35.

Smith, A. 2011. The transition town network: A review of current evolutions and renaissance. *Social Movement Studies* 10(1): 99-105.

Smith, J. and Positano, S. 2010. *The self-destructive affluence of the first world: The coming crises of global poverty and ecological collapse.* New York: Edwin Mellen.

Spaargaren, G. 2003. Sustainable consumption: A theoretical and environmental policy perspective. Society and Natural Resources 16(8): 687-701.

Taylor, P.J. 2012. 'Transition towns and world cities: Towards green networks of cities. *Local Environment* 17 (4):495-508.

Tomaney, J. 2013. Parochialism – a defence. Progress in Human Geography 37(5): 658-672.

Trainer, T. 2009. Transitioning to where? *Arena Magazine* 102: 11-12.

Trainer, T. 2010a. *The transition to a sustainable and just world.* Envirobook, Sydney.

Trainer, T. 2010b. The transition towns movement: Its huge significance and a friendly criticism. Available at: http://www.culturechange.org/cms/index.php?option=com_c

ontent&task=view&id=605&Itemid=1 (accessed 18 January 2013).

Trainer, T. 2012. De-growth: Do you realise what it means, *Futures* 44: 590-599.

Trainer, 2013a. Can Europe Run on Renewable Energy? A Negative Case. *Energy Policy* 63: 845-850.

Trainer, 2013b. Can the World Run on Renewable Energy' *Humanomics* 29(2): 88-104.

Transition Network. 2011. Transition Network diversity newsletter. Available at: http://www.transitionnetwork.org/tags/transition-network-diversity-newsletter (accessed 18 January 2013).

Transition Network. 2013a. 'What does transition network do?' Available at: http://www.transitionnetwork.org/about (accessed 18 January 2013).

Transition Network. 2013b. 'Transition initiatives map'. Available at: http://www.transitionnetwork.org/initiatives/map (accessed 2 December 2013).

Trapese Collective. 2008. *The Rocky road to a real transition: The transition towns movement and what it means for social change*. London: Trapse collective. Available at: http://trapese.clearerchannel.org/resources/rocky-road-a5-web.pdf (accessed 18 January 2013).

Turner, G. 2012. 'Are we on the cusp of collapse?' Updated comparison of *The limits to growth* with historical data'. *Gaia* 21(2): 116-124.

Tverberg, G. 2012. 'Oil supply limits and the continuing financial crisis'. *Energy* 37(1): 27-34.

United Nations (UN). 2010. *Global biodiversity outlook 3*. Available at: http://www.cbd.int/doc/publications/gbo/gbo3-final-en.pdf (accessed 20 December 2013).

United Nations Department of Social and Economic Affairs (UNDSEA). 2012. 'World Population Prospects: The 2012 Revision'. Available at: http://esa.un.org/wpp/ (accessed 10 September 2013).

Walker, B. and Salt, D. 2006. *Resilience thinking: Sustaining ecosystems and people in a changing world*. Washington: Island Press.

Walker, B., Holling, C.S., Carpenter, S.R., and Kinzig, A. 2004. 'Resilience, adaptability and transformability in socio-ecological systems'. *Ecology and Society* 9(2) Available at: http://www.ecologyandsociety.org/vol9/iss2/art5/ (accessed 29 July 2013).

Walker, J. and Cooper, M. 2011. 'Genealogies of resilience: From systems ecology to the political economy of crisis and adaptation'. *Security Dialogue* 42(2): 143-160.

Welsh, M. 2013. 'Resilience and responsibility: governing uncertainty in a complex world'. *The Geographical Journal*. doi: 10.1111/geoj.12012

Wilson, G.A. 2012. 'Community resilience, globalization and transitional pathways of decision-making'. *Geoforum* 43: 1218-1231.

Zolli, A. 2012. 'Learning to bounce back'. *The New York Times*, November 2012. Available at: http://www.nytimes.com/2012/11/03/opinion/forget-sustainability-its-about-resilience.html?_r=2& (accessed 2 December 2013).

Zolli, A. and Healy, M. 2013. *Resilience: Why things bounce back*. New York, NY: Simon and Schuster.

12

LOOKING BACKWARD FROM THE YEAR 2099
Ecozoic reflections on the future

It's all a question of story. We are in trouble just now because we ... are in between stories. The old story, the account of how the world came to be and how we fit into it, ... sustained us for a long period of time. It shaped our emotional attitudes, provided us with life purposes, and energised action. It consecrated suffering and integrated knowledge. We awoke in the morning and knew where we were. We could answer the questions of our children. ... [But now the old story] is no longer effective. Yet we have not learned the new story.

                    – Thomas Berry

Preamble

Thomas Berry was a visionary. He told new stories about the universe and our place in it, stories not only about where we have been and where we seem to be going, but also stories about where we could go, if only we exercised our freedom in different ways. Indeed, story, myth, and narrative played a central role in Berry's thinking, as the epigraph to this essay indicates.

Every individual life and every society is an enactment of a story people tell themselves about the nature and purpose of their existence and of the world they live in. These stories shape our experiences and guide our thoughts and actions – for better or for worse, consciously or unconsciously. Needless to say, Berry was deeply troubled by the dominant story of our times. Put simply, he felt it was a story of Earth as a limitless resource to be exploited for human gratification, a story which not only degraded the integrity of our living planet but also promoted a materialistic attitude to life by equating happiness and wellbeing with increased opportunities to accumulate and consume. Berry tried to provoke us into re-considering this story. He tried to unsettle and inspire us, by telling new stories. As one of its defining features, Berry's Earth scholarship is a reminder of the significance of story.

In this essay, rather than offering a close reading of Berry's writings in Earth Jurisprudence, I have dared to experiment with story, inspired by those writings. Due to the unconventional nature of my undertaking, I have avoided direct reference to Berry's writings, but the influence of those writings should be clear, everywhere lying just beneath the surface. In an attempt to build upon Berry's Earth scholarship and contribute in some modest way to the Great Work, I will tell a story of the future, a possible future that was conceived of in between the poles of pessimism and optimism but which is ultimately based upon a faith in the human spirit to meet the challenges of creating an Ecozoic era. Though I cannot be sure Berry would have agreed with all the conclusions drawn or speculations made, I believe he would have been sympathetic to my general undertaking.

What follows is an attempt to look back on the 21st century from the vantage point of the year 2099. It takes the form of an essay, entitled 'The Path to Entropia', written for the journal *Possibility* by Lennox Kingston, a 90-year-old retired Professor of Legal and Political History. Motivated by various themes in Earth Jurisprudence, the essay reviews how attitudes toward consumption and economic growth underwent a radical shift over the course of the 21st century and how this affected, through legal transformation, the social, political, and economic order of late capitalism. Particular attention is given to the legal evolution of property rights and the cultural movements that made this evolution possible. Whether the changes described are a cause or effect of a shift in human consciousness in relation to Earth is a question that I leave open for future reflection. I dedicate this experimental story to the memory of Thomas Berry.

THE PATH TO ENTROPIA
Lennox Kingston
Possibility 81(9) 2099

1. Past, Present, Future

The Ecozoic movements, which emerged with loud warnings in the final decades of the 20th century and which promised so much in the early decades of the 21st century, ultimately failed to prevent corporate profiteers and the consumer class from having a devastating and irreversible impact on global ecosystems and biodiversity. Scientists, who used to categorise geological ages into periods of millions of years, now commonly use the term 'Anthropocene' to refer to the last 300 years only. During this geological blink-of-an-eye, human economic activity violently degraded the planet in many ways, including pervasive deforestation and the mass extinction of species, climate destabilisation, soil erosion, ocean acidification and depletion, and the near exhaustion of many non-renewable resources, most notably oil. Though recent decades of sustained and dedicated commitment to the Great Restoration seem to have stabilised the biosphere and lessened the threat of ecosystemic collapse, our world has changed and there is no going back. History will never forget that fateful day when our species witnessed the last fragments of the polar ice cap melt away, stamping our age with a new image of Earth. It was in 1968 when the Apollo spaceship first captured those iconic pictures of our fragile planet floating mysteriously through the dark heavens of outer space. Fewer than 100 years later human beings had altered that cosmological scene.

We need not review here the catastrophic effect rising sea levels had on the lives of millions of environmental refugees, to say nothing of the other humanitarian crises, including the Water Wars, which were also causally linked to climate change. Nor is there any need to contribute a word further to the massive literature on the breakdown of global economic institutions during the Lost Years of 2031-34, from which the International Monetary Fund, the World Bank, and most transnational corporations never recovered. We know about these tragic, destabilising events all too well. But as the 21st century draws to a hesitant close – not with a bang but with a sigh of relief – there may be some value in looking back on our long, uncertain, and painful recovery from these events, if only so that we may better understand the present as we look to the future. It is a recovery which we must attribute primarily to all those in the Ecozoic movements who, despite repeated, harrowing disappointments, kept fighting tirelessly for the cause they knew to be just.

2. The Rise and Demise of Growth Economics

For most of human history – romantic myths aside – the vast majority of human beings lived lives oppressed by material deprivation and insecurity. Generally speaking, human existence was an ongoing struggle for little more than bare subsistence, and for several millennia the standard of living of the average person in civilised centres did not rise significantly. But then, in 1712, the steam engine was invented and the First Industrial Revolution was set into motion, catalysed by market forces. Suddenly the energy stored in the planet's fossilised fuels was released in an explosion of mechanised economic activity. The result was that the wealth of nations – primarily Western nations, at least at first – began to grow at exponential rates that previous generations would not have thought possible.

Within those nations that progressed from circumstances of widespread poverty to circumstances of moderate or comfortable material security, the human lot seemed to improve considerably. Although there were always costs, sometimes great costs, associated with economic growth – factory labour, pollution, deforestation, social dislocation, and so on – for many years these costs were generally outweighed, in terms of human wellbeing, at least, by the huge material benefits that resulted. This initial success led to the entrenchment of what political and economic historians now refer to as 'the growth model of progress'.

Put simply, the growth model assumed that the overall wellbeing of a society was approximately proportional to the size of its economy, because more money or higher Gross Domestic Product (GDP) meant that more individual or social 'preferences' could be satisfied via market transactions. No matter how rich a society became, growing the economy was thought to be the only effective way to eliminate poverty, reduce inequality and unemployment, properly fund schools, hospitals, the arts, scientific research, environmental protection programmes, and so on. In other words, the underlying social problem (even within the richest nations) was believed to be a lack of money, and thus for more than two centuries economic growth was heralded across the political spectrum as the goal toward which societies should direct their collective energy. The notion of a macroeconomic 'optimal scale' was all but unthinkable. It was assumed that a bigger economy was always better.

This growth model of progress, as we now know, turned out to be dangerously flawed, although dislodging it from the social imagination proved exceedingly difficult. John Stuart Mill, writing in 1848, was one of the first to point out that the costs of economic growth may one day outweigh the benefits, at which time, he argued, the most appropriate form of government would be 'the stationary state'. By this he meant a condition of zero growth in population and physical capital stock, but with continued improvement in technology and in what he called 'the Art of Living'. This aspect of his oeuvre, however – today his most famous – was either ignored or summarily dismissed by his contemporaries, and for several generations it lay forgotten in the intellectual dustbin. Growth scepticism was revived and updated in the late 1960s by the economist Ezra Mishan, and developed further in the 1970s and beyond by Donella Meadows, Ernst Schumacher, Herman Daly, and Fred Hirsch, among many others. But although these theorists attained a certain notoriety within the intelligentsia and certain counter-cultures, for a long time their work had no significant politico-economic impact. Economic growth remained the overriding objective of governments across the globe.

In the late 20th century and early 21st century, as the costs of economic growth became more pronounced and harder to tolerate, the undercurrent of growth scepticism slowly strengthened and began entering the intellectual mainstream. Many rigorous and credible sociological studies showed that, from about the 1970s onward, economic growth in most Western societies had stopped contributing significantly to human wellbeing. That is, it became apparent that a rise in material 'standard of living' (measured by per capita income) was no longer strongly correlated with 'quality of life' (measured by subjective wellbeing). Indeed, economic growth had even begun undermining many of the things upon which wellbeing depended, such as responsive democratic institutions, social solidarity, spiritual and aesthetic experience, and stable, functioning ecosystems. The clear implication of these findings was that economic growth should no longer be the primary measure of policy and institutional success within Western societies. But, again, the impact of this scholarship was very limited, at least for a time. Corporate interests ensured that growth economics remained firmly entrenched in the political realm, and well into the 21st century the reigning orthodoxy was that the answer to almost every problem – including environmental problems – was *more economic growth.*

Below we will review the broad legal and political transformations that eventually helped free the world from this growth fetish. Before doing so, however, we should direct our attention to the cultural movements that put those transformations on the political agenda and which were the driving force behind their implementation. Admittedly, this inquiry is bound to oversimplify the catalysts of change, because the extensive institutional restructuring that occurred over the 21st century doubtless had an infinite array of causes. Nevertheless, historians generally accept that within Western societies, at least, there were two causes of particular significance: the first being a destabilising but ultimately productive disillusionment with top-down politics; the second being a radical change in attitudes toward material consumption. Let us briefly consider these matters in turn.

The onset of chronic disillusionment with top-down or 'representative' politics is typically traced back to the years 2007-09. During these years there were two events of global significance which tested the capacity of democratic systems to function for the common good. The first was the Global Financial Crisis (GFC); the second was the United Nations' Climate Change Conference held in Copenhagen, Denmark.

The GFC had its roots in the so-called 'credit crunch', when a loss of confidence by US investors in the value of sub-prime mortgages caused a liquidity crisis, precipitated by expensive oil. Due to unscrupulous lending by several mega-banks – a process which had been insufficiently regulated and, indeed, had been systematically encouraged – a huge number of homeowners in the US found that they were unable to meet their mortgage repayments. But when the housing market crashed, banks found that the repossessed houses and land were worth less than what the bank had originally loaned out. This resulted in the liquidity crisis. The consequence was that it became increasingly difficult to obtain loans, investments dried up, and consumer confidence was shattered, all of which ended up having hugely negative impacts on the global economy. Moreover, many of the mega-banks were on the brink of collapse. Because those banks were considered 'too big to fail', however, governments were essentially forced to bail out the very institutions which caused the crisis in the first place. This approach proved to be efficacious, in the sense, at least, that over the next two years the global economy slowly recovered, at least superficially, not without great hardship to many millions of people. But as 'business as usual' seemed to resume, there was the deeply troubling sense that nothing of any significance had been done to rein in the vast powers of privately owned financial institutions or to protect people from history repeating itself. In short, Western governments of the time proved to be either impotent in the face of corporate power or unwilling to confront it.

Much the same can be said of the pivotal Climate Change Conference held in Copenhagen during December 2009. By this stage the state of scientific research meant that it was no longer credible to deny the reality of climate change or to deny the potentially catastrophic consequences – later realised, of course – of failing to significantly reduce global carbon emissions without delay. Despite the clarity and force of the scientific warnings, however, the Copenhagen conference lacked any real sense of urgency and was considered a despairing failure both by and for the Ecozoic movements. Eventually, a weak, non-binding Emissions Trading Scheme was agreed to, heralded by some as the salvation of Earth, but the very method of trying to use market mechanisms to solve a problem essentially caused by markets was doomed to failure – and fail it did. Looking back we see that Copenhagen was a great crossroad for humanity, a final opportunity to take climate change seriously. Vested interests in the economic status quo, however, were able to keep growth capitalism firmly on track, leading not to a decline but, for too many years, a continued rise in emissions.

Whether it was due to impotence, incompetence, or sheer unwillingness to face the facts, it must be said that at Copenhagen the political response to the ecological crisis – the response from the Western nations, in particular – was a profound dereliction of duty. Not only that, its short-sightedness was economically irrational, because the financial costs of taking genuine preventative action at that stage would have paled in comparison to the costs of what lay ahead. At this time democratic rule may still have been 'of the people', but there was a growing suspicion that it was no longer 'by the people' or 'for the people'.

And so it was that Western citizens began to lose faith, as never before, in representative democracy. The most significant political decisions of the age were widely perceived to be dishonourable capitulations before corporate power. Furthermore, the ballot box seemed to provide no avenue for redress, because it was understood to merely offer the choice between two or three essentially corporate parties. In such destabilising circumstances, one of two things tends to happen: either democratic subjects violently overthrow the unrepresentative government, or those subjects take government into their own hands at the local level. For several years, as the collective rumbling grew to a crescendo, political commentators were unsure which course of action would prevail, and some even voiced their concerns about the prospect of wholesale collapse of democratic processes and the rise of fascist or totalitarian politics in the West. More pessimistically still, others predicted the collapse of human civilisation itself.

But rather than a violent revolutionary movement, what in fact emerged was a highly-agitated (though inspired) grassroots democratic culture based on local participation, community activism, and personal responsibility. Though the essential structure of representative democracy remained in place, how it functioned changed in almost unrecognisable ways. Most notably, the Local Life Networks and the Online Referenda which today structure government so effectively, and which are able to instruct Members of Parliament so precisely and efficiently, would have been considered utopian dreams not so long ago. Leaving the details aside, however, our present point is simply that the disillusionment with top-down politics gave birth to an activist, grassroots culture, animated by the belief that another world was possible. Through sophisticated organisational techniques, this culture was able to change the nature of representative democracy by taking the power out of the hands of corporations and placing it in the hands of the people. This transition naturally faced fierce resistance from the economic elite, who had grown accustomed to getting their own way. But the tide of participatory democracy proved to be unstoppable. As corporate influence over governments faded, new space opened up within Western democracies, and elsewhere, for radical political change.

Of course, the mere possibility of radical political change did not guarantee that anything much would change, nor, if change were to come about, did it imply a particular direction. But when democratic processes are functioning sufficiently well, changes to the legal and political structure of a society tend to reflect cultural values, like a 'magic mirror', to revive Kermit Hall's old metaphor. This notion that 'law reflects culture' leads us to the second major reason, mentioned earlier, for the demise of growth economics in the West – namely, the radical transformation in attitudes toward material consumption that occurred during the second and third decades of this century.

The legal and political structures of growth capitalism depended, among other things, upon a culture of consumption – that is, upon a populace driven by an insatiable craving for more consumer goods and services. Though such commodity fetishism was observable in Western societies almost from the onset of industrialisation, it was really in the decades after World War II (during the era sometimes referred to as 'postmodernity') when consumption became a truly acute and debilitating social practice. A collective psychological disorder by our standards, commodity fetishism reached its zenith at the beginning of this century, establishing a materialistic culture without *any* sense of sufficiency. For reasons we still do not wholly understand, life in postmodernity was structured around the pursuit of luxuries and comforts merely, and no matter how rich people became, it never seemed to be enough.

Unsurprisingly, during this era the West entered a phase of social decay. Despite unprecedented levels of material wealth and sophisticated technologies, most Westerners during these times were working longer hours than they had in the past, and aside from working and sleeping, Westerners generally spent more time watching television than doing anything else. The division of labour reached an extreme, which may have efficiently maximised economic growth, but it also meant that people became wholly dependent on the market and thus were locked upon a consumerist treadmill that had no end and attained no lasting satisfaction.

Furthermore, urban sprawl led to highly artificial living environments that disconnected people from a community of neighbours and from any real engagement with nature. This was the culture that transnational corporations celebrated as the ultimate fulfilment of human destiny, the peak of civilisation.

So long as most people felt that a higher material 'standard of living' was needed to increase 'quality of life', growth capitalism was politically safe. However, what is kept alive by the citizenry can also, through a change in consciousness, be transformed by it. This subversive thesis was famously advanced during the counter-cultural movements of the 1960s and 1970s, and was neatly captured in their slogan 'revolution by consciousness'. But it was not until the so-called 'New Generation' counter-cultural movements of the late 2010s and early-to-mid-2020s that a 'revolution by consciousness' genuinely threatened to become a socio-political reality. Of those counter-cultural movements, one in particular, which came to be known as the Voluntary Simplicity Movement, deserves our immediate attention, as it undermined growth capitalism and consumer culture most directly. Its unexpected emergence and impact remains a subject of fascination amongst cultural historians, even if the radical ideas upon which it was based seem rather mundane in an age, such as our own, that accepts them unquestioningly as expressing the plainest commonsense. Let our examination, then, be brief.

The emergence of the Voluntary Simplicity Movement was inextricably intertwined with the rise of grassroots politics, which we have seen was a reaction against the undemocratic influence corporations had on 'political representatives'. But it was not enough simply to wrestle political power from corporations; the grassroots culture had to know what to do with power should it succeed in attaining it, and thus it needed a guiding philosophy. Furthermore, because the grassroots culture upheld 'personal action' and 'community action' as the means to social and political transformation, people realised that they needed to seriously explore, en masse, ways they could oppose growth capitalism in their daily lives. An attractive, meaningful, and coherent philosophy of living was found in the theory and practice of voluntary simplicity. Before proceeding, it may be helpful to present a short statement of this philosophy: first, so that we appreciate its stark contrast with consumerism, and second, to make explicit the ethics of consumption that came to inform the (soon-to-be-considered) politics beyond growth economics.

The following definition serves our purposes. It is taken from the introduction to an early anthology on voluntary simplicity, published 90 years ago at the height of consumer culture:

Voluntary simplicity is a post-consumerist living strategy that rejects materialistic lifestyles of consumer culture and affirms what is often called 'the simple life', or 'downshifting'. The rejection of consumerism arises out of the recognition that ordinary Western-style consumption habits are destroying the planet; that lives of high consumption are unethical in a world of great human need; and that the meaning of life does not and cannot consist in the consumption and accumulation of material things. Extravagance and acquisitiveness are thus considered a despairing waste of life, not so much sad as foolish, and certainly not deserving of the social status and admiration that they seem to attract today. The affirmation of simplicity arises out of the recognition that very little is needed to live well – that abundance is a state of mind, not a quantity of consumer products or attainable through them.

Sometimes called 'the quiet revolution', this approach to life involves providing for material needs as simply and directly as possible, minimising expenditure on consumer goods and services, and directing progressively more time and energy toward pursuing non-materialistic sources of satisfaction and meaning. This generally means accepting a lower income and a lower level of consumption, in exchange for more time and energy to pursue other life goals, such as community or social engagements, family time, artistic or intellectual projects, more fulfilling employment, political participation, sustainable living, spiritual exploration, reading, conversation, contemplation, relaxation, pleasure-seeking, love, and so on – none of which need to rely on money, or much money. The grounding assumption of voluntary simplicity is that human beings are inherently capable of living meaningful, free, happy, and infinitely diverse lives, while consuming no more than an equitable share of nature. Ancient but ever-new, the message is that those who know they have enough are rich.

According to this view, personal and social progress is measured not by the conspicuous display of wealth or status, but by increases in the qualitative richness of daily living, the cultivation of relationships, and the development of social, intellectual, aesthetic, and spiritual potentials. As Duane Elgin has famously defined it, voluntary simplicity is 'a manner of living that is outwardly simple and inwardly rich, . . . a deliberate choice to live with less in the belief that more life will be returned to us in the process'.

Voluntary simplicity does not, however, mean living in poverty, becoming an ascetic monk, or indiscriminately renouncing all the advantages of science and technology. It does not involve regressing to a primitive state or becoming a self-righteous puritan. And it is not some escapist fad reserved for saints, hippies, or eccentric outsiders. Rather, by examining afresh our relationship with money, material possessions, the planet, ourselves, and each other, the simple life of voluntary simplicity is about discovering the freedom and contentment that comes with knowing how much consumption is truly 'enough'. And this might be a theme that has something to say to everyone, especially those of us who are every day bombarded with thousands of cultural and institutional messages insisting that 'more is always better'. Voluntary simplicity is an art of living that is aglow with the insight that 'just enough is plenty'.

The spirit of late capitalist society, however, cries out like a banshee for us to expend our lives pursuing middle-class luxuries and coloured paper, for us to become faceless bodies dedicated to no higher purpose than the acquisition of 'nice things'. We can embrace that comfortable unfreedom if we wish, that bourgeois compromise. But it is not the only way to live.

Voluntary simplicity presents an alternative.

Of course, this 'art of living' was not by any means new. The virtues of moderation and enlightened material restraint had been integral to almost all ancient wisdom and spiritual traditions, with prominent advocates including Lao Tzu, Confucius, Buddha, the Stoics, Jesus, Mohammad, St. Francis, the Quakers, John Ruskin, the New England Transcendentalists (especially Henry David Thoreau), Gandhi, Richard Gregg, Helen and Scott Nearing, and many of the indigenous peoples around the world. But in postmodernity, when consumption was glorified and luxury admired as never before, voluntary simplicity acquired a special significance.

Exactly why the Voluntary Simplicity Movement became a powerful oppositional force in the second and third decades of this century remains something of a mystery, as noted above. Few saw it coming or even recognised the signs of its emergence until it had already arrived. Notions of simplicity spread, here and there, person to person, community to community, as if by means invisible. Perhaps the idea just gave people hope. The movement had no leader, as such, though it developed strong social networks. It received almost no support from mass media. Even politicians, despite their rhetoric of sustainability, were reticent to promote simplicity for fear that widespread reductions in personal consumption would slow economic growth. But still the light of simplicity began to dawn gradually over the whole.

Perhaps Theodore Roszack, writing in the depths of consumer culture, was the most prescient:

> There is one way forward: the creation of flesh-and-blood examples of low-consumption, high-quality alternatives to the mainstream pattern of life. This we can see happening already on the counter cultural fringes. And nothing – no amount of argument or research – will take the place of such living proof. What people must see is that ecologically sane, socially responsible living is *good* living;

that simplicity, thrift, and reciprocity make for an existence that is free.[1]

In the end, the nature of any society is shaped primarily by the countless number of small decisions made by private individuals. With respect to the Voluntary Simplicity Movement, those small decisions, those small acts of simplification – insignificant though they may have seemed in isolation – were ultimately of revolutionary significance when added up and taken as a whole. But this 'quiet revolution', as it came to be known, was not like revolutions of the past. It originated with the individual and with culture. It did not need violence to succeed, and it could not have been successfully resisted by violence. And it changed the politico-legal structure only as its final act.[2]

3. Politicising the Economy: The Emergence of Radical Democracy

By the end of the 2020s, the Voluntary Simplicity Movement had become a significant oppositional force, and it would continue to strengthen and expand every year. Though it had not, at this stage, achieved the cultural paradigm shift it sought, and though its political impact had so far been quite modest, the line between counter-culture and mainstream had certainly blurred, which is always a sign of great social transition. Within large sectors of Western societies attitudes to consumption changed drastically, encouraged, it should be noted, by very hard economic times. Luxurious and extravagant lifestyles, once almost universally admired and envied, had come to be seen by many as tasteless ostentation, improper in an age of human and ecological need, and certainly not a reliable path to personal wellbeing. Furthermore, simple living had become a socially accepted alternative lifestyle, which made stepping out of the mainstream much less isolating, thus hastening the demise of consumer culture. All this had discernable social and ecological benefits. The suburbs, in particular, were slowly transforming into bastions of home production and local food production.

Nevertheless, despite significant cultural transformation in attitudes to consumption, around this time many within the Voluntary Simplicity Movement came to a troubling realisation. It

[1] Theodore Roszack, *Where the Wasteland Ends: Politics and Transcendence in Postindustrial Society* (1972): 422.
[2] See Charles Reich, *The Greening of America* (1970).

was becoming apparent that even those who genuinely wished to embrace voluntary simplicity as an oppositional living strategy were finding the *practice* of simplicity extremely challenging, especially in urban centres. Put otherwise, it seemed that political and economic institutions, and social infrastructure, were functioning to lock many people into high-impact consumerist lifestyles, despite their desire for a simpler way of life. There had, of course, always been an undercurrent within the Voluntary Simplicity Movement that insisted that personal action alone was never going to be enough to achieve sustainability and social justice – that political engagement was necessary. But few had appreciated quite how hard it would be to create a simpler form of life from within an institutional framework based on materialistic values and imperatives to grow. By the late 2020s, however, it had become obvious to all that the socio-cultural movement away from consumerism needed to be supplemented and facilitated by a politico-legal movement away from growth economics, and that latter transition is the one to which we must now turn our attention.

Before we review the specific structural reforms that resulted from the gradual politicisation of the Voluntary Simplicity Movement, there is a somewhat abstract matter in political and legal theory that ought to be addressed, albeit briefly. It concerns the nature of property rights and the ways in which property rights were perceived to limit state power. We must not forget, after all, that in the first half of the 21st century, 'neoliberalism' was the dominant political ideology, one of the central assumptions of which was that, prima facie, the state had no right to interfere in the economy. This assumption had certain problematic implications for those seeking deep political and economic change. Let us consider those implications, for together they represent the last major obstacle that had to be overcome on the path to revolutionary reform.

When participants in the Voluntary Simplicity Movement first began seriously advocating political reform of the economy, they faced three fundamental objections arising out of neoliberal ideology: 1) that the reforms advocated would result in a property system that was no longer a private property system (and, if true, this was widely considered to be a knock-down argument, politically speaking); 2) that the reforms, by interfering in the property system, would violate the liberally revered 'private sphere' into which the state purportedly had no right to enter; and 3) that the reforms would arbitrarily interfere with the natural result of voluntary transactions made within the neutral and non-coercive 'free market' system.

These objections were not new and, indeed, they had been fairly well answered in the 20th century by other progressive intellectual movements such as Legal Realism, Critical Legal Studies, and Social Relations Theory. Accordingly, the Voluntary Simplicity Movement did not really need to develop new intellectual tools to respond to those objections, but it certainly needed to, and did, campaign laboriously to weaken the hold neoliberalism had on the popular consciousness. The following excerpt is taken from an anonymous political pamphlet distributed by the Voluntary Simplicity Movement during its influential internet campaign of 2034-5. It is quoted at some length because it responds, quite directly, to the three objections stated above:

> Our detractors rely on an 'essentialist' view of property. They assume that there is a concept of property that, in fact, is the right one or the only one; that there is *a* conception of property that is *the* concept of property. But the indeterminacy critique has thoroughly discredited any such claim to essentialism. The 'bundle of rights' conception of property, in particular, though it is hardly a complete or uncontroversial picture, has shown that we cannot say that person owns a resource if and only if that person has certain specified rights, powers, liberties, and duties. In other words, the *concept* of property is one that has many *conceptions*. This means that private property can take the shape of many different 'bundles', and so it should not be conceived of as a fixed, static, or homogenous category, especially since each 'bundle' can be disaggregated into isolated 'sticks'. Furthermore, the 'sticks' themselves – such as the 'right to use', the 'right to exclude', the 'right to transfer', or the 'duty not to harm' – are far from absolute or self-defining.
>
> This, in short, is the great legacy of Legal Realism to which essentialist and absolutist property theorists have never developed a satisfactory response. It is also the legacy upon which our Politics of Entropia are founded, for it promisingly demonstrates that there can be private property/market systems that are radically different from growth capitalism as we know it, since 'private property' does not mean one thing, and neither does 'the market'. Another property system is possible.
>
> Our detractors also claim that our political agenda would involve illegitimate state interference in the property and market system. But this objection is analytically outdated. Critical Legal Studies (CLS) showed long ago that for property and property-related concepts (such as ownership, harm, rights, wealth, efficiency, free contract, duress, justice, and so on) to become concrete conceptions in legal reality, state institutions must be always and necessarily involved in defining property rights and market structures. One consequence of this is that the neoliberal demand for state 'non-intervention' in the so-called 'private economic sphere' – where property rights are said to be sacrosanct and self-regulating – is an impossible one, and transparently so. The state is necessarily implicated in the economy because (among

other things) it must: a) provide details on which incidents of ownership will form the 'bundle', what each incident entails, and in which circumstances; b) define the idea of 'freedom of contract', since it too is not self-defining; c) set other 'ground-rules' to the economy (such as, 'What can be property?'; 'What kind of entities can be agents in the market?'; and 'What happens when property rights conflict?'); and d) enforce the property rights created by a), b), and c). As one critical theorist noted: 'The question is not whether to regulate owners; the question is what kind of property system to create in the first place.'[3] 'Hands off' is simply not an option.

This critique of the private/public distinction exposes how often the distinction between the 'free market' and 'regulatory systems' breaks down, a point another theorist has expressed in the following way: 'There is no nonarbitrary way to differentiate the law *constituting* a market, from the law supposedly *regulating* or *intervening in* the market.'[4] This critique is significant because it answers the neoliberal lament that property rights are violated whenever the state 'interferes' in the economy. Again, the state is *necessarily* implicated in the economy, and so reformers are entitled to question whether society may be better off if the state implicates itself in different ways and on a different basis. What is clear is that this reformist approach – which may include 'revolutionary reform' – cannot be dismissed in advance on the basis of an essentialist view of 'private property' or 'the market', or on the basis that the state ought to stay out of the 'private economic sphere', since both essentialism and the private/public distinction clearly lie in ruins.

Some detractors within the positivist tradition, however, accept that the state is indeed required to define the legal rules governing market transfers, private property, and voluntary contracting – since they are not self-defining – but argue that the rules set up by the state must be *neutral*. Legal rules that are neutral, the argument goes, would simply facilitate the voluntary exchange of private property rights in a free market, and thereby allow individuals to pursue their own preferences and visions of the good life without having the state impose its preferences or values upon them. Regulators and reformers, according this view, are seen as politically biased people who try to use state apparatus to impose their own subjective preferences and values on others, and who try to bring about a distribution of wealth and power other than that which naturally results when individuals voluntarily exchange property rights in a free market.

The indeterminacy critique, however, renders this neoliberal view incoherent also. As outlined above, the state is required to

---

[3] Joseph Singer, *Entitlement: The paradoxes of property* (2000): 7.
[4] Stuart Banner, 'Conquest by contract: Wealth transfer and land market structure in colonial New Zealand' 34 *Law and Society Review* 47: 53.

make all sorts of *definitional choices* about what the abstract property and property-related concepts mean in economic reality, and these choices have significant implications for what type of society results. What CLS made perfectly clear, however, is that these choices can never be *neutral* – first, because there is no objective or apolitical standpoint from where those choices could be made, and second, because such choices always allocate wealth and power between individuals and groups in society. For these reasons it is wrong to disclaim all responsibility for the social and environmental consequences of those allocations and blithely say that they are the natural result of free choices made within a neutral and non-coercive market framework. To stress the so-called neutrality of the 'free market', and to deny that political, value-laden, choices inevitably go into its formation, is ideological. It is a perspective that deflects attention away from the political choices benefiting some individuals, groups, and interests at the expense of others, and it unduly limits what reformative options appear democratically available. It can make the existing property regime (including its concentrations of wealth and structures of power) seem 'natural' or 'right' or 'just the way the world is', when in fact that regime is a contingent creation of our choosing, which we have made, and which can be democratically remade.

The choice is ours, if we choose it.

The fundamental point here – a rather obvious one to us – is that property rights are not static or determinate entities that exist independently of the state, but are evolving and highly malleable creatures of legal convention. It follows that property rights are also inescapably value-laden and context-dependent, meaning that their legitimacy must be constantly reassessed as society or the environment changes. Indeed, the greater the changes in context, the greater the need for the reassessment, and perhaps revision, of property rights. These ideas, as they came to be widely understood and accepted, functioned to radicalise Western democracies by politicising the economy in new ways. It was this shift in political consciousness that allowed democratic citizens to see that they had the right and the power to design (or redesign) the economic framework within which they live their lives, an insight which neoliberal ideology had repressed for far too long.

During this time, as noted above, the Voluntary Simplicity Movement was entering the cultural mainstream and beginning to demand some political recognition – sounding the death knell for growth capitalism. Attitudes to consumption had undergone a huge shift toward material simplicity, and the time was ripe for the political manifestation of this new sensibility. Furthermore, by this stage the myriad problems of social and ecological overconsumption had intensified, meaning that a political response could no longer be delayed. The Voluntary Simplicity Movement did not waste this opportunity to call for a politics of sustainable consumption, a politics beyond growth economics. And, at last, the call did not fall on deaf ears.

The world was ready for change.

4. A Politics of Property Beyond Growth Economics

What follows is a review of the matrix of 'revolutionary reforms' which resulted from the gradual politicisation of the Voluntary Simplicity Movement in Western societies over the course of the 21st century. Obviously, different nations evolved in different ways, at different times, and these differences were sometimes considerable. Indeed, throughout the Great Transition openness to plurality was, and still is, considered a virtue. Nevertheless, if we look at the world at the beginning of this century and compare it with how it is at the end, it cannot be denied that there has been a recognisable and coherent paradigm shift in law, politics, and economics, especially with respect to Western-style systems of property. In what follows an attempt is made to outline, with a very broad brush, the most significant features of the new paradigm, beginning with the new indicators of progress that were so instrumental in deposing growth economics. Deferring to convention, this new paradigm will be referred to as 'Entropia', which is not a place, as such, so much as it is the idealised social, economic, and political order which guided and motivated many of the radical law reform movements during this century.

4.1. *Beyond GDP: Alternative indicators of progress*

We saw earlier that during the era of growth capitalism, increasing GDP was the overriding objective of governments. It was an era when economists, policymakers, judges, reporters, and the wider public generally relied on GDP as a shorthand indicator of a nation's progress ('the growth model of progress'). But GDP is merely a sum of national spending which makes no distinctions between transactions that add to wellbeing and those that diminish it; it does not take any account of ecological damage or wealth distribution; and anything that is not recorded as a market transaction is excluded from its accounts, such as domestic work, volunteering, and leisure. For these reasons, among others, GDP is a highly defective measure of how well-off a society is and a poor indicator of policy and institutional success. When this was eventually recognised and exposed, scholars began developing alternative, much more nuanced measures of societal progress. One such measure, which has gradually received official recognition and respect, is known as the Genuine Progress Indicator (GPI). Arguably, this development symbolises better than any other the transition from growth capitalism to Entropia.

The 'extended accounts' of the GPI begin with total private consumption expenditure and then make reductions for things such as poverty, polarised income distribution, crime, resource depletion, pollution, environmental damage, and so on, and additions for things such as domestic work, volunteering, increases in leisure, public infrastructure, and the like. The aim is to measure, as accurately as possible, the 'genuine progress' of a society, not simply the growth of its GDP. Although the GPI remains an imperfect tool, and so must be employed cautiously and tentatively, the significance of it replacing GDP as a measure of progress can hardly be over-stated. In essence, public support of the GPI means that political parties can campaign for policy and institutional reforms that are likely to genuinely improve wellbeing, even if those reforms would slow or even reduce economic growth. Once upon a time, of course, implementing reforms that would negatively affect growth rates was tantamount to committing political suicide. But by distinguishing genuine progress from economic growth, that changed. In particular, new space opened up within the political arena for the following legal reforms in property relations.

4.2. *Basic income as a new property right*

One of the deepest and most enduring criticisms levelled at capitalist societies was that, no matter how rich they became, there always remained an underclass of people who were unemployed and poverty-stricken. To permit members of an affluent society to live without any secure livelihood seems to us to be an evident moral abomination, but majority opinion among earlier generations took it to be regrettable but permissible, perhaps even necessary. Even strong varieties of the 'welfare state' were unable to provide all with the economic security which we regard as necessary to live a fully human life of freedom and dignity, because welfare payments could be denied, delayed, or revoked, for any number of reasons. The politics of Entropia boldly confronted this serious problem with remarkable directness, by gradually introducing what is called a 'Basic Income System', otherwise known as a 'Simplicity Entitlement'.

Although there is considerable variety in forms of Basic Income, the core idea is relatively straightforward. In its idealised form, every permanent resident would receive a periodic (e.g., fortnightly) stipend sufficient to live at a culturally defined minimal standard of economic security, generally at a level marginally above the culturally specific 'poverty line'; that is, enough to live simply, securely, and with dignity, though, as two commentators put it, 'extremely modestly'. The Basic Income is guaranteed by the state, is unconditional on the performance of any labour, and is universal (excepting only those incarcerated). Parents are the custodians of children's grants (which are typically somewhat lower than adult grants). Within a fully developed Basic Income System most other state transfers can be abolished – unemployment benefits, family allowances, pensions, and so on – because the Basic Income grant is sufficient to provide everyone with a decent, though minimal, subsistence. Economic insecurity, whether from incapacity or unemployment, is therefore essentially eliminated. Even minimum wage laws can be somewhat relaxed, because all earning above the Basic Income is discretionary. Other kinds of programmes remain, such as subsidies for people with special needs, as do universalistic programmes, such as public education and health care. In many jurisdictions, the Basic Income entitlement is increasingly being described as a 'new' property right.

The feasibility of a Basic Income System was historically doubted for two main reasons. The first objection was that making the Basic Income unconditional on the performance of any labour would give rise to a society of 'free-riders' and ultimately lead to economic collapse. This pessimistic outlook, however, has been proven unjustified. Few would be surprised to hear that the 'free-rider' problem does exist to a certain extent today – that is, there are indeed some who live off the Basic Income but who choose not to contribute to society in any discernable way. However, it turns out that human beings, by and large, are social creatures, who find being engaged in their community's work more meaningful and fulfilling than being isolated, idle, and parasitic on the community. Furthermore, the very small minority that choose not to contribute in any way prove to be a tolerable burden – certainly more tolerable than the levels of poverty which persisted within the property systems of late capitalism. A large majority of citizens remain in some form of paid employment, and the percentage that do not are typically engaged in other forms of socially necessary and beneficial work, such as raising children, working in community gardens or local energy centres, volunteering at the esteemed and well-organised Centres for Social Service, or exchanging labour for housing through the Organisation for Affordable and Sustainable Housing.

The second objection concerned the feasibility of financing a Basic Income System, an issue that is obviously of great importance, although it was and remains a matter of political commitment more than a financing issue. Basic Income entitlements did create a new and significant financial burden on the public purse; however, changes to public spending as well as significant tax reforms have been sufficient, in many of the wealthier jurisdictions, at least, to gradually raise the Basic Income to a minimal level of dignified subsistence. Those jurisdictions around the globe that are still transitioning toward a subsistence-level Basic Income System are often called 'Guaranteed Income Systems' (which guarantee a certain level of income, but below subsistence levels, meaning that some supplementary income is still necessary through earnings). Another method several nations have used to progress toward a Basic Income System is to establish a Negative Income Tax System, which differs from a Basic Income in that it provides a tax credit (typically beginning at low levels and increasing over time) to those with low incomes, providing such low-earners with a minimum income but by an alternative route. These approaches of incrementally raising the level of Guaranteed Income or Negative Income Tax to establish a fully developed system of Basic Income were key both to the financial viability and the political attractiveness of the Basic Income policy objective.

It is worth noting that a Basic Income System or one of its varieties does tend to slow growth in the economies in which they operate, for the reason that such systems – consonant with the predictions of orthodox economic theory – inevitably provide fewer incentives for citizens to dedicate so much of their energy to productive activity. But because the wealthiest nations today are no longer anxious to grow, and many are even voluntarily transitioning by way of degrowth to a steady state economy, the whole question of maximising incentives is much less pressing. Indeed, the level at which governments set a Basic or Guaranteed Income can be a device to control, to a certain extent, the level of growth/degrowth in an economy.

The social benefits of the Basic Income were profound and far-reaching. Beyond eliminating poverty and economic insecurity – which were the primary functions of a Basic Income System – its gradual institution also strengthened the bargaining position of workers, because it gave them a livelihood that was independent of their paid employment and thus more power to demand decent working conditions. It also meant that people did not have to accept alienating, exploitative, or degrading jobs just to survive; nor was there any real pressure to sacrifice social and political autonomy in order to achieve economic security. Furthermore, introducing the Basic Income was effectively an acknowledgement of the worth of unpaid caring work and other forms of social contribution, thereby extending economic citizenship beyond participants in the traditional labour market. For these reasons, among others, the legal restructuring of property relations based upon the notion of Basic Income has done much to create more democratic and egalitarian societies. By structurally promoting 'simple living', the Basic Income has also had ecological benefits.

4.3. *Progressive income tax and the maximum wage*

In general, the property systems of Entropia are shaped by highly progressive income or consumption taxes which fund a considerable portion of the state's policies, including the Basic Income entitlement. Progressive forms of taxation were in place even within the paradigm of growth capitalism, so there is little need to address the matter of justification in any detail. Put simply, progressive taxation is justified primarily on the dual grounds of equity and utility. That is, because it is equitable for the richest to pay more than the poorest to fund the state's policies, and because the diminishing marginal utility of money means that the more money one has, the less utility or happiness one can buy with each further dollar (i.e., one dollar is more valuable to a poor person than to a rich person), some redistribution is an efficient use of resources. What distinguished the politics of Entropia from growth capitalism was how progressive taxation was used to effectively create a 'maximum wage' or 'income cap'. Let us consider this central development.

Just as most at the beginning of the 20th century had trouble imagining how their ancestors could have stomached slavery, so we at the end of the 21st century are dismayed by the truly excessive incomes that some executives, managers, shareholders, doctors, lawyers, and other professionals received not so long ago. We cannot understand why it was ever permitted for some incomes to reach into the millions or tens of millions of dollars when many workers – sometimes even those working in the same enterprise – received little more than an (insecure) subsistence wage. We consider such disparities plainly objectionable on many grounds: they undermine democracy and social solidarity, they encourage grossly extravagant lifestyles, and they simply cannot be justified by any appeal to proportional merit or social contribution. The politics of Entropia, of course, never advocated anything like strict equality in incomes. Much inequality remains. However, it is widely taken for granted today that *some* limits must be placed on individual incomes, and a simple restructure of progressive income tax policy provided a straightforward method for doing so.

An income tax is 'progressive' when the tax rate increases as the taxable income increases. In theory, at least, all income over a certain amount could be taxed completely, thereby creating a 'maximum wage' or 'income cap'. Although only New Zealand's Remuneration Justice Act 2038 has actually gone this far, all of the Western economies have gradually established a top income bracket which is taxed more than 90% (which, strictly speaking, does not place any 'cap' as such on incomes, but functions in a similar way). The income level of the top tax bracket also varies between nations – often starting high, for political reasons, and then decreasing – but today it generally sits quite stably around 10 to 15 times the level of the Basic Income.

One might have thought that the introduction of such policies would have been politically controversial in the extreme, given the history of limitless incomes, but it turned out that this was not the case. Although there were certainly loud objections from advocates of the 'free market', various referenda were held which un- ambiguously demonstrated that the policies had overwhelming public support, doubtless owing to the fact that the maximum wage would only limit the incomes of a very small minority of people. Political representatives, accordingly, had no choice but to follow the will of the people.

4.4. *Worker cooperatives*

Capitalist economic relations paradigmatically involved workers selling their labour to the owners of productive assets and those owners then selling the commodities produced for more than the cost of the labour that went into making them, thereby making a 'profit'. We attribute to Karl Marx, more than any other, the thesis that this capitalist mode of production and exchange exploits workers. It is exploitative, Marx argued, because workers are paid less for their labour than the value of the commodities they produce. The solution he proposed was to abolish all private ownership of productive assets and replace it with state ownership; that is, to replace capitalism with communism.

Many involved in the politics of Entropia were sympathetic to (without wholly subscribing to) the view that workers, to varying extents, were exploited under the capitalist mode of production and its legal superstructure; yet, for various reasons, they did not see state ownership of productive assets as the solution. Rather than state communism, what emerged instead were various forms of 'market-socialist' property systems in which worker cooperatives are increasingly the dominant economic form. These enterprises are owned by their workers and democratically operated on a 'one person, one vote' basis, thereby avoiding the exploitative relationships which Marx and others criticised so vehemently. The cooperatives still fall within the private property paradigm, however, because workers still have individual ownership interests in them, and the state does not determine what the cooperatives produce. Furthermore, the economy is still based on market exchanges, because cooperatives gain income by selling their goods and services to customers. In doing this, they compete with other cooperatives (and other small businesses of the allowable types). The primary difference with growth capitalism is that large corporate entities employing non-shareholders have largely disappeared.

The transition to this type of 'stakeholder society' was facilitated both by public policy and cultural changes, each promoting the other in a dialectical fashion. When governments decided that broadening the ownership base of the economy was to be a policy goal, the first step in that direction was often to make the tax rates for worker cooperatives extremely attractive compared to the tax rates for the traditional 'owner-shareholder' corporate entities. Governments also began explicitly preferring worker cooperatives when contracting with the private sector, and whenever possible government spending was directed toward worker cooperatives. Various types of development banks were also created through which governments began funding new businesses that were required to establish themselves as worker cooperatives. Collectively, these strategies, and many others, were able to create fertile conditions in which worker cooperatives could take root, multiply, and flourish. It was arguably a shift in consumer attitudes, however, that was the deepest driver of change. When private individuals began choosing to direct their expenditure toward cooperative enterprises, the old corporate structures gradually withered away as a natural consequence of market forces. This is a powerful reminder that how we spend our money is how we vote on what exists in the world.

The emergence of worker cooperatives has been one of the most significant developments in the transition toward Entropia. It has expanded democratic decision-making beyond representative politics to include the everyday realm of economics, giving people much more control over their lives. Though democratising the internal workings of business enterprises has created new inefficiencies – e.g., decision-making can be slower – the fact that workers now have a real stake in the businesses within which they work has also created new forms of efficiency and fostered a new ethics of productivity and collective responsibility. The material rewards of production are also distributed more evenly, though strict equality is rarely practised (or expected). Beyond these appealing features, worker cooperatives have also functioned to be more ecologically sensitive than the old corporate forms, because businesses owned and managed by local citizens take more care than 'absentee owners' to ensure business practices do not harm the environment. Finally, cooperatives also seem to have engendered a greater sense of social solidarity and community, as workers belong to and participate in stable associations of people with common interests and a shared economic identity.

4.5 Land law and the duty not to harm

Although all of the reforms described above had ecological benefits, more direct and immediate legal and political action was needed to adequately confront the ecological crisis. The difficulty here was the enduring influence of the neoliberal conception of property, which resisted state regulation in the economy. It was a remarkably simple question, however, which gave rise to a radically new approach: Do property owners have the right to use land in ecologically unsustainable ways? Although the response came dangerously late, lawmakers eventually answered that question in the negative. Let us consider the general line of argument.

To question whether a person or entity possesses a property right to engage in a particular activity is to acknowledge, as we must, that property rights are not absolute but in some sense always limited. Outdated imagery aside, ownership does not and cannot entail the right to 'do as one pleases' with the property one owns, for that would be plainly self-defeating. It would allow others to use their property in ways that harmed one's own property or indeed oneself, and thus even the most hard-nosed libertarians have always accepted that the ownership of property necessarily entails a 'duty not to harm'. As Hohfeld explained long ago, this 'duty not to harm' places limits on the 'right to use'.

One important consequence of this is that state regulation which prevents 'harmful use' cannot be considered a violation of property rights, because property holders simply do not have the right to harm others or the property of others. In other words, such preventative action would not be 'taking' anything that owners ever held (or properly held), from which it follows that in such circumstances no right to compensation could arise. What this means, also, is that regulation of the property system which prevents 'harmful use' should not be understood to be *changing* the prior regime, but only *maintaining and enforcing* the 'rightful scope' of the prior regime in which the duty not to harm was always recognised.

This blurs the distinction between 'property' and 'regulation'. Regulation is normally conceived of as something that *interferes* with property rights. But when the state intervenes in the property system to stop 'harmful use', then such intervention is not so much the *regulation* of property as it is the *maintenance* or *protection* of property. And this more accurate reframing of the issue has been of rhetorical significance to ecological reformers, especially in the first quarter of this century when 'regulation' was such a dirty word.

In the midst of the ecological crisis, when nothing less than Nature's life-support systems were at risk of collapsing, lawmakers realised that they needed to pay much more attention to the duty of property holders not to cause 'harm'. Exactly what constitutes harm, at any given time, is indeterminate and often contentious, of course, but that just means that it is a concept that must be defined democratically, for the common good. As one pioneering legal ecologist at the turn of the century noted: 'Harm ... is an elastic, vague concept that we can define in whatever way we deem wise. ... By redefining harm we can [for example] challenge and end land uses we don't want.'[5] This theorist added, however, with an air of caution, that 'government wields breathtaking power when it can define harm however it sees fit.'[6] That was (and remains) true, but as Nature was being degraded as never before there were far greater risks in the government not doing enough to enforce the 'duty not to harm' than there were in it doing too much.

As the problems of overconsumption, loss of biodiversity, and climate change intensified, the meaning of the 'duty not to harm' inevitably expanded, narrowing the rightful scope of property rights. By intervening in the property system to enforce this 'duty not to harm', the state was not actually *changing* the prior regime, properly understood, but only *maintaining* the 'rightful scope' of the prior regime in which the duty not to harm was always recognised. Accordingly, such preventative action or maintenance was not 'taking' anything that owners ever held (or properly held), from which it followed that in such circumstances no right to compensation could arise.

---

[5] Eric Freyfogle, *On private property: Finding common ground on the ownership of land* (2007): 115.

[6] Ibid.

To provide a famous, ground-breaking example of this approach, we need only note the case of Australia, which, in 2025, was the first nation to pass legislation to the effect that coal mining and the logging of old-growth forests were no longer acceptable uses of land, and would be faded out (with minor exceptions). Unsurprisingly, powerful economic agents at this time cried out piously about the alleged violation of their property rights; all the more so when they received little or no compensation. But slave owners once cried out in the same vein, and their claims to compensation were also properly ignored. In short, once lawmakers decided that property law had been wrong to protect certain use rights, and that no such rights did or should exist, it was considered contradictory to grant compensation as if the property rights did exist after all. As the preamble to the Australian *Land Ethics (Amendment) Act 2025* still reads: 'The government does not accept for compensation purposes the very baseline that regulatory protection recognises as wrongful.'[7]

4.6 *Inheritance and bequest*

Another key feature in the transition from growth capitalism to the politics of Entropia was the revolutionary reforms that took place in relation to the laws of inheritance and bequest. A few words will suffice to convey the essence of these changes and their salutary effects.

Opposition to the laws of inheritance and bequest was as old as the laws themselves. Allowing huge concentrations of wealth to be passed down a family line, from generation to generation, was often criticised for being an inequitable relic of feudalism that somehow survived the transition to capitalism. The overthrow of feudalism was driven, after all, by distaste for the arbitrary birthright privileges (of wealth, status, and power) that were bestowed upon the 'nobility'. Simultaneously, one of the bedrock principles of political liberalism which shaped the post-feudal world was a commitment to 'equality of opportunity', that is, to the belief that success in life should be based as far as possible on merit, not accident, chance, or caste. Yet, despite entrenching arbitrary privileges and keeping concentrations of wealth intact for reasons other than merit, the laws of inheritance and bequest endured for hundreds of years after the transition to capitalism, almost as if they were essential to a private property system.

---

[7] For an early defence of this position, see Margaret Radin, *Reinterpreting Property* (1993).

But essential they are not. Private property is a concept that has many conceptions. According to one persistent conception (useful though incomplete), property is a 'bundle of rights'. What is clear is that the 'bundle of rights' can be reconfigured, sometimes significantly, while remaining a private property system, and over the last century private property has indeed been significantly reconfigured. In various ways (discussed below), the right to bequeath one's property upon death has been disaggregated from the bundle of rights associated with property ownership. And when that right goes, so too does any alleged right of potential beneficiaries to inherit property. The politics of Entropia have shown not only that there can be private property systems that do not recognise the right to bequeath or inherit property, but also that such revised systems better accord with the arguments (based on freedom, justice, utility, security, and so on) used to justify private property in the first place.

Nevertheless, despite the conceptual possibility and normative attractiveness of a private property system that does not recognise the rights of inheritance and bequest, reconfiguring the 'bundle of rights' in that manner required political tact. Rather than an outright abolition of those inheritance and bequest laws, in most jurisdictions it proved to be politically more attractive to gradually increase inheritance taxes and gift taxes. In fact, even today, bequest and inheritance are still technically recognised in most of the advanced economies, where allowances are properly made for dependents (children, parents, and grandparents who are in need of support), as well as certain other exceptions (such as limited gifts to charities). But beyond providing for the essential needs of dependents, which is very limited in our age of the Basic Income, and other minor exceptions, a citizen's property upon death is generally taxed in excess of 90%. This effectively (though not technically) disaggregates the right of bequest from the bundle of rights associated with ownership. It is perhaps surprising that only in England, where the roots of feudalism were deepest, have inheritance and bequest been abolished outright. In that jurisdiction, a citizen's property upon death is now distributed by the Justice Tribunal, which was established in 2042. It is a system that has acquired wide support. Whether other jurisdictions eventually follow the English example remains to be seen.

Whether through taxation or outright abolition, disaggregating inheritance and bequest from the institution of private property has been a landmark achievement on the path to Entropia. Not only has it contributed greatly to the democratic ideals of equality of opportunity in life and a broad-based distribution of wealth, it also provided (and still provides) states around the world with the public resources necessary to adequately confront the ecological crisis and adapt to climate change. In fact, many political parties, particularly in Western Europe, campaigned for the reform of inheritance and bequest laws on the very basis that the bulk of the new tax revenues would be directed toward environmental initiatives. Indeed, it would be fair to say that the transition to clean and renewable energy systems that we saw over the first half of this century was funded, to a large extent, by the proceeds of the property and tax reforms related to inheritance and bequest.

4.7. *Working hours*

The reforms outlined above represent the most significant structural changes that occurred over the last century to Western-style property systems. Before concluding our review of the paradigm shift, it is important to note one final revolutionary reform, this time in labour law, which is considered central to the politics of Entropia.

Over the last century working hours in the West have dramatically decreased, representing a culture-wide exchange of money for time. This was partly due to cultural changes in attitudes to consumption (i.e., the less one consumes the less one needs to work to support one's lifestyle), but it was also facilitated by structural changes. Economic theory posits that actors in an economy should be free to maximise their happiness (or 'utility') by selling as much or as little of their time (or 'labour-power') as they want. Under growth capitalism, however, there were structural biases that functioned to promote over-work (i.e., working hours that were not 'optimal' or 'utility maximising'), such as laws which treated the 40-hour work week as 'standard' and which excluded part-time workers from many of the non-pecuniary benefits enjoyed by those who work full-time. The effect of these structural biases was essentially to force many people to work longer hours than they wanted or needed to, which gave rise to cultures that tended to overconsume resources and under-consume leisure. This led to higher GDP per capita, of course, but often at the cost of quality of life, and the planet.

During the 21st century, led by Western European nations, many jurisdictions first introduced the 35-hour work week, then the 28-hour work week, and in places even the 21-hour work week. In a progressive response to pressures arising from the GFC, the US state of Utah, for example, shifted to a four-day work week for all public employees. Almost immediately it was reported that the resulting pattern of work reduction led to 'significant environmental benefits, with reduced transport and energy costs'. Furthermore, the extra day off also led to a 'dramatic increase in community volunteering'. Many governments around the world have shown leadership in this regard, by down-shifting most government positions to a reduced work week and by providing tax incentives to private employers which do the same.

As well as reducing the standard work week, labour laws have also been broadly reformed to better protect those in part-time employment and those who wish to job-share. In many places these policies have gone a long way to eliminating unemployment (because labour is systematically spread); furthermore, the increase in leisure has resulted in many other social and ecological benefits, including healthier and happier populations with more time to pursue their private passions and enjoy their civic responsibilities, and with lower ecological footprints (because they are consuming and travelling less).

Those who complained that these work policies would not maximise GDP per capita were obviously missing the point. The point of an economy is to efficiently promote quality of life, and if a smaller economy promotes quality of life by providing increased leisure but less money for its participants, then a smaller economy is the most economically rational option to choose. In a word, this is the rationality of degrowth.

4.8 Miscellaneous

There is much more to be written, of course, about the nature of our new, sufficiency-based civilisation and its economic and political structures. Volumes of work, for example, could be written on how we managed the debt 'jubilee' or how our new, community-run banking and financing systems work, which provide no-interest credit to enterprises that clearly serve the common good. It would be worthwhile, on another occasion, to recount in more detail how we reduced our military expenditure as our foreign aid increased; or how we restructured our food and transport systems; abolished advertising in public spaces; introduced resource caps; and conducted education campaigns about simple living and the value of increased self-sufficiency. But for now, this author must tend to his garden.

5. Conclusion: The Law of Progressive Simplification

According to Arnold Toynbee's 'Law of Progressive Simplification', as a civilisation evolves it will come to transfer increasing increments of energy and attention from the material (energy, money, possessions, etc.) to the non-material side of life (relationships, contemplation, community, art, and so on). If we accept this aspect of Toynbee's conception of history, which posits simplicity of living as the peak of civilisation, then ours has ultimately been a century of progress. As Toynbee and others predicted, nature compelled us to revert to a stable state on the material plane and thus we found ourselves forced to turn to the realm of the spirit to satisfy our hunger for infinity. As the dust settles upon the path we have travelled this century, we look back and gain a new prospect of the world and our place in it. When placed in the context of history, the changes we have seen have surely been as great as the transition from feudalism to capitalism.

If there is one lesson that humanity will take from this difficult century, it will be that legal and political reforms in property relations which slow or even have a negative impact on growth, and which thereby lower 'standard of living' (measured by per capita income), can actually increase 'quality of life' (measured by subjective wellbeing). Put otherwise, the lesson is that lower productivity is a small price to pay for unprecedented wellbeing, the advancement of distributive justice, and enhanced ecological conditions. Looking back we see how easy it would have been to avoid so much suffering and destruction had we only realised this earlier, or, rather, had we only acted earlier upon what we knew very well.

Of course, despite huge advances, our world today is far from perfect. Global poverty has not been eradicated and it is probably too early to claim that the ecological crisis is over. In particular, we will still need to adapt as the climate changes further, and the countless tonnes of carbon deposited in the atmosphere by earlier generations may still have unforeseeable impacts on global ecosystems. But genuine and significant progress has un-questionably been made. Far from signifying the end of history, however, it is clear that this moment in time, like every moment, is simply the beginning of the future. And that is the challenge which confronts us, which has always confronted us.

Appendix

COLLECTED ESSAYS VOLUME I

PROSPEROUS DESCENT: CRISIS AS OPPORTUNITY IN AN AGE OF LIMITS

Samuel Alexander

Published by the Simplicity Institute in May 2015

CONTENTS PAGE

CHAPTER SUMMARIES OF *PROSPEROUS DESCENT*

Chapter 1 lays the foundation for the book by presenting an evidenced-based critique of techno-optimism. Most people today, including many environmentalists, assume that technological advancement will eventually 'decouple' our economic growth from environmental impact, thereby allowing us to grow our economies without limit while at the same time reducing ecological impact. This position – which I am calling techno-optimism – is the foundation of dominant conceptions of 'sustainable development' and the primary reason so many people assume there are no 'limits to growth'. If this techno-optimism is justifiable, sustained economic growth may eventually solve global poverty and raise the living standards of all, without destroying the necessary ecosystems that sustain life as we know it. But it is not justifiable. The opening chapter presents a critique of techno-optimism, showing it to be without evidential foundation and dangerously flawed. There are limits to growth – limits which in fact seem to be upon us – and we ignore them at our own peril. The implication is that any adequate response to today's overlapping crises requires a global shift away from growth economics toward a macroeconomics 'beyond growth'.

Chapter 2 reviews the key thinkers and movements in the emerging paradigm of 'post-growth' economics. It begins by presenting a brief overview of the conventional growth paradigm, in order to later highlight, by way of contrast, some of the most prominent features of the alternative paradigm. A substantial literature review of post-growth economics is then provided, after which, some of the outstanding issues in this emerging paradigm are outlined. This chapter raises questions about what prospects this alternative paradigm has for the economics of growth; what significance it may have if it were ever to succeed; and what the implications could be if it were to remain marginalised. The chapter concludes by outlining a research agenda of critical issues.

Chapter 3 outlines the sociological, ecological, and economic foundations of a macroeconomics 'beyond growth', focusing on the idea of degrowth. Degrowth opposes conventional growth economics on the grounds that growth in the highly developed nations has become socially counter-productive, ecologically unsustainable, and uneconomic. Stagnating energy supplies and rising prices also suggest an imminent 'end of growth'. In response to growth economics, degrowth scholars call for a politico-economic policy of *planned economic contraction*, an approach which has been broadly defined as 'an equitable downscaling of production and consumption that increases human wellbeing and enhances ecological conditions'. After defining growth economics and outlining the emerging case for degrowth, this chapter considers the feasibility of a macroeconomics beyond growth and sketches an outline of what such a macroeconomics might look like as a politico-economic programme.

Chapter 4 is based on the idea that a degrowth process of planned economic contraction depends on, and must be driven by, a culture of 'simple living' – or, as the title of this chapter puts it, 'degrowth implies voluntary simplicity'. Be that as it may, this chapter shows that things are not that simple. Our lifestyle decisions, especially our consumption practices, are not made in a vacuum. They are made within social, economic, and political *structures of constraint*, and those structures make some lifestyle decisions easy or necessary and other lifestyle decisions difficult or impossible. These structures can even 'lock' people into high consumption lifestyles. Change the social, economic, and political structures, however, and different consumption practices would or could emerge. This chapter seeks to deepen the understanding of the relationship between consumer behaviour and the structures which shape that behaviour, in the hope that the existing barriers to sustainable consumption can be overcome or avoided.

Chapter 5 outlines in more detail the theory and practice of 'voluntary simplicity'. This term defies easy definition but can be preliminarily understood as a way of life in which people choose to restrain or reduce their material consumption, while at the same time seeking a higher quality of life. For reasons discussed in previous chapters, there is a desperate need for alternative practices and narratives of consumption beyond those prevalent in the most developed regions of the world today, and increasingly people see voluntary simplicity or 'simple living' as a coherent and attractive alternative to the 'work-and-spend' cycle of consumer culture. After addressing issues of definition, justification, and practice, this chapter concludes by considering some objections that can be levelled against voluntary simplicity, both as a living strategy and as a nascent social movement.

Chapter 6 presents a sympathetic critique of Ted Trainer's vision of 'The Simpler Way', which he has been developing and refining for several decades. Trainer's essential premise is that overconsumption in the most developed regions of the world is the root cause of our global predicament, and upon this premise he argues that a necessary part of any transition to a sustainable and just world involves the consumer class adopting far 'simpler' lifestyles in terms of material and energy consumption. That is the radical implication of our global predicament that most people seem unwilling to acknowledge or accept, but which Trainer does not shy away from, and, indeed, which he follows through to its logical conclusion. Trainer's complex position can be understood to merge and build upon various strains of socialist, anarchist, and environmentalist thinking. Of particular importance is his critical analysis of the literature on renewable energy, which he argues does not support the assumption that renewable energy can sustain consumer societies. If Trainer is correct, sustainability implies moving toward societies with far lower energy demands than the developed economies, with all that this implies about reduced consumption and production. Needless to say, this directly contradicts the techno-optimism of most sustainability discourse, which assumes that existing and projected energy demands can easily and affordably be met with renewable energy.

Chapter 7 provides a review of the peak oil situation and offers a response to recent claims that 'peak oil is dead'. The analysis shows that oil issues remain at the centre of global challenges facing humanity, despite recent claims of oil abundance, and that the challenges are only going to intensify in coming years as competition increases over the world's most important source of fossil energy. The main issue, however, is not whether we will have enough oil, but whether we can afford to produce and burn the oil we have.

Chapter 8 provides an outline and analysis of various explanations for why the price of oil has fallen so dramatically between June 2014 and February 2015 (the time of writing). The main conclusion defended is that so-called 'cheap oil' (at ~$50 per barrel) is just as problematic as expensive oil (at $100+ per barrel), but for very different social, economic, political, and environmental reasons. Just as expensive oil suffocates industrial economies that are dependent on cheap energy inputs to function, cheap oil merely propagates and further entrenches the existing order of global capitalism that is in the process of growing itself to death.

Chapter 9 presents the most important theoretical contribution of the book, but it is a contribution that I suggest has hugely significant practical implications. The analysis revisits Joseph Tainter's theory of complexity and collapse and responds to his argument that 'voluntary simplification' (which is essentially Tainter's term for degrowth or the simpler way) is not a viable path to a stable civilisation. Tainter argues forcefully, I admit, that in order to solve the problems facing our species we will need increased energy supplies, and on that basis he rejects the strategy of voluntarily reducing consumption. While I accept many aspects of Tainter's profound theoretical framework, this chapter ultimately rejects his conclusion, arguing that we are at a stage in our civilisational development where increasing energy consumption is now causing some of the primary problems that energy consumption is supposed to allow us to solve. In order to 'solve' some of the central crises of our times – in particular, in order to solve the problem of diminishing marginal returns on complexity which Tainter argues has led to the collapse of civilisations throughout history – I maintain that we must embrace a process of voluntary simplification. The primary contribution of this chapter lies in showing why Tainter's dismissal of this strategy is misguided and that, in fact, voluntary simplification is the only alternative to collapse.

Chapter 10 is a thought experiment based on a 'collapse scenario', which attempts to explore the lifestyle implications of what Paul Gilding has called a 'Great Disruption'. The question the chapter poses is this: how would an ordinary member of the consumer class deal with a lifestyle of radical simplicity? By radical simplicity I do not mean poverty. Rather, I mean a very low but biophysically sufficient material standard of living. This chapter argues that radical simplicity, in this sense, would not be as bad as it might first seem, provided we were ready for it and wisely negotiated its arrival, both as individuals and communities. The aim of this chapter is to provoke readers to reflect deeply on the question of what material standard of living is really necessary to live a full, human life. If it turns out that much less might be needed than is commonly thought, then in our age of ecological overshoot, this should provide us with further grounds for attempting to minimise our consumption and move toward lifestyles of sufficiency. If we do not choose this path, then my concern is that lifestyles of radically reduced consumption will be soon enough imposed upon us, but in ways that are unlikely to be experienced positively. As Thoreau once said, 'when a dog runs at you, whistle for him' – which I interpret as suggesting that we should embrace those things that necessarily await us whether we want those things or not. Nietzsche expressed a similar point: *amor fati* ('love thy fate').

Chapter 11 is the most philosophical of these collected essays, and is also the longest. It is placed toward the end because it may also be the least accessible, but I include it because I am convinced that the issues it raises are of the utmost importance. The chapter summarises then applies the ethical writings of Michel Foucault to the theory and practice of voluntary simplicity, drawing in particular on his notion of an 'aesthetics of existence'. Foucault argued that 'the self' is socially constructed. So far as that is true, inhabitants of consumer societies have probably internalised the social and institutional celebration of consumer lifestyles to varying degrees, and this will have shaped our identities and worldviews, often in subtle, even insidious, ways. But Foucault also argued that 'the self', as well as being shaped by society, can act on itself and change itself through a process of 'self-fashioning'. This raises the ethical question: what type of person should one create? Given that overconsumption is driving many of the world's most pressing problems, it may be that ethical activity today requires that we critically reflect on our own subjectivities in order to *refuse who we are* – so far as we are uncritical consumers. This Great Refusal would open up space to create new, post-consumerist forms of subjectivity, which is surely part of the revolution in consciousness needed in order to produce a society based on a 'simpler way'. After outlining Foucault's ethics and situating them in the context of consumption practices, the chapter concludes by describing several 'techniques of the self' that could be employed by those who wish to practise the idea of voluntary simplicity as an aesthetics of existence.

Chapter 12, the final chapter, is a short essay which was delivered at the Festival of Ideas, at the University of Melbourne, Australia in October 2013. It looks back from the year 2033 to consider how a transition to a low-carbon society might transpire, based on the notion that a crisis is also an opportunity.

ABOUT THE AUTHOR

Dr Samuel Alexander is a lecturer at the University of Melbourne, Australia, teaching a course called 'Consumerism and the Growth Economy: Interdisciplinary Perspectives' in the Masters of Environment. He is also co-director of the Simplicity Institute and research fellow at the Melbourne Sustainable Society Institute, publishing widely on issues related to voluntary simplicity, degrowth and post-growth economics, energy descent, and transition strategies. He is author of *Prosperous Descent: Crisis as Opportunity in an Age of Limits* (2015), *Entropia: Life Beyond Industrial Civilisation* (2013), editor of *Voluntary Simplicity: The Poetic Alternative to Consumer Culture* (2009), and co-editor of *Simple Living in History: Pioneers of the Deep Future* (2014). He blogs at www.simplicitycollective.com and posts most of his writings at www.thesufficiencyeconomy.com.

OTHER BOOKS FROM THE SIMPLICITY INSTITUTE

Prosperous Descent: Crisis as Opportunity in an Age of Limits (2015)
Samuel Alexander

Simple Living in History: Pioneers of the Deep Future (2014)
edited by Samuel Alexander and Amanda McLeod

Entropia: Life beyond Industrial Civilisation (2013)
Samuel Alexander

The Hidden Door: Mindful Sufficiency as an Alternative to Extinction
(2013) Mark A. Burch

FOR MORE INFORMATION, SEE THE SIMPLICITY INSTITUTE

www.simplicityinstitute.org